Computer Architecture with Python and ARM

Learn how computers work, program your own, and explore assembly language on Raspberry Pi

Alan Clements

BIRMINGHAM—MUMBAI

Computer Architecture with Python and ARM

Group Product Manager: Kunal Sawant
Publishing Product Manager: Akash Sharma
Senior Editor: Nisha Cleetus
Technical Editor: Jubit Pincy
Copy Editor: Safis Editing
Project Coordinator: Manisha Singh
Proofreader: Safis Editing
Indexer: Pratik Shirodkar
Production Designer: Shankar Kalbhor
Business Development Executive: Kriti Sharma
Developer Relations Marketing Executive: Sonia Chauhan

First published: July 2023

Production reference: 2281123

Published by Packt Publishing Ltd.
Grosvenor House
11 St Paul's Square
Birmingham
B3 1RB, UK.

ISBN 978-1-83763-667-9

www.packtpub.com

Writing the dedication is the hardest part of writing a book. Of all the people you have known, who do you honor? I would like to dedicate this book to four people who have smoothed my path through life, have been my friends, have set an example, and have made my life worth living.

To my wife, Sue, who has been my companion and soulmate for over half a century and has provided so much help with my writing.

To Samuel Gatley, my oldest school friend, who provides me with inspiration and, like all good friends, is always there to speak to.

To Derek Simpson, who was my Dean at Teesside University for many years and continues to be a friend. Derek is the most selfless person I've ever met and is always willing to help anyone and everyone.

To Patricia Egerton, a former colleague and friend who had faith in me when I lacked it and propelled me to make a career decision that changed the course of my life.

Contributors

About the author

Dr. Alan Clements taught computer architecture for over 30 years at The University of Teesside. Alan has written several major university texts on computer architecture. He was also an active member of the IEEE Computer Society for two decades and ran its Computer Society International Design Competition for over 10 years. Alan was second vice president of the society for a year.

Since retiring, Alan has thrown himself into photography and has exhibited his work several times in the UK, Spain, and Venice.

About the reviewers

Sri Manikanta Palakollu is a proficient full-stack developer who has acquired expertise in various technologies, such as Java, AEM, Python, C++, C, JavaScript, TypeScript, MERN, databases, machine learning, and deep learning. He has also authored many articles on diverse domains such as AI, machine learning, programming, data science, and cybersecurity. He has published his articles on various platforms, such as Medium, HackerNoon, and Analytics Vidhya. He has offered technical guidance for many books from well-known publishers, such as Packt and Apress, and penned a book named *Practical System Programming with C*. He has also mentored more than 5,000 students in various coding hackathons hosted by different organizations and institutions.

Aleksei Goriachikh is a mathematics master's degree holder with a diverse professional background. Prior to entering the semiconductor industry, he conducted research in computational mathematics and optimization and participated in the development of a geometric kernel for CAD systems. Throughout his time in the semiconductor industry, Aleksei has been involved in performance optimization, library development, and autonomous driving projects. His current professional interest lies in pre-silicon modeling, where he leverages virtual simulations to optimize semiconductor devices before fabrication.

Table of Contents

Part 1: Using Python to Simulate a Computer

1

2

6

TC1 Assembler and Simulator Design 119

7

Extending the TC1 185

8

Simulators for Other Architectures   223

Part 2: Using Raspberry Pi to Study a Real Computer Architecture

9

Raspberry Pi: An Introduction   279

10

A Closer Look at the ARM   321

11

ARM Addressing Modes   341

12

Subroutines and the Stack   355

Appendices – Summary of Key Concepts   371

Index   381

Other Books You May Enjoy   388

Preface

A fundamental thread of computer science is computer architecture. This topic was once called computer hardware and is concerned with the physical computer itself; that is, the **central processing unit** (**CPU**), memory, buses, and peripherals. Computer hardware contrasts with computer software, which applies to the programs, applications, and operating systems that computers execute.

Most users are no more concerned with computer hardware and architecture than drivers worry about the operation of their vehicles' carburetors. However, a knowledge of computer architecture is useful in many ways, ranging from how efficiently you operate your computer to maximizing its security. A good analogy is with pilots. They learn how to fly an aircraft, and a knowledge of how its engines operate is considered absolutely vital in handling abnormal situations, prolonging the engine life, and minimizing fuel consumption.

Computer architecture is a large subject and is broadly divided into three interrelated areas: **instruction set architecture** (**ISA**), computer organization, and computer hardware. The ISA represents the programmer's view of the computer; that is, it's an abstract model of what a computer does (rather than how it does it). For example, the programmer is interested in a computer's instruction set, which includes operations such as `add P,A,B`, which adds A to B and puts the sum in P. This book explains computer architecture by demonstrating how you can write a program that simulates a computer.

The part of computer science that deals with how a computer implements the actions of its architecture is called computer organization and is largely beyond the scope of this text. Computer organization is concerned with the gates and circuits of the computer.

An author can't do justice to all the aspects of a computer in one book. Here, I am interested in tackling one topic: the ISA. I am going to introduce the computer's instruction set and explain what it does. I will also discuss different types of instruction sets; for example, the ARM processor found in most mobile phones is very different from the Intel and AMD processors at the heart of PCs and laptops. In the second part of this book, we will concentrate on a specific computer and look at a real-world architecture, the ARM processor.

This book is different. There are books on computer architecture. There are books on Python. There are books on the Raspberry Pi computer. Here, we combine all three of these topics. However, I don't do this in a superficial way leaving the reader with a shallow and unsatisfactory knowledge of each topic.

My intention is to introduce a computer architecture and its instruction set. That is, I am going to explain how a computer works at the level of its native instructions (called assembly language). I describe what an instruction does and how it is read, interpreted (i.e., decoded), and then executed (implemented). I will also discuss the type of operations computers implement.

So, how does Python fit into this scheme? Python is a popular high-level programming language that is freely available for use on the PC, Apple Mac, and Raspberry Pi. Moreover, Python is probably the easiest computer language to learn, and it is remarkably powerful.

People learn by doing. I have decided to include sufficient Python for the reader to construct a simple computer simulator that can read a machine-level computer instruction and execute it. Because I will show how this Python simulator works, students can build computers to their own specifications. They can experiment with instruction sets, addressing modes, instruction formats, and so on. They can even build different types of computers to their own specifications, for example, by using **complex instruction set computer** (**CISC**) or **reduced instruction set computer** (**RISC**) architectures. CISC and RISC offer two different philosophies of computer design. Essentially, RISC computers have fixed-length instructions that permit only register load and store memory operations, whereas CISC computers can have variable-length instructions and permit direct data operations on memory. In reality, the distinction between RISC and CISC is more complex. The first generation of microprocesses all conformed to CISC philosophy.

Readers can build computers because they can write a program in Python that will execute the target language of a specific computer architecture and they can design that target language themselves.

One of the most popular computer architectures is the ARM processor found in countless mobile applications and even Apple laptops. Not only is this an economically dominant processor family but it's also very popular in education because of its interesting and innovative architecture and its relatively gentle learning curve. Even better, this is the processor used by the low-cost Raspberry Pi computer. You can run ARM code on Raspberry Pi using software tools that come with the computer. You can also run Python programs on Raspberry Pi with free software. Consequently, Raspberry Pi provides students with an excellent low-cost machine that lets them study core hardware topics with no further investment in hardware or software.

Who this book is for

For many years, I have taught computer architecture and have used simulators to teach assembly language. This approach demonstrates what instructions do but not how they do it or how they are designed, decoded, and executed. I decided to create a simple instruction simulator for class use. This book evolved from that project.

My target audience can be divided into four main groups, as follows:

- Students who are taking a computer architecture course and would like to enhance their experience of computer architecture by experimenting with their own CPUs by means of simulation. This approach would increase the depth of their knowledge of computer architecture and enhance their understanding of the trade-offs that the computer designer faces.

- The non-computer specialist, the layperson, and the enthusiast who would like to know how computers work. By using Python as the design language and providing an introductory course on Python, I have attempted to make the book accessible to those with little or no experience in programming.

- The Raspberry Pi user. Raspberry Pi has had an immense impact on computer science education. This book provides a brief introduction to Raspberry Pi and shows how it is possible to write assembly language programs in the ARM's native language. Moreover, Raspberry Pi also provides an environment (Python and its tools) that allows the reader to understand and simulate computers.

- The reader wanting to learn Python. Although this is not a formal course on Python, it provides a goal-oriented introduction to Python; that is, it applies Python to an actual example. This approach avoids the breadth of a conventional course and enables the reader to construct a practical application with a relatively shallow learning curve.

- I have not assumed that a beginner reader has absolutely no knowledge of computers at all. This book assumes a very basic knowledge of binary arithmetic and number bases and the basic concepts of Boolean variables.

What this book covers

- *Chapter 1, From Finite State Machines to the Computers*, introduces the notion of digital computers via the finite state machine that is used to model simple control systems. From there, we introduce the concept of algorithms and programs. Once we know what we want a computer to do, we can think about what we need to implement a computer.

- *Chapter 2, High-Speed Introduction to Python*, provides the initial background in Python that is required to take the first steps on the way to implementing a computer using Python.

- *Chapter 3, Data Flow in a Computer*, demonstrates how information flows around a computer during the execution of a program. It is this data flow that we have to implement when we are simulating a program in software.

- *Chapter 4, Crafting an Interpreter – First Steps*, begins the journey to a simulator. Now that we have been introduced to the concept of a computer and a little Python, we can go further and describe the fundamental ideas behind a computer simulator. In this chapter, we also look at the nature of computer instructions.

- *Chapter 5, A Little More Python*, expands our knowledge of Python and introduces us to vital topics such as Python's dictionaries, which provide tools that greatly simplify the design of a computer simulator.

- *Chapter 6, TC1 Assembler and Simulator Design*, is the heart of this book. Here, we discuss the components of a simulator and then provide a program that can simulate a hypothetical teaching computer, TC1.

- *Chapter 7, Extending the TC1*, adds further facilities to the simulator, such as data checking and creating new instructions.

- *Chapter 8, Simulators for Other Architectures*, looks at different types of computer architecture and describes alternative simulators.

- *Chapter 9, Raspberry Pi – An Introduction,* changes course. Here, we look at the popular Raspberry Pi and the ARM processor at its core. In particular, we learn how to enter a program in ARM assembly language and run it in debugging mode.

- *Chapter 10, A Closer Look at the ARM,* examines ARM's instruction set in greater detail and provides a foundation for writing programs in assembly language.

- *Chapter 11, ARM Addressing Modes,* looks at the addressing modes of the ARM in greater detail and explains some of its special features.

- *Chapter 12, Subroutines and the Stack,* is really an extension of the previous chapter because we look at the way in which the ARM uses its addressing modes to implement stack operations, which are so important in assembly language programming.

To get the most out of this book

This book is split into two parts. The first part develops a computer simulator in Python and the second part provides a brief introduction to Raspberry Pi and uses it as a vehicle to teach ARM assembly language programming.

I used a PC with Windows to develop the Python programs. The reader may use a Windows-based system, an Apple Mac, or any Linux-based computer to develop Python. All the necessary software is freely available.

You can, of course, use Raspberry Pi itself to develop Python.

In order to write ARM assembly language programs and debug them, you need a Raspberry Pi. This is a single-board computer and requires a power supply, keyboard, mouse, and monitor. I have used both the Raspberry Pi 3 Model A+ and Raspberry Pi 4 Model B versions.

The software required to develop Python programs is freely available from `https://www.python.org`. The Raspberry Pi single-board computer is not sold with an operating system. You must either buy an SD card with the operating system installed or download it yourself. Details are given at `https://www.raspberrypi.com/documentation/computers/getting-started.html`.

If you are using the digital version of this book, we advise you to type the code yourself or access the code from the book's GitHub repository (a link is available in the next section). Doing so will help you avoid any potential errors related to the copying and pasting of code.

Download the example code files

You can download the example code files for this book from GitHub at `https://github.com/PacktPublishing/Computer-Architecture-with-Python-and-ARM`. If there's an update to the code, it will be updated in the GitHub repository.

We also have other code bundles from our rich catalog of books and videos available at `https://github.com/PacktPublishing/`. Check them out!

Conventions used

There are a number of text conventions used throughout this book.

`Code in text`: Indicates that words in text are not plain English words, but are words belonging to a program.

The `break` instruction breaks out of the `while` loop (that is, execution continues beyond the end of the loop - it's a sort of short-circuit mechanism).

In order to draw your attention to features in code, we sometimes use bold font or shading to highlight features. Consider the following example:

The text following # is in a non-monospaced font and is a comment ignored by the computer:

```
for i in range (0,6):            # Repeat six times
```

Get in touch

Feedback from our readers is always welcome.

General feedback: If you have questions about any aspect of this book, email us at `customercare@packtpub.com` and mention the book title in the subject of your message.

Errata: Although we have taken every care to ensure the accuracy of our content, mistakes do happen. If you have found a mistake in this book, we would be grateful if you would report this to us. Please visit `www.packtpub.com/support/errata` and fill in the form.

Piracy: If you come across any illegal copies of our works in any form on the internet, we would be grateful if you would provide us with the location address or website name. Please contact us at `copyright@packt.com` with a link to the material.

If you are interested in becoming an author: If there is a topic that you have expertise in and you are interested in either writing or contributing to a book, please visit `authors.packtpub.com`.

Share Your Thoughts

Once you've read *Computer Architecture with Python and ARM*, we'd love to hear your thoughts! Scan the QR code below to go straight to the Amazon review page for this book and share your feedback.

https://packt.link/r/1-837-63667-2

Your review is important to us and the tech community and will help us make sure we're delivering excellent quality content.

Download a free PDF copy of this book

Thanks for purchasing this book!

Do you like to read on the go but are unable to carry your print books everywhere?

Is your eBook purchase not compatible with the device of your choice?

Don't worry, now with every Packt book you get a DRM-free PDF version of that book at no cost.

Read anywhere, any place, on any device. Search, copy, and paste code from your favorite technical books directly into your application.

The perks don't stop there, you can get exclusive access to discounts, newsletters, and great free content in your inbox daily.

Follow these simple steps to get the benefits:

1. Scan the QR code or visit the link below

https://packt.link/free-ebook/9781837636679

2. Submit your proof of purchase
3. That's it! We'll send your free PDF and other benefits to your email directly

Part 1: Using Python to Simulate a Computer

In this part, you will be introduced to two threads: the digital computer and the programming language Python. The purpose of this book is to explain how a computer works by constructing a computer in software. Because we assume that the reader will not have a knowledge of Python, we will provide an introduction to Python. However, we will cover only those topics relevant to building a computer simulator are explored. The topics of the structure and organization of a computer and Python programming are interleaved. Once we have introduced the TC1 (Teaching Computer 1) simulator, the two final chapters will first explore ways of enhancing the simulator's functionality, and then look at simulators for alternative architectures.

This section comprises the following chapters:

- *Chapter 1, From Finite State Machines to Computers*
- *Chapter 2, High-Speed Introduction to Python*
- *Chapter 3, Data Flow in a Computer*
- *Chapter 4, Crafting an Interpreter – First Steps*
- *Chapter 5, A Little More Python*
- *Chapter 6, TC1 Assembler and Simulator Design*
- *Chapter 7, Extending the TC1*
- *Chapter 8, Simulators for Other Architectures*

1

From Finite State Machines to Computers

In this chapter, you will discover the fundamental nature of computers. Our goal is to explain what makes a computer a computer. These concepts are important because you can't understand how a computer works until you appreciate the implications of its sequential nature.

Once we've introduced the concept of digital systems, the next chapter will demonstrate how a computer operates by fetching instructions from memory and executing them. After that, we will introduce Python and demonstrate how you can write a program to simulate a computer and observe its operations. This book is all about learning by doing; by building a computer with software, you will learn how it operates and how to extend and modify it.

The remainder of this book will look at a real computer, a Raspberry Pi, and show you how to write programs for it and observe their execution. In doing so, we will move on from simulating a hypothetical computer to learning about a real computer.

A computer is a *deterministic symbol processing* machine. But what does that mean? *Deterministic* tells us that a computer always behaves in the same way when operating under the same conditions (that is, programs and inputs). If you use a computer to evaluate $\sqrt{2}$, you will always get the same result, no matter how many times you perform the operation. Not all systems are deterministic – if you toss a coin, the sequence of heads and tails is not predictable.

When we say that a computer is a *symbol processing machine*, we mean that it takes in symbols and operates on them to provide new symbols as an output. These symbols are anything that can be represented in digital form: letters, words, numbers, images, sound, and video. Consider a computer that's playing chess. The input symbols that are received by the program correspond to the moves made by a player. The program operates on the input symbols according to a set of rules and produces an output symbol – the computer's move.

Although we've just provided a theoretical definition of a computer, it is important to appreciate that programming involves translating information in the real world into symbols that can be manipulated by a computer – writing a set of rules (that is, a program) that tells the computer how to manipulate the symbols, and then converting the output symbols into a form that is meaningful to a human. The symbols that are processed by a computer have no intrinsic meaning to the computer – a certain pattern of bits (that is, the symbol) might represent a number, a name, a move in a game, and so on. The computer processes these bits to produce a new pattern of bits (that is, an output symbol) that has a meaning only to the programmer or user.

We are going to pose a simple problem and then solve it. Our solution will lead us to the concepts of algorithms and computers, and also introduce key concepts such as discrete digital operations, memory and storage, variables, and conditional operations. By doing this, we can determine the types of operations a computer needs to perform to solve a problem. After this, we can ask, "How can we automate this? That is, how can we build a computer?"

It's a trite statement, but once you understand a problem, you're well on the way to finding a solution. When you first encounter a problem that requires an algorithmic solution, you have to think about what you want to do, rather than how you are going to do it. The worst approach to problem solving is to start writing an algorithm (or even actual computer code) before you have fully explored the problem. Suppose you were asked to design a cruise control system for an automobile. In principle, this is a very simple problem with an equally simple solution:

```
IF cruise control on THEN keep speed constant
                     ELSE read the position of the gas pedal
```

Couldn't be simpler, could it? Well, what happens if you've selected cruise control and someone pulls out in front of you? You could brake, but this algorithm would attempt to keep the speed constant while you are braking by applying full throttle at the same time. Alternatively, you might suggest that the act of braking should disengage the cruise control mechanism. But is the cruise control to be disengaged permanently, or should the automobile accelerate to its previous speed once the braking action has ceased? You have to think about all the aspects of the problem.

Even if you design a correct algorithm, you have to consider the effect erroneous or spurious data will have on your system. One of the most popular criticisms of computers is that they produce meaningless results if you feed them with incorrect data. This idea is summed up by the expression **garbage in, garbage out** (**GIGO**). A well-constructed algorithm should detect and filter out any garbage in the input data stream.

In this chapter, we will introduce the following topics:

- The finite state machine
- Solving a problem algorithmically

Technical requirements

You can find the programs used in this chapter on GitHub at https://github.com/PacktPublishing/Computer-Architecture-with-Python-and-ARM/tree/main/Chapter01.

The finite state machine

There are remarkably few fundamental concepts that you need to know about to understand what a digital computer does and how it operates. One of the most important concepts is discrete, which lies at the heart of both computer operation and computer programs.

Computers operate on discrete data elements – that is, elements whose values are chosen from a fixed and finite range of values. We use discrete values in everyday life – for example, the letters of the Roman alphabet that belong to the set {A…Z}. A letter is never between two possible values. It's the same with the days of the week; you can have one of seven days, but you can't have a day that is slightly Monday or just a little bit bigger than Wednesday. In the case of computers, the fundamental data element is the bit, which can only have values of 0 or 1, and all its data structures are represented by strings of 1s and 0s.

As well as discrete data values, we can have discrete points in time. Imagine that time moves in one direction, from one discrete point to another discrete point. Nothing exists between two discrete points in time. It's a bit like a digital clock that goes from 12:15:59 to 12:16:00. There's nothing in between.

Now, imagine state space, which is a grandiose term for all the states a system can be in (for example, a plane can be in the climbing, descending, or level flight state). States are a bit like time, except that you can go forward or backward between discrete points in state space. If there are a limited number of possible states, a device that models the transitions between states is called a **finite state machine** (**FSM**). An elevator is a finite state machine: it has states (position at the floors, doors open or closed, and so on) and inputs (the elevator call buttons, floor selection buttons, and door open and close buttons).

Before we take a serious look at FSMs, let's begin with a simple example of how to use FSMs to describe a real system. Consider the TV of yesterday, which is a device with two states: on and off. It is always in one of these two states, and it can move between these states. It is never in a state that is neither on nor off. Modern TVs often have three states – on, *standby*, and off– where the standby state provides a fast-on mechanism (that is, part of the electronics is in an active on state, but the display and sound system are powered down). The standby state is often called the sleep state or idle state. We can model discrete states using a diagram. Each state is represented by a labeled circle, as demonstrated in *Figure 1.1*:

Figure 1.1 – Representing the three states of a television

Figure 1.1 shows the three states, but it doesn't tell us the most important information we need to know: how we move between states. We can do this by drawing lines between states and labeling them with the event that triggers a change of state. *Figure 1.2* does this. Please note that we are going to construct an incorrect system first to illustrate some of the concepts concerning FSMs:

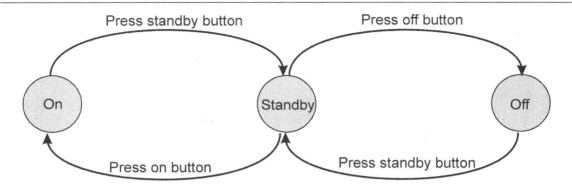

Figure 1.2 – Representing the states of a television with transitions

In *Figure 1.2*, we labeled each transition by the event that triggers it; in each case, it's pressing a button on the remote controller. To go from off to on, you have to first press the standby button and then the on button. To go between on and standby, you must press the on button or the standby button.

We've forgotten something – what if you are already in a state and you press the same button? For example, let's say the TV is on, and you press the on button. Also, what's the initial state? *Figure 1.3* rectifies these omissions.

Figure 1.3 has two innovations. There is an arrow to the off state marked *Power on*. This line indicates the state the system enters when you first plug it into the electricity supply. The second innovation in *Figure 1.3* is that each state has a loop back to itself; for example, if you are in the on state and you press the on button, you remain in that state:

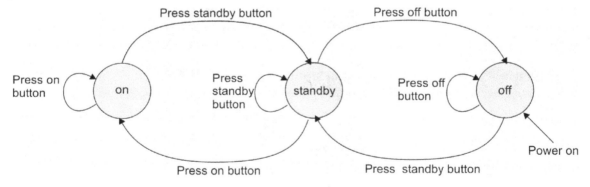

Figure 1.3 – The TV control with initialization

The state diagram shown in *Figure 1.3* has both a logical error and an ergonomic error. What happens if you are in the off state and press the on button? If you are in the off state, pressing the on button (in this system) is incorrect because you have to go to standby first. *Figure 1.4* corrects this error by dealing with incorrect inputs:

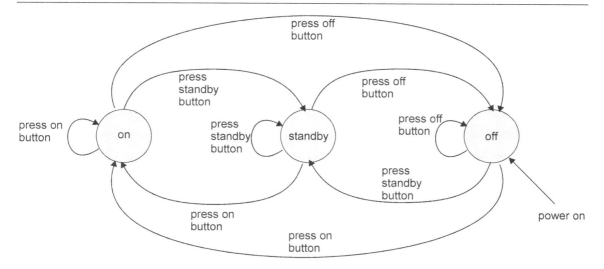

Figure 1.4 – The TV control with wrong button correction

Figure 1.4 now provides correct operations from any state and includes the effect of pressing buttons that cause no change of state. But we still have the ergonomic error – that is, it's a correct design that behaves in a way that many would consider poor. The standby state is a convenience that speeds up operations. However, the user does not need to know about this state – it should be invisible to the user.

Figure 1.5 demonstrates the final version of the controller. We've eliminated a standby button, but not the standby state. When the user presses the on button, the system goes directly to the on state. However, when the user presses off when in the on state, the system goes to the standby state. From the standby state, pressing the on button results in the power on state, while pressing off results in the power off state. Note that the same action (pressing off) can have different effects, depending on the current state:

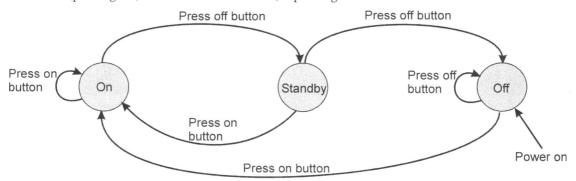

Figure 1.5 – The TV control with a hidden standby state

We've labored with this example because the notion of FSMs is at the heart of all digital systems. All digital systems, apart from the most trivial, move from state to state, depending on the current input and past states. In a digital computer, the change-of-state trigger is the system clock. A modern computer operating at a clock speed of 4 GHz changes state every 0.25×10^{-9} s or every 0.25 ns. Light traveling at 300,000 km/s (186,000 mph) moves about 7.5 cm or 3 inches during a clock cycle.

Traffic lights example

Let's look at a second example of an FSM. A classic example of an FSM is traffic lights at a crossroads. Consider an intersection with traffic moving north-south or east-west. The traffic may move in only one direction at a time. Assume that this is a system with a clock and a change of state is permitted every minute:

Current State of the Lights	Traffic in the North-South Direction	Traffic in the East-West Direction	Action to Be Taken On the Next Clock	Next State of the Lights
North-south	None	None	No traffic, no change	North-south
North-south	None	One or more	East-west, forces change	East-west
North-south	One or more	None	North-south, no change	North-south
North-south	One or more	One or more	East-west, forces change	East-west
East-west	None	None	No traffic, no change	East-west
East-west	None	One or more	East-west, no change	East-west
East-west	One or more	None	North-south, forces change	North-south
East-west	One or more	One or more	North-south, forces change	North-south

Table 1.1 – Traffic lights sequence table

Suppose the traffic is currently flowing north-south. At the next clock, it may either remain flowing north-south or the lights may change to allow east-west traffic. Similarly, if traffic is flowing east-west, at the next clock, it may either remain flowing east-west or the lights may change to permit north-south traffic.

We can use *Table 1.1* to describe this system. We have provided the current state of the lights (direction of traffic flow), indicated whether any traffic had been detected in either the north-south or east-west direction, the action to be taken at the next clock, and the next state. The traffic rule is simple: the lights remain in their current state unless there is pending traffic in the other direction.

We can now convert this table into the FSM diagram shown in *Figure 1.6*. Note that we have made the east-west state the power on state; this is an arbitrary choice:

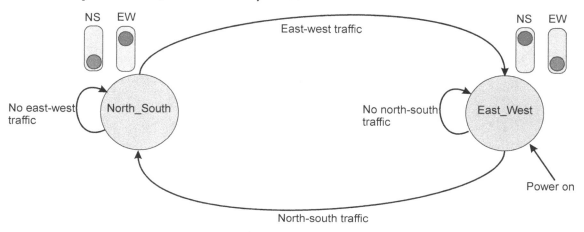

Figure 1.6 – A finite state machine for Table 1.1

What have we learned? The most important point is that a system is, at any instant, in a particular state and that a transition to another state (or a transition back to the current state) is made according to a defined set of conditions. The FSM has several advantages, both as a teaching tool and a design tool:

- It uses a simple intuitive diagram to describe a system with discrete states
- The state transition diagram (if correct) provides a complete and unambiguous way of describing a system
- The FSM is also an abstract machine in the sense that it models a real system, but we don't have to worry about how the FSM is implemented in real hardware or software
- Any FSM can be implemented either in hardware or software; that is, if you can define a state diagram on paper, you can build the circuit in dedicated hardware or write the program to run on a general-purpose computer

I have included a brief introduction to FSMs because they can be considered a precursor to the digital computer. An FSM is designed to carry out a specific task; this is built into its hardware. A computer has some of the characteristics of an FSM but you can program the transitions between states.

Solving a simple problem algorithmically

Now that we've introduced FSMs, we will describe a problem, solve it, and then construct our computer. A bag contains a mixture of red and white tokens. Suppose that we take a token at a time out of the bag and continue until we have removed three consecutive red tokens. We want to construct an algorithm that tells us to stop removing tokens from the bag when three reds in a row have been detected.

Before creating an algorithm, we'll provide an FSM for this problem:

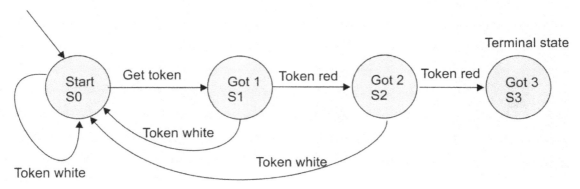

Figure 1.7 – FSM for a three-token detector

As you can see, there are four states. We begin in state S0. Each time a token is received, we move to the next state if it's red, and back to the initial state if it's white. Once we've reached state S3, the process ends. Now, we'll perform the same operation algorithmically.

If a white token is represented by the symbol W, and a red token by R, a possible sequence of tokens might be RRWRWWWWRWWRRR (the sequence is terminated by the three Rs). An algorithm that tells us when to stop removing tokens can be written in the following form:

- Line 1: Get a token from the bag
- Line 2: If the token is white, then go back to line 1
- Line 3: Get a token from the bag
- Line 4: If the token is white, then go back to Line 1
- Line 5: Get a token from the bag
- Line 6: If the token is white, then go back to Line 1
- Line 7: Success – three consecutive red tokens have been taken out of the bag

As you can see, the algorithm is expressed in plain English. It is read from top to bottom, line by line, and the action specified by each line is carried out before the next line is processed. In this algorithm, each line has a unique name (that is, Line 1, Line 2, and so on). Labeling a line enables us to refer to it; for example, when the algorithm states that we must go back to Line 1, this means that the next step to be carried out is specified by Line 1, and we continue carrying out actions from Line 1 onward. This algorithm is not entirely satisfactory – we haven't checked that the bag contains only red and white tokens, and we haven't dealt with the situation in which we run out of tokens before we locate the sequence we're looking for. At the moment, we are not concerned with these details.

There's no single solution to this problem – more often than not, lots of algorithms can be constructed to solve a given problem. Let's derive another algorithm to detect a sequence of three consecutive red tokens:

Line 1: Set the total number of consecutive red tokens found so far to 0

Line 2: Get a token from the bag

Line 3: If the token is white, then go back to Line 1

Line 4: Add 1 to the number of consecutive red tokens found so far

Line 5: If the number of consecutive red tokens is less than 3, then go back to Line 2

Line 6: Success – 3 consecutive red tokens have been taken out of the bag

This algorithm is more versatile because it can easily be modified to detect any number of consecutive red tokens simply by changing the value of 3 in Line 5 of the algorithm.

Figure 1.8 presents this algorithm diagrammatically in the form of a flowchart that shows the sequence of operations that take place when executing an algorithm. Lines with arrowheads indicate the sequence in which operations are carried out. Boxes indicate the actions themselves, and diamonds represent conditional actions. The expression in the diamond is evaluated to yield either "yes" or "no," and control flows in one direction or another. In general, flowcharts are well suited to depicting simple algorithms, but they are regarded as very unsuitable for complex algorithms. A flowchart for a complex algorithm looks like a bowl of spaghetti – but without the spaghetti's inherent clarity and organization.

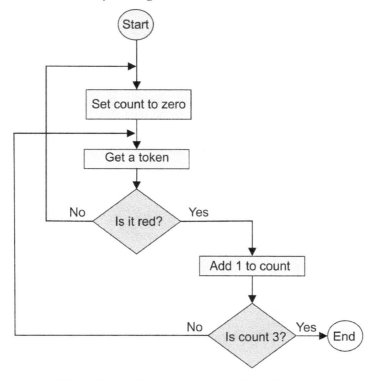

Figure 1.8 – An algorithm represented by a flowchart

Constructing an algorithm

The next step is to provide an *algorithm* that tells us how to solve this problem clearly and unambiguously. As we step through the sequence of digits, we will need to keep track of what's happening, as *Table 1.2* demonstrates:

Position in sequence	0	1	2	3	4	5	6	7	8	9	10	11	12	13
New token	R	R	W	R	W	W	W	W	R	W	W	R	R	R
Is it red?	Y	Y	N	Y	N	N	N	N	Y	N	N	Y	Y	Y
Number of reds	1	2	0	1	0	0	0	0	1	0	0	1	2	3

Table 1.2 – A sequence of tokens selected at random

Pseudocode is a term that's applied to a method of expressing an algorithm in something that falls between plain English and a formal programming language. The following pseudocode expresses the actions we need to perform. The initialization operations that we perform once at the beginning are in normal typeface, while the repetitive actions defined by REPEAT...UNTIL are in bold. We will look at these operations in detail when we introduce Python:

```
1.      Set numRed to 0
2.      Set maxRed to 3
3.      REPEAT
4.          Get a token
5.          IF its color is red
6.          THEN numRed = numRed + 1
7.          ELSE numRed = 0
8.      UNTIL numRed = maxRed
```

This pseudocode employs two constructs found in many high-level computer languages: the REPEAT...UNTIL construct in lines 3 to 8, and the IF...THEN...ELSE construct on lines 5 to 7. REPEAT...UNTIL lets you carry out an action one or more times, while IF...THEN...ELSE lets you choose between one of two possible courses of action.

The IF...THEN...ELSE construct is central to the operation of digital computers and you will encounter it many times in this book.

The next step is to introduce Python so that we can write a program to implement this algorithm. Then, we can start to look at the computer. The following code shows a Python program and its output when executed. We haven't introduced Python yet. The purpose of this program is to demonstrate how close it is to the preceding algorithm and the simplicity of Python:

```
Sequence = ['W','R','R','W','R','W','W','W','W','R','W','W','R','R','R']
numRed = 0
maxRed = 3
count  = 0
```

```
while numRed != maxRed:
    token = sequence[count]
    if token == 'R':
        numRed = numRed + 1
    else: numRed = 0
    print('count', count,'token',token,'numRed',numRed)
    count = count + 1
print('Three reds found starting at location', count - 3)
```

The `while numRed != maxRed:` line means *carry out the block of indented operations, so long as (*`while`*) the value of* `numRed` *is not equal to* `maxRed`. The `!=` Python operator means *not equal*.

This is the output when the program is executed. It correctly identifies three consecutive reds and indicates the location of the first run in the run of three:

```
count  0 token  W numRed 0
count  1 token  R numRed 1
count  2 token  R numRed 2
count  3 token  W numRed 0
count  4 token  R numRed 1
count  5 token  W numRed 0
count  6 token  W numRed 0
count  7 token  W numRed 0
count  8 token  W numRed 0
count  9 token  R numRed 1
count 10 token  W numRed 0
count 11 token  W numRed 0
count 12 token  R numRed 1
count 13 token  R numRed 2
count 14 token  R numRed 3
Three reds found starting at location 12
```

Summary

In this first chapter, we introduced the concept of a computer via an FSM. A state machine is an abstraction of any system that can exist in one of several states at any instant. State machines are defined in terms of the states and the transitions between states. We introduced state machines as a precursor to digital systems. State machines introduce the notion of discrete states and discrete times. A state machine moves from one state to another at discrete instants in time. This mirrors the action of a program where actions (change of state) take place only when an instruction is executed.

State machines can model systems as simple as traffic lights to a game of chess or a computer program. We also introduced the idea of algorithms – that is, a set of rules used to solve a problem. Later in this book, we'll explain how computers can implement algorithms.

In *Chapter 2*, we'll provide a brief overview of n. We've chosen this language because it has a remarkably shallow learning curve, is very powerful (it does a lot with a few lines of code), is taught in many universities, and is freely available to run on PCs, Macs, and Raspberry Pi systems.

2

High-Speed
Introduction to Python

This chapter introduces Python and demonstrates how to write a program in Python to solve the type of problem we described in *Chapter 1*. We are not going to delve deeply into Python in this chapter, but we will cover Python sufficiently to enable you to simulate and modify a computer to incorporate your own ideas.

Traditionally, a computer program has been compared to a cookery recipe because they are analogous. Strictly speaking, this statement applies only to procedural languages such as Python, Java, and C. Functional languages such as Lisp do not conform to this strictly sequential paradigm and are beyond the scope of this text

A recipe is a sequence of *operations* (i.e., actions or steps) that are carried out *in order* on the *ingredients* used by the recipe. A program is the same; it is a sequence of operations (instructions) that are carried out, in order, on data. The instructions of a program are carried out, one by one, sequentially, from top to bottom, arranged exactly like a page of printed text. It's also possible to repeat a group or block of instructions several times, and you can even skip past or ignore blocks of instructions.

The analogy between a recipe and a program is surprisingly accurate. In a recipe, you can have *conditional* instructions such as, "*If the sauce is too thick, then add more water.*" In programming, you can have conditional instructions such as, "*If x is 0, then add 1 to y.*" Similarly, in cooking, you can express repetitive action by expressions such as, "*Beat the mixture until stiff.*" In computing, repetition can be expressed using constructs such as, "*Subtract 1 from z until z = 0.*"

In this chapter, we will cover the following topics:

- Reading programs
- Getting started with Python
- Python's data types
- Mathematical operators
- Names, values, and variables
- Comments

- The list – a Python key data structure
- Functions in Python
- Conditional operations and decision-making
- Reading data from a file
- Translating a token detector algorithm into Python
- Computer memory
- Register transfer language

Technical requirements

You can find the programs used in this chapter on GitHub at `https://github.com/PacktPublishing/Computer-Architecture-with-Python-and-ARM/tree/main/Chapter02`.

The requirements to write a program in Python and run it are minimal. Python is an open source language and is freely available for the PC, Mac, and Linux platforms. All the information you need to set up a Python environment on your computer system can be found on the home page at `https://www.python.org`.

Remarkably, you do not need any other software to construct a computer simulator in Python. The Python package comes with Python's **Integrated Learning and Development Environment** (**IDLE**) that lets you edit a Python program, save it, run it, and debug it.

There are alternatives to IDLE that let you create Python source files supported by Python platforms. These alternatives are generally more sophisticated and targeted at the professional developer. For the purposes of this chapter, IDLE is more than sufficient, and nearly all the Python programs in this text were developed with IDLE.

Alternative IDEs are Microsoft's Visual Studio Code, Thonny, and Geany. All these IDEs are freely available. Thonny was developed for the Raspberry Pi, which we will use in later chapters:

- Visual Studio Code: `https://code.visualstudio.com/download`
- Geany: `https://www.geany.org/`
- Thonny: `https://thonny.org`

Reading programs is not easy for the beginner because you don't know how to interpret what you see. The following section describes some of the typography and layout conventions we will use in this chapter to make the meaning of programs more clear and to highlight the features of a program.

Reading programs

In order to help you follow the programs, we have adopted two different type fonts – a variable-width font (where letters have different widths, such as the bulk of the text here) and a mono-spaced font, such as the Courier font found on old mechanical typewriters `that looks like this`.

The reason for using a mono-spaced font to represent code is twofold. First, it tells the reader that a word is computer code and not just part of the narrative text. Second, spacing in computer programs is important for readability, and mono-spaced fonts line up letters and numbers on adjacent rows neatly in columns. The following is an example of code from a later chapter to demonstrate this point. The proportionally-spaced text to the right, prefixed by #, indicates that the text is not code but a plain-language comment:

```
elif litV[0]   == '%': literal = int(litV[1:],2)      # If first % convert binary to integer
elif litV[0:2] == '0B':literal = int(litV[2:],2)      # If prefix 0B convert binary to integer
elif litV[0:1] == '$': literal = int(litV[1:],16)     # If $, convert hex string to integer
elif litV[0:2] == '0X':literal = int(litV[2:],16)     # If 0x convert hex string to integer
```

We have occasionally used shading or a bold font to distinguish one feature of a piece of code from another. For example, `x = y.`**`split('.')`** uses a bold font to emphasize the `split` function.

Consider the following example. The gray text indicates reserved words and symbols in Python that are necessary to specify this construct. The numbers in bold black are values supplied by the programmer. The text following # is in a non-monospaced font and is a comment ignored by the computer:

```
for i in range (0,6):        # Repeat six times
```

In this example, we use shading to emphasize a feature – for example, `rS1 = int(inst[2][1])` draws your attention to the first parameter, `[2]`.

Getting started with Python

Before we look at Python in more detail, we will provide a brief introduction to getting started with Python and demonstrate a short program. Although we have not even introduced the basics of the language, Python programs are remarkably easy to follow.

Python is a computer language such as C or Java and, like every computer language, it has its advantages and disadvantages. We have chosen to use Python because it is free and universal, there's a vast amount of information about it, and, most importantly, it has a very shallow learning curve. Indeed, Python has become one of the most popular languages used in computer science education.

Python was conceived by the Dutch computer scientist Guido van Rossum, and the stable Python 2.0 was released in 2000. Today, Python is promoted by the Python Software Foundation, a body of volunteers whose aim is to develop the language as a public service.

The high-level language programs in this text were written in Python on a PC. To install Python, you need to go to its home page at `https://www.python.org` and follow the instructions. There are several versions of Python because it is continually growing. The two main branches are Python 2 and Python 3; I will be using the latter. Python is continually updated and new versions are introduced. I started with Python 3.6, and at the time of writing, we're up to Python 3.11. However, new incremental versions do not offer radical changes, and many of the new features are not used by the Python version in this book.

Loading the Python packages provides you with a Python documentation library, a Python interpreter, and a Python editor called the IDLE. All this is freely available. IDLE allows you to perform a cycle, *edit a program, run it, and debug it* until you are happy with the result. I also used the freely available Thonny IDE, which I found even easier to use. Using an IDE lets you develop a program, run it, and then modify it, without having to switch between separate editors, compilers, and runtime environments.

Late in the writing of this book, Graeme Harker introduced me to **Visual Studio Code** (**VS Code**). This is a popular integrated development system developed by Microsoft that supports several languages, including Python, and which runs on several platforms, including Windows, Linux, and macOS. VS Code is a very powerful IDE indeed and includes facilities that go beyond those of IDLE.

Consider the example of an IDE (in this case, IDLE) in *Figure 2.1*. Suppose we want to create a four-function calculator that performs simple operations such as 23 x 46 or 58 - 32. I've chosen this example because it is really a very simple computer simulator. *Figure 2.1* is a screenshot taken after a Python program has been loaded using the `file` function. You can also directly enter a Python program from the keyboard.

If we click on **File**, a new editing window is opened, and we can write our program. The Python code inputs a first number, an operator, and a second number and displays the result of the calculation. Then, it repeats. When you enter *E* instead of +, -, /, or *, it terminates the execution and prints a message.

Like most high-performance IDE systems, IDLE uses color to help you to read a program. Python lets you add a commentary to the program because code is not always understandable. Any text following a # symbol is ignored. In this case, the code is understandable, and these comments are not necessary.

You have to save a program before you can run it. Saving a program from IDLE automatically appends `.py`, so that a file named `calc1` is saved as `calc1.py`.

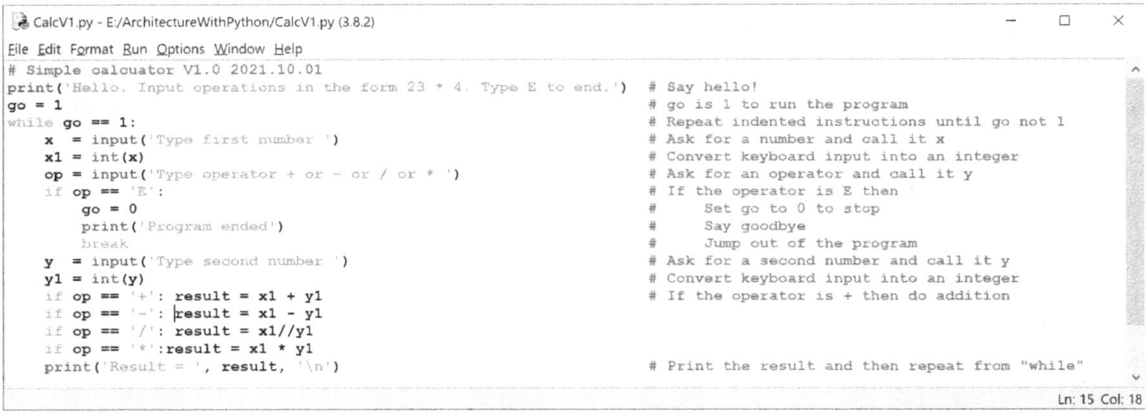

```
CalcV1.py - E:/ArchitectureWithPython/CalcV1.py (3.8.2)                                    —    □    ×
File Edit Format Run Options Window Help
# Simple calculator V1.0 2021.10.01
print('Hello. Input operations in the form 23 * 4. Type E to end.')   # Say hello!
go = 1                                                                # go is 1 to run the program
while go == 1:                                                        # Repeat indented instructions until go not 1
    x  = input('Type first number ')                                  # Ask for a number and call it x
    x1 = int(x)                                                       # Convert keyboard input into an integer
    op = input('Type operator + or - or / or * ')                     # Ask for an operator and call it y
    if op == 'E':                                                     # If the operator is E then
        go = 0                                                        #    Set go to 0 to stop
        print('Program ended')                                        #    Say goodbye
        break                                                         #    Jump out of the program
    y  = input('Type second number ')                                 # Ask for a second number and call it y
    y1 = int(y)                                                       # Convert keyboard input into an integer
    if op == '+': result = x1 + y1                                    # If the operator is + then do addition
    if op == '-': result = x1 - y1
    if op == '/': result = x1//y1
    if op == '*':result = x1 * y1
    print('Result = ', result, '\n')                                  # Print the result and then repeat from "while"
                                                                                                    Ln: 15 Col: 18
```

Figure 2.1 – A screenshot of a Python program in IDLE

Figure 2.1 shows the layout of Python programming, including the all-important *indentation*, which is a key feature of Python and indicates which operations belong to a particular command.

Here's a brief description of the program. We will cover this material in greater detail later. `while` heads a group of indented instructions that are repeated until some condition stops being true. In this case, the instructions are executed as long as the `go` variable is `1`.

The `if` statement defines one or more operations that are executed if `if` is true. In this case, if the input is `'E'`, the `go` variable is set to `0`, and the indented operations after `while` are no longer executed.

The `break` instruction breaks out of the `while` loop (that is, execution continues beyond the end of the loop – it's a sort of short-circuit mechanism).

Finally, the `int (x)` function converts a keyboard character into an integer – for example, `int ('27')` converts the two keys, 2 and 7, into the integer, `27`. We will discuss all this in greater detail later.

To run the program, you select the **Run** tab and then click on **Run module**, or you just enter F5. The following demonstrates the effect of running this program. The text in bold is the text I entered using the keyboard:

```
Hello. Input operations in the form 23 * 4. Type E to end.
Type first number 12
Type operator + or - or / or * +
Type second number 7
Result =  19

Type first number 15
Type operator + or - or / or * -
Type second number 8
Result =  7

Type first number 55
Type operator + or - or / or * /
Type second number 5
Result =  11

Type first number 2
Type operator + or - or / or * E
Program ended
```

The purpose of this brief demonstration is to show how a Python program is entered and executed. In practice, no programmer would write the preceding code. It is inefficient. It does not deal with errors (what happens if you type @ instead of *, or $ instead of 4?). Even worse, to stop the program, you have to enter a dummy number before entering E to end the program. I leave it as an exercise for you to convert this program into a version that is more user-friendly.

We've demonstrated a trivial Python program. The next step is to introduce the data with which Python operates – that is, we show how Python handles numbers and text.

Python's data types

A recipe uses *ingredients* that fall into distinct groups (fruit, vegetables, nuts, cheeses, spices, etc.). A computer program uses data that falls into groups called *types*. Some of the main data types used by Python are as follows:

- **Integer**: This uses whole numbers, such as 0, 1, 2, and so on. Integers also include negative numbers -1, -2, -3, and so on. Positive integers are also known as natural numbers.

- **Float**: These are numbers with a decimal point (e.g., 23.5 and -0.87). These are also called *real* numbers. Surprisingly, we will not be using real numbers in this text.

- **Character**: A character is one of the keys on a computer keyboard – for example, Q, Z, a, $, and @. Computer languages often indicate a character by putting it in inverted commas – for example, 'R'. In practice, Python does not have an explicit character type.

- **String**: A string is a sequence of characters – for example, `'This'` or `'my program'`. Python doesn't have a character type because it treats a character as a string of length 1. Python allows you to use single or double quotes interchangeably – for example, x = `'this'` and x = `"this"` are identical in Python. This mechanism allows you to type x = "The boy's books" (i.e., you can use an apostrophe without it being treated as a quotation mark). In computing, the term *string* is rather like the English term *word*. A string is any sequence of characters – for example, `'time'` and `'!££??'` are legal Python strings. Recall that a string of length 1 is a single character – for example, 'Q'. You can have a string of length zero – that is,''. Here, you have two quotation marks with nothing in between. This indicates an empty string.

- **bool**: Python has a Boolean type, bool, which has only two values, `True` and `False`. The bool type is used in Boolean logic expressions. It is also used in comparisons – for example, the English expression, "Is *x* greater than *y*?" has two possible outcomes – True or False. If you type `print(5 == 5)` in Python, it will print True because the == means "*is the same as?*" and the result is True.

Each data element used in a program is given a *name* so that we can access it. The programmer chooses names for variables, and a good programmer chooses sensible names that indicate what the variable is. No one calls a variable `qZz3yT`. Names must begin with a letter, and then they may have any sequence of letters and numbers – for example, `alan`, `alan123`, and `a123lan` are legal Python names, whereas `2Alan` or `Al@n` is not legal. However, the underscore may be used in a name – for example, `time_one`. By convention, Python uses lowercase for the first character of variables and function names. Uppercase first letters are reserved for class names (which we will not use in this text). This restriction is a programming convention – that is, an error will not occur if you give a variable a name beginning with an uppercase letter.

Now that we've introduced data elements, we next describe some of the operations you can apply to numeric data. These are essentially the arithmetic operators we encountered in high school, except for division, which has three variations.

Mathematical operators

Computers can perform the four standard arithmetic operations – addition, subtraction, multiplication, and division. For example, we can write the following:

```
X1 = a + b    Addition
X2 = a - b    Subtraction
X3 = a * b    Multiplication
X4 = a / b    Division
```

The symbol for multiplication is * (the asterisk) and not the conventional x. Using the letter x to indicate multiplication would lead to confusion between the letter x and x as a multiplication operator.

Division is more complicated than multiplication because there are three ways of expressing the result of x ÷ y. For example, 15/5 is 3, and the result is an integer. 17/5 can be expressed in two ways – as a fractional value (i.e., a float) 3.4, or as 3 remainder 2. In Python, the division operator provides a float result if the result is not an integer (e.g., 100/8 = 12.5).

As well as the division operator, /, Python has two other division operators – // and %.

Python's // is a *floor integer* divide that generates an integer result by rounding down to the nearest integer. For example, the operation x = 17//5 gives the result 3 and the fractional part (the remainder) is discarded. Note that x = 19//5 gives the result 3 because it *rounds down*, even though 4 is the closest integer. If you were to execute x = -19//5, that would give the result -4 because it rounds *down* to the closest integer.

The % symbol is the *modulus* operator and provides the remainder after division. For example, x = 17%5 gives the result 2. Suppose, on Monday, someone said they were visiting you in 425 days. What day of the week is that? 425%7 is 5, which indicates Saturday. We can use % to test whether a number is odd or even. If you write y = x%2, then y is 0 if the number is even and 1 if it is odd.

Names, values, and variables

Computers store data in their memory. Each data element has two values associated with it – **where** it is, and **what** it is. In computer terms, *where* corresponds to the location (address) of the data in memory, and *what* corresponds to the value of that data. This is not rocket science, and matches everyday life – for example, I might have a bank account numbered 111023024 containing $890. Here, 111023024 is the "where," and the $890 is the "what."

Now, suppose I write 111023024 + 1. What exactly do I mean? Do I mean to add 1 to the account number to get 111023025 (which is a different account), or do I mean to add $1 to the number in this account numbered 111023024 to get $891? In everyday life, this is something that's so obvious we just don't think about it. In computing, we have to be a little more careful and think clearly about what we are doing.

Data elements are called **variables** because their values can be changed. A variable has an address (location) in memory. A programmer doesn't have to worry about the actual location of data; the operating system takes care of that for them automatically. All they have to do is to come up with a name for the variable. For example, let's take the following:

```
totalPopulation = 8024
```

When you write this, you define a new variable that you've called `totalPopulation` and have told the computer to store the number `8024` at that location. You don't have to worry about all the actions involved in doing this; that's the job of the operating system and compiler.

Let's summarize. A variable is a name that refers to some value stored in memory. Let's say you write the following:

```
totalPopulation = totalPopulation + 24
```

Here, the computer reads the current value in the memory location assigned to the name `totalPopulation`. It then adds 24 to this value, and finally, stores the result in `totalPopulation`.

In the next section, we look at user comments and program layout in a little more detail.

Comments

Because computer languages can be terse and confusing to the human reader, they let you add comments that are ignored by the computer (i.e., they are not part of the program). In Python, any text on the same line following the # symbol is ignored. In the following examples, we've put that text in a different font to emphasize that it's not part of the program. First, consider the following Python expression:

```
hours = 12              # Set the value of the variable hours to 12
```

This code creates a new data element called `hours` and gives it the integer value `12`. *Figure 2.2* illustrates the structure of this line.

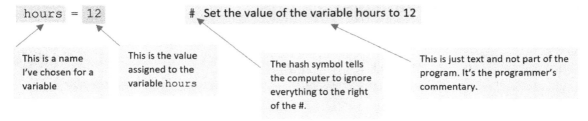

Figure 2.2 – The structure of a statement with a comment

Let's say you were then to write the following:

```
allTime = hours + 3      # Add 3 to the hours and assign a result to a new variable, allTime
```

Then, the computer would read the value of the name on the right-hand side of the expression (i.e., `hours`) and substitute its value with 12. Then, it would add 3 to get 12 + 3 = 15, storing this new value in a memory location called `allTime`. The text following # is ignored by the computer and serves only to help humans understand the program.

Many computer languages use the = symbol differently from how we were taught in high school. In school algebra, '=' means "*the same as,*" so that $x = y + 2$ means that the value of x and $(y + 2)$ are identical. If the value of y is 12, then the value of x is 14.

In programming, the statement `x = y + 2` indicates that the value of $y + 2$ is calculated and then *transferred* to x. If a programmer writes `x = x + 2`, it means to add 2 to `x`. If this were a mathematical equation, we could write $x - x = x - x + 2$, which simplifies as the nonsensical expression 0 = 2. In Python, the = symbol does NOT mean equals!

In Python, the = symbol means "*assign to.*" A better symbol is ←, so that $x ← y + 2$ expresses clearly what we are doing. Some languages such as Pascal use the symbol pair := to indicate assignment. Sadly, the back arrow is not on keyboards, and we are stuck with =. Note that, in Python, a *statement* is a command such as `print ()` or an assignment such as `x = 4`. An *expression* is a combination of variables or values and operations that returns a result.

As we've seen, Python has a special symbol for "*is the same as,*" and that symbol is '=='. Never confuse = and ==. It is very easy to write `if x = 5` instead of `if x == 5` and wonder why your program gives the wrong result.

Consider the following example of a simple Python program, where we calculate the area of a circle. The names `radius`, `pi`, and `area` are all chosen by the programmer. We could have used other names, but these are more obvious to the reader:

```
radius = 2.5                 # Define the radius as 2.5
pi = 3.142                   # Define the value of pi
area = pi*radius*radius      # Calculate the area of a circle
print (area)                 # The print function prints the value of the area on the display
```

Recall that a Python name consists of letters and (optionally) numbers and underscores, but the first character in the name must be a letter and not a number. Uppercase and lowercase letters are regarded as being different in Python – that is, `tesT22` and `test22` are different names. It is good practice to choose meaningful names because that makes it easier to read a program. Consider the following:

```
wagesFred = hoursWorkedFred*12 + hourOvertimeFred*18
```

The preceding expression is verbose but clear to a human reader. This is an example of *camelCase*, a popular term for names that consist of words joined without spaces, using a capital letter to indicate each word in the chain, `asWeAreDoingNow`. Remember that Python variables and labels do not start with a capital letter (that's a convention and not a requirement).

There are two classes of data elements – constants and variables. A *constant* is given a value when it is first named, and that value cannot be changed – for example, if you define x = 2 as a constant in a language such as C, the value of *x* is fixed (e.g., the expression x = 3 would be illegal). A *variable* is an element that can be modified. Python does not support constants.

Let's calculate the sum of the first *n* integers, $s = 1 + 2 + 3 + ... + n$. Algebra tells us that the sum of *n* integers is $n(n + 1)/2$. We can convert this into the following Python program:

```
n = int(input("How many integers are you adding? "))
s = n * (n + 1)/2
print("Sum of ",n, " integers is",s)      # We used double quotes " instead of single
```

This three-line Python program asks for an integer, performs the calculation, and prints the result. Let's suppose we don't know the formula for the sum of the first *n* integers. We can do it the hard way by adding them up one by one. The Python code to do this is given in *Listing 2.3*.

We have not covered all aspects of this program in detail yet. It is given here to demonstrate the essential simplicity of Python. However, note that Python allows you to request input from the keyboard and provide a prompt at the same time.

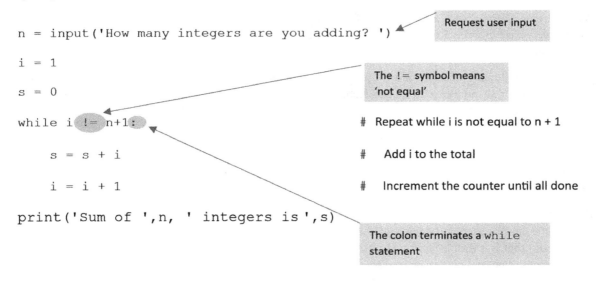

```
n = input('How many integers are you adding? ')      ◄  Request user input

i = 1
                                                         The != symbol means
s = 0                                                    'not equal'

while i != n+1:   ◄                                   #  Repeat while i is not equal to n + 1

    s = s + i                                         #  Add i to the total

    i = i + 1                                         #  Increment the counter until all done

print('Sum of ',n, ' integers is ',s)
                                                         The colon terminates a while
                                                         statement
```

Figure 2.3 – A Python program to add the first n integers

Our next topic introduces one of Python's key elements – a feature that is immensely powerful and flexible and one that makes Python such a popular language, especially for beginners. We will describe the list.

The list – a Python key data structure

We now introduce Python's *list*, which that groups together a sequence of elements. We show how the elements of a list can be accessed. Because the list is such a key feature, we will return to it several times, each time introducing new features.

A data structure is an ordered collection of data elements. The term *ordered* indicates that the position of a data element matters – for example, in everyday life, the week is ordered because the sequence of the days is fixed. A *table*, a *stack*, a *queue*, a *list*, a *heap*, a *pile*, a *file*, and an *array* all embody the idea of a data structure. In English, a *sackload* of books implies an *unordered* collection of items. Python does have a special data structure for unordered items, called a set. We will not use sets in this chapter.

Like any other object, the programmer assigns a name to a list. The following Python list gives the result of eight consecutive exams taken by a student, expressed as a percentage:

```
myTest = [63, 67, 70, 90, 71, 83, 70, 76]
```

We have given the list a meaningful name, `myTest`. In Python, a list is enclosed in square brackets and the items are separated by commas. Lists can grow (items added to them) and shrink (items removed). You can have an empty list – for example, `abc = []`.

The whole point of a list is to be able to access individual items and manipulate them – for example, we might want to find the highest result or the lowest result, or the average in the `myTest` list. Therefore, we need to specify the location of an item. Mathematicians use *subscripts* for this task – for example, they may write $myTest_5$. Unfortunately, computer science arose in the dark age of the mechanical courier typewriter script, when different fonts, colors, italics style, and subscripts didn't exist. So, we have to use the symbols that are on all keyboards to indicate a location within a list.

Python indicates the position of an item in a list (or other data structures) by means of *parentheses* – for example, element 3 in `myTest` is expressed as `myTest[3]`. The first element of a list is position 0 because computers count from zero. The first value in `myTest` is `myTest[0]`, which is 63. Similarly, the last result is `myTest[7]`, which is 76. We have 8 results, numbered 0 to 7.

Python is a more flexible language than some. In Python, the list is a *"one size fits all"* data structure. If you want to put different types of items in a list, you can. Other computer languages require a list to have identical items (e.g., all integers, all floats, or all strings). The following example demonstrates some legal lists in Python. As you can see, you can even have a list of lists:

```
roomTemps = [15,17,14,23,22,19]                         # A list of six integers
words     = ['this', 'that', 'then']                    # A list of three strings
x47       = [x21,timeSlot,oldValue]                     # A list of three variables
opCodes   = [['add',3,4],['jmp',12,1],['stop',0,0]]     # A list of three lists
mixedUp   = [15,time,'test',x[4]]                       # A list of mixed elements
inputs    = []                                          # An empty list
```

Note that we have aligned the *equals* symbols in a column on the left. This is not a feature of Python. Nor is it a requirement. We do it because it makes the code easier to read and makes debugging easier.

Let's return to the shopping list example and call the list `veg1`. We can set up this list with the following:

```
veg1 = ['potatoes', 'onions', 'tomatoes']        # A list of three strings
```

The individual items in this list are in quotation marks. Why? Because they are strings – that is, text. Without quotations, the items would refer to variables that were defined earlier, such as the following:

```
opClass = 4                          # Define opClass
addOp   = ['add', opClass]           # A list with an instruction name and its class
```

Slicing lists and strings

Here, we will demonstrate how you can take a string or a list and extract data elements (i.e., the slices) from a string or a list. The individual characters of a string can be accessed – for example, if `y = 'absde'`, then `y[0] = 'a'`, `y[1]= 'b'`, `y[2]= 's'`, , and so on.

Python lets you select the last element in a string or list by using the - 1 *index* – for example, if you write `x = y[-1]`, then `x = 'e'`. Similarly, `y[-2]` is `'d'` (i.e., the next but one from the end).

You can select a slice of a string or list using the `list[start:end]` notation. The slice specified by `[start:end]` selects elements from `start` to `end - 1` that is, you specify the end as the element *after* the last element you require. If `q = 'abcdefg'`, then the `r = q[2:5]` slice assigns `r = 'cde'`.

The expression `z = q[3:]` refers to all elements from 3 to the end of the list, and assigns `'defg'` to `z`. This is a remarkably useful feature because it allows us to take a text string such as `s='R14'` and extract the numeric value of the register with `t=int(s[1:])`. The expression `s[1:]` returns a substring from the second character to the end – that is, `'R14'` becomes `'14'`. This value is a string type. The `int('14')` operation converts the string type to an integer type and returns 14.

The `len` function returns the length of a string. If `y='absde'`, `p=len(y)` returns 5 because there are 5 characters in the string.

Consider a list of assembly language instructions – `ops=['ADD', 'MUL', 'BNE', 'LDRL']`. If we write `len(ops)`, we get the result 4, because there are 4 strings in the `ops` list. Suppose we write `x=ops[3][2]`. The value of `ops[3]` is `'LDRL'`, and the value of `LDRL[2]` is `'R'`. In other words, we can extract one or more characters from a string in a list of strings. The `x[a][b]` notation means to take item `a` of list `x` and then take item `b` of that element.

We have used functions such as `print()` and `len()`. We will now discuss functions in a little more detail. Later, we show you how you can define your own functions as well as use Python's built-in functions.

Functions in Python

Before continuing, we need to introduce the concept of a function in a high-level language. In high school math, we encounter functions such as *sqrt(x)*, which is an abbreviation of *square root* and returns the square root of *x* – for example, *sqrt(9) = 3*. Computer languages have borrowed the same concept.

Python provides functions that are built into the language. You call a function to perform a specific operation (it's a bit like subcontracting in the real world) – for example, `len()` operates on strings and lists. If you call `len(x)` with the list x, it will return the number of items in that list. Consider the following:

```
toBuy = len(veg1)        # Determine the length of list veg1 (number of items in it)
```

This takes the list we called `veg1` and counts the number of items in it, copying that value to the `toBuy` variable. After this operation has been executed, the value of `toBuy` will be the integer 3, since there are 3 items in `veg1`.

Let's say you write the following:

```
q = 'abcdefgh'
print(len(q))
```

Then, the number printed is 8 because there are eight characters in the string q.

Let's suppose we have another list of food items:

```
fruit1 = ['apples', 'oranges', 'grapes', 'bananas']
```

Let's add together the number of items in the two lists. We can do that with the following:

```
totalShopping = len(veg1) + len(fruit1)
```

This expression calculates the length of both lists (getting the integers 3 and 4, respectively), adds them together, and assigns the value 7 to the `totalShopping` variable. You can print this on the screen by using the `print()` function:

```
print('Number of things to buy ', totalShopping)
```

This expression consists of the Python word `print`, which displays something on the screen. The parameters used by `print` are enclosed in parentheses, separated by commas. A parameter in quotes is a string and is printed literally as it is. Remember that Python lets you use either single or double quotation marks. A parameter that is a variable is printed as its value. In this case, the value of the `totalShopping` parameter is 7. This expression would display the following:

```
Things to buy 7
```

Consider the following expression (we've shaded the text to be printed). Variables whose values will be printed are in bold to improve understanding:

```
print('Total items to buy', totalShopping, 'These are: ', fruit1)
```

What would this print? The output would be the following:

```
Total items to buy 7 These are: ['apples', 'oranges', 'grapes', 'bananas']
```

Is this what you would have expected? You might have been looking for a list in the order of apples, oranges, grapes. But what you asked for was the `fruit1` Python list, and that is exactly what you got (hence the brackets, and quotation marks around each item in the list). If we wanted to print the list as `apples, oranges, grapes, bananas`, we would have had to first convert the list of strings into a single string item (which we will discuss later). However, for the impatient among you, here's how it's done using the `join()` function:

```
fruit1 = ['apples', 'oranges', 'grapes', 'bananas']
print('Fruit1 as list = ', fruit1)
fruit1 = (' ').join(fruit1)              # This function joins the individual strings
print('Fruit1 as string = ', fruit1)
```

The output from this code is the following:

```
Fruit1 as list =  ['apples', 'oranges', 'grapes', 'bananas']
Fruit1 as string =  apples oranges grapes bananas
```

Next, we will discuss the very item that makes a computer a computer – the conditional operation that selects one of two or more possible courses of action, depending on the result of a test.

Conditional operations and decision-making

And now for the biggie – the conditional operation. Let's consider the following recipe:

1. Take two eggs.
2. Separate the whites.
3. Add sugar.
4. Beat until stiff.

These actions are carried out sequentially. The first three actions are simple operations. The fourth action is very different from the previous three, and it is this action that gives the computer its power. It's an operation that performs one of two actions, depending on the outcome of a test. In this case, the eggs are beaten, then tested. If they are not sufficiently stiff, the beating is continued, they are retested, and so on.

What makes a computer so powerful is its ability to take decisions. Without a *decision-making* capacity, a computer could not respond to its environment; it could perform only the same calculation over and over again. The foundation of human intelligence is also decision-making. If you play chess, you use decision-making to choose the next move on the basis of the current board positions. The move you make is the one that will give you the best chance of winning from your current situation.

It's the same with a computer. At any point in a program, the computer can be given two alternative courses of action. Depending on the outcome of a test, the computer chooses one of these courses of action to take and then carries out the appropriate operations for that decision.

A typical conditional operation is the `if` statement. In Python, this can be expressed as the following:

```
z = 9                   # Set z to 9
if x > 5: z = 20        # If x is greater than 5, then make the value of z equal to 20.
```

We've put the condition in bold, and the action is shaded. The action is carried out if, and only if, the condition is true. If the condition is not true, the action is ignored. For example, if x is 6, the value of z will be 20. If x is 4, the value of z will remain at 9.

Computers perform simple tests whose outcome is one of the two Boolean values, `True` or `False`. More often than not, the test asks, "*Is this variable equal to zero?*"

In Python, the `if` statement has the following form:

```
if condition: action        # The colon is mandatory, and indicates the end of the condition
```

The only two reserved Python elements are `if` and the colon. The term `condition` is any Python expression that returns the `True` or `False` value, and `action` is any block of instructions the computer will execute if the condition is `True`. Some programmers put the action on a new line. In this case, the action MUST be indented, such as the following *Figure 2.4*:

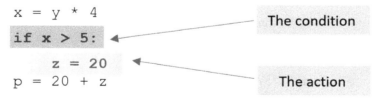

Figure 2.4 – A Python program to add the first n integers

Although Python lets you use any indentation, good practice suggests the indentation be four spaces.

The condition is `x > 5`, and the action is `z = 20`. The condition is a Boolean logic expression that yields one of two outcomes – True if x is greater than 5 and False if x is not greater than 5.

Using a conditional expression in Python

A Python program to control the temperature of a room might look something like this:

```
cold = 15                           # Define the temperature at which we turn on the heater
hot = 25                            # The temperature at which we turn on the cooler
nowTemp = getTemp()                 # getTemp() is a function that reads the thermometer
if nowTemp < cold: heat(on)         # If too cold, then turn on the heater
if nowTemp > hot:  cool(on)         # If too hot, then turn on the cooler
if nowTemp > cold: heat(off)        # If not cold, then turn off the heater
if nowTemp < hot:  cool(off)        # If not hot, then turn off the cooler
```

Typical Boolean conditions are as follows:

```
x == y
x != y
x >  y
x <  y
```

These four conditions are *equal to*, *not equal to*, *greater than*, and *less than*, respectively. Remember that the expression $x == y$ reads, "*Is x equal to y?*" Consider the following example (using the Python IDLE interpreter):

```
>>> x = 3
>>> y = 4
>>> x == y
False
>>> x + 1 == y
True
```

Examples of if statements

A variable, x, varies between 0 and 9, inclusive. Let's say we want y to be 0 if x is less than 5, 1 if $x > 4$ and $x < 8$, and 2 if $x > 7$. We can express this as follows:

```
if x < 5: y = 0
if x > 4 and x < 8: y = 1       # A compound test. Is x greater than 4 AND x is less than 8
if x > 7: y = 2
```

The second `if` statement tests two conditions together by using an `and` operator. Both conditions, $x > 4$ and $x < 8$, must be true for the whole expression to be true.

We can also use Python's `or` operation, which means if any of the conditions are true. You can write complex conditions such as the following:

```
if (x > 4 and x < 8) or (z == 5): y = 1
```

As in conventional arithmetic, it is necessary to use parentheses to ensure that operations are carried out in the appropriate sequence.

We can test this code by generating sequential values of *x* and printing the corresponding value of *y*, as the following code in *Figure 2.5* demonstrates. The first statement executes the indented block for x is 0 to 9 (one less than the range given):

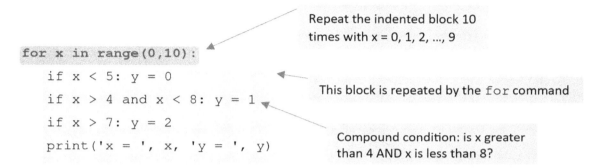

Figure 2.5 – Demonstrating iteration

The output from this code is the following:

```
x =   0 y =   0
x =   1 y =   0
x =   2 y =   0
x =   3 y =   0
x =   4 y =   0
x =   5 y =   1
x =   6 y =   1
x =   7 y =   1
x =   8 y =   2
x =   9 y =   2
```

Python's if ... else

The preceding code is correct, but it's not efficient. If the result of the first if is true, the other if statements can't be true, and yet they are tested. What we need is a test in which if it is true, we perform the appropriate action. If it is not true, we perform a different action. We have a word for this in English – it's called "else":

Consider the following:

```
if    x < 5:         # Is x less than 5?
      y = 0          # If x is less than 5, then y = 0
else:
      y = 3          # otherwise, y is 3
```

Python has an `elif` (else if) statement that allows multiple tests. We can use `elif` to perform another `if` if the result of the first `if` is false. Consider the preceding code using `elif`:

```
if    x < 5:                  # Is x less than 5?
      y = 0                   # If x is less than 5, then y = 0
elif  x > 4 and x < 8:        # If x is not less than 5, test whether it's between 5 and 7
      y = 1                   # If x is between 5 and 7, then set y to 1
elif  x > 7:                  # If both previous tests fail, then test whether x is 8 or more
      y = 2
print('x and y ', x, y)
```

In this case, the computer drops out of this construct as soon as one of the conditional tests is true. It does exactly the same as the preceding example using `if` statements, but it is more efficient because it terminates as soon as a condition is satisfied. That is, once any of the tests yields true, its associated action is carried out, and then control passes to the next statement after the `if` ... `elif` sequence (in this case, `print`).

The great thing about programming is that there are many ways of doing the same thing. Suppose we know that a variable, x, is always in the range from 0 to 10, and we want to know the value of y for each x (using the preceding algorithm). We can calculate the value of y as we did previously by using conditional statements and programming.

We can implement the algorithm without using an `if` statement by creating a *lookup table* that provides the value of y for any x. Let's call this table `lookupY` and load it with the values of y for x inputs from 0 to 10. *Table 2.1* gives the value of y for each possible x.

Input x	Output y
0	0
1	0
2	0
3	0
4	0
5	1
6	1
7	1
8	2
9	2
10	2

Table 2.1 – Using a lookup table to perform a Boolean operation

We can code this `lookup` operation in Python in just two lines:

```
lookup   = [0,0,0,0,0,1,1,1,2,2,2]        # Create a lookup table
y = lookup[x]                             # Read the value of y from the lookup table
```

When we simulate a computer, we need to load programs to be simulated. The next section describes how we can read a source file (in text format) from memory into the simulator.

Reading data from a file

When testing an assembler or simulator, you need to enter the test data (the source program). This can be done in three ways.

- Include the data in the program – for example, `myProg = ['add r1,r2', 'inc r1', 'beq 7']`
- Get the text from the keyboard – for example, `myProg = input('Type program ')`
- Create a text file in memory and read it from your program

The first two techniques are great for testing a very short program but less so for a long source program. The third technique means that you write your source code using your favorite text editor, save it as a `.txt` file, and then read that file in your assembler.

I often put the name of my test program in my assembler during development work to avoid typing the name (because I'm working on the same source file most of the time). Let's suppose my file is called `c.txt`:

```
myFile = 'E:/simPython/c.txt'        # This is my source text file on my computer
with open(myFile,'r') as sFile:      # Open the file for reading (indicated by 'r')
    newFile = sFile.readlines()      # Read the code and copy to newFile.
```

In the preceding code, the `myFile` variable provides the name of the source file as a string. Then, the `with open` operation opens and reads `myFile`. This operation also closes the file after use. The preceding code opens `c.txt` for reading and creates a new file, `sFile`.

The `open` function can be used in three ways, as follows:

```
open('thisFile')                # Open a file
open('thatFile', 'r')           # Open a file for reading
open('thatFile', 'w')           # Open a file for writing
```

It is good practice to close a file after you have used it, with `filename.close()`. Because the `with open` operation automatically closes a file at the end of an operation, it is not necessary to call the `close()` function.

The `readlines()` function operates on `sFile` to create a file, `newFile`, containing a list of the lines of my source code. The following fragment of code demonstrates reading a file from disk and cleaning up the end-of-line sequences in a text file. That's because text files are stored with an `'\n'` sequence at the end of each line, and this sequence must be removed because it is not part of the source program. We will return to string processing later:

```
#                                                   # Test reading a file
with open("E:\simPython.txt",'r') as example:       # Open the file for reading
    theText = example.readlines()                    # Read the file example
print('The source file ',theText)                    # Display the file
for i in range(0,len(theText)):                      # This loop scans the file
    theText[i] = theText[i].rstrip()                 # rstrip() removes end-of-file markers
print('The source file ',theText)
```

The following is the output from this code. You can see how the '\n' sequences have been removed:

```
%Run testRead.py
The source file  ['# test file\n', 'NOP\n', ' LDRL 5\n', ' NOP\n', 'STOP']
The source file  ['# test file', 'NOP', ' LDRL 5', ' NOP', 'STOP']
```

We've provided enough information to demonstrate a short Python program that implements the simple sequence detector we described earlier.

Translating a token detector algorithm into Python

We can readily translate our pseudocode to detect a sequence of red tokens in a stream of read/write tokens as follows. In this fragment of Python, you are invited to enter first the number of red tokens to detect, and then r or w to indicate the color of each token. Once the appropriate number of tokens has been detected, the program terminates:

```
# Simple algorithm to detect consecutive tokens

maxRed = int(input("How many red tokens are you looking for? "))

go = 1
numRed = 0

while go == 1:
    y = input("Which token is it? Red or white? ")
    if y == 'w': numRed = 0
    else:        numRed = numRed + 1
    if numRed == maxRed: go = 0

print(maxRed, "Reds found")
```

The output of this program for a sequence I entered was the following:

```
How many red tokens are you looking for? 3
Which token is it? Red or white? r
Which token is it? Red or white? r
Which token is it? Red or white? w
Which token is it? Red or white? r
Which token is it? Red or white? w
Which token is it? Red or white? w
Which token is it? Red or white? w
Which token is it? Red or white? r
Which token is it? Red or white? r
Which token is it? Red or white? r
3 Reds found
```

A computer has three essential elements – an **arithmetic and logical unit** (ALU) that performs all arithmetic and logical operations on data, a memory that holds programs and data, and a control unit that reads the instructions from memory and executes them. In the next section, we will introduce some of the basic concepts of memory.

Computer memory

Now, we are going to introduce the *concept of memory*, the mechanism that holds programs and data. Real or *physical* memory is implemented as DRAM, flash memory, and disk drives. This memory is part of a computer's hardware. We do not cover physical memory in this book. Instead, we will discuss *abstract memory* and how it is modeled by Python. This is the programmer's view of memory.

All data is stored in physical memory, and all the data structures designed by a programmer must be mapped onto physical memory. The mapping process is the job of the operating system, and this book does not deal with the translation of abstract memory addresses into real memory addresses.

Consider the following Python list:

```
friends = ['John', 'Jenny', 'Rumpelstiltskin']
```

These three strings have the [0], [1], and [2] addresses in the `friends` list. The operating system maps these elements onto the physical memory storage locations. These strings each require a different number of physical memory locations because each one has a different length. Mercifully, computer users do not have to worry about any of that. That is the job of the operating system.

We will now take a brief look at the concept of memory because you have to understand the nature of memory in order to understand how computers work, and how to write programs in assembly language.

First, consider our own memories. Human memory is a strange and *inexact* thing. An *event* triggers the recall or *retrieval* of a data element that we call a *memory*. The event may be a question that someone asks you, or it may be something that *reminds* you of an episode that took place in the past. Often, we remember information only partially, or even incorrectly.

Human memory seems to be accessed by matching an event against stored information. That is, our memory is *associative* because we associate one memory with another. A computer's memory operates in a very different way and is best thought of as a *table* or *list* of stored items. You need to know where an item is on the list (its address) in order to access it. We will soon meet a Python memory, which is associative and called a *dictionary*. You don't access a dictionary with an address but, instead, with a *key* that is associated with the required data element.

Figure 2.6 shows how a program to find the number of red tokens in a string of tokens is stored in a hypothetical memory. I must stress that the program is conceptual rather than actual because real computer instructions use rather more primitive machine-level instructions than these. This figure, called a *memory map*, shows the location of information within the memory. It's a *snapshot* of the memory because it represents the state of the memory at a particular instant. The memory map also includes the *variables* used by the program and a string of digits. The stored program computer stores instructions, variables, and constants in the same memory.

Figure 2.6 demonstrates that each location in the memory contains either an *instruction* or a *data element*. Numbers 0 to 23 in the first column are *addresses* that express the position of data elements and instructions within the memory (addresses start from 0 rather than 1 because 0 is a valid identifier).

The program is in locations 0 to 8, the variables in locations 9, 10, and 11, and the data (the tokens) in locations 12 to 23. You can regard the computer's memory as a table of *items*, and the location of each item is its address – for example, memory location 1 contains the instruction `Set numRed to 0`, location 10 contains the value of the `numRed` element, and location 11 contains the value of the current data element (`R` or `W`). Locations 12 onward are in bold font to indicate that they contain the values of the sequence of tokens we operate on.

0	Set i to 12
1	Set numRed to 0
2	new = memory[i]
3	i = i + 1
4	IF new = red
5	THEN numRed = numRed + 1
6	IF i = 23
7	THEN Stop
8	**JUMP to 2**
9	i
10	numRed
11	new
12	**R (the first token)**
13	**R**
14	**W**
15	**R**
16	**R**
	...
23	**R (the last token)**

This is an abstract view of a von Neumann computer memory. It shows that instructions and data are stored in the same memory and items are stored in consecutive locations.

An alternative computer structure is the Harvard computer where data and programs are stored in different memories. Today, that distinction is blurred because some computers store data and programs in the same DRAM immediate access store, but separate data and programs on chip in different cache memories.

In practice, all physical memory locations are the same size (typically 32 bits or 4 bytes).

Data is stored in binary form and instructions are in machine code and not the high-level language instructions shown here.

Figure 2.6 – The memory map

Figure 2.6 is an abstract view of a computer's memory for teaching purposes. Real memory is an array of locations, each of the same size (typically, 16, 32, or 64 bits). Individual instructions may occupy one, two, or more consecutive locations, depending on the actual size of the data.

Although we will not describe physical memory in any detail, a few comments will help to distinguish it from abstract memory. *Figure 2.7* illustrates the organization of actual computer *memory* (e.g., DRAM). The processor provides memory with an address on the *address bus* and a control signal that selects either a *read* or a *write* cycle. In a *read cycle*, the memory puts data onto the *data bus* for the CPU to read. In a *write cycle*, data from the CPU is stored in the memory. Information enters or leaves memory (or any other functional part of a computer system) via a port. A real computer has a hierarchy of memory systems implemented with different technologies – for example, DRAM for main memory, SSD for the much slower secondary storage, and high-speed cache for frequently used data and instructions. In this book, we deal with only abstract memory implemented in Python and not real physical memory. The job of the operating system is to integrate the abstract memory addresses used by the programmer with the real physical addresses of data in memory.

A computer's main store is composed of high-speed **random-access memory** (**RAM**) that can be written to or read from. It is invariably composed of *dynamic* semiconductor memory, DRAM (today, it's DDR4 and DDR5 technology), and the size of a typical PC's RAM generally ranges from 4 GB for tablets to 64 GB for high-performance systems. RAM is volatile, which means that its data is lost when you switch it off (in comparison with flash memory, which retains data).

The term *dynamic* in the DRAM acronym describes its storage mechanism (as a charge on a capacitor, which leaks away and has to be periodically written back). From a user's point of view, DRAM provides very cheap, large-volume storage. From a designer's point of view, DRAM poses particular design problems because of its operating characteristics. An alternative to DRAM is **static RAM** (**SRAM**), which is easier to use and faster than DRAM but is far more expensive, preventing its use in PCs, except for special applications such as cache memory. Cache memory is a special high-speed memory that contains frequently used data.

Secondary (physical) storage is a **hard disk drive** (**HDD**) or **solid-state drive** (**SSD**). Both these store large quantities of data and are far slower than the DRAM of the main store. Computers do not directly access the secondary store. The operating system transfers data, a page at a time, from the SSD/HDD to a computer's main store. This is invisible to the user.

The next step in describing abstract memory is to introduce a notation, called RTL, which is often employed to describe or define memory transactions.

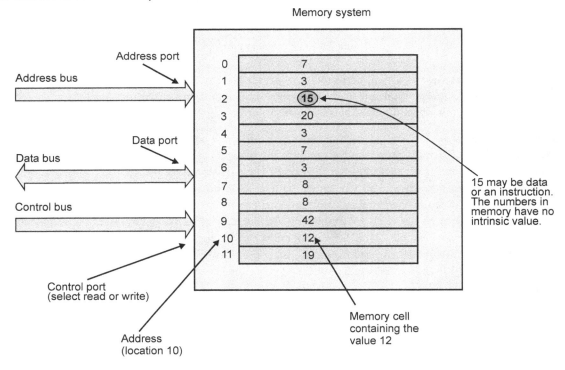

Figure 2.7 – The memory system

Register transfer language

Describing computer operations in words is often cumbersome. Here, we will introduce **register transfer language** (**RTL**), which makes it easy to define computer operations. RTL is neither an assembly language nor a programming language. It is a notation.

It is important to distinguish between a memory *location* and its *contents*. Register transfer language uses square brackets, [ ], to indicate the *contents* of a memory location. The expression [15] = maxRed is interpreted as *the contents of memory location 15 contain the value of maxRed*. If we wish to give the memory a name, we can write, for example, dram[15] rather than just [15].

The ← symbol indicates a *data transfer*. For example, the expression [15] ← [15] + 1 is interpreted as *the contents of memory location 15 are increased by 1 and the result is put back in memory location 15*. Consider the following RTL expressions:

```
a.    [20] = 5
b.    [20] ← 6
c.    [20] ← [6]
d.    [12] ← [3] + 4
e.    [19] ← [7] + [8]
f.    [4] ← [[2]]
```

Expression (a) states that the contents of memory location 20 are equal to the number 5. Expression (b) states that the number 6 is put into (*copied* or *loaded* into) memory location 20. Expression (c) indicates that the contents of memory location 6 are copied into memory location 20.

Expression (d) indicates that 4 is added to the contents of location 3, and the sum is put in location 12. Expression (e) indicates that the sum of the contents of locations 7 and 8 are added and put in location 19.

Expression (f) indicates that the contents of location 2 are used to access memory to read a value, which is an address. The contents of that second address are put in location 4. This expression is the most interesting because it introduces the notion of a *pointer*. The value of memory location 2, [2], is a pointer that indicates (points to) another memory location. If we perform [2] ← [2] + 1, the pointer now points to the next location in memory. We will return to this when we discuss indirect addressing (also called pointer-based addressing or indexed addressing).

The "←" RTL symbol is equivalent to the conventional assignment symbol, "=", used in some high-level languages. RTL is not a computer language; it is a notation used to define computer operations.

Nested square brackets such as [[4]] indicate the contents of the memory location, whose address is given by the contents of memory location 4. This is called indirect addressing. Figure 2.8 demonstrates how location 4 points at location 12, which contains the value of the required data – that is, 9.

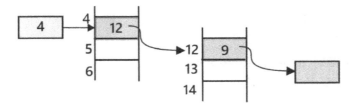

Figure 2.8 – Pointer-based addressing

An example of the use of RTL

Let's look at an example of the way that RTL can be used. *Figure 2.9* illustrates a small abstract memory with 12 locations.

Address	Data
0	6
1	2
2	3
3	4
4	5
5	2
6	8
7	1
8	5
9	2
10	1
11	5

Figure 2.9 – An example of the memory map of an abstract memory

We wish to evaluate the expression X = 3 + [4] + [1+[3]] + [[10]] + [[9]*3]. This expression can be evaluated by summing its components, as follows:

- The first element in the sequence is the literal 3
- The expression [4] represents the contents of memory location 4 – that is, 5.
- The expression [1+[3]] represents [1 + 4] = [5] = 2
- The expression [[10]] represents [1], which is 2
- The expression [[9]*3] represents [2*3] = [6] = 8

The final value is 3 + 5 + 2 + 2 + 8 = 20.

The next step is to simulate abstract memory in Python.

Simulating memory in Python

We now demonstrate how computer memory can be simulated in a Python program. To simulate a computer's main memory (the immediate access store, often called DRAM), we just create a Python list. A typical PC has over 4G memory locations (2^{22}). Here, we will create tiny memories that are easy to simulate. If we call the memory mem, we can create a memory with eight locations and initialize them to zero with the following:

```
mem = [0,0,0,0,0,0,0,0]          # Create 8-location memory. All locations set to zero
```

This initialization mechanism is inconvenient if you have much larger memory. If so, you can use a Python facility that lets you create a list and fill it with identical elements. Let's consider the following:

```
mem = [0]*128                    # Create memory with 128 locations, all set to 0
```

To demonstrate simple operations on the memory, we'll load two numbers into the simulated memory, retrieve them, add them, and store the result in memory using RTL notation:

```
mem[3]  ← 4                      # Load location 3 with 4. Note this is RTL not Python
mem[5]  ← 9                      # Load location 5 with 9
sum     ← mem[3] + mem[5]        # Add contents of locations 3 and 5, and put result in sum
mem[6]  ← sum                    # Store sum in location 6
```

We can translate this into Python and print the contents of location 6 as follows:

```
mem = [0]*8                      # Create memory with 8 locations, all set to 0. This is Python
mem[3] = 4                       # Load location 3 with 4
mem[5] = 9                       # Load location 5 with 9
sum    = mem[3] + mem[5]         # Add locations 3 and 5 and assign result to sum
mem[6] = sum                     # Store sum in location 6
print('mem[6] =', mem[6])        # Print contents of location 6
print('Memory =', mem)           # Print all memory locations
```

As you can see, Python is remarkably close to RTL notation. Now, let's use data in memory as a pointer. Recall that a pointer is a value that points to another location in memory. *Figure 2.10* shows an eight-location memory map with five integers stored in the memory.

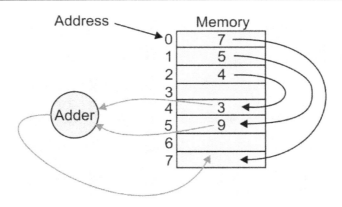

Figure 2.10 – A memory map of an addition operation

We will perform the following operation, first in RTL and then in Python:

mem[mem[0]]← mem[mem[1]] + mem[mem[2]]

Alternatively, if we use the simplified RTL where "mem" is understood, we can write this as follows:

[[0]]← [[1]] + [[2]]

This operation adds the contents of the memory location pointed at by the contents of location 1 to the contents of the memory location pointed at by the contents of memory location 2, putting the result in the contents of the memory location pointed at by memory location 0. We can express this in Python as follows:

```
mem = [7,5,4,0,3,9,0,0]          # Preset the memory. Unspecified locations are set to 0
pointer0 = mem[0]                # Get pointer 0 to result
pointer1 = mem[1]                # Get pointer 1 to source 1
pointer2 = mem[2]                # Get pointer 2 to source 2
source1  = mem[pointer1]         # Get source data 1
source2  = mem[pointer2]         # Get source data 2
result   = source1 + source2     # Do the addition
mem[pointer0] = result           # Store result at the location pointed at by pointer 0
print('Memory =', mem)           # Print all memory locations
```

This program will print the contents of memory as Memory = [7, 5, 4, 0, 3, 9, 0, 12]. As you can see, memory location 7 has changed from its initial value of 0 to the value 12 – that is, the sum of the contents of memory locations 5 and 4.

Summary

One of the main themes of this book is writing a program to simulate a computer so that you can run programs on a computer you designed yourself. To do this, it is necessary to write a simulator in a suitable high-level language. We chose Python because of its availability, simplicity, and power.

This chapter has provided a brief overview of Python by introducing the data structures and flow-control features you need to design a computer simulator. We have covered the basics of Python in sufficient detail for you to follow simple programs that don't use any of Python's more esoteric features.

Two important and very fundamental features of Python are the string (which is important, as simulation involves text processing) and the list. The list is simply a sequence of elements separated by commas and enclosed by square brackets. What is special about Python's lists is that the elements can be any data elements, and they are easy to access – for example, element 10 of list x is simply x[10]. Equally, character 5 of string x = 'a test' and is expressed as [5] and is 'i'. Like all computer languages, Python numbers elements from 0.

We also looked at the function, a piece of code that can be called from anywhere in a program to carry out some operation. You don't need functions. However, if you do the same thing often, calling a chunk of code to do the job makes the program easier to read and debug.

We demonstrated a very simple Python program to simulate memory and took our first step on the way to a simulator.

However, Python's strength (simplicity) is also a weakness. More complex languages ensure correctness by providing strict rules – for example, strong typing where you must declare the type of each variable and then use it accordingly. A very common Python pitfall is wrong indenting. Code in a loop or if construct is indented to show it belongs to whatever construct guards it. If you make a mistake with indenting while editing a program, it will either crash or behave very differently from what you intended.

In *Chapter 3*, we look at the basic structure of a **central processing unit** (**CPU**) and demonstrate how an instruction is read from memory, decoded, and executed.

3
Data Flow in a Computer

In this chapter, we will learn how a computer executes an instruction. We have to understand how a computer operates internally before we can simulate its behavior in Python. We will also introduce the concept of a computer instruction (the smallest operation that it can be commanded to perform) and show you what a computer instruction looks like.

What is a computer? How does it work? What does it do? We will answer these questions by demonstrating how a computer can be designed using Python, and how programs can be run on this simulated computer. Here, we are interested only in how a computer behaves at the machine level – that is, the type of operations it carries out. We are not concerned with the internal design of the computer or how the computer is implemented electronically (i.e., the circuits used to build a computer).

We will cover the following topics in this chapter:

- The instruction set architecture (ISA)
- The Von Neumann architecture
- An assembly-level program
- The machine-level instruction

Technical requirements

You can find the programs used in this chapter on GitHub at https://github.com/PacktPublishing/ Computer-Architecture-with-Python-and-ARM/tree/main/Chapter03.

The Instruction Architecture Level (ISA)

In this section, we will show how a computer can be described in different ways and explain that this book is about computers from the point of view of their instruction sets and capabilities.

The term *computer* means different things to different people. To an engineer, a computer is a collection of circuits that perform a certain function; to a pilot, it's a machine that flies an aircraft from one airport to another and can land it in thick fog.

Table 3.1 demonstrates the hierarchy of computer languages and structures. At the top you have the actual application for which the computer is used. At this level, the application may be a user-selected program (flight simulator), or it may be a program that runs on an embedded system (e.g., an ATM). Communication with that application is universal and independent of the actual computer on which the application runs.

Level	Realization	Universality
1. Application	Word, Excel, Photoshop, and flight sim	Universal
2. High-level language	Python, Java, C++	Universal
3. Assembly language	ADD r1,r2, and r3	Computer family
4. Binary (machine code)	001110101111000010101011110001010 binary	Computer family
5. Circuit (microprocessor)	Gates, adders, counters, and memory	Specific family member
6. Silicon	The physical silicon chip	Specific chip

Table 3.1 – The hierarchy of computer languages and systems

Below the application level, you have the high-level language used to build the application. This language may be Python, Java, C++, and so on. High-level languages were designed to enable programmers to build applications that run on different types of computers. For example, a program written in Python will run on any machine for which a Python interpreter or compiler is available. Before the introduction of high-level languages, you had to design the application for each specific computer.

Most computers are currently unable to directly execute high-level languages. Each computer has a native language that is understood by a computer family (e.g., Intel Core, Motorola 68K, ARMv4, and MIPS). These languages are related to the structure of the computer and its hardware, which is expressed by a computer's ISA. This level is represented by two layers in *Table 3.1*, *assembly language and machine code*.

The layer below the high-level language is the assembly language level, which is a human representation of the computer's binary machine code. People can't remember or easily manipulate strings of 1s and 0s. Assembly language is a textual version of machine code. For example, the assembly language operation ADD **A**,B,C means add B to C and put the result in A (i.e., A = B + C) and might be represented in machine code as 00110101011100111100001010101010.

The *machine code* layer is the binary code that the computer actually executes. In the PC world, a machine-code program has the .exe file extension because it can be *executed* by the computer. All computers execute binary code, although this layer is different for each type of computer – for example, Intel Core, ARM, and MIPS are three computer families, and each has its own machine code.

Although the assembly language layer is a representation of the machine code layer, there is a difference between these two layers. The assembly language layer includes facilities to help a programmer write programs, such as the ability to define variable names and to link independently written modules into a single machine-code program.

Below the machine-code layer are the electronic circuits, which are generically called microprocessors, or just chips. This is the hardware that companies such as Intel make, and it's this hardware that reads programs from memory and executes them. In general, this layer cannot be programmed or modified any more than you can change the number of cylinders in your car's engine.

Today, some digital systems do have circuits that can be modified electronically – that is, it is possible for the circuits of a computer to be restructured by changing the routing of signals through a circuit called a **field programmable gate array (FPGA)**. The FPGA contains a very large number of gates and special-purpose circuit blocks that can be interconnected by programming. An FPGA can be programmed to perform dedicated applications such as signal processing in medical or aerospace systems.

At the electronic circuit level, it's possible to have different versions of the same set of circuits. For example, a microprocessor can be realized using 7 nm or 14 nm device technology (these figures express the basic size of components on the chip, and smaller is better). The two circuits may be operationally identical in every way, but one version may be faster, cheaper, more reliable, or use less power than the other.

This book is about assembly language and machine code layers, and the layers in *Table 3.1* allow us to write programs that are executed by a computer. By the end of this book, you will be able to design your own machine code, your own assembly language, and your own computer.

In the 1940s and 1950s, all programming was done in assembly language (or even machine code). Not today. Writing assembly language programs is tedious and very challenging. Computer scientists have created high-level languages such as C++, Java, Python, and Fortran. These languages were developed to allow programmers to write programs in a near-English language that expresses more powerful ideas than assembly language. For example, in Python, you can print the text `"Hello World"` on the screen with the instruction `print("Hello World.")`. If you wanted to do that in assembly language, you would have to write out, say, 100 individual machine-level instructions. Moreover, the Python version will run on all computers, but the machine-level version has to be written for each specific computer type.

The high-level language's secret is the *compiler*. You write a program in a high-level language and then compile it to the machine code of the specific computer you want to run it on. You may come across the term *interpreter*, which performs the same function as a compiler. A compiler translates an entire high-level language program into machine code, whereas an interpreter performs the translation line by line, executing each line as it is interpreted.

Writing code in assembly language is not popular today (outside academia). However, it has the advantage that (in principle) you can write optimized code that runs faster than compiled code.

A principal theme of this book is *learning by doing*. We will explain what a computer is, introduce the instructions it executes, and then show how it can be built (i.e., simulated) in a high-level language. We will call the program we are going to construct **TC1 (Teaching Computer 1)**. This program will execute the assembly language of a hypothetical computer. You will be able to write a program in assembly language, and the TC1 program will read the instructions and execute them as if they were running on a real TC1 computer.

When you run the program, you can execute instructions one by one and observe their outcomes v – that is, you can read the values of data in registers and memory as the program runs. The purpose of this computer is not to perform useful computing functions but to show what instructions look like and how they are executed.

This computer demonstrates how instructions are executed and how to use assembly language. Moreover, you can modify the instruction set of the computer to create your own special-purpose instructions. You can remove instructions, add new instructions, extend instructions, and even change the format of instructions. TC1 was designed to enable students that study computer architecture to understand instruction formats, instruction decoding, and instruction complexity. It is also very helpful to understand addressing modes (i.e., how data is located in memory), such as pointer-based addressing. We will discuss these topics in more detail later.

TC1 has several useful facilities that are not present in conventional computer instruction sets. For example, you can directly input data into the computer from the keyboard, and you can load random numbers into memory. This allows you to create data for testing purposes.

First, we need to introduce the prototype computer, the so-called von Neumann machine, which was created in the 1940s and 1950s and became the template for most modern computers. In reality, there's been quite a departure from the pure von Neumann architecture, but we still tend to use the term to distinguish between other classes of computers (e.g., analog computers, neural networks, and quantum computers).

ISAs – the Naming of Parts

Before we introduce the structure of a computer, we need to introduce several terms that you need to know:

- **Bit**: The smallest unit of data in a computer is the bit, which is 0 or 1. You can set a bit to 0, to 1, or toggle it (flip it over).

- **Word**: A word is a group of bits – typically, 8, 16, 32, or 64. In general, the word is the basic unit of data that the computer operates on. An instruction such as ADD **a**, b, c executed on a 64-bit computer would add the 64-bits of word b to the 64-bits or word c and put the 64-bit result in word a. The a, b, and c variables refer to storage locations in either memory or registers.

- **Instruction**: A machine-level instruction is the most primitive operation that a programmer can specify and defines a single action carried out by the computer. Even more primitive level operations may exist on the silicon, but a programmer cannot directly access these. Instructions largely fall into three classes – data movement that copies data from one place to another, arithmetic and logical operations that process data, and instruction sequence commands that determine the order in which instructions are carried out (necessary to implement decisions of the form *if this, then do that*).

- **Immediate access memory**: This is often just called memory or RAM or DRAM by many programmers. It is where programs and data are stored during the execution of a program. The term *random access memory* today means the same thing. However, strictly speaking, the term *random* indicates that the access time for a memory element chosen at random is the same for every element (unlike, say, magnetic tape, where the access time depends on where data is on the tape).

- **Register**: A register is a single-word memory element that is located on the chip. It is used to store frequently accessed data. Because there are typically 8 to 64 registers on a chip, it requires only 3 to 6 bits to specify a given register, rather than the 32 or 64 bits typically used to access a memory location. Most computer operations act on the contents of registers rather than the main memory. There is no universal convention for the naming of registers. In this chapter, we will generally use for register names – for example, INC r3 increments the contents of register r3 by 1.

- **Address**: The location of a data item in memory is called its address. Modern computer addresses are typically 32 bits or 64 bits long. However, 8- and 16-bit computers are frequently used in embedded control applications (e.g., toys, TVs, washing machines, and automobiles).

- **Literal**: A literal value is just that, an actual value. If you have an instruction ADD **a**,b,5 where 5 is a literal, then it means, add the 5 integer to b. Some computers use a # to indicate a literal – for example, ADD **a**,b,#12 means, add the number 12 to the contents of memory location b.

- **Move**: This is the most inaccurate word in computing. In plain English, it indicates that something was at A and then ends up at B – simplicity itself. In computing, the term *move* indicates that something that was at A ends up at B, as well – that is, it is now in both A and B. In other words, programmers use *move* to mean *copy*. If you *move* data from a register to memory, the data remains in the register and is *copied* to memory. We will introduce the prototype computer in the following section.

The next step is to introduce the notion of the von Neumann computer, which can be regarded as the grandfather of most modern computers. The mathematician von Neumann was one of the authors of *The First Draft Report on the EDVAC* in 1945, which characterized the structure of the digital computer.

The von Neumann architecture

The prototype computer is often called a stored program von Neumann machine. It has a program in memory that is executed instruction by instruction sequentially. Moreover, the program is stored in the same memory as the data that the computer operates on. This structure is named in honor of one of the pioneers of computing, John von Neumann. Once you understand the von Neumann machine, you understand all computers.

Figure 3.1 illustrates a simplified von Neumann machine that contains three basic elements:

- A memory that holds the program and any data used by the program
- A set of registers that each holds one word of data (in *Figure 3.1*, there is one register, r0)
- An **arithmetic and logic unit (ALU)** that performs all data processing

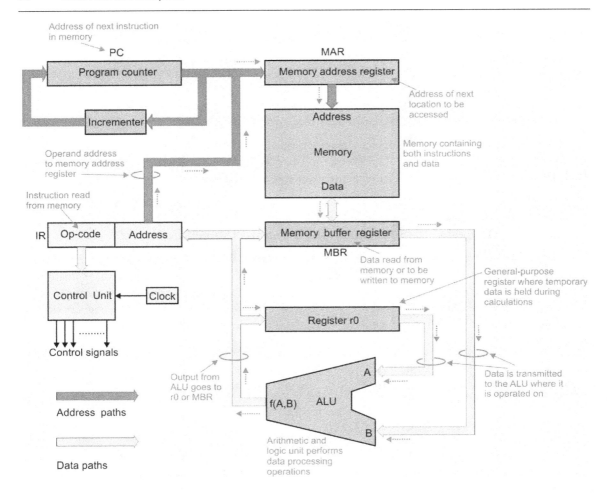

Figure 3.1 – The von Neumann architecture

The memory contains instructions to be executed. Both data and instructions are stored in binary form, although we will often show operations in assembly language form for ease of reading. Each instruction is read from memory, decoded, and interpreted (i.e., executed). The principal simplification of *Figure 3.1* is the lack of a means of executive conditional operations (i.e., if… then). We will fix that later.

Figure 3.1 looks complicated. It's not. We'll explain its operation step by step. Once we see how a computer operates in principle, we can look at how it may be implemented in software. We describe the operation of a very simple, so-called *one-and-a-half* address machine, whose instructions have two operands – one in memory and one in a register. Instructions are written in the form ADD **B**,A, which adds A to B and puts the result in B. Either A or B must be in a register. Both operands may be in registers. The term *one-and-a-half address* machine is a comment about the fact that the memory address is 16 to 32 bits and selects one of millions of memory locations, whereas the register address is typically 2 to 6 bits and selects only one of a small number of registers.

Instead of introducing the computer all at once, we will build up a CPU step by step. This approach helps demonstrate how an instruction is executed because the development of the computer broadly follows the sequence of events taking place during the execution of an instruction. Real computers don't execute an instruction from start to finish. Today's computers *overlap* the execution of instructions. As soon as one instruction is fetched from memory, the next instruction is fetched before the previous instruction has completed its execution. This mechanism is called *pipelining* and is a major aspect of a modern computer's organization. Pipelining is analogous to the automobile production line, where computer instructions are executed in stages so that several instructions may be in the process of being executed at the same time. We will begin with the address paths that are used to locate the next instruction to be executed. In this book, we will not cover pipelining because it is a factor or implementation and not an instruction set design.

The address path

An address is a number representing the location of an item of data within memory. *Figure 3.2* shows only the address paths needed to read an instruction from memory.

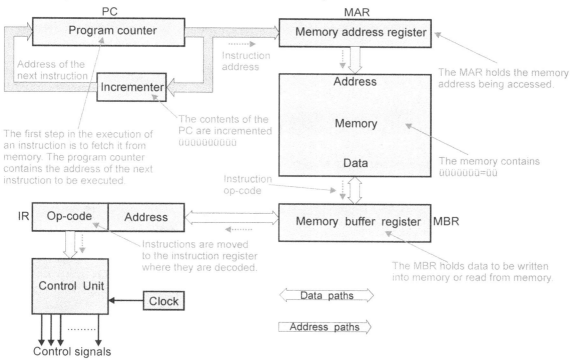

Figure 3.2 – The CPU's address paths

An address path is a data highway that moves addresses between the CPU and memory. The address tells memory where we want to read data from, or where we want to store it. For example, the instruction ADD **r0**,234 indicates the operation *read the contents of memory location 234, add them to the contents of register r0, and then put the result in r0. Figure 3.2* omits the data paths required to execute instructions to avoid clutter.

There are three types of information flow in a computer – address, data, and control. Data comprises the instructions, constants, and variables stored in memory and registers. Control paths comprise the signals that trigger events, provide clocks, and determine the flow of data and addresses throughout the computer.

Reading the instruction

Before the CPU can execute an instruction, the instruction must be brought from the computer's memory. We begin our description of the way in which a program is executed with the CPU's *program counter* (also called *instruction pointer* or *location counter*). The expression *program counter* is a misnomer. The program counter doesn't count programs or anything else, but instead contains the address of the next instruction in memory to be executed.

The program counter *points* to the next instruction to be executed. If, for example, [PC] = 1234 (i.e., the PC contains the number 1234), the next instruction to be executed will be found in memory location 1234.

Fetching an instruction begins with the contents of the program counter being moved to the memory address register (i.e., [MAR] ← [PC]). Once the contents of the program counter have been transferred to the memory address register, the contents of the program counter are incremented and moved back to the program counter, as follows:

[PC] ← [PC] + 1.

The PC increment is 1 because the next instruction is one location on. Real computers are normally byte-addressed – that is, the bytes are numbered sequentially 0, 1, 2, 3 … Modern computers have 32- or 64-bit data words – that is, 4- or 8-byte words. Consequently, real computers increment the PC by 4 or 8 after each instruction.

After this operation, the program counter points to the *next* instruction while the current instruction is executed.

The **memory address register (MAR)** holds the address of the location in the memory into which data is written in a write cycle, or from which data is read in a read cycle.

When a *memory read cycle* is performed, the contents of the memory location specified by the MAR are read from the memory and transferred to the **memory buffer register (MBR)**. We can represent this read operation in RTL terms as follows:

[MBR] ← [[MAR]]   @ A read operation (example of indirect addressing)

We interpret the `[[MAR]]` expression as *the contents of the memory whose address is given by the contents of the MAR*. The memory buffer register is a temporary holding place for data received from memory in a read cycle, or for data to be transferred to memory in a write cycle. Some texts refer to the MBR as the **memory data register (MDR).** At this point in the execution of an instruction, the MBR contains the bit pattern of the instruction to be executed.

The instruction is next moved from the MBR to the **instruction register (IR),** where it is divided into two fields. A *field* is part of a word in which the bits are grouped together into a logical entity – for example, a person's name can be divided into two fields, the given name and the family name. One field in the IR contains the *operation code* (opcode) that tells the CPU what operation is to be carried out. The other field, called the *operand field*, contains the address of the data to be used by the instruction. The operand field can also provide a constant to be employed by the operation code when immediate or literal addressing is used – that is, when the operand is an actual (i.e., literal) value and not an address. For our current purposes, the register address is considered to be part of the instruction. Later, we will introduce computers with multiple registers. Real computers divide the instruction into more than two fields – for example, there may be two or three register-select fields.

The **control unit (CU)** takes the opcode from the instruction register, together with a stream of clock pulses, and generates signals that control all parts of the CPU. The time between individual clock pulses is typically in the range 0.3 ns to 100 ns (i.e., 3×10^{-10} to 10^{-7} s), corresponding to frequencies of 3.3 GHz to 10 MHz. The CU is responsible for moving the contents of the program counter into the MAR, executing a read cycle, and moving the contents of the MBR to the IR.

Instructions are executed in a two-phase *fetch-execute cycle*. During the *fetch phase*, the instruction is read from memory and decoded by the control unit. The fetch phase is followed by an *execute phase*, in which the control unit generates all the signals necessary to execute the instruction. The following RTL notation describes the sequence of operations that take place in a fetch phase. FETCH is a label that serves to indicate a particular line in the sequence of operations. The notation IR_{opcode} means the operation-code field of the instruction register. We use # to indicate a comment in Python and @ in assembly language to be compatible with ARM's convention. Some assemblers use a semicolon to indicate a comment field:

```
FETCH  [MAR]  ←  [PC]          @ Copy contents of the PC to the MAR
       [PC]   ←  [PC] + 1      @ Increment the contents of the PC to point to next instruction
       [MBR]  ←  [[MAR]]       @ Read the instruction from memory
       [IR]   ←  [MBR]         @ Move the instruction to the instruction register for processing
       CU     ←  [IRopcode]    @ Transmit the opcode to the control unit
```

The following is an example of how we can code the fetch cycle as a function in Python, together with the code needed to test it. We define a 12-bit instruction with a 4-bit opcode and an 8-bit address. The memory has 16 locations, and we load the first two with dummy values to test the program. The Python expression p >> q takes the binary value p and shifts it q places right, and & performs a logical AND. We will discuss this in more detail later. For example, **011**000001010 >> 8 becomes **0110**. This extracts the opcode. Similarly, 0b011011111010 & 0b111111111111 = 0b000000001010 to extract the address:

```
                                # Testing the fetch cycle
mem = [0] * 16                  # Set up 16 locations in memory
pc = 0                          # Initialize pc to 0

mem[0] = 0b011000001010         # Dummy first instruction (opcode in bold) 0b indicates binary value
mem[1] = 0b100011111111         # Dummy second instruction

def fetch(memory):              # Fetch cycle implemented using a function
    global pc                   # Make pc global because we change it
    mar = pc                    # Copy pc to mar
    pc = pc + 1                 # Increment the pc ready for next instruction
    mbr = memory[mar]           # Read instruction from memory
    ir = mbr                    # Copy instruction to instruction register
    cu = ir >> 8                # Shift instruction 8 places right to get the operation code
    address = ir & 0xFF         # Mask opcode to 8-bit address
    return(cu, address)         # Return instruction and address

opCode,address = fetch(mem)     # Do a fetch cycle
print('pc =', pc - 1, 'opcode =', opCode, ' Operand =', address)
opCode,address = fetch(mem)     # Do a fetch cycle
print('pc =', pc - 1, 'opcode =', opCode, ' Operand =', address)
```

In the preceding code, the numeric 0b011000001010 value is expressed in binary form by the 0b prefix. Similarly, the 0xFF notation indicates a number in hexadecimal form – that is, 255 in decimal or 11111111 in binary form.

The function is tested by calling it twice with opCode, address = fetch(mem). Python lets us receive the two returned parameters, opcode and address, on one line. Note how closely the Python code follows the RTL. In practice, you would not write this code. We don't need the MAR and MBR registers. I included them to help model the hardware. We can simply write the following:

```
ir = mem[pc]                    # Read current instruction into ir
pc = pc + 1                     # Increment program counter ready for next cycle
cu = ir >> 8                    # Extract the opcode
address = ir & 0xFF             # Extract the operand address
```

The CPU's data paths

Having sorted out the fetch phase, let's see what else we need to execute instructions. *Figure 3.3* adds data paths to the CPU of *Figure 3.2*, plus an address path from the address field of the instruction register to the memory address register. Other additions are a data register, r0, and an ALU that does the actual computing. The operations it performs are typically arithmetic (add, subtract, multiply, and divide) and logical (AND, OR, EOR, and shift left or right).

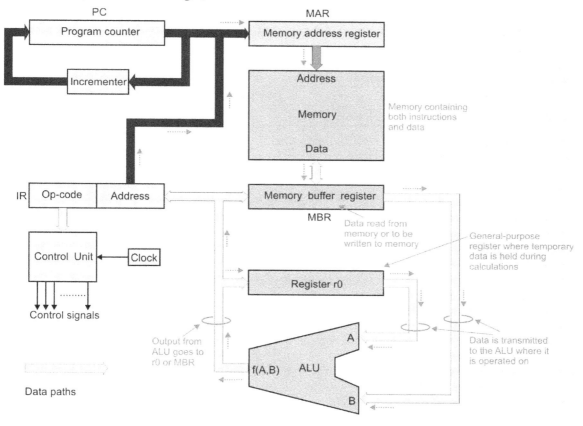

Figure 3.3 – The CPU's address and data paths

The data register, r0, holds temporary results during a calculation. You need a data register (i.e., an accumulator) because *dyadic* operations with two operands such as ADD use one operand specified by the instruction, and the other register is the contents of a data register. ADD **r0**, P adds the contents of the memory location, P, to the contents of the general-purpose register, r0, and deposits the sum in the data register, destroying one of the original operands. The arrangement of *Figure 3.3* has one general-purpose data register that we've called r0. A real processor, the ARM, has 16 registers, r0 to r15 (although not all of them are general-purpose data registers).

Typical data movement instructions

All computers have data move instructions that transfer (i.e., copy) data from one place to another. These are the simplest instructions because they don't involve processing data. Data movement instructions vary from computer to computer. Here, we will provide a few typical examples that will help you follow the examples in this chapter. Note that we will use different conventions in this text. For example, we will sometimes prefix a literal by # (e.g., ADD **r1**, #6) and sometimes add the suffix L to the instruction (e.g., ADDL **r1**, 6). This is because there are several standards/conventions in use in computing, and they vary from computer to computer. The following are simply generic examples of code. Note the duplication of load a literal. Some processors use move and some use load:

Mnemonic	Example	Name	RTL	Comment
MOV	MOV **r1**, r4	move register	[r1] ← [r4]	Copy register r4 to register r1
MOVL	MOVL **r1**, 5	move literal	[r1] ← 5	Copy the integer 5 to register r1
LDR	LDR **r3**, 12	load register	[r3] ← [12]	Load r3 with contents of memory location 12
LDRL	LDRL **r0**, 13	load literal	[r0] ← 13	Load register r0 with the integer 13
STR	STR r4, **8**	store register	[8] ← [r4]	Store contents of r4 in memory location 8

Table 3.2 – Typical data movement instructions

Data processing instructions

Let's look at a typical data-processing operation. We can represent an ADD **r0**, X instruction with the RTL expression:

```
[r0] ← [r0] + [X]          @ Add the contents of the memory
                             location X to register r0
```

The ALU is the workhorse of the CPU because it performs all calculations. Arithmetic and logical operations are applied to the contents of a data register and the contents of a data register or the MBR. The output of the ALU is fed back to the data register or to the MBR.

The fundamental difference between arithmetic and logical operations is that logical operations don't generate a carry when bit a_i of word A and bit b_i of B are operated upon. *Table 3.2* provides examples of typical arithmetic and logical operations.

Operation	Class	Typical mnemonic
Addition	Arithmetic	ADD (a = b + c)
Subtraction	Arithmetic	SUB (a = b - c)
Negation	Arithmetic	NEG (a = -b)
Multiplication	Arithmetic	MUL (a = b * c)
Division	Arithmetic	DIV (a = b / c)
Divide by 2	Arithmetic	ASR (a = b / 2)
Multiply by 2	Arithmetic	ASL (a = b * 2)
AND	Logical	AND (a = b & c)
OR	Logical	OR (a = b | c)
NOT	Logical	NOT (a = !b)
EOR	Logical	EOR (a = b ⊕ c)
Shift left	Logical	LSL (shift all bits left a = b << 1)
Shift right	Logical	LSR (shift all bits right a = b >> 1)

Table 3.3 – Typical arithmetic and logical operations

A logical shift treats an operand as a string of bits that are moved left or right. An arithmetic shift treats a number as a signed 2s complement value and propagates the sign bit during a right shift (i.e., the sign bit is replicated and duplicated). Most of these operations are implemented by computers such as the 68K, Intel Core, and ARM.

Another look at the data flow

Let's have another look at data flow in a computer to cement the basic concepts together. In *Figure 3.4*, we have a computer that supports operations involving three registers (a hallmark of computers such as the ARM). Here, we have three registers, r1, r2, and r3. The block labeled *adder* is part of the ALU and serves to add two numbers to produce a sum. Instruction LDR **r2**, X loads the contents of memory address X into register r2. Instruction STR r1, **Z** stores the contents of register r1 in memory address Z.

The instruction ADD **r1**, r2, r3 reads the contents of registers r2 and r3, adds them together, and deposits the result in register, r1. Since it's not clear which register is the destination register (i.e., the result), we use a bold font to highlight the destination operand, which is normally the leftmost operand.

Figure 3.4 shows several fundamental components of a computer. This is, essentially, the same as the more detailed structures we used to demonstrate the fetch/execute cycle. Here, we are interested in data flow into and out of memory.

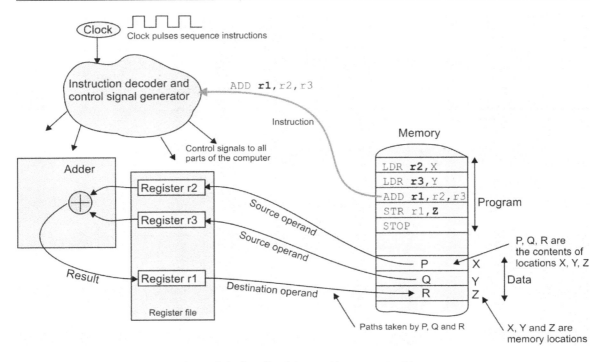

Figure 3.4 – Details of the von Neumann machine

The elements of interest are as follows:

- A clock that generates timing pulses. All operations take place when triggered by the clock.

- An interpreter or control unit that takes an instruction, together with a stream of clock pulses, and converts it into the actions required to perform the required operation. In *Figure 3.4*, the interpreter routes the contents of registers r2 and r3 to the adder, makes the adder add the two values together, and then routes the result from the adder to the destination register.

- The program in memory. Data is loaded from memory into registers r2 and r2. Then, r2 and r3 are added together and the result is put in r3. Finally, the contents of r3 are moved to memory.

Now that we've covered the basic structure of a computer and introduced some instructions, the next step is to look at a complete program that carries out a specific function.

An assembly-level program

Having developed our computer a little further, in this section, we will show how a simple program is executed. Assume that this computer doesn't provide three-address instructions (i.e., you can't specify an operation with three registers and/or memory addresses) and we want to implement the high-level language operation Z = X + Y. Here, the *plus* symbol means arithmetic addition. An assembly language program that carries out this operation is given in the following code block. Remember that X, Y, and Z are symbolic names referring to the *locations* of the variables in memory. Logically, the store operation should be written STR Z,r2, with the destination operand on the left just like other instructions. By convention, it is written as STR r2,Z, with the source register on the left. This is a quirk of programming history:

LDR **r2**,X   Load data register r2 with the contents of memory location X

ADD **r2**,Y   Add the contents of memory location Y to data register r2

STR r2,**Z**   Store the contents of data register r2 in memory location Z

Eight-bit computers had a one-address machine, requiring a rather cumbersome sequence of operations just to carry out the simple act of adding two numbers. If we had a computer with a three-address format, we could have written the following:

ADD **Z**,X,Y   Add the contents of X to the contents of Y and put the result in Z

Three-address machines are *potentially* faster than one-address machines because they can do in one instruction things that take other machines three operations. Unfortunately, it is a factor of technological development that on-chip registers are faster than DRAM, and computer designers try to keep data in registers on-chip as much as possible.

The reality is more complicated. Accessing memory is slow compared to accessing registers. This is a property of the hardware. Consequently, it is more efficient to keep data in registers.

The way in which the CPU operates can best be seen by examining the execution of, say, ADD **r2**,Y in terms of register-transfer language. In the following code block, we describe the operations carried out during the fetch and execute phases of an ADD **r2**,Y instruction:

```
FETCH [MAR] ← [PC]                    Move the contents of the PC to the MAR
      [PC]  ← [PC] + 1                Increment the contents of the PC
      [MBR] ← [[MAR]]                 Read the current instruction from the memory
      [IR]  ← [MBR]                   Move the contents of the MBR to the IR
      CU    ← [IRopcode]              Move the opcode from the IR to the CU

ADD   [MAR] ← [IRaddress]             Move the operand address to the MAR
      [MBR] ← [[MAR]]                 Read the data from memory
      ALU   ← [MBR], ALU ← [r2]       Perform the addition
      [r2]  ← ALU                     Move the output of ALU to the data register
```

Operations sharing the same line are executed simultaneously.

During the fetch phase, the opcode is fed to the control unit by CU ← [IR_{opcode}] and used to generate all the internal signals required to place the ALU in its addition mode. When the ALU is programmed for addition, it adds together the data at its two input terminals to produce a sum at its output terminals.

Operations of the form [PC] ← [MAR] or [r2] ← [r2] + [MBR] are often referred to as *microinstructions*. Each assembly-level instruction (e.g., MOV, ADD) is executed as a series of microinstructions. Microinstructions are the province of the computer designer. In the 1970s, some machines were user-microprogrammable – that is, you could define your own instruction set.

We can test the execute phase by extending the fetch phase code. The following Python code provides three instructions – load a register with a literal, add memory contents to the register, and stop. We have also made the Python code more compact – for example, you can put expressions in a function's return statement. In this example, we return two values: ir >> 8 and ir & 0xFF. The operation x >> y takes the binary value of x and shifts the bits y places right; for example, 0b0011010110 >> 2 gives 0b0000110101. The shaded part of the code is the machine-level program we execute:

```
# Implement fetch cycle and execute cycle: include three test instructions
mem = [0] * 12                          # Set up 12-location memory
pc = 0                                   # Initialize pc to 0
mem[0] = 0b000100001100                  # First instruction load r0 with 12
mem[1] = 0b001000000111                  # Second instruction add mem[7] to r0
mem[2] = 0b111100000000                  # Third instruction is stop
mem[7] = 8                               # Initial data inlocation 7 is 8

def fetch(memory):                       # Function for fetch phase
    global pc                            # Make pc a global variable
    ir = memory[pc]                      # Read instruction and move to IR
    pc = pc + 1                          # Increment program counter for next cycle
    return(ir >> 8, ir & 0xFF)           # Returns opCode and operand

run = 1                                  # run = 1 to continue
while run == 1:                          # REPEAT: The program execution loop
    opCode, address = fetch(mem)         # Call fetch to perform fetch phase
    if   opCode == 0b1111: run = 0       # Execute phase for stop (set run to 0 on stop)
    elif opCode == 0b0001:               # Execute phase for load number
        r0 = address                     # Load r0 with contents of address field
    elif opCode == 0b0010:               # Execute phase for add
        mar = address                    # Copy address in opCode to MAR
        mbr = mem[mar]                   # Read the number to be dded
        r0 = mbr + r0                     # Do the addition
    print('pc = ',pc - 1, 'opCode =', opCode, 'Register r0 =',r0)
                                         # We print pc – 1 because the pc is incremented
```

The output from this code is as follows:

```
pc =   0 opCode = 1  Register r0 = 12
pc =   1 opCode = 2  Register r0 = 20
pc =   2 opCode = 15 Register r0 = 20
```

Note that the Python term `elif` is short for *else if.* The preceding case says, *"Is the opcode stop. If not, is the opcode load. If not, is the opcode add."* This allows for a sequence of tests. We discuss `elif` in more detail later.

Executing conditional instructions

So far, we've looked at the structure of a CPU capable of executing programs in a purely *sequential* mode – that is, the computer can execute only a stream of instructions, one by one, in strict order. We introduced conditional behavior in the previous chapter, and now we will extend the CPU so that it can execute instructions, such as `BEQ Target` (a branch on a zero flag set to `Target`), that are able to execute instructions out of sequence.

The computer in *Figure 3.1* lacks a mechanism to make choices or repeat a group of instructions. To do this, the CPU must be able to execute *conditional branches* or *jumps.* The block diagram of *Figure 3.5* shows the new address and data paths required by the CPU to implement conditional branches.

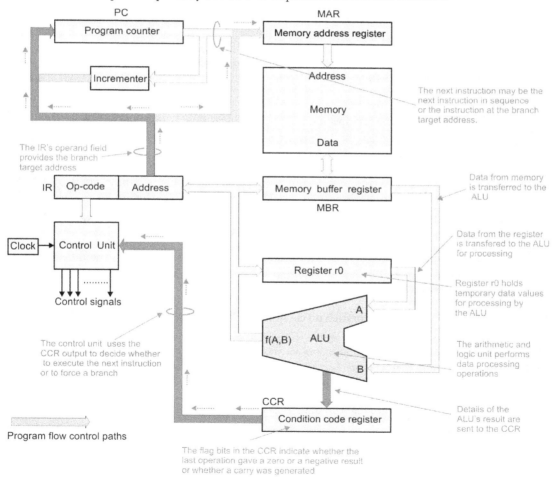

Figure 3.5 – Information paths in the CPU and conditional instructions

Three items have been added to our computer in *Figure 3.5*. These are highlighted:

- A **condition code register (CCR)**
- A path between the CCR and the control unit
- A path between the address field of the instruction register and the program counter.

The *condition code register* or *processor status register* records the ALU state after each instruction has been executed, and updates the carry, negative, zero, and overflow flag bits. A conditional branch instruction interrogates the CCR's flags. The CU then either executes the next instruction in sequence or branches to another instruction. Let's look at the details of the conditional branch. The following is a reminder of the CCR bit functions:

- C = Carry: A carry occurs when an operation in n bits yields an n+1 bit result (e.g., when your car odometer winds round from 999...9 to 000...0). In 8-bit computer terms, this is when 11111111 + 1 = 0000000 carry 1.
- Z = Zero: This is set if the last operation generated a zero result.
- N = Negative: This is set if the last result generated a negative result in 2s complement arithmetic – that is, set if the most significant bit of a word is 1 (for example, 00101010 is positive and 10101010 is negative when the number is viewed as a two's complement value).
- V = Overflow: This is set if the last operation resulted in an arithmetic overflow, which occurs in two's complement arithmetic if the result is outside its allowable range. In this text, we generally don't implement the V-flag for the sake of simplicity.

The condition code register is connected to the control unit, enabling an instruction to interrogate it. For example, some instructions test whether an operation yielded a positive result, whether the carry bit was set, or whether an arithmetic overflow occurred. We need a mechanism that does one thing if the result of the test is `true` and does another thing if the result of the test is `false`.

The final modification included in *Figure 3.5* is the addition of a path between the operand field (i.e., the target address) of the instruction register and the program counter. It's this feature that enables the computer to respond to the result of its interrogation of the CCR.

A *conditional branch* instruction such as **branch on carry set (BCS)** tests the carry bit of the CCR, and if the bit tested is clear, the next instruction is obtained from memory in the normal way. If the bit tested is set, the next instruction is obtained from the location whose *target address* is in the instruction register. In the preceding description, we said that a branch is made if a bit of the CCR is set; equally, a branch can be made if the bit is clear (branches can also be made on the combined state of several CCR bits).

Branch operations can be expressed in register-transfer language in the following form:

```
IF condition THEN action
```

Typical machine-level conditional operations expressed in RTL are as follows:

1.   Branch on carry clear (jump to the target address if the carry bit in the CCR is 0)

   BCC target: IF [C] = 0 THEN [PC] ← [IR$_{address}$]

2.   Branch on equal (jump to the target address if the Z bit in the CCR is 1)

   BEQ target: IF [Z] = 1 THEN [PC] ← [IR$_{address}$]

Both these actions have an `ELSE` condition, which is the default `[PC] ← [PC] + 1`.

An example of a conditional branch in assembly language is as follows:

```
        SUB   r0,x      @ Subtract the contents of memory location x from register r0
        BEQ   Last      @ If the result was zero, then branch to Last; otherwise, continue
          .             @ Execute here if branch not taken
          .
Last                    @ Target address of branch (if taken)
```

The final step in extending the computer architecture is the introduction of data paths to permit literals to be loaded into a register – that is, to load a register with a number that is in the instruction rather than from memory. The z-bit can be confusing. The z-bit is set to 1 if a result yields zero, and it's set to 0 if the result is not zero.

Dealing with literal operands

Computer instructions such as ADD `r0,abc` refer to an operand somewhere within the CPU's memory. Sometimes, we want to use an instruction such as ADD `r0,#12,` where the source operand supplies the *actual value* of the data being referred to by the opcode part of the instruction – in this case, 12. Although the symbol # appears as part of the operand when this instruction is written in mnemonic form, the assembler uses a different opcode code for the following:

ADD   `r0,#literal` and ADD   `r0,address`.

The instruction ADD   `r0,#12` is defined in RTL as [r0] ← [r0] + 12.

Note that we use two conventions for literals. One is ADD   `r0,#12` and the other is ADD**L**   `r0,12`. This matches typical instruction sets.

Figure 3.6 shows that an additional data path is required between the operand field of the IR and the data register and ALU to deal with literal operands. *Figure 3.6* includes three general-purpose registers, `r0, r1,` and `r2`. In principle, there is nothing stopping us from adding any number of registers. However, the number of internal registers is limited by the number of bits available to specify a register in the instruction. As you can see, three data buses, A, B, and C, are used to transfer data between the registers and ALU.

The structure of *Figure 3.6* can implement instructions with more complex addressing modes than the simple direct (absolute) addressing we have used so far. Consider MOV **r1**, [r0], which copies the contents of the memory location whose address is in r0. Here, r0 is a pointer to the actual data. This instruction can be implemented by the following sequence of micro-operations:

MOV	[MAR]	←	[r0]	Move the source operand address to the MAR
	[MBR]	←	[[MAR]]	Read the actual operand from memory
	[MAR]	←	[MBR]	Copy the address back to the MAR
	[r1]	←	[[MAR]]	Copy the data from memory to r1

This sequence has been simplified because, as you can see from *Figure 3.6*, there is no direct path between register r0 and the MBR. You would have to put the contents of r0 onto bus A, pass the contents of bus A through the ALU to bus C, and then copy bus C to the MAR.

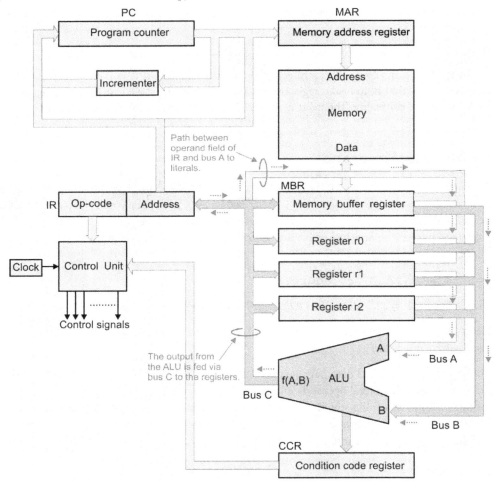

Figure 3.6 – Modifying the CPU to deal with literal operands

Let's extend our Python code to include both literal operations and conditional operations. The following Python code implements a load register with literal instruction, an add/subtract, a conditional branch on zero, and a stop. Here, we use LDRL to indicate a literal, rather than prefixing the literal with #. The program to be executed is as follows:

Address	Mnemonic	Instruction	Binary code	Note
0	LDRL r0,9	load r0 with the literal 9	**0001**00001001	[r0] ← 9
1	SUB r0,7	subtract mem [7] from r0	**0011**00000111	[r0] ← [r0] - mem[7]
2	BEQ 6	branch on zero to 6	**0100**00000110	if z = 1 [PC] ← 6
3	STOP	top execution	**1111**00000000	
4				
5				
6	STOP	top execution	**1111**00000000	

Table 3.4 – Caption

To implement a load register, we simply move the literal in the instruction to the register. The subtraction tests the result and sets the zero-status bit, z, to 1 if the result is 0 and 0 if it is not. The conditional branch tests the z-bit and loads the pc with the literal from the instruction if z = 1.

```
                                      # Simple program to test a branch instruction
mem = [0] * 12                        # Set up a 12-location memory
pc = 0                                # Initialize program counter to 0
mem[0] = 0b000100001001               # First instruction loads r0 with 9 (i.e., 1001)
mem[1] = 0b001100000111               # Second instruction subtracts mem[7] from r0
mem[2] = 0b010000000110               # Third instruction is BEQ 6 (branch on zero to 6)
mem[3] = 0b111100000000               # Fourth instruction is stop
mem[6] = 0b111100000000               # Seventh instruction is stop
mem[7] = 9                            # Initial data in location 7 is 9
                                      # Fetch returns opcode and address
def fetch(memory):                    # This function, fetch, gets the instruction from memory
    global pc                         # Declare pc as global because we modify it in the function
    ir = memory[pc]                   # Read the instruction from memory
    pc = pc + 1                       # Now point to the next instruction
    return(ir>>8, ir&0xFF)            # Return the opcode and address

z = 0                                                  # Clear z bit initially
run = 1                                                # run = 1 to continue
while run == 1:                                        # Main loop REPEAT until stop found
    pcOld = pc                                         # Save current pc for display
    opCode, address = fetch(mem)                       # Perform fetch to get opcode
```

```
if    opCode == 0b1111: run = 0                # Test for stop
elif opCode == 0b0001: r0 = address           # Test for load literal
elif opCode == 0b0010: r0 = r0 + mem[address] # Test for add
elif opCode == 0b0011:                         # Test for subtract
    r0 = r0 - mem[address]                     # Do subtraction
    if r0 == 0: z = 1                          # Update z flag on subtract
    else:        z = 0
elif opCode == 0b0100:                         # Test for branch on zero
    if z == 1: pc = address                    # If BEQ, load PC on zero flag

print('pc = ',pcOld,'opCode =',opCode,'\tRegister r0 =',r0,'z = ',z)
                                               # The '\t' performs a tab operation
```

The output from this Python code is as follows:

```
pc =   0 opCode = 1  Register r0 = 9 z =  0
pc =   1 opCode = 3  Register r0 = 0 z =  1
pc =   2 opCode = 4  Register r0 = 0 z =  1    z = 1 so branch taken
pc =   6 opCode = 15 Register r0 = 0 z =  1
```

We load the literal 9 into r0, subtract the contents of memory location 7 (which contains 9), and then branch to location 6 if the result was 0. And that's what happens.

Having described the structure of a computer, the next step is to look at the instructions that are executed by a computer.

The machine-level instruction

Having described how a computer works, we now take a closer look at the computer. We are interested in what an instruction does and what resources it needs (i.e., data locations or constants). A low-level computer operation (i.e., machine code or assembly language) operates on binary data in memory or registers. Although computers have become millions of times faster over the decades, the nature of the low-level instruction has hardly changed.

Many first-generation microprocessors (e.g., 8080, 6800, Z80, and 6502) of the 1970s and 1980s used 8-bit instructions that had to be chained together to create a more practical instruction – for example, 8-bit microprocessors provide 16-bit instructions by chaining together two consecutive 8-bit instructions.

The second generation of microprocessors, such as Intel's 8086 and Motorola's 68000, had 16-bit instructions. These too were chained together to create sufficiently long instructions to perform all the necessary operations. Indeed, the 68000 actually chained up to five consecutive 16-bit words to create a gigantic 80-bit instruction. Modern high-performance microprocessors (e.g., ARM, MIPS, and RISC-V) have 32-bit or 64-bit instructions that provide a full instruction set without the need to chain consecutive instructions. The CISC approach to chaining instructions together to increase the number of opcodes was a great idea at the time. However, it reduces performance by making it difficult to execute instructions in parallel because a computer does not know where the boundaries lie between instructions until they have been decoded.

Later in this book, we will take a brief look at the concept of multi-length instruction sets.

Instruction types and formats

Now, we will describe the type of primitive operations computers perform. First, a surprise. How many different instructions does a computer need? I mean, how many does it need to solve any problem that can be solved by a computer, today, tomorrow, and at any point in the future? The remarkable answer is one. Yes, you can solve any problem with the permutations of one single instruction.

According to Wikipedia, the SBNZ a,b,c,d instruction *("subtract and branch if not equal to zero")* subtracts the contents at address a from the contents at address b, stores the result at address c, and then, if the result is not 0, transfers control to address d (if the result is equal to zero, the execution proceeds to the next instruction in sequence). Expressed in RTL, the SBNZ instruction is as follows:

```
[c] ← [b] – [a]
if [c] != 0: [pc] ← d
else: [pc] ← [pc] + 1
```

All computation can be done using this single instruction alone. In practice, such a computer would be impossibly inefficient and impractical. However, it hints that a large and complex set of instructions is not necessarily required to build a computer. Most computers today have a relatively modest number of instructions. However, some computer designers now create optimized special-purpose instruction set enhancements for specific applications (e.g., graphics, signal processing, and AI).

From the first computer to today's chips with over 10 billion transistors, computers have had instruction sets that include the following three classes of operation. *Table 3.3* gives the name of the instruction group, an example of an operation in Python, and a typical assembly language instruction.

Instruction Group	Typical Python Code	Assembly Language
Arithmetic and logical	c = (a + b) * c	ADD **r1,r2,r3**
Data movement	x = y	MOV **r1,r2**
Conditional	if x == 4: y = 7	BEQ next

Table 3.5 – Instruction classes

The TC1 that we are going to design has a 32-bit instruction and can provide up to 2^{32} = 4,294,967,296 unique instructions. In practice, the instruction provides memory addresses, numerical constants (i.e., literals), and register numbers, which means that the number of unique instructions you can define is a lot smaller.

TC1 has a 32-bit instruction but only a 16-bit data word. This arrangement makes it easier to design and understand the computer, and you can load a 16-bit data word with a single 32-bit instruction. Computers with 32-bit instructions and data have to use convoluted methods to load 32-bit data words, as we shall see when we introduce the ARM.

It may seem strange that I allow a binary number to be specified as either 0b1101 or %1101, and I allow hexadecimal numbers to be formatted as 0x1AC or $1AC. I did this for two reasons. The first is that I was brought up in a Motorola world where the % and $ prefixes were used, but now I live in a C world where the 0b and 0x prefixes are used. Habit makes % and $ more natural for me. Secondly, I want to show you that you can choose your own formats and conventions.

TC1's instruction set is designed for simplicity rather than computational elegance. The instruction set is realistic in terms of the concepts it involves but not in terms of its implementation. For our purposes, we have given all instructions in identical formats. In a real computer, there are usually several classes of instruction, each with its own format. By having a single format, we can simplify instruction decoding and execution.

A 32-bit instruction set is used by many high-performance microprocessors and is ideal for demonstration and teaching purposes. Typically, computers use the same size for data elements as they do for instructions. TC1 uses 32-bit instructions but 16-bit data elements because it is easier for students to read and manipulate 16-bit values than 32-bit values (modifying the TC1 computer to operate with 32-bit data would be a very easy task).

In order to write a machine-level program for TC1, you would have to hand-code each instruction into a 32-bit binary sequence. This is easy to do, but it's horribly tedious. We have also designed a simple assembler that allows you to write instructions in assembly language form. The TC1 assembler translates an instruction in the form ADD **r7**, r2, r3 into a binary string such as 00000011110100110000000000000000.

Normally, an assembler is a separate piece of code from a simulator. You provide the assembler with a *source file* (in text format), and the assembler creates a *binary code file* that the simulator executes. The TC1 assembler is part of the simulator, so you don't have to worry about creating binary files for the simulator.

We have made the TC1 assembler as simple as possible to reduce the level of complexity and keep the final Python program reasonably short. It would take a lot more high-level language code to write a comprehensive assembler. This assembler performs no error-checking on the source program (i.e., it doesn't detect an error when you mistype something). It supports the use of symbolic values for variables and addresses – that is, you can write BEQ loop rather than BEQ 7, where the symbolic name loop labels line number 7.

The TC1 assembler allows you to enter numbers in decimal, binary, or hexadecimal formats – for example, you can write LDRL **r0**, 255, LDRL **r0**, 0xFF, or LDRL **r0**, %11111111. The operation LDRL means, "*load a register with a literal (i.e., an actual) value.*" In each case, the instruction puts the binary value for 255 in register r0.

All computers operate on data that is either in memory or in one of a few on-chip registers. Typically, a computer has between 2 and 32 on-chip registers. The TC1 computer has eight registers, r0 to r7.

Computer instructions have many different formats, depending on the architecture of the computer. The two fundamental formats are as follows:

- CISC-style operations allow general instructions to access memory (e.g., ADD **r3**,1200 means, add the contents of memory location 1,200 to register 3)

- RISC-style: All data-processing operations are between registers (e.g., ADD **r1**,r2,r3), and the only memory accesses are *load a register from memory and store a register in memory*

Typical assembly language instruction formats that we will use in our first computer are as follows:

Format	Mnemonic	Action
Two address	MOV **r0**,r1	Copy the contents of register r1 to register r0
Three address	ADD **r0**,r1,r2	Add the contents of register r1 to r2 put the result in r0
Literal	ADDL **r0**,r1,24	Add literal 24 to r1 and put the result in r0
Branch	BEQ 5	If z-bit set, jump to instruction at address 5
Load register indirect	LDRI **r0**,[r1,10]	Load r0 with the contents of memory at address r1 + 10

There is no universal assembly language format, and conventions differ from assembler to assembler (even for the same machine). For example, one assembly language might use the format MOV **r1**,r2 to load r1 with r2, and the other might use it to load r2 with r1 – that is, the destination can be on the left or the right. I put the destination for operands on the left, which appears to be the more common convention. I also put the destination in bold font as a reminder.

A simple example of a program that adds together the first 10 integers is shown in the following code snippet in a hypothetical assembly language. This is not the most efficient way of writing this fragment of code; it's just intended as a demonstration. The version of the TC1 assembler we design here accepts uppercase or lowercase characters, and either a space or a comma can be used as a separator – for example, you can happily write the following:

```
lOOp aDdL r1 R2,r3 or

Loop ADDL R1,r2,R3.
```

Consider the following example of TC1 assembly language. Note that I use @ to indicate a comment field because that is the standard for the ARM assembly language, which we will introduce later. We will continue to use the # symbol for comments in Python.

```
        LDRL  r0,0      @ Load register r0 with 0 (the sum)
        LDRL  r1,0      @ Load register r1 with 0 (the counter)
Loop    ADDL  r1,r1,1   @ Increment the counter in r1
        ADD   r0,r0,r1  @ Add the count to the sum in r0
        CMPL  r1,10     @ Compare the count with 10
        BNE   Loop      @ Branch back to Loop until all numbers added
```

CISC and RISC

In this book, we use the terms RISC and CISC repeatedly. These two terms are vital to the understanding of a modern computer. They describe two different approaches to the implementation of a computer. The early 1980s saw the CISC versus RISC war when two different architectures competed for the computing market. The term **complex instruction set computer (CISC)** is analogous to the term *analog watch*. When the digital watch was invented, watches with moving hands suddenly became analog watches in order to distinguish them from digital watches. Similarly, the term *complex instruction set computer* didn't exist until it was coined to contrast with the new **reduced instruction set computer (RISC)**.

From the moment computers were invented, they just grew. As technology advanced, new features were just bolted onto existing computers. Someone once said that if the aircraft had developed like the computer, every jumbo jet would have had a 1903 Wright Flyer at its core. This approach wasn't cost-effective because technology had changed so dramatically that the design of computers needed to be reconsidered. In particular, memory capacity had grown exponentially, and the cost per bit had plummeted. Similarly, the 8- and 16-bit wordlengths gave way to the 32- and 64-bit instruction sets. Doing things the old way was not efficient.

First- and second-generation microprocessors were *accumulator*-based. They applied operations to an accumulator on the processor and a memory location. Instructions were called *one-and-a-half addresses* because they had a memory address and an accumulator address (since there were only a few accumulators, they were jokingly referred to as having "*half an address*"). To perform C = A + B (where A, B, and C are memory addresses), you would have to write the following:

```
LDA A          @ Load accumulator with A
ADD B          @ Add B to the accumulator
STA C          @ Store the accumulator in C
```

Passing all data through the accumulator creates a bottleneck. Because computer speed increased faster than memory speed, programmers wanted to keep as much data on-chip as possible.

The RISC solution adopted a *register-to-register* architecture. The only operations permitted on memory are the transfer of data between a register and memory. Instead of having one or two accumulators, RISC processors have 16 or 32 registers. The preceding code on a RISC processor can be typically represented by the following:

```
LDR r0,[r1]    @ Load r0 with data pointed at by r1
LDR r2,[r3]    @ Load r2 with data pointed at by r3
ADD r4,r0,r2   @ Add r0 and r2, result in r4
STR r4,[r5]    @ Store r4 in memory pointed at by r5
```

All data movement is between memory and a register, and data-processing operations apply only to registers. Instructions have three operands.

RISC computers introduced other enhancements, such as overlapping the execution of instructions (called *pipelining*). Many in the 1980s expected Intel's CISC computers to die out. They didn't. Intel cleverly incorporated RISC features into its CISC processors. AMD designed a RISC architecture that took Intel's CISC instructions and translated them into a sequence of RISC commands before executing them.

To summarize, CISC processors have instruction sets that perform operations between an operand in memory and one in a register. All RISC data-processing operations take place between operands in registers. The only memory operations RISC processors permit are *loading a register from memory and storing a register in memory*.

Two ways of representing literals

Assemblers differ in how they represent instructions because assemblers developed rapidly over a few short years in competitive industries. Each manufacturer designed an assembler for their own microprocessors. Some adopted a left-to-right convention with the destination operand on the right, and some adopted a right-to-left convention with the destination operand on the right. Consequently, one manufacturer's mov a,b meant a ← b, and another's meant b ← a. Similarly, mnemonics were also unstandardized – for example, MOVE, MOV, and LDA all define a copy operation.

Since the assembler is just a human-readable version of machine code, it doesn't actually matter how we represent an instruction. It's the binary code that gets executed, irrespective of how we represent it in text form. However, from a teaching and learning perspective, the variations in conventions are a nuisance. Consider the representation of a literal value in an instruction.

Some assemblers represent a literal by using a special instruction – for example, ADD r1,r2,r3 for a three-register addition, and ADDL r1,r2,24 for a literal operand. Other assemblers use the *same* mnemonic in both cases but prefix the literal by a symbol to indicate that it's a literal operation – for example, ADD r1,r2,#25. Some assemblers use # to indicate a literal and others use %.

In this text, we've used the ADDL convention in the design of some simulators, but we will use the # convention when we introduce the ARM processor because that's used by ARM assemblers. In retrospect, if I were writing this book again, I think I might have been tempted to use only one representation, the # symbol. However, by using ADD and ADDL, I was able to simplify the Python code because the *decision point* between register and literal operands was made when examining the mnemonic, not when examining the literal.

Summary

In this key chapter, we introduced the von Neumann computer with its fetch-execute cycle, where an instruction is read from memory, decoded, and executed in a two-phase operation. It is precisely these actions that we will learn to simulate in later chapters in order to build a computer in software. We have looked at the flow of information as an instruction is executed. The model of the computer we introduced here is the traditional model and does not take into account current technology that executes multiple instructions in a pipeline.

We also looked at the instruction format and described how it has several fields – for example, the opcode that defines the operation and the data required by the operation (e.g., addresses, literals, and register numbers). You will eventually be able to design your own instructions (thereby defining the computer's instruction set architecture) and create a computer that will execute these instructions.

While describing the operation of a von Neumann computer, we introduced sufficient Python code to show the direction we are heading in and hint at how simulation can be carried out.

In the next chapter, we will begin to look more closely at the concept of an interpreter that reads a machine-level instruction and carries out its intended actions.

4

Crafting an
Interpreter – First Steps

In this chapter, we'll take our first steps toward constructing a computer simulator by constructing a very primitive simulator that can execute only a single instruction. Once we've taken this step, we can move on by gradually enhancing this simulator.

The key topics that we'll cover in this chapter are as follows:

- Designing a minimal computer with one instruction
- Designing a simple simulator that can decode and execute several instructions
- The instruction set of a general-purpose computer called TC1
- Handing bits in Python (Boolean operations)
- Decoding an instruction in binary form into its component parts
- Executing an instruction after it has been decoded
- Arithmetic operations in a computer
- Designing functions in Python
- Branch and flow control instructions in computer instruction sets

Collectively, these topics cover three areas. Some topics expand our knowledge of Python to help us construct a simulator. Some topics introduce the instruction set of a typical digital computer that we call TC1 (TC1 simply means *Teaching Computer 1*). Some topics cover the actual design of TC1 in Python.

This chapter will introduce the computer simulator and look at some basic building blocks. The actual simulator will be presented in *Chapter 6*.

Technical Requirements

You can find the programs used in this chapter on GitHub at `https://github.com/PacktPublishing/Computer-Architecture-with-Python-and-ARM/tree/main/Chapter04`.

An ultra-primitive one-instruction computer

Our first *one-instruction interpreter* demonstrates both instruction decoding and execution, which are key to all simulators. This computer has a memory with nine locations, mem[0] to mem[8], arranged as a list of integers. The contents of the memory are preset to mem = [4,6,1,2,7,8,4,4,5]. The memory locations are 0 to 8 and are read left to right in the list; for example, memory location 0 contains a value of 4, location 1 contains a value of 6, and location 8 contains a value of 5.

The computer has an array of eight registers, r[0] to r[7]. These are specified in Python via the following:

```
r = [0,0,0,0,0,0,0,0]          #. Define a list of 8 registers and set them all to 0.
```

The single instruction we are going to execute is add r[4],mem[3],mem[7]. This instruction adds the contents of memory location 3 to the contents of memory location 7 and puts the sum in register 4. We have chosen to begin with a single-instruction computer because it can be expressed in a few lines of Python code and yet it performs many of the actions required of a real computer simulator.

We have defined this add memory to memory operation as a demonstration. It's not part of any real computer language. Interestingly, it's more complex than most real computer instructions because it uses memory-to-memory operations rather than register-to-register operations.

We are going to write the Python code necessary to read this instruction in text form and carry out the action it defines. The two shaded lines in the following code take this instruction and split it into a list of tokens that can be processed. A token is an element in an instruction (just as a sentence in English can be split into tokens that we call words). The tokens here are 'add', 'r[4]', 'mem[3]', and 'mem[7]'.

This instruction reads the contents of mem[3], which is 2; reads the contents of mem[7], which is 4; adds them together to get 2 + 4 = 6; and then stores the value 6 in register 4. After this instruction has been executed, the value of register r[4] should be 6:

```
mem =   [4,6,1,2,7,8,4,4,5]    # Create a 9-location memory. Fill with some data
r =     [0,0,0,0,0,0,0,0]      # Create a set of 8 registers, all initialized to 0
inst    = 'add r[4],mem[3],mem[7]'   # inst is our solitary instruction, stored as a string
inst1   = inst.replace(' ',',')      # Step 1: Replace any space with a comma
inst2   = inst1.split(',')           # Step 2: Split instruction into tokens at each comma
token0  = inst2[0]             # Step 3: Get token0 via the 'add' instruction
token1  = inst2[1]             # Step 4: Get token1, register 'r[4]'
token2  = inst2[2]             # Step 5: Get token2, 'mem[3]'
token3  = inst2[3]             # Step 6: Get token3, 'mem[7]'
value1  = int(token1[2])       # Step 7: Get the register number as an integer
value2  = int(token2[4])       # Step 8: Get the first memory number as an integer
value3  = int(token3[4])       # Step 9: Get the second memory number as an integer
if token0 == <add>:            # Step 10: Test for an 'add' instruction
  r[value1] = mem[value2] + mem[value3] # Step 11: If ADD, then add the contents of the memory
print('Registers: ',r)
```

The `inst1 = inst.replace(' ',',')` operation takes the instruction and replaces a space with a comma to get `'add r[4],mem[3],mem[7]'`. This is now a string with the tokens separated by commas.

The next step is to create a list of tokens so that we can access the individual components of the instruction. The effect of `inst2 = inst1.split(',')` is to create a list of strings:

```
inst2 = ['add', 'r[4]', 'mem[3]', 'mem[7]']
```

The `split()` method takes a string and creates a list of strings using the delimiter specified as a parameter. If `y = x.split('!')`, the value of `y` is a list of strings and the separator is `!`. An example of the use of `split()` is shown here:

```
>>> x = 'asssfg! !    !,!!rr'
>>> x
'asssfg! !    !,!!rr'
>>> y = x.split('!')
>>> y
['asssfg', ' ', '    ', ',', '', 'rr']
```

The `token2 = inst2[2]` line gives `token2 = 'mem[3]'`; that is, the fourth token.

The `value2 = int(token2[4])` line gives `value2 = 3` because the second slice is the 3 in the `'mem[3]'` string. Note that we use the `int()` function to convert the characters 4, 3, and 7 into integer values. When going from strings to numeric operations, you have to remember to convert between character and integer types.

If we execute this program, we get the following output:

```
Registers:  [0, 0, 0, 0, 6, 0, 0, 0]      Output from the program. The correct value is in r4
```

Now that we've introduced the fundamental components of a simulator, the next step is to construct a computer that can handle more instructions, albeit a tiny subset of typical operations. However, this is a subset that includes all categories of real computer operations.

Building a simple computer interpreter in Python

We can take the concept of a simulator a step further and execute a program with multiple instructions using the concepts we just developed. Consecutive instructions are executed by reading them from program memory, one by one, and using a program counter to keep track of where we are in the program.

Please be aware of a possible source of confusion when we refer to a *program*. We are writing a program in the high-level language Python to simulate a computer. That simulated computer runs a program written in assembly language. Consequently, the term program can refer to two different entities. It should be clear from the context which one we are referring to.

Note that pseudocode is not a computer language, but a method of expressing a computer algorithm in almost plain English. So, a piece of pseudocode can represent either a high-level language such as Python or an assembly language.

In the following example, the source program of assembly language instructions is expressed as a Python list, where each instruction is a string:

```
prog=['LDRL r0 0','LDRL r1 0','ADDL r1 r1 1','ADD r0 r0 r1','CMPL r1 10', \
      'BNE 2','STOP']
```

The effect of these instructions is as follows:

LDRL r0 0	Load r0 with literal 0
ADDL r1 r1 1	Add 1 to r1 and put the result in r1
ADD r0 r0 r1	Add r1 to r0 and put the result in r0
CMPL r1 10	Compare the contents of r1 with literal 10
BNE 2	Branch to instruction 2 if the last result is not 0
STOP	Stop

To simplify the Python code, we've used spaces as separators – for example, LDRL r0,0 is written as LDRL r0 0.

Real computers store assembly language instructions as strings of 32- or 64-bit binary numbers. We're going to directly execute the assembly language instructions from the text string to avoid having to translate text into binary and then interpret the binary as instructions. Here, we have one goal: to demonstrate how a program is executed.

The computer on which the preceding assembly-level code runs has only a handful of instructions, although it is very easy to add extra instructions. Throughout this text, the term *opcode* or operation code indicates the binary code (or text version) of an assembly language instruction such as ADD or BNE. The structure of the simulator program in pseudocode is as follows:

```
prog=['LDRL r0 0','LDRL r1 0','ADDL r1 r1 1','ADD r0 r0 r1', \
      'CMPL r1 10','BNE 2','STOP']
Define and initialize variables (PC, registers, memory)
while run == True:
    read instruction from prog
    point to next instruction (increment program counter)
    split instruction into fields (opcode plus operands)
    if  first field = op-code1 get operands and execute
    elif first field = op-code2 get operands and execute
    elif first field = op-code3 . . .
    . . .
    else declare an error if no instruction matches.
```

This assembly language program, `prog` (provided as a list in the simulator code), uses a conditional branch, `BNE 2`, to jump back to instruction 2 if the previous operation result was not 0. The assembly language version in the Python program in the following section uses a symbolic name, `Loop`, to indicate the target of the branch, but the actual code uses a literal 2. We will look at how symbolic names such as `Loop` are handled later.

Python code for a primitive simulator

The following is the Python code for this simulator. The initial series of comments on lines 0 to 6 show the assembly language pro :

```
#                                  @ Test fetch/execute cycle
#0        LDRL  r0 0               @ Load register r0 with 0 (the sum)
#1        LDRL  r1 0               @ Load register r1 with 0 (the counter)
#2  Loop  ADDL  r1 r1 1            @ REPEAT Increment counter in r1. Loop address = 2
#3        ADD   r0 r0 r1           @ Add the count to the sum in r0
#4        CMPL  r1 10              @ Compare the count with 10
#5        BNE   Loop               @ Branch back to Loop until all numbers added (BNE 2)
#6        STOP                     @ Terminate execution

prog=['LDRL r0 0','LDRL r1 0','ADDL r1 r1 1','ADD r0 r0 r1','CMPL r1 10', \
      'BNE 2','STOP']

r = [0] * 8                        # Initialize r[0], r[1], ... r[7] and initialize to 0
z = 0                              # Z is zero flag: if a compare result is 0, z = 1
run = True                         # Run flag True to execute
pc = 0                             # Pc is program counter, initially 0

while run == True:                 # The fetch/execute loop
    inst = prog[pc]                # Read next instruction from memory
    oldPC = pc                     # Save the old value of the the pc (program counter)
    pc = pc + 1                    # Point to the next instruction
    inst = inst.split(' ')         # Split divides the instruction into tokens (separate fields)

    if inst[0] == 'ADD':           # Test for ADD rd,rS1,rS2 instruction
        rd  = int(inst[1][1])      # Get dest, source 1 and source 2
        rS1 = int(inst[2][1])
        rS2 = int(inst[3][1])
        r[rd] = r[rS1] + r[rS2]    # Add reg 1 and 2 sum in destination register

    elif inst[0] == 'ADDL':        # Test for ADD literal instruction, ADDL
        rd  = int(inst[1][1])      # If found, get destination register
        rS1 = int(inst[2][1])      # Now get source 1 register
        literal =  int(inst[3])    # Now get the literal
```

```
          r[rd] = r[rS1] + literal    # Add reg 1 and literal

    elif inst[0] == 'BNE':            # Test for branch on not zero
        if z == 0:                    # If z is 0 (last register not zero)
            pc = int(inst[1])         # Get branch destination from operation

    elif inst[0] == 'CMPL':           # Test register for equality with a literal
        z = 0                         # Set z flag to 0 (assume not equal)
        rVal = r[int(inst[1][1])]     # Register value
        intVal = int(inst[2])         # Literal value
        if rVal == intVal: z = 1      # If reg value =s literal, z=1

    elif inst[0] == 'LDRL':           # Test for load literal into register operation
        rd = int(inst[1][1])          # Get destination register
        data = int(inst[2])           # Test literal value
        r[rd] = data                  # Store literal in destination register

    elif inst[0] == 'STOP':           # Test for STOP instruction
        run = False                   # If STOP found, then set run flag to False
        print('End of program reached')

    else:                             # If we end up here, not a valid instruction
        run = False                   # So set run flag to False and stop
        print('Error: illegal instruction ',inst)
    print('PC = ',oldPC,'r0 = ',r[0],'r1 = ',r[1],'z = ',z)    # Print results
                                      # Repeat loop until Run = False
```

The interesting part of the code is extracting the operands from the instruction. Consider the ADDL r1 r2 3 instruction, which means add a literal to the source register and put the sum in the destination register. The destination register is r1, the source register is r2, and the literal is 3.

The Python inst = inst.split(' ') operation converts a string into a list of substrings using a space as a separator. Therefore, the new value of inst is the following list:

```
inst = ['ADDL', 'r1', 'r2', '3']   # An instruction converted into a list of substrings
```

We can now examine the four fields of this list; for example, inst[0] = 'ADDL' gives us the actual instruction mnemonic.

Suppose we want to get the contents of the source register, r2. The source register is in the third position in the list at ['ADDL', 'r1', 'r2', '3']; that is, inst[2]. Let's write rS1 = inst[2]. The value of rS1 is 'r2'.

We want the register number (that is, 2) as an integer, so we have to get the second character of r2 and convert it into an integer. We can do this in the following way:

```
rS1 = int(rS1[1])                    # get second character of the rS1 string and convert it into an integer
```

We can combine these two expressions into one as follows.

```
rS1 = int(inst[2][1])                # inst[2][1], which gets character 1 of substring 2.
```

The tiny computer we have created executed only five different instructions, but it includes many of the most important components of a real computer. This computer directly executes instructions from their assembly language form, rather than from their binary code. The next step is to look a little more closely at instruction sets before we can build a more realistic machine.

Having constructed a simulator, the next step is to look at the type of instructions a computer can execute.

In the next section, we will develop an instruction set for the TC1 computer. As well as providing a practical example of instruction set design, we will demonstrate how instructions are divided into multiple fields and each field supplies some information about the current instruction.

The TC1 instruction set

In this section, we will introduce the key component of our demonstration computer: its instruction set. This computer, TC1, has many of the functions of a real computer and is easy to understand and modify. We will begin by introducing the TC1 instruction set encoding.

To simplify this, we can use separate programs and data memories. This departure from the traditional von Neuman model allows us to have a 32-bit program memory and a 16-bit data memory. Moreover, we don't have to worry about accidentally putting data in the middle of the program area.

A typical instruction has several fields; for example, operation code, registers, and literals (that is, constants). However, the number of bits in each field must add up to the total length of the instruction.

Modern computers normally employ different formats for each class of instruction. This optimizes the allocation of op-codes to bits; for example, a branch instruction may have a 4-bit opcode and a 28-bit literal field, whereas a data-processing instruction may have a 17-bit opcode and three 5-bit register-select fields.

For the sake of simplicity, the TC1 computer has a single, fixed format. All instructions have the same number of fields, and fields are the same size for each instruction. An instruction, as shown in *Figure 4.1*, is made up of an operation *class* plus an opcode, three register fields, and a literal field. *Figure 4.1* shows the opcode field as 7 bits, with a 2-bit opcode class and a 5-bit actual opcode.

The structure of this instruction format is inefficient because if an instruction does not access a register, the three register select fields are wasted. In a three-register instruction such as ADD r_d, r_{S1}, r_{S2}, the r_d register is the destination, r_{S1} is source register 1, and r_{S2} is source register 2:

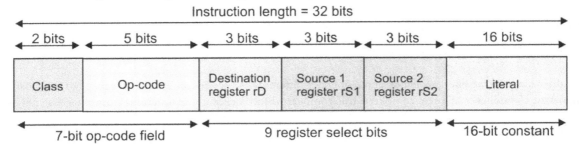

Figure 4.1 – TC1 instruction format (RISC style)

We devote 16 bits to the literal field so that we can load a constant into memory with a single instruction. That leaves 32 - 16 = 16 bits to allocate to all the other fields.

TC1 has a three-register format, which is typical of load and store computers such as ARM and MIPS. If we have eight registers, it takes 3 x 3 = 9 bits to specify all three registers. After allocating 16 bits to the literal and 9 bits to the register selection, we are left with 32 - (16 + 9) = 7 bits to specify up to 128 different possible instructions (2^7 = 128).

The opcode field itself is divided into four categories or classes, which take two bits, leaving 7- 2 = 5 for the instructions in each category. *Table 4.1* defines the categories (class) of instructions:

Class	Group	Comments
0 0	Special operation	Operations that perform functions such as STOP or read the keyboard
0 1	Data transfer	Operations that copy data from one place to another
1 0	Data processing	Arithmetic and logic data-processing operations
1 1	Flow control	Operations that control the sequencing of instructions, such as BEQ

Table 4.1 – TC1 instruction classes

Table 4.2 illustrates the TC1 instruction set. The first column (**Binary Code**) provides the 7-bit instruction code; for example, 01 00001 loads a register with the contents of a memory location. The leftmost two bits are separated to indicate the instruction group:

Binary Code	Operation	Mnemonic	Instruction Format rrr = Rd, aaa = rS1, bbb = rS2	Code Format
00 00000	Stop operation	`STOP`	00 00000 000 000 000 0	0 0 0 0
00 00001	No operation	`NOP`	00 00001 000 000 000 0	0 0 0 0
00 00 010	Get a char from the keyboard	`GET   r0`	00 00010 rrr 000 000 0	1 0 0 0
00 00011	Get a random character	`RND   r0`	00 00011 rrr 000 000 L	1 0 0 1
00 00100	Swap bytes in the register	`SWAP  r0`	00 00100 rrr 000 000 0	1 0 0 0
00 01000	Print a hex value in the register	`PRT   r0`	00 01000 rrr 000 000 0	1 0 0 0
00 11111	Terminate program	`END`	00 11111 000 000 000 0	0 0 0 0
01 00000	Load register from register	`MOV   r0,r1`	01 00000 rrr aaa 000 0	1 1 0 0
01 00001	Load register from memory	`LDRM  r0,L`	01 00001 rrr 000 000 L	1 0 0 1
01 00010	Load register with literal	`LDRL  r0,L`	01 00010 rrr 000 000 L	1 0 0 1
01 00011	Load register indirect	`LDRI  r0,[r1,L]`	01 00011 rrr aaa 000 L	1 1 0 1
01 00100	Store register in memory	`STRM  r0,L`	01 00100 rrr 000 000 L	1 0 0 1
01 00101	Store register indirect	`STRI  r0,[r1,L]`	01 00101 rrr aaa 000 L	1 1 0 1
10 00000	Add register to register	`ADD   r0,r1,r2`	10 00000 rrr aaa bbb 0	1 1 1 0
10 00001	Add register to literal	`ADDL  r0,r1,L`	10 00001 rrr aaa 000 L	1 1 0 1
10 00010	Subtract register from register	`SUB   r0,r1,r2`	10 00010 rrr aaa bbb 0	1 1 1 0
10 00011	Subtract literal from register	`SUBL  r0,r1,L`	10 00011 rrr aaa 000 L	1 1 0 1
10 00100	Multiply register by register	`MUL   r0,r1,r2`	10 00100 rrr aaa bbb 0	1 1 1 0
10 00101	Multiply literal by register	`MULL  r0,r1,L`	10 00101 rrr aaa 000 L	1 1 0 1
10 00110	Divide register by register	`DIV   r0,r1,r2`	10 00110 rrr aaa bbb 0	1 1 1 0
10 00111	Divide register by literal	`DIVL  r0,r1,L`	10 00111 rrr aaa 000 L	1 1 0 1
10 01000	Mod register by register	`MOD   r0,r1,r2`	10 01000 rrr aaa bbb 0	1 1 1 0
10 01001	Mod register by literal	`MOD   r0,r1,L`	10 01001 rrr aaa 000 L	1 1 0 1
10 01010	AND register to register	`AND   r0,r1,r2`	10 01000 rrr aaa bbb 0	1 1 1 0
10 01011	AND register to literal	`ANDL  r0,r1,L`	10 01001 rrr aaa 000 L	1 1 0 1
10 01100	OR register to register	`OR    r0,r1,r2`	10 01010 rrr aaa bbb 0	1 1 1 0
10 01101	OR register to literal	`ORL   r0,r1,L`	10 01011 rrr aaa 000 L	1 1 0 1
10 01110	EOR register to register	`EOR   r0,r1,r2`	10 01010 rrr aaa bbb 0	1 1 1 0
10 01111	EOR register to literal	`EORL  r0,r1,L`	10 01011 rrr aaa 000 L	1 1 0 1
10 10000	NOT register	`NOT   r0`	10 10000 rrr 000 000 0	1 0 0 0
10 10010	Increment register	`INC   r0`	10 10010 rrr 000 000 0	1 0 0 0
10 10011	Decrement register	`DEC   r0`	10 10011 rrr 000 000 0	1 0 0 0

Binary Code	Operation	Mnemonic	Instruction Format rrr = Rd, aaa = rS1, bbb = rS2	Code Format
10 10100	Compare register with register	CMP r0,r1	10 10100 rrr aaa 000 0	1100
10 10101	Compare register with literal	CMPL r0,L	10 10101 rrr 000 000 L	1001
10 10110	Add with carry	ADC r0,r1,r2	10 10110 rrr aaa bbb 0	1110
10 10111	Subtract with borrow	SBC r0,r1,r2	10 10111 rrr aaa bbb 0	1110
10 11000	Logical shift left	LSL r0,L	10 10000 rrr 000 000 0	1001
10 11001	Logical shift left literal	LSLL r0,L	10 10000 rrr 000 000 L	1001
10 11010	Logical shift right	LSR r0,L	10 10001 rrr 000 000 0	1001
10 11011	Logical shift right literal	LSRL r0,L	10 10001 rrr 000 000 L	1001
10 11100	Rotate left	ROL r0,L	10 10010 rrr 000 000 0	1001
10 11101	Rotate left literal	ROLL r0,L	10 10010 rrr 000 000 L	1001
10 11110	Rotate right	ROR r0,L	10 10010 rrr 000 000 0	1001
10 11111	Rotate right literal	RORL r0,L	10 10010 rrr 000 000 L	1001
11 00000	Branch unconditionally	BRA L	11 00000 000 000 000 L	0001
11 00001	Branch on zero	BEQ L	11 00001 000 000 000 L	0001
11 00010	Branch on not zero	BNE L	11 00010 000 000 000 L	0001
11 00011	Branch on minus	BMI L	11 00011 000 000 000 L	0001
11 00100	Branch to subroutine	BSR L	11 00100 000 000 000 L	0001
11 00101	Return from subroutine	RTS	11 00101 000 000 000 0	0000
11 00110	Decrement and branch on not 0	DBNE r0,L	11 00110 rrr 000 000 L	1001
11 00111	Decrement and branch on zero	DBEQ r0,L	11 00111 rrr 000 000 L	1001
11 01000	Push register on the stack	PUSH r0	11 01000 rrr 000 000 0	1000
11 01001	Pull register off the stack	PULL r0	11 01001 rrr 000 000 0	1000

Table 4.2 – TC1 Instruction encoding (the 4 code format bits are not part of the opcode)

The rightmost column is called **Code Format** and is not part of the instruction. This code can be derived from the opcode (as we shall see) and tells the simulator what information is required from the instruction. Each bit of the code format corresponds to an operand. If a bit in the code format is 1, the corresponding operand in the instruction must be extracted. The order of the code format bits (left to right) is destination register, source register 1, source register 2, literal; for example, code 1001 tells the assembler that the instruction requires a destination register and a 16-bit literal. Code 0000 tells us that the instruction contains no operands at all.

We chose these instructions to demonstrate a range of operations. Many of these instructions are typical of a RISC computer such as ARM (that is, we don't include operations on data in memory). Note that later, we'll introduce a simulator for a memory-to-register instruction set that allows operations such as ADD r1,12, where 12 is a memory location.

Some instructions in *Table 4.2* don't exist on a real computer; for example, read a character from the keyboard. We added that to simplify debugging and experimentation. Similarly, TC1 can generate a random number, a feature not found in most computer instruction sets. However, it's useful for generating random test data. Some instructions, such as subroutine calls and returns, implement more sophisticated operations, which we shall encounter later.

The column labeled **Operation** in *Table 4.2* describes the instruction in words; the third column provides the instruction's mnemonic, where L indicates a literal value (that is, a 16-bit constant).

The fourth column (**Instruction Format**) defines the instruction's encoding in binary. The fields containing rrr, aaa, and bbb show the location of the three register select fields. The rightmost field (0 or L) represents 16 bits of the literal. We show 0 if all bits are 0, and L if a 16-bit literal is required by the instruction. If a register field is not required, the corresponding field is filled with zeros (although it doesn't matter what value these bits are because they are not used by the instruction).

Remember that the four bits in the rightmost column are not part of the opcode or instruction itself. These bits show which fields are required by the current instruction: the destination register (rrr), the source 1 register (aaa), the source 2 register (bb), and the literal, L. For example, code 1100 indicates that the instruction has a destination register and a single source register.

Explaining some of the instructions

Some of the instructions in *Table 4.2* are typical of real processors. Several instructions have been included to provide useful facilities such as generating a random number for testing purposes. This section describes several of the instructions in *Table 4.2*.

STOP terminates instruction processing. Most modern computers don't have an explicit STOP operation.

NOP does nothing other than advance the program counter. It's a dummy operation that is useful as a marker in code, a placeholder for future code, or as an aid to testing.

GET reads data from the keyboard and offers a simple way of getting input from the keyboard into a register. This is useful when testing programs and is not a normal computer instruction.

RND generates a random number. It's not in computer instruction sets but provides an excellent means of generating data internally when testing your code.

SWAP exchanges upper- and lower-order bytes – for example, 0x1234 becomes 0x3412.

The load and store instructions move data between memory and registers. The difference between members of this class is the direction (store is computer-to-memory, while load is memory-to-computer), size (some computers allow byte, 16-bit, or 32-bit transfers), and addressing mode (using a literal value, an absolute address, or an address from a register).

MOV copies one register to another – for example, MOV r3,r1 copies the contents of r1 to r3. MOV is, essentially, an a load register with register (LDRR) instruction.

LDRL loads a register with a literal value – for example, LDRL r3,20 loads register r3 with 20.

LDRM loads a register with the contents of a memory location specified by a literal address. LDRM r1,42 loads r1 with the contents of memory location 42. This instruction does not exist on modern RISC processors. Most modern processors do not allow you to access an absolute memory address,

LDRI, the load register indexed (or load register indirect) instruction, loads a register with the contents of a memory location specified by the contents of a register plus a literal address. LDRM r2,[r3,10] loads r2 with the contents of the memory location whose address is given by the contents of r3 plus 10. This instruction is the standard RISC load operation.

STRM, the store register memory instruction, stores a register at the location specified by a literal address. STRM r2,15 stores register r2 at memory location 15. RISC processors don't implement this instruction.

STRI, the store register indexed instruction, stores a register at the location specified by a register plus a literal. STRI r2,[r6,8] stores r2 at the memory location whose address is r6 plus 8.

The STR, STRM, and STRI instructions are anomalous because they write the source and destination operands in the reverse order to LDR (and all other processor operations); that is, if you write LDR r0,PQR, you should write STR PQR,r0 to indicate the reverse data flow. But, by custom and practice, we don't.

DBNE We added the decrement and branch on not zero instruction for fun because it reminds me of my old Motorola days. The 68000 was a powerful microprocessor (at the time) with a 32-bit architecture. It has a decrement and branch instruction that is used at the end of a loop. On each pass around the loop, the specified register is decremented, and a branch back to a label is made if the counter is not -1. DBNE r0,L decrements r0 and branches to the line numbered L if the count is not zero.

Register indirect addressing

Two instructions require a special mention because they are concerned not with operations on data but with accessing data in memory. These are LDRI and STRI, both of which use register indirect addressing. In *Table 4.2*, the 0b0100011 opcode corresponds to LDRI (that is, load register *indirect*). This instruction doesn't give you the actual address of the operand; it tells you where the address can be found. The register indirect addressing mode is also called pointer-based or indexed addressing. The operand address in memory is given by the contents of a register plus an offset; that is, r[rD]=mem[r[rS1]+lit]. If we use bold and shading, we can make its interpretation a little easier:

```
r[rD] = mem[r[rS1]+lit]
```

Figure 4.2 demonstrates the effect of the LDRI r1,[r0,3] TC1 instruction, where pointer register r0 contains 100 and the operand is accessed at memory address 100 + 3 = 103:

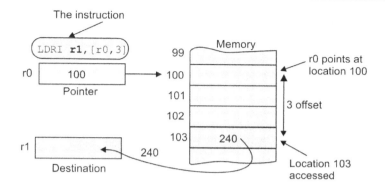

Figure 4.2 – Register indirect addressing

This addressing mode lets you modify addresses while the program is running (because you can change the contents of the pointer, r0). Pointer-based addressing makes it possible to step through a list of items, element by element, simply by incrementing the pointer. Here's an example:

```
LDRI   r1, [r2,0]      @ Get the element pointed at by r2. Here the offset is 0
INC    r2              @ Increment r2 to point to the next element
```

We access the element pointed at by r2 (in this case, the offset is 0). The next line increments r2 to point to the next element. If this sequence is executed in a loop, the data will be accessed element by element.

Computers implement both arithmetic and Boolean (logical) operations. In the next section, we'll briefly look at how Python can be used to simulate logical operations at the assembly language level.

Bit-handling in Python

In this section, we'll look at how Python deals with the fundamental component of all computer data: the bit. Because simulated computers operate at the level of bits, we have to look at how bits are manipulated in Python before we can construct a simulator that can perform logical operations such as AND and OR.

Computers can operate on entire words as a single entity, or on the individual bits of a word. Consequently, we have to be able to perform both bit operations and word operations to simulate a computer.

Python lets you input data and display it as a binary string of bits. You can operate on individual bits of a string using Boolean operators, and you can shift the bits of a word left and right. You have all the tools you need in Python. We are now going to look at Python, which lets you operate on the individual bits of an integer.

Because the simulator will operate on binary numbers, we have to exploit several Python facilities; for example, a binary value is indicated by prefixing it with 0b. If you want to use the binary equivalent of 15, you must write 0b1111 and use it just like a decimal number. The following two operations have the same effect:

```
x = y + 0b111        # Addition using a binary integer
x = y + 15           # Addition using a decimal integer
```

Two important binary operators are >> (shift right) and << (shift left). Shift expressions are written as p >> q or p << q, where p is the number to be operated on and q is the number of bit positions shifted. Consider the following example:

```
x = 0b1110110
x = x << 2
```

This shifts x two places left to give the new value 0b111011000. All the bits have moved two places left and 0s have been entered at the right-hand end to fill the newly vacated positions. The shifted version of x now has nine bits, rather than seven. However, when we simulate a computer, we have to ensure that, whatever we do, the number of bits in a word remains constant. If a register has 16 bits, any operation you perform on it must yield 16 bits.

We can take two words and perform Boolean (bitwise) operations on them; for example, C = A & B ANDs together words A and B by calculating $c_i = a_i \cdot b_i$ for each bit in the word (that is, for i = 0 to 7). Consider the following:

```
x = 0b11101101 & 0b00001111
```

Truth table for AND		
x	y	z=x & y
0	0	0
0	1	0
1	0	0
1	1	1

This gives x = 0b000001101, because ANDing a bit with 0 gives a 0 result, and ANDing a bit x with 1 gives x, because 1 & 0 = 0 and 1 & 1 = 1, as the truth table demonstrates.

In Python, hexadecimal numbers are prefixed with 0x; for example, 0x2F1A. We use hexadecimal numbers in Python programs because they are shorter than binary numbers. Here is an example:

```
0x1234 = 0b0001001000110100
0xA0C2 = 0b1010000011000010
0xFFFF = 0b1111111111111111
```

Consider the following fragment of Python code:

```
x = 0b0011100101010011    # A 16-bit binary string we are going to process
y = (x >> 8) & 0xF        # Shift x right 8 places and mask it to 4 bits
print('y is ',bin(y))     # Print the result in binary form using bin()
```

The output from this code is y is 0b1001.

Python uses more than 16 bits to represent numbers. To simulate binary arithmetic in TC1, we must constrain Python's numbers to 16 bits. We have to work with the longer words provided by Python and chop them down to 16 or 32 bits as necessary. Consider the following:

```
x = 0xF009       # Set up 16-bit number    1111000000001001
y = x << 2       # Shift left twice to get  111100000000100100 = 0x3C024 (18 bits)
y = y & 0xFFFF   # Constrain to 16 bits to get  1100000000100100 = 0xC024
```

Shifting the 16-bit word left two places made it an 18-bit word. ANDing it with the 0b1111111111111111 binary value forces it to 16 significant bits.

Operator precedence in Python

Now, we have to re-learn something that we learned about in high school arithmetic: operator precedence. When you use several operators in an expression, you have to be aware of operator precedence; that is, which operations are performed before others. For example, is 4 * 5 + 3 equal to 23 or 32? All computer languages have a hierarchy of operator precedence. The partial list of operator precedence for Python is as follows, with the highest precedence first. We often use parentheses to make the meaning of expressions clearer, even if it's not required – for example, (xxx << 4) & (yyy << 2):

( )	Parentheses	Highest precedence
~	Negation	
*, /, %	Multiplication, division, modulus	
+, -	Addition, subtraction	
<<, >>	Bitwise shift left, right	
&	Logical (bitwise) AND	
^	Logical (bitwise) XOR	
|	Logical (bitwise) OR	
<, <+, >, >+, <>, !=, ==	Boolean comparisons	Lowest precedence

In the next section, we'll look at how an instruction, which is a string of 1s and 0s, is decoded and the appropriate operation that's performed.

Next, we'll take a major step in constructing a simulator – that is, decoding a machine-level binary instruction to extract information about the operation it is going to simulate.

Decoding and executing an instruction

In this section, we'll look at a few examples of how instructions are encoded and decoded. Consider the ADD r1,r2,r3, operation (where the codes for registers rD, rS1, and rS2 are shaded), which is defined in RTL as follows:

[r1] ← [r2] + [r3]

Table 4.2 shows that the encoding of ADD r1,r2,r3 is 10 00000 001 010 011 0000000000000000.
The corresponding 4-bit format code that defines the registers to be used is 1110 because we use three
registers and no literal field (remember that this 4-bit format code is not part of the opcode but is used by
the assembler to interpret the instruction).

The following Python code shows how we can decode an instruction to extract five variables: the operation
code (binOp); the three registers, rD, rS1, and rS2; and a literal. Decoding is performed by shifting the
bits of the instruction right to move the required field into the least significant position and then ANDing it
with a mask to remove any other fields. Consider, xxxxxxx xxx 010 xxx xxxxxxxxxxxxxxxx. If we
shift this string 19 places right, we get 00000000000000000000xxxxxxxxxx010. The zeros have been
shifted in, and the three bits we're interested in are right-justified in the least significant bits. If we AND this
with 0b111 to select only the three least significant bits, we get 00000000000000000000000000000010
– that is, the required register value is now right-justified and we can use it:

```
binOp = binCode >> 25          # Extract the 7-bit opcode binOp by shifting 25 bits right
rD    = binCode >> 22 & 0b111  # Extract the destination register as rD. 0b111 is a mask
rS1   = binCode >> 19 & 0b111  # Extract source register 1 as rS1
rS2   = binCode >> 16 & 0b111  # Extract the source register 2 as rS2
lit   = binCode & 0xFFFF       # Extract the low-order 16 bits (the literal) as lit
op0 = r[rD]                    # Read contents of destination register operand 0 as op0
op1 = r[rS1]                   # Read contents of source 1 register as op1
op2 = r[rS2]                   # Read contents of source 2 register as op2
```

The shift-right operator in Python is >> and the bit-wise logical AND operator is &. The mask is expressed
as a string of bits (rather than a decimal number) because ANDing with binary 111 is clearer than ANDing
with decimal 7. In Python, a binary value is preceded by 0b, so 7 is represented by 0b111. The literal is
ANDed with 16 ones, expressed as 0xFFFF. We use binary for short fields, and hex value for long fields. It's
just personal preference.

The binCode >> 22 & 0b111 expression shifts the bits of binCode 22 places right, and then bitwise
ANDs the result with 000...000111. Because of operator precedence, the shifting is performed first. Otherwise,
we would have written (binCode >> 22) & 0b111. We often use parentheses, even when not strictly
necessary, to stress operator precedence.

Note that we extract all fields, even though they may not be required by each instruction. Similarly, we read
all three register's contents. This approach simplifies the Python code, at the cost of efficiency.

Consider extracting the destination register field, rrr. Suppose that the instruction is ADD r1,r2,r3, and
the opcode is 10000000010100110000000000000000. We have put alternate fields in bold font and
the destination field is shaded to make it easier to read. Performing a 22-bit right shift moves the destination
register into the least-significant bits and leaves us with

00000000000000000000001000000001   (after shifting 22 places right).

Now, if we perform the AND operation with 111 (all bits to the left are zero), we get the following:

```
00000000000000000000001000000001        (after shifting 22 places right)
00000000000000000000000000000111        (the three-bit mask)
00000000000000000000000000000001        (The result; the 1 in bit position 9 has been removed)
```

We have now isolated the first register field to get 001, which corresponds to register r1. The final three lines of the program to decode an instruction are as follows:

```
op0 = r[rD]        # Operand 0 is the contents of the destination register
op1 = r[rS1]       # Operand 1 is the contents of source register 1
op2 = r[rS2]       # Operand 2 is the contents of source register 2
```

These instructions use the register addresses (rD, rS1, and rS2) to access registers; that is, the instruction specifies which registers are to be used. For example, if op0 = r[5], register r5 is operand zero, the destination register. If an instruction does not specify a register, the unused field is set to zero.

Once an instruction has been decoded, it can be executed. Fortunately, executing most instructions is remarkably easy. Consider the following examples:

```
if   opCode == 0b0100010: r[rD] = lit             # Load register with literal
elif opCode == 0b0100001: r[rD] = mem[lit]        # Load register from memory
elif opCode == 0b0100011: r[rD] = mem[op1 + lit]  # Load register indirect
elif opCode == 0b0100100: mem[lit] = r[rD]        # Store register in memory
```

This fragment of code demonstrates the execution of four instructions from the load and store (that is, memory access) group. The Python if … elif construct tests each opcode in turn. The first line compares the 7-bit opcode with the binary value 0100010, which corresponds to the LDRL (load a register with a literal value) instruction. Incidentally, in the final version of TC1, we made the code easier to read by comparing operations with the actual mnemonic; for example, 'LDRL' is easier to read than its code, 0b100010.

If there is a match, the code following the colon is executed, (r[rD] = lit). If not, the next line uses the elif command to compare the opcode with 010001. If there is a match, the code after the colon is executed. In this way, the opcode is compared with all its possible values until a match is found.

Suppose the instruction's opcode is 0100010, and the r[rD] = lit line is executed. This Python operation transfers the value of the 16-bit literal provided in the instruction to the destination register specified in the instruction. In RTL terms, it carries out r[rD] ← lit and is used by the programmer to load an integer into a register. Let's say the binary pattern of the instruction code is as follows:

```
01 00010 110 000 000 0000000011000001,
```

Here, the 16-bit literal is loaded into register r6 to implement LDRL r6,193.

Arithmetic and logical operations

The arithmetic and logical group of operations do all the work (data processing) in a program. They include arithmetic operations (addition, subtraction, and multiplication), as well as logical operations (AND, OR, EOR, and NOT). These are three-operand instructions, apart from NOT; for example, AND r3,r0,r5 performs a bitwise AND between the bits of r0 and r5, and puts the result in r3.

The following fragment of Python code shows how TC1 interprets four instructions in this group. There are two pairs of instructions: addition and subtraction. Each pair consists of a register-to-register operation and a register-with-literal operation; for example, ADD r1,r2,r3 adds the contents of registers r2 and r3 together, whereas ADDL r1,r2,L adds the contents of a 16-bit literal to the contents of register r2. We don't do the arithmetic here. Instead, we call a function called alu(f,a,b) to perform the required action. The next section will show you how to create your own functions:

```
elif opCode==0b1000000:  reg[dest]=alu(1,reg[src1],reg[src2])   # Add register to register
elif opCode==0b1000001:  reg[dest]=alu(1,reg[src1],literal)     # Add literal to register
elif opCode==0b1000010:  reg[dest]=alu(2,reg[src1],reg[src2])   # Subtract register from register
elif opCode==0b1000011:  reg[dest]=alu(2,reg[src1],literal)     # Subtract literal from register
```

If you were to write the full Python code required to execute each operation, it would require several lines of code per instruction. An addition operation such as reg[dest] = reg[src1] + reg[src2] appears simple enough, but there is more to an arithmetic operation.

To explain why, we need to discuss the role of conditional flag bits. Recall that computers make decisions regarding whether to execute the next instruction in sequence, or whether to jump to a different place in the code (that is, an if...then...else construct). The decision whether to take the if branch or the else branch is determined by the outcome of an arithmetic or logical operation (this includes compare operations).

The result of an arithmetic or logical operation is tested and used to set or clear condition code flags. These flags are usually the negative, zero, carry, and overflow flags and are written as n, z, c, and v. For example, if an operation is x = p − q and the result is x = 0, then the z-bit (zero bit) is set to 1. Similarly, if an operation yields a result that cannot be represented in 16 bits, the carry bit, c, is set. Because most computers use two's complement arithmetic, the negative flag, n, is set if the result is negative in two's complement terms (that is, its most significant bit is 1). The v-bit indicates arithmetic overflow and is set if the result is out of range. This means that two positive numbers have been added and the result is negative, or two negative numbers have been added and the result is positive.

Table 4.3 demonstrates how 4 bits can be allocated to the numbers 0 to 15 (unsigned) or -8 to 7 (signed two's complement). It's up to the programmer to choose the convention. However, the arithmetic remains the same for both conventions.

Consider 0110 + 1100, which is 10010 (or 0010 in 4 bits). If we interpret these figures as unsigned, the calculation gives us 6 + 12 = 2, which is incorrect, because the result 18 cannot be represented in 4 bits. If we consider these as signed values, the calculation is 6 + -4 = 2 and the result is correct:

8	4	2	1	Unsigned value	Signed value
0	0	0	0	0	0
0	0	0	1	1	1
0	0	1	0	2	2
0	0	1	1	3	3
0	1	0	0	4	4
0	1	0	1	5	5
0	1	1	0	6	6
0	1	1	1	7	7
8	4	2	1		
1	0	0	0	8	-8
1	0	0	1	9	-7
1	0	1	0	10	-6
1	0	1	1	11	-5
1	1	0	0	12	-4
1	1	0	1	13	-3
1	1	1	0	14	-2
1	1	1	1	15	-1

Table 4.3 – A representation of 4-bit values in signed and unsigned forms

Two's complement arithmetic – a note

There are several ways of representing negative numbers in binary arithmetic. One of the oldest is called sign and magnitude, where a number is prefixed by 0 if it's positive and 1 if it's negative. This is not used today in binary arithmetic (except for floating-point numbers).

Two's complement notation is used by almost all modern computers to represent signed integers. In two's complement arithmetic, if N is a positive number in n bits, the value of -N is given by 2^{n-1}. The two's complement of N can be calculated easily by inverting the bits and adding 1. For example, if N = 000110 in six bits, the value of -6 is represented by 111010.

The advantage of two's complement arithmetic is that addition and subtraction are performed in the same way. If you add a two's complement value to another number, the result is correctly calculated. For example, if we add 9 (that is, 001001) to the previous value of -6, we get 001001 + 111010 = 1000011, which is +3 in six bits. The carry-out (in bold font) is discarded.

Zero, carry, and sign bits

The carry and sign bits are used to determine whether a result is in range or out of range. In signed arithmetic, the result of a two's complement addition of S = A+B is out of range, if the sign bits of A and B are both 0 and the sign bit of S is 1, or if the sign bits of A and B are both 1 and the sign bit of S is 0. Consider addition and subtraction using four bits. Two's complement arithmetic is used, and the leftmost bit is the sign bit. In each case, we've performed a two's complement addition on signed numbers. The results give us the state of the flag bits:

```
 +0101                              +5 + -5 = 0
 +1011
 10000 Z = 1, N = 0, C = 1, V = 0
                        The result is zero and the Z-bit is set. The C bit is 1, and N, V bits are clear

 +1101                              -3 + -3 = -6
 +1101
 11010 Z = 0, N = 1, C = 1, V = 0  The result is negative, N = 1, and a carry is generated, C = 1

 +1101                              -3 + +5 = +2
 +0101
 10010 Z = 0, N = 0, C = 1, V = 0  The result is positive and the carry bit is set

 +0101                              +5 + 6 = -5
 +0110
  1011 Z = 0, N = 1, C = 0, V = 1
                        Two positive numbers are added and the result is negative. V is set

  1010                             -6 + -4 = +7
 +1100
 10111 Z = 0, N = 0, C = 1, V = 1
                        Two negative numbers are added and the result is positive. V is set
```

How do we know whether a number is signed or unsigned? We don't! There is no difference. If you use signed numbers, you must interpret the result as a signed value. If you use unsigned numbers, you must interpret the result as an unsigned value. For example, in four bits, 1110 is both -2 and +14, depending on how you look at it.

The next topic deals with how we handle groups of repetitive operations. If the same sequence of operations is going to be used more than once in a program, it makes sense to combine them into a group and invoke that group whenever you need it. In Python, this group of actions is called a function.

Functions in Python

We will now describe Python's functions. We've already used functions that are part of the language, such as len(). In this section, we'll do the following:

- Explain why functions are useful
- Provide an example of a function to implement an ALU
- Explain how variables can be private to a function or shared between functions (scope)
- Describe how parameters are passed to functions
- Describe how a function returns a result

Writing the Python code to deal with each arithmetic or logical operation implemented by a simulator would be tedious because so much code would be replicated by individual instructions. Instead, we can create a Python function (that is, a subroutine or procedure) that carries out both the arithmetic/logic operation and the appropriate flag-bit setting.

Consider a Python function called alu(f,p,q) that returns an integer that is a function of the f, p, and q parameters. The operation to be performed is passed to the procedure as an integer, f. The function also updates the z and n flag bits. This is a simplified version of the actual function we will use and will provide just two operations, add and subtract, and update only two flag bits:

```
def alu(f,p,q):             # Define the alu function with the f, p, and q input parameters
    global z,n              # Declare flags as global
    if f == 1: r = p + q   # If f (the operation) is 1, do an addition
    if f == 2: r = p - q   # If f is 2, do a subtraction
    z, n = 0, 0            # Clear zero and negative flags
    if r & 0xFFFF == 0: z = 1   # If the result is 0 in 16 bits, then z = 1
    if r & 0x8000 != 0: n = 1   # If result is negative (msb = 1), then n = 1
    return (0xFFFF & r)    # Ensure result is restricted to 16 bits
```

The function is introduced by def, its name, and any parameters followed by a colon. The body of the function is indented. The first parameter, f, selects the operation we wish to perform (f = 1 for addition and 2 for subtraction). The next two input parameters, p and q, are the data values used by the function. The last line of the function returns the result to the function's calling point. This function can be called by, for example, opVal = alu(2,s1,s2). In this case, the result, opVal, would be the value of s1 - s2.

We also update two flag bits, z and n. Initially, both z and n are set to zero by z, n = 0, 0. (Python allows multiple assignments on the same line; for example, a,b,c = 1,5,0 sets a, b, and c to 1, 5, and 0, respectively.)

You can pass data to a function via parameters and receive a result via return(). However, you can declare variables in a function as global, which means they can be accessed and modified as if they were part of the calling program.

`return()` is not mandatory because some functions don't return a value. You can have multiple `return()` statements in a function because you can return from more than one point in a function. A return can pass multiple values because Python permits multiple assignments on a line; for example, see the following:

```
this, that  = myFunction(f,g)    # Assign f to this and g to that
```

Testing for a zero result can easily be done by comparing the result, r, with 0. Testing for a negative result is harder. In two's complement arithmetic, a signed value is negative if the most significant bit is 1. We are using 16-bit arithmetic, so that corresponds to bit 15. We can extract bit 15 by ANDing the result, r, with the binary value of 1000000000000000 by writing `r&0x8000` (the literal is expressed in hex form as 0x8000, which is mercifully shorter than the binary version).

To call the function, we can write the following:

```
if opCode == 0b1000000: r[rD] = alu(1,r[rS1],r[rS2])
```

We test for opcode 1000000 and call the `alu` function if it corresponds to ADD. The function is called with the `f = 1` parameter for addition; the numbers to be added are the contents of the two source registers. The result is loaded into the `r[rD]` register. In the current version of TC1, we use the opcode to look up the mnemonic and then apply the test if `mnemonic == 'ADD':`. This approach is easier to read and can use the mnemonic when displaying the output during tracing.

We have made the z and n variables global (that is, they can be changed by the function and accessed externally). If we didn't make them global, we would have to have made them return parameters. In general, it is regarded as a better practice to pass variables as parameters rather than making them global.

Functions and scope

Variables are associated with *scope* or *visibility*. If you write a program without functions, variables can be accessed everywhere in the program. If you use functions, life becomes rather more complex.

If you declare a variable in the main body, that variable will be visible in functions (that is, you can use it). However, you cannot change it in the function and then access the new value outside the function. What goes on in the function stays in the function. If you wish to access it from outside the function, you must declare it as *global*. If you write `global temp3`, then the `temp3` variable is the same variable both in and outside the function.

If you create a variable in a function, that variable cannot be accessed outside the function because it's private to the function (a local variable). You can create a variable with the same name in another function or the body of the program, but the variable in this function has no effect on variables with the same name outside the function.

If you create a variable in a function that you want to be visible outside the function, you have to declare it as global in the function. Consider the following code:

```
def fun_1():                # A dummy function
    p = 3                   # p is local to fun_1 and set to 3
    global q                # q is global and visible everywhere
    print('In fun_1 p =',p) # Print p in fun_1
    print('In fun_1 q =',q) # Print q in fun_1
    q = q + 1               # q is changed in this function
    p = p + 1               # p is changed in this function
    r = 5                   # set local variable r to 5
    return()                # You don't need a return

p = 5                       # p is defined in the body
q = 10                      # q is defined in the body
print('In body: p =',p, 'q =',q )  # Print current values of p and q
fun_1()                     # Call fun_1 and see what happens to p and q
print('In body after fun_1 q =',q, 'after fun_1 p = ',p)
```

After running this code, we get the following. As you can see, the function changes q because it is global, whereas p does not change since it is a local variable in the function:

```
In body: p = 5 q = 10
In fun_1 p = 3
In fun_1 q = 10
In body after fun_1 q = 11 after fun_1 p =  5
```

Here is a summary of the rules:

- If you don't change it in a function, you can use it anywhere

- If you declare it in a function, it's all yours and private to the function

- If you want to change it in the function and use it outside the function, then declare it as global in the function

This means that variables such as the z and n condition code flags can be accessed in a function. If you wish to change them in a function, they must be declared as global by using the following command:

```
global z,n
```

If a function returns a value, it ends with `return(whatever)`. If you don't return a value from a function, the `return` statement is not necessary. However, we usually include a `return()` that returns nothing, and then we explicitly mark the end of the function.

Although the use of global variables is supported by Python, some programmers avoid them because global variables make it too easy to accidentally change a variable in a function and not notice it, leading to headaches when debugging a faulty program. They argue that all variables should be passed to a function as a parameter.

In the next section, we'll describe the very thing that makes a computer a computer – its ability to take two different courses of action, depending on the outcome of an operation.

Branches and flow control

All microprocessors have flow control instructions; for example, the unconditional branch, BRA XYZ, means execute the next instruction at address XYZ. A typical conditional instruction is BNE XYZ, which implements taking the branch to the instruction at location XYZ, if and only if, the z flag is not set. The BNE mnemonic means "branch on not equal" because the z-bit is evaluated by comparing two values using subtraction. Consider the following example, which uses the TC1 assembly language:

```
       LDRL  r2,0      @ Load r2 (the sum) with 0
       LDRL  r0,5      @ Load r0 (the loop counter) with 5
       LDRL  r1,1      @ Load r1 (the register added to the sum) with 1
Loop   ADD   r2,r2,r1  @ Repeat: add r1 to r2
       INC   r1        @ Increment r1 so that we add 1, 2, 3 ... as we go round the loop
       DEC   r0        @ Decrement the loop counter in r0
       BNE   Loop      @ Until loop counter = 0
       STOP            @ Program completed
```

Load register with a literal (LDRL) is used three times to load r2 with 0, r0 with 5, and r1 with 1. In the line labeled Loop, we add r2 to r1 and put the result in r2. On its first execution, r2 becomes 0 + 1 = 1.

The next two lines increment r1 and decrement r0 so that r1 becomes 2 and r0 becomes 4. When we decrement r0, the z-flag is set if the result is zero. Since r2 initially contains 5 and then 4 after decrementing, the result is not zero and the z-flag is not set.

When BNE is executed, the z-flag is tested. If it is not zero, a branch is taken to the line labeled Loop and the same batch of four instructions are executed again. When the BNE is encountered a second time, the z-bit is still zero, because this time the decrement went from 4 to 3. Eventually, r0 contains 1 and is decremented to 0. The z-bit is then set. When BNE is next executed, the branch to loop is not taken, and the next instruction in the sequence, STOP, is executed. The loop is repeated 5 times. This program evaluates 1 + 2 + 3 + 4 + 5 = 15, which is the result in r2.

Branch addresses can be a little complicated. You can provide an absolute address; for example, BRA 24 jumps to the instruction at memory location 24. Most computers use a relative address, which is relative to the current instruction. For example, in this case, we would branch three instructions back from the current location (that is, the BNE instruction). So, you might think that the relative address is -3. It is a negative address because it is backward from the current address. Since the program counter has already been incremented to point to the next instruction, the branch back is -4. So, the literal field of the BNE loop would be -4.

The following fragment of code demonstrates testing four branch instructions and their implementation. In this example, we are using relative addressing for the branch; that is, the target address is specified with respect to the program counter. The first branch, BRA, is an unconditional branch and the next value of pc is calculated. All the others are conditional branches, and pc is changed only if the required condition is met. Note that the last operation is BMI, which means branch on minus, although some call it branch on negative (which has the same meaning):

```
if   opCode == 0b1100000:            pc = 0xFFFF & (pc + literal) # Branch always
elif opCode == 0b1100001 and z == 1: pc = 0xFFFF & (pc + literal) # Branch on zero
elif opCode == 0b1100010 and z == 0: pc = 0xFFFF & (pc + literal) # Branch on not zero
elif opCode == 0b1100011 and n == 1: pc = 0xFFFF & (pc + literal) # Branch on minus
```

The pc is incremented by pc + literal. However, since backward branches are represented in two's complement form, it is necessary to AND the result with 0xFFFF to force it to 16 bits to generate the correct value. This is because we are simulating 16-bit arithmetic using a computer language, Python, that represents numbers with more than 16 bits. This is just an unfortunate consequence of computer arithmetic that you have to be aware of when simulating binary arithmetic.

In the next chapter, we will return to Python and extend our ability to handle data structures and use Python's functions.

Summary

We started this chapter by designing a computer simulator. However, we haven't created a final product yet. Instead, we looked at some of the issues involved, such as the nature of an instruction set and the structure of an opcode.

We examined how an instruction can be decoded and how it can be executed. We also took the opportunity to broaden our knowledge of Python and introduced Python's bit-manipulation facilities, which let us implement machine-level instructions that operate on bits.

We also introduced an important component of Python, known as a function, which allows the programmer to create a self-contained unit of code that can be called to perform a specific job from many points in a program. Functions are vital to modern programming because they facilitate elegant design by bundling a complex sequence of operations into a unit, which you call to carry out a task.

In *Chapter 5*, we'll return to Python and look at some topics in a little more depth – in particular, lists. Lists are probably Python's most interesting and important feature.

5

A Little More Python

We've introduced Python and we've been using it. In this chapter we increase our knowledge of Python and extend some of the concepts we have encountered, and also introduce new features. In particular, we examine data structures, starting with the way in which lists of elements or strings of characters can be processed. This chapter paves the way for *Chapter 6,* where we complete the design of a computer simulator. But, before that, we provide a note on the terminology we use when discussing features of Python.

We will discuss the following topics:

- Statements and expressions
- More string features
- List comprehensions
- String processing
- Repetition and looping
- The dictionary
- Functions
- Lists of lists
- Imports
- Indenting in Python

Technical requirements

You can find the programs used in this chapter on GitHub at https://github.com/PacktPublishing/Computer-Architecture-with-Python-and-ARM/tree/main/Chapter05.

This chapter requires no new resources in addition to previous chapters. All that is required is a computer with a Python IDE. The same is true of all chapters until we reach *Chapter 9,* which deals with Raspberry Pi.

> **Statements and Expressions**
>
> An *expression* is a combination of values and operators that can be evaluated to provide a result; for example `(p+q)*7 - r`. A Boolean expression is a combination of values and logical operators that yields the value `True` or `False`; for example, `p > q`.
>
> A *statement* is a Python operation that must be evaluated by an interpreter; that is, it's an action. Typical Python statements involve `if`... `for`... actions. These two terms are often used in formal definitions; for example, the definition of an `if` statement is as follows:
>
> ```
> if <expr>:
>     <statement>
> ```
>
> Angle brackets are used in descriptions of the language to indicate *something that will be replaced by its actual value*; for example, a valid `if` statement is as follows:
>
> ```
> if x > y:
>     p = p + q
> ```
>
> In this case the *expression* is `x > y` and the *statement* is `p = p + q`.

More string features

Now we're going to extend our ability to manipulate strings. The string is one of Python's most important data structures and is at the heart of all the programs we write in this book. Python's string-handling facilities make it one of the most powerful and easy-to-use text-processing languages. A string is indicated by quotes, which may be either single or double; for example, `x = "Two"` and `y = 'One'` are Python strings. Python's ability to use two string terminators means that we can create strings like "Alan's book" (i.e., use the apostrophe as a normal grammar element).

During the execution of a Python program, you can read a string from the keyboard and also provide a prompt in the following way.

```
x = input(' Please type something ')
```

Executing this command displays `'Please type something'` on the screen, waits for your input, and then assigns the string you typed to variable `x`. This mechanism is very useful when simulating a program, because you can provide input as the program runs. Note that the input string must be terminated by hitting the *Enter* key.

String processing

You can change (substitute) characters in a string by using the method `replace`. For example, suppose we wish to replace all occurrences of `'$'` in the string `price` with `'£'`:

```
price =  'eggs $2, cheese $4'
price = price.replace('$', '£')          # Replace $ by £ in the string price
```

If we print `price`, we now get `'eggs £2, cheese £4'`.

Other string methods are `upper()` (convert text to upper case), `lstrip()` (remove leading characters), and `rstrip()` (remove trailing characters). Let `x ='###this Is A test???'`. Consider the following sequence:

```
x = x.lstrip('#')        # Remove left-hand leading '#' characters to get x = 'this Is A test???'
x = x.rstrip('?')        # Remove right-hand trailing '?' characters to get x = 'this Is A test'
x = x.lower()            # Convert to lower-case to get x = 'this is a test'
```

This sequence produces `x ='this is is a test'`.

Strings are *immutable*. You cannot change them once they are defined. In the preceding code, it looks as if we have modified x by removing leading and trailing characters and converting upper case to lower case. No! In each case we have created a *new* string with the same name as the old string (i.e., x).

If you were to enter `y = 'Allen'` and try to edit it to read `'Allan'` by changing the 'e' to 'a' using the expression `y[3] = 'a'`, you would get an error, because you would have tried to change an immutable string. However, you could legally write `y = y[0:3] + 'a' + y[4]` to create a new string y with the value `'Allan'`.

The addition symbol, +, performs addition in *arithmetic* and *concatenation* in string processing; for example, `x = 4 + 5` gives 9, whereas `x = '4' + '5'` gives `'45'`. This action is called *operator overloading* and indicates the extension of a function, when, for example, the function is applied to different objects.

The TC1 assembler uses the following string methods to remove spaces before an instruction, enable users to employ upper- or lower-case, and allow the use of a space or comma as a separator. For example, this code fragment lets you write either `r0, [r1]` or `R0,R1` with the same meaning. The code below shows how TC1 takes a line of the input (i.e., an assembly instruction) and simplifies it for later conversion to binary:

```
line = line.replace(',',' ')     # Allow use of a space or comma to separate operands
line = line.replace('[','')      # Allow LDRI r0,[r2] or LDRI r0,r2 First remove '['
line = line.replace(']','')      # Replace ']' by null string.
line = line.upper()              # Let's force lower- to upper-case
line = line.lstrip(' ')          # Remove leading spaces
line = line.rstrip('\n')         # Remove end of line chars. End-of-line is \n
```

Suppose an instruction is entered in string form as `'    ADD r0,R1, r3'`. This has leading spaces, upper- and lower-case text and commas, and is converted to `'ADD R0 R1 R3 '` by the above sequence of operations. The next step is to convert the string into individual *tokens* for analysis by the assembler. We can do this with the `split()` method. which converts a string into a list of strings separated by the character in the parentheses. Note that the default parameter is a space. If `s = 'ADD R0 R1 R2'`, then `s.split()` or `s.split(' ')` results in this:

```
s = ['ADD', 'R1', 'R2', 'R3']     # A list of four tokens, each of which is a string
```

We now have a list consisting of four separate strings; that is, a command followed by three parameters. We can access each of these strings using index notation:

```
T1 = s[0]                    # This is the mnemonic 'ADD'
T2 = s[1]                    # This is the destination register 'R1'
T3 = s[2]                    # This is the first source register 'R2'
T4 = s[3]                    # This is the second source register 'R3'
```

We can now perform operations on the tokens:

```
if T1 == 'STOP': then run = 0    # If the instruction is stop then halt processing
firstReg = int(T2[1:])           # Get the register number as an integer
```

The second statement uses `T2[1:]` to convert string `'R2'` into a new string `'2'` by removing the first character. The slice notation `[1:]` is interpreted as "All characters following the first." This lets us deal with one- or two-digit values like R2 or R23. Since there are only 8 registers, we could have written `[1:2]`. Using `[1:]` allows the extension 16 registers in a future version of TC1 without changing the code.

We have to use the *integer* function `int` to convert the register number from a string into its value as an integer. When learning Python, a common mistake is to forget to convert a string to an integer:

```
regNum = input('Please enter register number >>>')
contents = reg[regNum]
```

This code would generate an error. Because `regNum` is created as a string, holding the value you typed. However, in the second line, the program is expecting an integer as a list index. You have to write `reg[int(regNum)]` to convert the numeric string into an integer value.

Example – text Input

Here's a simple example of text input with Python using a simple `.txt` file. The source file is this:

```
@ This is text
NOP
  NOP


NOP
NOP

END
```

This file was processed by Python as follows. I use the address it had on my computer. This is read into a variable sFile:

```
myFile = 'E:\\ArchitectureWithPython\\testText.txt'
with open(myFile,'r') as sFile:
    sFile = sFile.readlines()              # Open the source program
print (sFile)
```

The output from this code fragment is as follows:

```
['@ This is text\n', 'NOP\n', ' NOP\n', ' \n', 'NOP\n', '\n', 'NOP\n', 'END']
```

We now have a Python list of strings, each corresponding to one line of the source text. Note that each line ends with an end-of-line (i.e., \n) and any spaces in the text are included. For example, there's a totally empty line and an empty line with a space. We have to take account of these when dealing with the input.

Having increased our ability to manipulate text strings, in the next section we look at one of Python's most interesting features: the facility to perform a sequence of operations on a string or a list in just one line of code with list comprehension.

List comprehensions

We now introduce a very powerful feature of Python, the *list comprehension*. It's not powerful because of what it can do, but because of how succinct it is. A list comprehension lets you take a list and process it in a single line. We take a look at list comprehensions, because they are so useful in processing text; for example, you can use a list comprehension to take a line of text and replace all double-spaces with single spaces, or convert all lower-case characters to upper-case characters.

List comprehensions can be applied to any iterable. An iterable is a structure that you can step through, such as a list, a string, or a tuple. The simplest form of list comprehension is this:

```
x = [i for i in y]
```

Here, x and y are strings (or lists). The text in bold represents Python reserved words and punctuation. The variable i is a user-chosen variable used to step through the list. We could have used any name instead of *i*; it simply doesn't matter. Consider the following example:

```
lettersList = [i for i in 'Tuesday']
```

The iterable being processed is the string 'Tuesday' and it is copied a character at a time to lettersList. This returns lettersList as the list of characters ['T','u','e','s','d','a','y']. We have turned a string into a list of characters.

We can create a more sophisticated version of the list comprehension as follows:

```
x = [expression for i in y if condition]
```

where `expression` is a Python expression, and `condition` is a Boolean condition. We step through the iterable, `y`, looking at each element and selecting it subject to a condition, processing it according to the expression, and then putting it in a new list. That's an awful lot of work in a single line. Consider this:

```
y = 'this$is$a$test'
x = [i for i in y if i != '$']
```

The condition is *if item i from y is not equal to '$'*. This list comprehension says, "Copy the characters in string y to string x, one-by-one, as long as the character isn't a `'$'` character." The result is this:

```
x =['t', 'h', 'i', 's', 'i', 's', 'a', 't', 'e', 's', 't'].
```

The original string has been replaced by a list of single-character strings, but with every `'$'` removed.

Let's look at three examples of list comprehensions:

1. The first example demonstrates how empty lines (i.e., ") can be removed from the input. We can copy all lines apart from those equal to the null or empty string " "with:

    ```
    sFile = [i for i in sFile if i != '']     # Remove blank lines
    ```

    We've renamed the new list the same as the old one. There's no reason why we can't do this and it saves having to invent a new name for each of the list comprehensions.

2. The second example is this:

    ```
    sFile = [i.upper() for i in sFile]        # Convert to upper-case
    ```

    We apply the function `.upper()` to each element `i`. This expression converts a lower-case character into its upper-case equivalent; that is, it converts all strings to upper-case. The last list comprehension is this:

    ```
    sFile = [i.split() for i in sFile if i != '']
    ```

    The expression `i.split()` divides the source string into individual tokens (strings) at each space. This means we can then then process the line as a sequence of tokens. The condition `if i != ''` is used to remove empty strings by not copying them.

3. The third example removes empty lines.

    We've created a list of three instructions that has empty lines in it, denoted by ''. When we execute this list comprehension, we convert each string into a sublist and we remove the empty lines:

    ```
    sFile = ['ADD R1 R2 R3', 'BEQ LOOP', '', 'LDRL R2 4','']
    sFile = [i.split() for i in sFile if i != '']
    print(sFile)
    ```

The output from this code is as follows:

```
[['ADD', 'R1', 'R2', 'R3'], ['BEQ', 'LOOP'], ['LDRL', 'R2', '4']]
```

The tuple

We now introduce the tuple for the sake of completeness, although we make little use of it in this text. A list is a sequence of elements enclosed by square brackets; for example, `P = [1,4,8,9]`. A tuple is a sequence of elements separated by round brackets; for example, `Q = (1,4,8,9)`.

There is little difference between a tuple and a list; they are both data structures that hold a sequence of elements. However, a *tuple is immutable* and cannot be modified, unlike a list. A tuple is a read-only list and is used when you wish to store data that does not change. Although not relevant here, tuples do have implementation and performance advantages over lists; that is, if you have a list that is fixed, it is better to use a tuple.

Later, we will use tuples in dictionary structures, as here:

```
opCodes = {'add':(2,34), 'inc':(4,37)}
```

In this case, the values in bold are each two-component tuples. We could have used a list, but the tuple indicates a fixed structure that cannot change. If you were to use a list instead of a tuple, you would write this:

```
opCodes = {'add':[2,34], 'inc':[4,37]}
```

Repetition and looping

We now expand our knowledge of Python's repetition mechanism, a feature common to all high-level procedural languages. In this section we learn how to do the following:

- Repeat an action multiple times
- Use different data and parameters each time you carry out the action
- Iterate over elements in a list
- Use the `enumerate` function

Suppose we want to test whether a list includes a particular item. We can create a `for` loop to do this:

```
fruit1 = ['apples', 'oranges', 'grapes', 'bananas', 'peaches']
size = len(fruit1)              # Get length of the list
inList = False                  # inList is False until we find item
for i in range (0,size):        # Repeat for each item in list
    if fruit1[i] == 'grapes':
        inList = True           # Set flag to True if we find the item
```

This code first sets inList to False to indicate that the element 'grapes' has not been found. The for loop steps though all elements in the list, testing each one for the item we're looking for. If it is found, inList is set to True. This code works, but it is not good. If there are a million elements in the list and grapes the first one, the code still steps through the remaining 999,999 elements. This is horribly inefficient.

In the following example, we compare successive elements with a value, and stop if we find it. On each cycle, if the item is not found, we continue. If we find what we want, we jump out of the loop rather than continuing to the bitter end by testing every single item. When we do the comparison, if the current item is *not* equal to 'grapes', we set inList to False and the loop continues with the next element.

If we find 'grapes', the else part of the if statement sets inList to True and then uses a break statement to exit the loop and avoid further pointless cycles round the loop. A break in a for or while loop tells Python to exit the loop now and continue with the next instruction *after* the loop:

```
listSize = len(fruit1)
for i in range (0,listSize):
    if fruit1[i] != 'grapes': inList = False    # Is the item here?"
    else:                                        # If it is, drop out of the loop
        inList = True                            # Set flag on finding it
        break                                    # Jump out of the loop
```

The variable inList is just a flag that we can use later in the program; for example, we could write this:

```
if inList == False: print('Yes, we have no grapes')
if inList == True:  print('Grapes --- we got lots')
```

Another approach is to use the list operator in. If we have a list, we can check whether an item is a member of that list by using the following construct:

```
if      'grapes' in fruit1:
        inList = True
else: inList = False
```

The first line returns True if 'grapes' is in the list fruit1, and False otherwise. The in construct is very useful in testing whether an item belongs to a group of other items arranged as a list; for example, if all employees are in the list staff, then

sets worksHere to True if Smith is a valid employee name, and False otherwise.

```
if 'Smith' in staff:  worksHere = True
else:                 worksHere = False
```

Later we will use the `in` operator in to test whether an instruction is a member of a set, as here:

```
arithOps = ['ADD','SUB','MUL','DIV']        # Define list of arithmetic operations
.

.
if 'mnemonic' in arithOps:                  # Test whether instruction is arithmetic
    .

else:
```

Repetition and Iterables

Another version of the `for` loop iterates over the elements of a list as follows:

```
for i in anyList:                           # Operate on each element of the list one-by-one
    <body of loop>
```

The words in bold are the reserved Python words; the other words are user-defined variables. Here, the `i` is not a sequence-counting integer as it was in the previous example using `range()`. It is the value of each element (or iterable) in the list taken in turn. Consider the following example using a list of colors:

```
car = ['red', 'white', 'green' ,'silver', 'teal']
for color in car: print(color)             # Color is a loop variable; we could have used i.
```

This code steps through each element of the list `car` and prints out its value, as follows.

```
red
white
green
silver
teal
```

Consider an example using a list of computer operations. In this case we've taken a list of tuples, one for each of four op-codes. The tuple consists of an op-code string, an instruction type, and the number of operands required. This is just a demonstration. We could have used a list but chose a tuple to emphasize that the tuple values do not change:

```
opCodes = [('NOP','misc',0),('BEQ','flow',1),('LDR','move',2), \
           ('ADD', 'arith',3)]
for instruction in opCodes:                 # Step through the op-codes
    print(instruction)                      # Print the current op-code
    op     = instruction[0]                 # Extract the three tuple members
    group  = instruction[1]
    params = instruction[2]
    print(op, group, params)                # Print the three tuple values
    if op == 'BEQ': print('beq found')      # Demo! Print BEQ when we find it
```

The output of this code fragment is as follows:

```
('NOP', 'misc', 0)
NOP misc 0
('BEQ', 'flow', 1)
BEQ flow 1
beq found
('LDR', 'move', 2)
LDR move 2
('ADD', 'arith', 3)
ADD arith 3
```

We have now demonstrated that you can iterate through a list of any type in Python.

A particularly interesting feature of Python is looping with a *double index*. You can step through a list by numeric index, or by object name. This is useful when you want to step through by object name but would also like to know where it is in the list. The Python function `enumerate` permits this form of looping. It is easier to demonstrate the action of `enumerate` than to explain it. Consider the previous example of the list `car`:

```
car = [ 'red', 'white', 'green', 'silver', 'teal']
for color in enumerate(car):
    print (color)
```

The output from this code is as follows:

```
(0, 'red')
(1, 'white')
(2, 'green')
(3, 'silver')
(4, 'teal')
```

The iterator, `color`, has become a sequence of tuples with the element index and the corresponding value from the list. Remember that a tuple is like a list except that its elements are immutable and can't be changed. Here's a case where I would use an iterator name like *color*, rather than *i*, because it is more explicit/descriptive, and it is less easy to confuse with an integer.

An alternative form of enumeration uses two indices, one an explicit integer count and one an element count. In the following example, `count` is the explicit integer index and `color` is the enumeration index. Thus, `count` steps 0, 1, 2 etc., and `color` steps red, white, green ...:

```
for count, color in enumerate(car):
    print ('count = ', count, 'Color =', color)
```

This produces the following output:

```
count =  0 Color = red
count =  1 Color = white
count =  2 Color = green
count =  3 Color = silver
count =  4 Color = teal
```

Lists of lists

Here we extend the use of Python's most important data structure, the list. First, we demonstrate that a list can, itself, contain lists. Python lets you construct lists with any type of item; for example, x = [1,2,'test',v,True] defines a list with two integers, a string, a variable, and a Boolean constant. Since you can use any legal element in a list, you can create a *list of lists*. Consider this:

```
fruit = [['apple',2.35,150], ['orange',4.10,200], ['banana',3.65,70]]
```

This is a list of three items and each item is a list itself (shaded); for example, the first item in this list is the list ['apple',2.35,150]. Each sub-list consists of a string naming the fruit, the price of the fruit, and the current stock level.

Suppose we want to know the price of oranges; we could write something like this:

```
for i in range (0,len(fruit)):    # Step through the list of fruit. len(fruit) is 3
    if fruit[i][0] == 'orange':   # If the first element in the current item is 'orange',
        price = fruit[i][1]       # then get the second element in that item
        break                     # If we do find 'orange' we can break out of the loop
```

We use a for loop to step through the list of fruits. Then, when we've located the item we want (which is a list), we read the second item of that list. As you can see, we use two subscripts, first [i] and then [1].

Consider the following example of lists of lists:

```
testList = [[4,9,[1,6]],[8,7,[0,9]]]
```

This is not easy on the eye! Let's use bold font and shading to emphasize the components of the string:

```
testList = [[4,9,[1,6]], [8,7,[0,9]]]   # Each element in the list is itself a list
```

It's a list consisting of two items: [4,9,[1,6]] and [8,7,[0,9]]. Each of these items is itself a list consisting of three items: two integers and a list; for example, the elements of the first item are 4, 9 and the list [1,6].

If I were to write x = testList[1][2][1], what would the value of x be?

It would be 9, because `testList[1]` is `[8,7,[0,9]]` and `testList[1][2]` is `[0,9]` and `testList[1][2][1]` is 9. Think of this as a tree with branches! The first branch is element `[1]` of `testList`. The second branch is element `[2]` of that branch, and the third (final) branch is element `[1]` on that second branch. *Figure 5.1* illustrates the concept of embedded lists graphically.

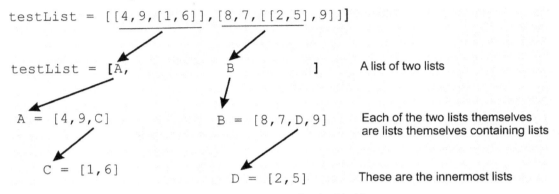

Figure 5.1 - Illustration of embedded lists

Consider a second example:

```
x = ['this', 'that', 'then']
```

What is `x[2][3]`? This expression yields `'n'`, because `x[2]` is `'then'`, and element 3 of that is `'n'`.

Indenting in python

We have been indenting code since we introduced Python. Now we re-emphasize the use of the indent in Python because it is so vital to correct programming. Most computer languages allow you to group statements together, as a block, for a particular purpose. Typically, the instructions in a group are executed as a batch, one by one. Such groups are often associated with conditional statements and loops.

Some languages indicate a block of instructions by enclosing them in curly brackets { }. Consider the following. It's not real code; it's just plain text designed to illustrate the layout of a program:

```
{some operations}
{main loop
{some other operations}
if x == 1 {Do this batch of operations}
repeat
{do these operations}
}
```

Here, you have several blocks of operations, which include nested blocks (i.e., a block within another block). Blocks are executed as if they were a single operation; that is, they are the computer equivalent of *subcontracting*.

Although it is not a programming requirement, it is normal to use indentation as a reading aid to make the code more understandable to people, as here:

```
{some operations}
{main loop
    {some operations}
    if x == 1
        {do this batch of operations}
    repeat
        {do these operations}
}
```

Python doesn't use brackets to indicate a block of consecutive operations. It requires that a block of code be indented (and the same indentation used for each member of the block). Failure to get the indentation right will either result in a failure to compile the program, or a program that doesn't do what you think it will do. Errors of indentation are one of the first things that the novice programmer encounters. An indentation error is very easy to miss. For example, if you accidentally create an indent or remove an indent while editing a program, you can easily get an error that takes a long time to locate.

A simple example of the use of blocks and indentation in Python is given below. Although any amount of indent is legal, by convention, an indent is normally four spaces. Each level of indentation is shaded. Note that the else in the last line belongs to the first if. If we had indented it further, it would belong to the second if:

```
x = 1
y = 2
if z == 4:
    s = 1
    b = 2
    if b == 3:
        g = 1
else: p = 7
```

The dictionary

In this section we introduce Python's dictionary mechanism, which makes writing simulators so easy. Here, you will learn how to create a dictionary that translates one thing into another, for example, translating the name of an instruction into its binary code. Here we learn about the following:

- The nature of a dictionary
- The advantages of a dictionary over the list
- The difference between a dictionary key and a dictionary value
- Inserting items in a dictionary
- Extracting items from a dictionary
- Using a dictionary to solve a problem

The dictionary is one of Python's most useful features, a feature that makes it so much easier to design simulators. The Python dictionary is an impressive data structure that is accessed by means of a *key*, rather than a location within the data structure. Instead of providing a location like myList[5], you look up an item in a dictionary in exactly the same way you use a dictionary in everyday life. You provide the dictionary with a name (which we call a *key*) and up pops the information *associated* with that name. Keys are unique; the same key can't appear more than once in a dictionary (just as social security numbers are unique).

A Python dictionary has the form {key1:value1, key2:value2, key3:value3}; for example, {'UK':44, 'USA':1, 'Germany':49, 'France':33} might be used to look up a country's international telephone prefix. The dictionary is enclosed in curly braces, and key:value pairs have a colon between the key and its value. The order of pairs in a dictionary does not matter, because an item is accessed by its *key* and not by its location in the dictionary.

The key is often a string, but that is not a requirement. In our computer simulator, the keys are usually the mnemonic codes of a computer language. The value associated with a key can be any legal Python data structure. In some of the simulators we create, we often specify the value as a tuple, which is an ordered list. For example, the dictionary entry 'INC':(8,16) has the key 'INC' and the value (8,16). Searching the dictionary using the key 'INC', returns the tuple (8,16). In this case, the value is the format of the instruction (i.e., 8), and its op-code (i.e., 16).

You could use a list as a value instead of a tuple, that is, 'INC':[8,16]. The only significant difference is that you can't change a tuple once it is defined.

You can check whether an item is in the dictionary by writing if key in dictionary, as follows:

```
if 'INC' in opCodes:          # This returns True if 'INC' is in opCodes
```

To obtain the information about a particular mnemonic, we can use the get method to read the value associated with the key. For example, opData = opCodes.get('INC') returns (8,16).

We can then access the two fields of the tuple associated with 'INC' as follows:

```
binaryCode  = opData[0]
formatStyle = opData[1]
```

If the requested key is not in the dictionary, the get method returns None. None is a Python reserved word and indicates a null value. Note that None is not zero or an empty string, it has its own type None. Consider the following:

```
if opCodes.get(thisInstruction) == None:  # Ensure that the instruction is valid
    print("Error. Illegal operation")
```

The following code uses the telephone prefix directory we described above to demonstrate how to use None to deal with errors. Note that this uses an infinite loop and terminates on an error. When None is detected, the break forces an exit from the infinite loop:

```
prefixes = {'UK':44, 'USA':1, 'Germany':49, 'France':33}
while True:                          # Infinite loop
    x = input('Country? ')          # Ask for the country
    y = prefixes.get(x)             # Look up the prefix
    if y == None:                   # If None print error message
        print('Prefix not found')
        break                       # And exit the loop
    else: print('Prefix = ',y)
print('Program terminated')
```

Python's dictionaries make it incredibly easy to implement symbolic names for labels and variables. Just create a dictionary with *name: value* pairs, and use the name to get the value associated with the label; for example, you might want to associate Hastings with the value 1066. Typical assemblers use *directives* to express this:

```
Hastings EQU 1066       @ Equate the Name "Hastings" to the value 1066
```

Later in your program, you might write LDRL **r0**,Hastings in order to load r0 with 1066. Suppose you have a table of names and values, namSub, that's set up as a dictionary:

```
namSub = {'Hastings':1066, 'Agincourt':1415, 'Trafalgar':1805}
```

If we wish to get the value associated with Hastings, we can write this:

```
x = namSub.get('Hastings')
```

The name will be translated into its value.

In what follows, we've written several fragments of Python code in order to demonstrate how the dictionary can be used. These examples demonstrate the setting up of a dictionary, adding information to it, and accessing it. When an assembly language program is run, some dictionaries are set up before it is executed, for example, the list of legal instructions. Some directories, such as the symbol table of names appearing in the assembly language program, will be constructed as the program runs.

The first directory in the example converts a register name into its register number; for example, a register name x can be converted to its register number y by y = regs.get(x). Of course, you don't need to use a dictionary. We could simply write y = int(x[1:]) to convert the string 'r6' into the integer 6 by using string processing. However, the dictionary method is more elegant and easier to follow. Moreover, it's more flexible:

```
regs = {'r0':0, 'r1':1, 'r2':2, 'r3':3, 'r4':4}    # Register name-to-number translation
symTab = {'start':0,'time':24,'stackP':'sp','next':0xF2}
                                    # Symbol table converts symbolic name to value
```

```
x0 = 'add r1,r2,r4'                # An example of an instruction in text form
x1 = x0.split(' ')                 # Split instruction into op-code and predicate
x2 = x1[1].split(',')              # Split the predicate into tokens
x3 = x2[0]                         # Get the first token of x2
if x3 in regs:                     # Is this a valid register?
    x4 = regs.get(x3)              # Use get() to read its value
print ('x0 = ',x0, '\nx1 = ',x1, '\nx2 = ',x2, '\nx3 = ',x3, '\nx4 = ',x4)

y0 = 'beq next'                    # Another example: instruction with a label
y1 = y0.split(' ')                 # Split into op-code and predicate on the space
y2 = y1[1]                         # Read the predicate (i.e.,'next')
y3 = symTab.get(y2)                # Get its value from the symbol table (i.e., 0xF2)
print('beq ',y3)                   # Print the instruction with the actual address

z = symTab.get('beq next'.split(' ')[1])   # We've done it all in one line. Not so easy to follow.
print('beq ',z)
print('Symbol table ', symTab)             # Print the symbol table using a print

symTab['nextOne'] = 1234                    # This is how we add a new key and value
print('Symbol table ', symTab)             # Here's the augmented symbol table

opCode = {'add':('Arith',0b0001,3),'ldr':('Move',0b1100,2), \
        'nop':('Miscellaneous',1111,0)}     # New directory. Each key has three values in a tuple
thisInst = 'ldr'                            # Let's look up an instruction
if thisInst in opCode:                      # First test if it's valid and in the dictionary
    if thisInst == 'ldr':                   # If it is:
        instClass = opCode.get('ldr')[0]    # Get first element of the instruction
        binaryVal = opCode.get('ldr')[1]    # Get the second element
        operands  = opCode.get('ldr')[2]    # Get the third element

print('\nFor opCode: ',thisInst, '\nClass = ', instClass, \
        '\nBinary code = ', bin(binaryVal), '\nNumber of operands = ',operands)

print('\nThis is how to print a directory')
                                            # Now print a formatted dictionary (key and value on each line)
for key,value in opCode.items():
    print(key, ':', value)
print()
for i,j in opCode.items():                  # Note that key and value can be any two variables
    print(i, ':', j)

theKeys = opCode.keys()                     # The function .keys() returns the keys in a dictionary
```

```
print('The keys are: ',theKeys)

test = {'a':0,'b':0,'c':0,'d':0}    # A new directory. The values are just integers
test['a'] = test['a'] + 1           # You can change a value! Use the key to locate it
test['d'] = test['d'] + 7

test1 = {'e':0, 'f':0}              # Here's a second dictionary.
test.update(test1)                  # Append it to test using .update()
print('Updated dictionary test is: ',test)    # Not convinced? Here it is then.
```

The following is the output after executing the above fragment of code:

```
x0 =  add r1,r2,r4
x1 =  ['add', 'r1,r2,r4']
x2 =  ['r1', 'r2', 'r3']
x3 =  r1
x4 =  1
beq  242
beq  242
Symbol table  {'start': 0, 'time': 24, 'stackPointer': 'sp', 'next': 242}
Symbol table  {'start': 0, 'time': 24, 'stackPointer': 'sp', 'next': 242,
               'nextOne': 1234}

For opCode:  ldr
Class =  Move
Binary code =  0b1100
Number of operands =  2

This is how to print a directory
add : ('Arith', 1, 3)
ldr : ('Move', 12, 2)
nop : ('Miscellaneous', 1111, 0)

add : ('Arith', 1, 3)
ldr : ('Move', 12, 2)
nop : ('Miscellaneous', 1111, 0)
The keys are:  dict_keys(['add', 'ldr', 'nop'])
Updated dictionary test is:  {'a': 1, 'b': 0, 'c': 0, 'd': 7, 'e': 0, 'f': 0}
```

Let's look at dictionaries in more detail with another example. The use of Python's dictionaries makes it easy to implement symbolic names for labels and variables. All we have to do is to create a dictionary with name: value pairs and use a name to get its associated value. Suppose we've read an instruction, say, 'ADD r4,r2,r3', and tokenized it into this:

```
predicate = ['r4','r2','r3']    # The list of parameters for the op-code
```

We can get the integer value of a register the hard way by using slicing:

```
rD = int([predicate[0]][1:])
```

Let's simplify the expression to make the explanation easier. Suppose we write this:

```
rD = predicate[0]
```

The value of rD is the string 'r4'. What we need to do is to isolate the '4' from 'r4' and then convert the character '4' to the integer 4.

We can write rD = rD[1:] to return all characters in the string except the initial 'r'. The final step is to convert to an integer, which we can do with rD = int(rD).

The [1:] means all the characters after the first character, r, which returns '4' if the register was 'r4'. We could have written [1:2] rather than [1:]. However, by using [1:], we can later increase the number of registers beyond 9 without changing the program. Putting all three steps together, we get this:

```
rD = int([predicate[0]][1:])
```

Let's use a dictionary to carry out the same action. Assume also that we've set up a directory for the registers:

```
regs = {'r0':0, 'r1':1, 'r2':2, 'r3':3, 'r4':4}    # Register names and values
```

Before processing a register name, we can test for a valid register symbolic name with this:

```
if predicate[0] in regs:
        <deal with valid name>
else: <deal with error>
```

Extracting the actual integer number of the register is easy:

```
rD = regs.get(predicate[0])
```

Finally, note that you can access a dictionary in two ways. Consider the following:

```
regs = {'r0':0, 'r1':1, 'r2':2, 'r3':3, 'r4':4}
aaa = regs.get('r3')
bbb = regs['r3']
print('Test aaa = ',aaa, 'bbb =',bbb)
```

This gives us this:

```
Test aaa =  3 bbb = 3
```

The advantage of get is that it returns None if the key is not found, whereas the other method creates a runtime error, called KeyError.

Functions revisited

This section looks at functions in a little more detail and demonstrates the use of the `global` statement to make parameters accessible outside a function.

Parameters can be passed to functions in parentheses in the function call, and results retrieved by a `return()` statement. Recall that variables created in a function are local to the function unless they are declared as global; that is, if you write x = 5 in a function, you have created a local variable x with the value 5. If there is an x outside the function, it is a different x. A value declared outside a function can be accessed inside the function provided it hasn't been declared as a local variable within the function.

The body of a function is indented from the initial `def` statement. A function does not need an explicit termination, because *indentation* takes care of that. Consider the following:

```
def adder(P,Q):                    # Adder function
    R = P + Q
    return (R)                     # Return the sum R

def subtractor(P,Q):               # Subtractor function
    global R                       # Make R global
    R = P - Q                      # No need to return a value

A, B = 7, 2                        # Note Python's multiple assignment
C = adder(A,B)                     # Do addition
subtractor(A,B)                    # Do subtraction (just call the function)
print('Sum =', C, 'Diff = ',R)
```

If we run this program we get the following:

```
Sum = 9 Diff =   5
```

As you can see, we can return a value as an argument in the return statement, or we can make it global. When we do use the global variables, we don't need to pass the parameters to or from the function.

Imports

This section shows how you can access operations that are not part of the Python language itself. These functions are not vital to writing a simulator, but they do provide some very useful facilities. We've included this short section to demonstrate how these facilities are accessed.

A strength of Python is that it includes several libraries of functions that you can access to facilitate the design of programs, for example, graphics. We don't need many external functions for our work. Here, we will demonstrate two: `random` and `sys`.

When simulating a computer, you often need data for testing. Typing it in is time-consuming. Fortunately, Python has a library of functions that generate random numbers. In order to use a library, you first have to import it. Consider the following:

```
import random              # Get the library (usually at the start of the program)
.
.
X = random.randint(0,256)  # Generate a random integer in the range 0 to 255
```

Function calls are usually of the form `library.action`. In this case, the library is `random` and the action is `randomint(a,b)`. The parameters `a` and `b` give the range of random integer values.

Another useful library is `sys`, which provides operating system functions such as `exit()`, which terminates a Python program and returns to its calling level. See this, for example:

```
import sys                 # Get the system library
.
.
if run == 0: sys.exit()    # If run is 0 then go home (exit the Python program)
```

We have now covered enough Python topics to begin to design a real computer simulator in the next chapter.

Summary

In this chapter, we've extended our knowledge of Python and introduced or expanded some of the features that demonstrate its power and versatility. For example, we've looked at the list and the string, the two data structures that are of most importance to us. We've also expanded on the use of loops and other repetitive structures.

We've introduced the dictionary, a delightfully elegant data structure that enables us to locate information by a key that describes it, rather than its location in the directory. For example, if we want to convert instruction names into binary op-code, we can create a dictionary and just look up the appropriate code for any mnemonic. This feature really does simplify the design of interpreters and assemblers.

We've also looked at one of Python's more unusual features: list comprehensions. These take a little getting used to, but they can make it much easier to process the text of assembly language instructions by cleaning up the input (for example, by removing spaces, or modifying punctuation and syntax).

In *Chapter 6* we put together the things we've learned about the operation of a computer and design an assembler and a simulator for a hypothetical computer called TC1.

6

TC1 Assembler and Simulator Design

In this chapter, we will put together the lessons we have learned in previous chapters and construct a computer simulator. The key topics we will cover in this chapter are as follows:

- Analyzing instructions
- Dealing with assembler directives
- Building the binary instruction
- The pre-TC1 (a prequel to the actual simulator)
- The TC1 simulator program
- A TC1 assembly language program
- TC1 postscript

By the end of this chapter, you should understand how a simulator is designed and be able to create one. The following two chapters concentrate on expanding the simulator and providing more facilities, such as error detection in the input.

Technical requirements

You can find the programs used in this chapter on GitHub at https://github.com/PacktPublishing/Computer-Architecture-with-Python-and-ARM/tree/main/Chapter06.

In order to construct a Python-based simulator, you need the same tools used in earlier chapters; that is, you require an editor to create the Python program and a Python interpreter. These are included in the freely available Python package we introduced in *Chapter 1*.

Analyzing instructions

In this section, we will look at the way in which we take a text string representing an assembly language instruction and process it to create binary code that can be executed by the simulator.

Interestingly, the assembler can be more complicated than the actual simulator. Indeed, we devote relatively little space to the simulator itself in this chapter. We don't actually need an assembler, because it's easy to hand-translate assembly-level operations into binary code; it's just a matter of filling in the fields of the 32-bit instruction format. For example, *load register R7 with the literal value 42* can be written as LDRL R7,42. This has a 7-bit opcode, 01 01010, the destination register is r7 (code 111), the two source registers are not used, and their fields can both be set to 000. The literal is 42, or 0000000000101010 as a 16-bit binary value. The binary-encoded instruction is as follows:

0001010111000000000000000000101010

It's easy to translate code by hand, but it's no fun. We are going to create an assembler that automates the process of translation and lets you use symbolic names rather than actual literals (constants). Consider the following example of assembly language code. This is written using *numeric values* (shaded), rather than symbolic names. This is not intended to be a specific assembly language; it is designed to illustrate the basic concepts:

```
        LDRL    R0,60           @ Load R0 with the time factor, 60
        .
        CMP     R3,R5           @ Compare R3 and R5
        BEQ     1               @ If equal, jump to next-but-one instruction
        ADD     R2,R2,4
        SUB     R7,R1,R2
```

In the following example, literals have been replaced with symbolic names. These are shaded:

```
Minutes EQU     60              @ Set up a constant
Test    EQU     4
        LDRL    R0,Minutes      @ Load R0 with the time factor
.
        CMP     R3,R5
        BEQ     Next
        ADD     R2,R2,Test
Next    SUB     R7,R1,R2
```

Python's dictionary structure makes the handling of symbolic names very easy indeed. The preceding shows the processing of a text file containing the assembly language. This file is called sFile and is simply a .txt file containing the assembly language instructions.

Processing the input

We will now look at how the raw input – that is, the text file containing the assembly language source code – can be processed. In principle, it would be nice to have a source file where the assembly language instructions were all perfectly formatted and laid out.

In reality, a program may not be formatted ideally; for example, there may be blank lines or program comments that need to be ignored.

We have designed this assembly language to allow considerable latitude in the writing of a TC1 program. In fact, it allows a free format that is not implemented by most real assemblers. We took this approach for several reasons. First, it demonstrates how to perform text processing, which is a fundamental part of the design of assemblers. Second, a free format means you don't have to remember whether to use uppercase or lowercase names and labels.

Some languages are case-sensitive and some are not. The assembly language we have designed is *case-insensitive*; that is, you can write either ADD `r0`,r1,r2 or ADD `R0`,R1,R2. Consequently, we can write the load register immediate assembly instruction in all the following forms to execute a *load register-indexed* operation:

LDRI R2,[R1],10 or

LDRI R2,r1,10 or

LDRI R2,[R1,10] or,

LDRI r2,r1,10

This level of freedom of notation is possible because the [] brackets are not actually necessary to identify the instruction; they are used in programs because programmers associate [r0] with indirect addressing. In other words, the brackets are there for the programmer, not the computer, and are redundant.

However, this level of freedom is not necessarily desirable because it could lead to errors and make it more difficult for one person to read another person's program. All design decisions come with pros and cons.

The following Python example includes a short embedded assembly language program. The Python code has been designed so that you can use either an assembly language program that is part of the assembler (this is just for testing and debugging purposes because it avoids having to go into a text editor every time you want to test a feature) or a program in text form on disk. In this example, we located the test program at E\:testCode.txt on my computer. When the demonstration text-processing code runs, it asks you whether the code is to come from disk or is the embedded code. Typing d reads the disk, and entering any other input reads the embedded code.

The filename of the assembly language program is testCode = 'E://testCode.txt'. A double backslash is used instead of the conventional filenaming convention in Python programs.

The text-processing program removes blank lines, converts text into uppercase (allowing you to write r0 or R0), and lets you use a comma or a space as a separator (you can write ADD R0,R1,R2 or ADD r0 r1 r2). We also remove surplus spaces before and after the instruction. The final result is a tokenized list; that is, ADD r0,r1,r2 is converted into the ['ADD','R0','R1','R2'] list. Now, the assembler can look up the instruction and then extract the information it requires (register numbers and literals).

In the following program, we used a new variable every time we processed a line in order to help you keep track of variables. The following is an example:

```
sFile2 = [i.upper() for i in sFile1]          # Convert in to uppercase
sFile3 = [i.split('@')[0] for i in sFile2]     # Remove comments
```

We've used different variable names for clarity. Normally, you would write:

```
sFile = [i.upper() for i in sFile]             #
sFile = [i.split('@')[0] for i in sFile]       #
```

We use file comprehension to remove comments in the code:

```
sFile3 = [i.split('@')[0] for i in sFile2]     # Remove comments
```

This is a rather clever trick and requires explanation. It copies each line of sFile2 to sFile3. However, the value copied for each line is i.split('@')[0], where i is the current line. The split('@') method divides the list into strings using '@' as a divider. If there is no '@' in the original string, the string is copied. If there is an '@', it is copied as two strings; for example, ADD R1,R2,R3 @ Sum the totals is copied to sFile3 as 'ADD R1,R2,R3','@ Sum the totals'. However, only the first element of the list is copied because of the [0] index; that is, only 'ADD R1,R2,R3' is copied and the comment is removed.

The text input processing block is given here:

```
testCode = 'E://testCode.txt'
altCode  = ['nop', 'NOP 5', 'add R1,R2','', 'LDR r1,[r2]', \
            'ldr r1,[R2]','\n', 'BEQ test @www','\n']
x = input('For disk enter d, else any character ')
if x == 'd':
    with open(testCode, 'r') as source0:
        source = source0.readlines()
    source = [i.replace('\n','') for i in source]
else:    source = altCode
print('Source code to test is',source)
sFile0 = []
for i in range(0,len(source)):              # Process the source file in list sFile
    t1 =  source[i].replace(',',' ')        # Replace comma with space
    t2 =  t1.replace('[',' ')               # Remove [ brackets
    t3 =  t2.replace(']',' ')               # Remove ] brackets
    t4 =  t3.replace('  ',' ')              # Remove any double spaces
    sFile0.append(t4)                       # Add result to source file
sFile1= [i for i in sFile0 if i[-1:]!='\n'] # Remove end-of-lines
sFile2= [i.upper() for i in sFile1]         # All uppercase
sFile3= [i.split('@')[0] for i in sFile2]   # Remove comments with @
sFile4= [i.rstrip(' ') for i in sFile3 ]    # Remove trailing spaces
```

```
sFile5= [i.lstrip(' ') for i in sFile4 ]          # Remove leading spaces
sFile6=[i for i in sFile5 if i != '']             # Remove blank lines
print ('Post-processed output',  sFile6)
```

The following are two examples of using this code. In the first case, the user input is d, indicating a disk program, and in the second case, the input is x, indicating the use of the embedded source program. In each case, the course and output values are printed to demonstrate the string-processing operations.

Case 1 – Disk input

```
For disk enter d, else any character d
Source code to test is ['diskCode', 'b', 'add r1,r2,[r3]', '', 'ADD r3 @
test', ' ', 'r2,,r3', ' ', 'gg']
Post-processed output ['DISKCODE', 'B', 'ADD R1 R2 R3', 'ADD R3', 'R2 R3',
'GG']
```

Case 2 – Using the embedded test program

```
For disk enter d, else any character x
Source code to test is ['nop', 'NOP 5', 'add R1,R2', '', 'LDR r1,[r2]', 'ldr
r1,[R2]', '\n', 'BEQ test @www', '\n']
Post-processed output ['NOP', 'NOP 5', 'ADD R1 R2', 'LDR R1 R2', 'LDR R1 R2',
'BEQ TEST']
```

The preceding code does not represent an optimum text-processing system. It was designed to demonstrate the basic process involved in manipulating text before you process it. However, these concepts will appear again in TC1.

Dealing with Mnemonics

What's in a name? How do we know that a NOP instruction stands alone, but an ADD instruction requires three registers? In this section, we begin a discussion of how assembly language instructions are processed in order to extract their meaning (i.e., convert them into binary form).

Consider the following fragment of TC1 assembly language:

```
ADD  R1,R3,R7          @ Three operands (three registers)
NOP                    @ No operands
LDRL R4,27             @ Two operands (register and a literal value)
```

When the assembler reads a line, it needs to know how to deal with the opcode and its operands. So, how does it know how to proceed? We can use Python's dictionary facility to solve this problem in a very simple way, by just looking in a table to see what information an opcode requires.

Recall that a dictionary is a set or collection of items, where each item has two components; for example, an English-German dictionary has items that consist of an English word and its German equivalent. The word you look up is called a *key* and that provides a *value*. For example, in the English-German dictionary, the item `'town':'Stadt'` consists of the key `town` and the value `Stadt`. A dictionary is a fancy name for a *look-up table*.

A dictionary in Python is defined by its punctuation (i.e., it doesn't require any special reserved Python words); it's a type of list enclosed by curly braces, `{ }`. Each list item consists of a key and its value separated with a colon. Successive items are separated with commas, exactly as in a list.

A *key* is used to access the appropriate value in a dictionary. In TC1, the key is the *mnemonic* used to look up the details of the instruction. Let's create a dictionary called `codes` with three keys that are strings representing valid TC1 instructions: `STOP`, `ADD`, and `LDRL`. This dictionary can be written as follows:

```
codes = {'STOP':P, 'ADD':Q, 'LDRL':R}          # P, Q, R are variables
```

Each key is a string terminated by a colon, followed by its value. The key doesn't have to be a string. In this case, it's a string because we are using it to look up mnemonics, which are text strings. The first `key:value` pair is `'STOP':P`, where `'STOP'` is the key and `P` is its value. Suppose we want to know whether `ADD` is a legal instruction (i.e., in the dictionary). We can test whether this instruction (i.e., key) is in the dictionary with the following:

```
if 'ADD' in codes:     # Test whether 'ADD' is a valid mnemonic in the dictionary
```

This returns `True` if the key is in the dictionary, and `False` otherwise. You can use `not in` to test whether something is *not* in a dictionary.

Python allows a key to be associated with any valid object, for example, a list. We could write, for example, the following `key:value` pair:

```
'ADD': [3, 0b1101001, 'Addition', '07/05/2021', timesUsed]
```

Here, the value associated with a key is a five-element list that associates the ADD mnemonic with the number of its operands, its binary encoding, its name, the date it was designed, and the number of times it was used in the current program (as well as being able to read a value from a dictionary, you can write to it and update it).

The following code sets up a dictionary that binds mnemonics to variables (preset to integers `1`, `2`, `3`, `4`):

```
P,Q,R,N = 1,2,3,4                                        # Set up dummy opcodes
validCd = {'STOP':P, 'ADD':Q, 'LDRL':R, 'NOP':N}         # Dictionary of codes
x = input('Please enter a code  ')                       # Request an opcode
if x not in validCd:                                     # Check dictionary for errors
    print('Error! This is not valid')
if x in validCd:                                         # Check for valid opcode
    print('Valid op ', validCd.get(x))                   # If found, read its value
```

In this example, we used the `get()` method to read the value associated with a key. If the key is `x`, its value is given by `validCd.get(x)`; that is, the syntax is `dictionaryName.get(key)`.

Assembly language contains instructions that are executed. However, it also contains information called *assembler directives* that tells the program something about the environment; for example, where to put data in memory or how to bind symbolic names to values. We will now look at assembler directives.

Dealing with assembler directives

In this section, we will learn about the following:

- What assembler directives do
- How to create a symbol table linking symbolic names to values
- How to access the symbol table
- How to update the symbol table
- Processing labels

We will demonstrate how the names the programmer chooses are manipulated and translated into their appropriate numerical values.

The first version of TC1 required you to provide actual values for all names and labels. If you wanted to jump to an instruction, you had to provide the number of lines to jump. It's much better to allow the programmer to write the following:

```
JMP next
```

Here, `next` is the label of the target line. This is preferred over writing the following:

```
JMP 21
```

Similarly, if the literal `60` represents minutes in an hour, write the following:

```
MULL R0,R1,MINUTES
```

This is preferred over the following:

```
MULL R0,R1,60
```

We need a means of *linking* `next` with `21` and `MINUTES` with `60`.

Python's *dictionary* structure solves this problem. We simply create `key:value` pairs, where `key` is the label that we want to define and `value` is its value. In this example, a dictionary for the preceding example would be `{'NEXT':21, 'MINUTES':60}`. Note this example uses *integers* as values. In this book, we will also use *strings* as values, because we input data in text form; for example, `'MINUTES':'60'`.

The EQU assembler directive equates a value with a symbolic name. For example, TC1 lets you write the following:

```
MINUTES EQU 60
```

Using the dictionary

The MINUTES EQU 60 assembler directive has three tokens: a label, a function (equate), and a value. We extract the 'MINUTES':60 dictionary pair from the source code and insert it into a dictionary called symbolTab. The following code demonstrates the procedure. The first line sets up a symbol table. We initialize it with a dummy entry, 'START':0. We've created this initial entry for testing purposes:

```
symbolTab = {'START':0}                             # Symbol table for labels
for i in range (0,len(sFile)):                      # Deal with equates
    if len(sFile[i]) > 2 and sFile[i][1] == 'EQU':  # Is token 'EQU'?
        symbolTab[sFile[i][0]] = sFile[i][2]        # If so, update table
sFile = [i for i in sFile if i.count('EQU') == 0]   # Delete EQU from source
```

The for loop (shaded) reads each line of the source code, sFile, and tests for lines where 'EQU' is the second token in the line. The len(sFile[i]) > 2 comparison ensures that this line has at least three tokens to ensure it's a valid equate directive. The text is in bold font.

We can perform two tests together by employing an and Boolean operator so that the test is true only if both conditions are true.

We check that the second token is 'EQU' with sFile[i][1] == 'EQU'. The sFile**[i]**[1] notation has two list indexes. The first, in bold, indicates line i of the source code, and the second index indicates token 1 of that line; that is, it is the second element.

If 'EQU' is found, we add (i.e., insert) the first token, [sFile[i][0]], into the symbol table as the key, and the third token, **sFile[i][2]**, as the value.

Consider the MINUTES EQU 60 source code line.

The key is sFile[i][0] and its value is sFile[i][2], because MINUTES is the first token on line i and 60 is the third token on line i. The stored key is 'MINUTES' and its value is 60. But note that the value 60 is in *string* form and not *integer* form. Why? Because the assembler directive is a string and not an integer. If we want the numeric value, we have to use int().

The final line of this block of code is as follows:

```
sFile = [i for i in sFile if i.count('EQU') == 0]
```

This line uses a list comprehension to scan the source file and delete any line with EQU, because only instructions are loaded in program memory. A line containing EQU is a directive and not an instruction. This operation uses the count method, i.count('EQU'), to count the number of times EQU appears in a line, and then deletes that line if the count isn't 0. The condition we test for before moving (i.e., keeping) a line is as follows:

```
if i.count('EQU') == 0:
```

Here, i is the current line being processed. The count method is applied to the current line and counts the number of occurrences of the 'EQU' string in the line. Only if the count is 0 (i.e., it isn't a line with an EQU directive) does that line get copied into sFile.

Because detecting an EQU directive, putting it in the symbol table, and removing it from the code are so important, we will demonstrate its operation with a little piece of test code. The following code fragment sets up a list of three instructions in sFile to test. Remember that sFile is a list of lists and each list is an instruction composed of tokens, each of which is a string:

```
sFile=[['test','EQU','5'],['not','a','thing'],['xxx','EQU','88'], \
       ['ADD','r1','r2','r3']]
print('Source: ', sFile)
symbolTab = {}                                  # Creates empty symbol table
for i in range (0,len(sFile)):                  # Deal with equates e.g., PQR EQU 25
    print('sFile[i]', sFile[i])
    if len(sFile[i]) > 2 and sFile[i][1] == 'EQU':  # Is the second token 'EQU'?
        print('key/val', sFile[i][0], sFile[i][2])  # Display key-value pair
        symbolTab[sFile[i][0]] = sFile[i][2]         # Now update symbol table
sFile = [i for i in sFile if i.count('EQU') == 0]   # Delete equates from source file
print('Symbol table: ', symbolTab)
print('Processed input: ',sFile)
```

The code in bold is the code we've discussed. The remaining code is made up of print statements used to observe the code's behavior. The key line in this code is as follows:

```
symbolTab[sFile[i][0]] = sFile[i][2]
```

This updates the symbol table by adding a key:value pair in the following format:

```
symbolTab[key] = value
```

When this code is run, it generates the following output:

```
Source [['test','EQU','5'],['not','a','thing'],['xxx','EQU','88'],
['ADD','r1','r2','r3']]
sFile[i] ['test', 'EQU', '5']
key/val test 5
sFile[i] ['not', 'a', 'thing']
sFile[i] ['xxx', 'EQU', '88']
key/val xxx 88
sFile[i] ['ADD', 'r1', 'r2', 'r3']
Symbol table {'test': '5', 'xxx': '88'}
Processed input [['not', 'a', 'thing'], ['ADD', 'r1', 'r2', 'r3']]
```

The final two lines give the symbol table and the post-processed version of sFile. The two equates have been loaded into the dictionary (symbol table) and the processed output has had the two equates stripped.

There are several ways to add new `key:value` pairs to a dictionary. We could have applied the `update` method to `symbolTab` and written the following:

```
symbolTab.update({[sFile[i][0]]:sFile[i][2]})
```

In a later example of an assembler, we will adopt a different convention for assembler directives and use the format `.equ name value` because this convention is adopted by ARM processors, as we'll see in later chapters. There is often more than one way of representing assembly directives, each with its own advantages and disadvantages (e.g., ease of coding or fitting in with particular standards and conventions).

Labels

The next step in processing the source file is to deal with labels. Take the following example:

```
      DEC    r1                         @ Decrement r1
      BEQ    NEXT1                       @ If result in r1 is 0, then jump to line NEXT1
      INC    r2                          @ If result not 0, increment r2
      .
NEXT1 .
```

In this example, the decrement operation subtracts 1 from the contents of register `r1`. If the result is 0, the `Z flag` is set. The next instruction is *branch on zero to NEXT1*. If $Z = 1$, a jump is made to the line labeled `NEXT1`; otherwise, the `INC r2` instruction immediately following `BEQ` is executed.

The binary program (machine code) generated by TC1 does not store or use labels. It requires either the actual address of the next instruction or its relative address (i.e., how far it needs to jump from the current location). In other words, we need to translate the `NEXT1` label into its actual address in the program.

This is a job for the dictionary. All we have to do is put a label in the dictionary as a key and then insert the corresponding address as the value associated with the key. The following three lines of Python demonstrate how we collect label addresses and put them in the symbol table:

```
1. for i in range(0,len(sFile)):            # Add branch addresses to symbol tab
2.     if sFile[i][0] not in codes:          # If first token not an opcode, it's a label
3.         symbolTab.update({sFile[i][0]:str(i)})   # Add pc value, i to sym tab as string
4. print('\nEquate and branch table\n')      # Display symbol table
5. for x,y in symbolTab.items():             # Step through symbol table
6.     print('{:<8}'.format(x),y)
```

The three lines, 1 to 3, define a `for` loop that steps through every line in the source code in `sFile`. Because we've processed the code to convert each instruction into a list of tokens, each line begins with either a valid mnemonic or a label. All we have to do is check whether the first token on a line is in the list (or dictionary) of mnemonics. If the first token is in the list, it's an instruction. If it's not in the list, then it's a label (we are ignoring the case that it's an error).

We perform the check for a valid mnemonic with the following:

```
2. if sFile[i][0] not in codes:
```

Here, `sFile[i][0]` represents the first item (i.e., token) of line `i` in the dictionary of mnemonics. The `not in` Python code returns `True` if the mnemonic is not in the dictionary called `codes`. If the test does return `True`, then we have a label and must put it in the symbol table with the following operation:

```
3. symbolTab.update({sFile[i][0]:str(i)})                    # i is the pc value
```

This expression says, "*Add the specified* `key:value` *pair to the dictionary called* `symbolTable`." Why is the value associated with the label given as `i`? The value associated with the label is the address of that line (i.e., the value of the program counter, `pc`, when that line is executed). Since we are stepping through the source code line by line, the counter, `i`, is the corresponding value of the program counter.

The `update` method is applied to the symbol table with **`sFile[i][0]`** as the key and `str(i)` as the value. The key is **`sFile[i][0]`**, which is the label (i.e., a string). However, the *value* of `i` is not a *string*. The value is an *integer*, `i`, which is the current line address. We convert the integer address into a string with **`str(i)`** because equates are stored in the table as strings (i.e., this is a design decision made by me).

The next two lines print the symbol table:

```
4. print('\nEquate and branch table\n')                      # Display symbol table
5. for x,y in symbolTab.items(): print('{:<8}'.format(x),y)  # Step through symbol table
```

The value of the symbol table is printed using a `for` loop. We extract a `key:value` pair by using the following:

```
5. for x,y in symbolTab.items():
```

The **`items()`** method steps through all the elements of the `symbolTab` dictionary and allows us to print each `key:pair` value (i.e., all names/labels and their values). The `print` statement displays eight characters, right justified, by using `{:<8}.format(x)` to format the value of `x`.

Having decoded an instruction, we next have to convert it into the appropriate binary code.

Building the binary instruction

The next step in the assembly process is to generate the appropriate binary pattern for each instruction. In this section, we show how the components of an instruction are put together to create a binary value that can later be executed by the computer.

Note that the code in this section describes some of the instruction processing involved in analyzing instructions. The actual simulator differs in minor details, although the principles are the same.

We first have to extract the mnemonic, convert it into binary, then extract the register numbers (where appropriate), and finally, insert the 16-bit literal. Moreover, because the assembler is in text form, we have to be able to deal with literals that are symbolic (i.e., they are names rather than numbers), decimal, negative, binary, or hexadecimal; that is, we have to handle instructions of the following form:

```
LDRL  r0,24            @ Decimal numeric value
LDRL  r0,0xF2C3        @ Hexadecimal numeric value
LDRL  r0,$F2C3         @ Hexadecimal numeric value (alternative representation)
LDRL  r0,%00110101     @ Binary numeric value
LDRL  r0,0b00110101    @ Binary numeric value (alternative representation)
LDRL  r0,-234          @ Negative decimal numeric value
LDRL  r0,ALAN2         @ Symbolic value requiring symbol table look-up
```

The assembler looks at each line of the source code and extracts the mnemonic. An instruction is a list of tokens (e.g., 'NEXT', 'ADD', 'r1', 'r2', '0x12FA', which is five tokens, or 'STOP', which is one token). The situation is made more complex because the mnemonic may be the *first* token, or the *second* token if the instruction has a label. In the following example, sFile contains the program as a list of instructions, and we are processing line i, sFile[i]. Our solution is as follows:

1. Read the first token, sFile[i][0]. If this token is in the list of codes, then it's an instruction. If it is not in the list of codes, it's a label, and the second token, sFile[i][1], is the instruction.

2. Get the instruction details. These are stored in a dictionary called codes. If the mnemonic is in the dictionary, the key returns a tuple with two components. The first component is the format of the instruction, which defines the required operands in the sequence rD, rS1, rS2, literal; for example, the code 1001 indicates an instruction with a destination register and a literal. The second component of the tuple is the value of the opcode. We use a decimal value for this (ideally, it should be binary for the sake of readability, but binary values were too long and made the text harder to read).

3. Read the register numbers from the tokens in the instruction; for example, ADD r3,r2,r7 would return 3,2,7, whereas NOP would return 0,0,0 (if a register field is not used, it is set to 0).

4. Read any literal and convert it into a 16-bit integer. This is the most complex operation because the literal may have one of the seven different formats described previously.

5. The discussion in this section refers to the TC1 program that is presented in full at the end of the chapter. Here, we present slices of that program and explain how they work and the steps in the assembly process.

Extracting the instruction and its parameters

The following fragment of code shows the beginning of the loop that scans the source code and creates the binary value. This code initializes variables, extracts the opcode as a mnemonic, extracts any labels, extracts the parameters required by the mnemonic, and looks up the opcode and its format:

```
for i in range(0,len(sFile)):                        # Assembly loop reads instruction
    opCode,label,literal,predicate = [],[],[],[]     # Initialize opcode, label, literal, predicate
    rD, rS1, rS2  = 0, 0, 0                           # Clear register-select fields to zeros
```

```
if sFile[i][0] in codes: opCode = sFile[i][0]      # If first token is a valid opcode, get it
else:                          opCode = sFile[i][1]    # If not, then opcode is second token
if (sFile[i][0] in codes) and (len(sFile[i]) > 1):  # If opcode valid and length > 1
    predicate = sFile[i][1:]
else:
    if len(sFile[i]) > 2: predicate = sFile[i][2:] \
                                   # Lines with a label longer than 2 tokens
form = codes.get(opCode)                  # Use mnemonic to read instruction format
if form[0] & 0b1000 == 0b1000:            # Bit 4 of format selects destination register rD
if predicate[0] in symbolTab:               # If first token in symbol tab, it's a label
        rD = int(symbolTab[predicate[0]][1:])  # If it is a label, then get its value
```

Lines 2 and 3 in the loop declare and initialize the variables and provide default values.

The first if...else statement on line 4 looks at the first token on line i of the source code, sFile[i][0]. If that token is in the codes dictionary, then sFile[i][0] is the opcode. If it isn't in the dictionary, then that token must be a label and the second token is the opcode (lines 4 and 5):

```
4.    if sFile[i][0] in codes: opcode = sFile[i][0]   # If first token is a valid opcode, get it
5.    else:                     opCode = sFile[i][1]   # If not, then it's the second token
```

If we encounter a label, we can convert it into its actual address, which is in symbolTab, using the following:

```
    if sFile[i][0] in symbolTab: label = sFile[i][0]   # Get label
```

Lines 6, 7, 8, and 9 extract the predicate from the assembly language. Remember, the predicate comprises the tokens following the mnemonic and consists of any registers and literal required by the instruction:

```
6. if (sFile[i][0] in codes) and (len(sFile[i])>1):  # Get everything after opcode
7.                      predicate = sFile[i][1:]      # Line with opcode
8. else:
9.    if len(sFile[i])>2: predicate = sFile[i][2:]    # If label and len > 2 tokens
```

We have to deal with two cases: the first token is the mnemonic and the second token is the mnemonic. We also check that the line is long enough to have a predicate. If there is a predicate, it is extracted by lines 7 and 9:

```
7.        predicate = sFile[i][1:]      # The predicate is the second and following tokens
9.        predicate = sFile[i][2:]      # The predicate is the third and following tokens
```

The notation [2:] indicates *everything from token 2 to the end of the line*. This is a very nice feature of Python because it doesn't require you to explicitly state the length of the line. Once we've extracted the predicate containing the register and literal information, we can start to assemble the instruction.

Next, we extract the current line's code format to get the information required from the predicate. Line 10, form = codes.get(opCode), accesses the codes dictionary to look for the mnemonic, which is in the opCode variable. The get method is applied to codes and the form variable receives the key value, which is the (`format`,`code`) tuple, for example, (`8`,`10`). The `form[0]` variable is the instruction format, and `form[1]` is the opcode:

```
10. form = codes.get(opCode)                       # Use opcode to read instruction format
11. if form[0] & 0b1000 == 0b1000:                 # Bit 3 of format selects destination reg rD
12.     if predicate[0] in symbolTab:              # Check whether first token is symbol table
13.         rD =int(symbolTab[predicate[0]][1:])   # If it's a label, then get its value
```

The second element of the tuple, `form[1]`, gives the 7-bit opcode; that is, `0100010` for `LDRL`. Lines `10` to `13` demonstrate how the destination register is extracted. We first use AND `form[0]` with `0b1000` to test the most significant bit that indicates whether a destination register, `rD`, is required by this instruction. If it is required, we first test whether the register is expressed in the form `R0`, or whether it's given as a name, for example, `TIME`. We have to do this because TC1 lets you rename registers by using the `EQU` directive.

You can check whether an item is in the dictionary by using **if** key **in** `dictionary`. Take the following example:

if `'INC'` in `opCodes`:

To obtain information about a particular mnemonic, we can use the `get` method to read the value associated with the key – for example, `format = opCodes.get('INC')`.

The preceding example returns `format = (8,82)`. `8` refers to the format code `0b1000` (specifying a destination register). `82` is the opcode for this instruction. We access the two fields of the value associated with `'INC'` with, for example, the following:

```
binaryCode  = format[0]
formatStyle = format[1]
```

We first test whether a register has a symbolic name in line `12` with. `if predicate[0] in symbolTab:` and, if it is in the symbol table, we read its value in line `13` with.

`rD = int(symbolTab[predicate[0]][1:])`

We interrogate the symbol table with a key, which is the first element of the predicate since the destination register always comes first in a TC1 assembly language instruction (e.g., in ADD `r4,r7,r2`, register `r4` is the first element). The register is given by `predicate[0]`. The `symbolTab[predicate[0]]` expression looks up the symbolic name and provides its value; for example, consider `TIME EQU R3`. The `INC TIME` assembly language instruction will look up `TIME` and return `R3`. We now have the destination operand, but it is a string, `'R3'`, and not a number. We just want `3` and have to use the `int` function to convert a number in string format into an integer value.

Let's simplify the Python expression to make the explanation easier. Suppose we write the following:

`destReg = symbolTab[predicate[0]]`

The value of `destReg` is the string representing the destination register. Assume that this is `'R3'`. What we need to do is to isolate `'3'` from `'R3'` and then convert the character `'3'` into the integer 3. We can write `destRegNum = destReg[1:]` to return all characters in the string except the initial `'R'`. The final step is to convert into an integer, which we can do with `rD = int(destRegNum)`.

Remember that `[1:]` means all the characters after the first character, `'R'`. Consequently, this returns `'3'` if the register was `'R3'`. We could have written `[1:2]` rather than `[1:]` since the number is in the range 1 to 7. However, by using the `[1:]` notation, we can later increase the number of registers beyond 9 without changing the program.

Putting all three steps together, we get `rD = int(symbolTab[predicate[0]][1:])`.

The following Python code shows the entire decoding process:

```
form = codes.get(opCode)                              # Use opcode to read type of instruction
if form[0] & 0b1000 == 0b1000:                        # Bit 4 of format selects destination register rD
    if predicate[0] in symbolTab:                     # Check whether first token is sym tab
        rD = int(symbolTab[predicate[0]][1:])    # If it is, then get its value
    else: rD = int(predicate[0][1:])                  # If it's not a label, get from the predicate
if form[0] & 0b0100 == 0b0100:                        # Bit 3 selects register source register 1, rS1
    if predicate[1] in symbolTab:
        rS1 = int(symbolTab[predicate[1]][1:])
    else: rS1 = int(predicate[1][1:])
if form[0] & 0b0010 == 0b0010:                        # Bit 2 of format selects register rS1
    if predicate[2] in symbolTab:
        rS2 = int(symbolTab[predicate[2]][1:])
    else: rS2 = int(predicate[2][1:])

if form[0] & 0b0001 == 0b0001:                        # Bit 1 of format indicates a literal
    if predicate[-1] in symbolTab:                    # If literal in symbol table, get it
        predicate[-1] = symbolTab[predicate[-1]]
    elif type(predicate[-1]) == 'int':                                    # Integer
        literal = str(literal)
    elif predicate[-1][0]    == '%':                                      # Binary
        literal=int(predicate[-1][1:],2)
    elif predicate[-1][0:2]  == '0B':                                     # Binary
        literal=int(predicate[-1][2:],2)
    elif predicate[-1][0:1]  == '$':                                      # Hex
        literal=int(predicate[-1][1:],16)
    elif predicate[-1][0:2]  == '0X':                                     # Hex
        literal=int(predicate[-1][2:],16)
    elif predicate[-1].isnumeric():                                       # Decimal
        literal=int(predicate[-1])
    elif predicate[-1][0]    == '-':                                      # Negative
        literal=(-int(predicate[-1][1:]))&0xFFFF
    else:  literal = 0                                                    # Default
```

This block of code performs the same sequence of operations three times, processing rD, then rS1 (the first source register), and then rS2 (the second source register) in the same way. The last section of this block of code (shaded)) is more complicated because we allow several representations of the literal. We use an if...elif structure to test for a symbolic literal, a binary literal, a hexadecimal literal, an unsigned decimal numeric literal, and finally, a negative decimal numeric literal.

The literal is a numeric constant used by an instruction. However, in the assembly language, the literal is represented by a text string; that is, if the literal is 12, it is the string '12' and not the numeric value 12. It has to be converted into numeric form by the int() function.

We initially decided to allow decimal, binary, or hexadecimal integers. Later, we included symbolic names because they are so easy to deal with using Python's dictionary. Suppose we have an instruction that has been tokenized into a mnemonic and a predicate that contains registers and a literal or symbolic name, for example, ['R1', 'R2' , 'myData']. Consider the following code:

```
if predicate[-1] in symbolTab:              # If literal is in symbol table, look up value
    predicate[-1] = symbolTab[predicate[-1]]  # Get its value from the symbol table
```

This takes the last element of the predicate (indicated by the [-1] index) and looks to see whether it's in the symbol table. If it isn't, the code tests for other types of literal. If it is in the symbol table, it is extracted and the myData symbolic name is replaced with its actual value.

The literal in the table may be an integer or a string. The following converts it into a string if it is a literal:

```
if type(predicate[-1])=='int': literal=str(literal)  # Integer to string
```

The if construct uses the type() function, which returns the type of an object. In this case, it will be 'int' if the object is an integer. The str() function converts an integer object into a string object.

This action may seem strange because we are converting an integer (which we want) into a string (which we don't want). The reason for this anomaly is that we are later going to test for hex, binary, and signed values that will be strings, and keeping all literals as strings simplifies the coding.

The following code demonstrates how three number formats are converted into integer form, ready for packing into the final 32-bit TC1 machine instruction:

```
if    predicate[-1][0]    == '%':  literal = int(predicate[-1][1:],2)
elif predicate[-1][0:2    == '0B': literal = int(predicate[-1][2:],2)
elif predicate[-1][0:1] == '$':  literal = int(predicate[-1][1:],16)
elif predicate[-1][0:2] == '0X': literal = int(predicate[-1][2:],16)
elif predicate[-1].isnumeric():  literal = int(predicate[-1])
```

Binary numbers are prefixed with either % or 0b in the TC1 assembly language, and hexadecimal values with $ or 0x. The constant is tested to see whether it's decimal, binary, or hex, and then the appropriate conversion is performed. Converting a binary string, x, into an integer, y, is done with y = int(x,2). The parameter in bold is the number base. In this case, it's 2 in binary format. In hexadecimal format, it's 16.

Let's look at the hex conversion. We have to make two selections: the token and then the specific characters of the token. Consider ADDL R1,R2,0XF2A4. The predicate is 'R1 R2 0XF2A4', which is tokenized as predicate = ['R1', 'R2', '0XF2A4'].

The value of predicate[-1] is '**0XF2A4**'. To test for a hexadecimal value, we have to look at the first two characters to see whether they are '0X'. Note 0X not 0x because TC1 converts input into uppercase. We could write the following:

```
lastToken = predicate[-1]          # Get the last token from the predicate
prefix = lastToken[0:2]            # Get the first two characters of this token to test for '0X'
```

We can save a line by combining the two list-index suffixes, [-1] and [0:2], into predicate[-1][0:2].

The third line of the code, elif predicate[-1].isnumeric(): literal=int(predicate[-1]), detects decimal strings and converts them into numeric form. Since decimal values don't have a prefix, we use the isnumeric method to test for a string that has a numeric value. This line is read as, "*If the last token in the predicate is numeric, then convert it into an integer value.*"

Finally, we have to deal with negative numbers (e.g., -5). If a literal is prefixed with -, the remaining string is read and converted into two's complement binary form in 16 bits. This is necessary because the TC1 computer represents signed integers in 16-bit two's complement form.

The generation of the final 32-bit binary code of an instruction is easy. We have an opcode and zero to four fields to insert. The fields are initially set to all zeros (the default values). Then, each field is shifted left to its required place in the instruction and inserted into the instruction by using a bit-wise OR operation. The code for this is as follows:

```
s2      = s2      << 16           # Shift source 2 16 places left
s1      = s1      << 19           # Shift source 1 19 places left
destReg = destReg << 22           # Shift destination register 22 places left
op      = op      << 25           # Shift opcode 25 places left
binCode = lit | s2 | s1 | destReg | op # Logical OR the fields
```

We could do all this in one line, as follows:

```
binCode = lit | (s2 << 16) | (s1 << 19) | (destReg << 22)| (op << 25)
```

In the next chapter, we'll return to the TC1 simulator and expand it. We'll also demonstrate how the TC1 simulator can be extended by adding new operations to the instruction set and some ways of printing the results of a simulator.

Before presenting the full TC1, we are going to demonstrate a simplified version that can execute an assembly language program, essentially the same as the TC1. However, this version has been designed to reduce the total complexity by leaving out features such as symbolic names or the ability to use different number bases when specifying a constant. In this case, all literals are simple decimal integers.

Intermission: The Pre-TC1

In order to provide a more complete overview of the operation of a CPU simulator, we are going to introduce a highly simplified, but complete, version to give you an idea of how things fit together, before we create a more complex system.

In this section, you will learn how to design a simulator without some of the complications associated with a fully fledged design.

This version of TC1, called TC1$_{mini}$, can execute assembly language. However, we use a fixed format for assembly-level instructions (input is case-sensitive) and a fixed literal format (no hexadecimal or binary numbers), and we don't support labels and symbolic names. This approach helps stop the details from getting in the way of the bigger picture.

The Simulator

The simulator supports register-to-register operations, such as ADD r1,r2,r3. Its only memory access is pointer-based, that is, LDRI r1, [r2] and STRI r1, [r2]. It provides increment and decrement instructions, INC r1 and INC r2. There are two compare operations: CMPI r1,5 and CMP r1,r2 (the former compares a register with a literal and the latter compares two registers). To keep things simple, the only status flag is z (zero) and this is used only by compare and subtract operations.

Three branch instructions are provided (unconditional branch, branch on zero, and branch on not zero). Since this simulator doesn't support symbolic names, a branch requires a literal to indicate the destination. Branching is relative to the current location of the branch instruction; for example, BRA 3 means jump to the instruction three locations forward, and BRA -2 means jump two instructions backward.

I did not provide a file-based program input mechanism (i.e., reading a source program as a text file). The assembly language program to be executed is embedded as a Python list of strings called sFile. You can readily modify this or substitute the code to input a file.

The opcodes are set up in a dictionary of the following form:

```
codes = {'STOP':[0], 'LDRL':[3], 'STRL':[7]}
```

The key:value pair uses a mnemonic as the key and a list with one item, the class of the instruction, as the value. The classes range from 0 (a mnemonic with no operands) to 7 (a mnemonic with a register and register indirect operand). We've not implemented TC1's 4-bit format code, which is used to determine the parameters required by an instruction, because that information is implicit in the class. Moreover, we do not assemble the instruction into a binary code. We read the mnemonic in text form and directly execute it.

When an instruction is read, it is first tokenized to create a list of one to four tokens, for example, ['CMPL', 'r3', '5']. When an instruction is read from the source, the class is determined and used to extract the required information from the tokens.

Once the mnemonic and register numbers/values and literal are known, a simple `if .. elif` structure is used to select the appropriate instruction and then execute it. Most instructions are interpreted in a single line of Python.

At the end of the instruction reading and execution loop, you are invited to hit a key to execute the next instruction in sequence. The data displayed after each instruction is the program counter, z-bit, instruction, registers, and memory location. We use only four registers and eight memory locations.

We have split this program into sections with brief descriptions between them. The first part provides the source code as a built-in list. It defines the instruction classes and provides a list of opcodes and their classes. We don't use a dictionary for this. However, we do provide dictionaries for the registers and their indirect versions to simplify analyzing instructions. For example, we can look up both `r1` and `r2` in the `LDRI r1, [r2]` instruction:

```
sFile = ['LDRL r2,1','LDRL r0,4','NOP','STRI r0,[r2]','LDRI r3,[r2]',   \
         'INC r3','ADDL r3,r3,2','NOP','DEC r3', 'BNE -2','DEC r3','STOP']
                                            # Source program for testing
# Simple CPU instruction interpreter. Direct instruction interpretation. 30 September 2022. V1.0
# Class 0: no operand              NOP
# Class 1: literal                 BEQ  3
# Class 2: register                INC  r1
# Class 3: register,literal        LDRL r1,5
# Class 4: register,register,      MOV  r1,r2
# Class 5: register,register,literal ADDL r1,r2,5
# Class 6: register,register,register ADD  r1,r2,r3
# Class 7: register, [register]    LDRI r1,[r2]
codes = {'NOP':[0],'STOP':[0],'BEQ':[1],'BNE':[1],'BRA':[1],  \
         'INC':[2],'DEC':[2],'CMPL':[3],'LDRL':[3],'MOV':[4],  \
         'CMP':[4],'SUBL':[5],'ADDL':[5],'ANDL':[5],'ADD':[6],  \
         'SUB':[6], 'AND':[6],'LDRI':[7],'STRI':[7]}
reg1  = {'r0':0,'r1':1,'r2':2,'r3':3}            # Legal registers
reg2  = {'[r0]':0,'[r1]':1,'[r2]':2,'[r3]':3}  # Legal pointer registers
r = [0] * 4                                 # Four registers
r[0],r[1],r[2],r[3] = 1,2,3,4               # Preset registers for testing
m  = [0] * 8                                # Eight memory locations
pc = 0                                      # Program counter initialize to 0
go = 1                                      # go is the run control (1 to run)
z  = 0                                      # z is the zero flag. Set/cleared by SUB, DEC, CMP
while go == 1:                              # Repeat execute fetch and execute loop
    thisLine = sFile[pc]                    # Get current instruction
    pc = pc + 1                             # Increment pc
    pcOld = pc                              # Remember pc value for this cycle
    temp = thisLine.replace(',',' ')        # Remove commas: ADD r1,r2,r3 to ADD r1 r2 r3
    tokens = temp.split(' ')                # Tokenize: ADD r1 r2 r3 to ['ADD','r1','r2','r3']
```

In the following section, we analyze an instruction to extract the values of the operands required by the instruction. This is achieved by looking at the instruction's op-class and then extracting the appropriate information (e.g., the register number):

```
mnemonic = tokens[0]                                    # Extract first token, the mnemonic
opClass = codes[mnemonic][0]                            # Extract instruction class
                                                        # Process the current instruction and analyze it
rD,rDval,rS1,rS1val,rS2,rS2val,lit, rPnt,rPntV = 0,0,0,0,0,0,0,0,0
                                                        # Clear all parameters
if opClass in [0]: pass                                 # If class 0, nothing to be done (simple opcode only)
if opClass in [2,3,4,5,6,7,8]:                          # Look for ops with destination register rD
    rD      = reg1[tokens[1]]                           # Get token 1 and use it to get register number as rD
    rDval   = r[rD]                                     # Get contents of register rD
if opClass in [4,5,6]:                                  # Look at instructions with first source register rS1
    rS1     = reg1[tokens[2]]                           # Get rS1 register number and then contents
    rS1val  = r[rS1]
if opClass in [6]:                                      # If class 6, it's got three registers. Extract rS2
    rS2     = reg1[tokens[3]]                           # Get rS2 and rS2val
    rS2val  = r[rS2]
if opClass in [1,3,5,8]:                                # The literal is the last element in instructions
    lit     = int(tokens[-1])                           # Get the literal
if opClass in [7]:                                      # Class 7 involves register indirect addressing
    rPnt    = reg2[tokens[2]]                           # Get the pointer (register) and value of the pointer
    rPntV   = r[rPnt]                                   # Get the register number
if mnemonic == 'STOP':                                  # Now execute instructions. If STOP, clear go and exit
    go = 0
    print('Program terminated')
```

This is the instruction execution part of the program. We use a series of comparisons of the mnemonic with the opcodes and then directly execute the instruction. Unlike TC1, we do not convert the mnemonic into binary code and then execute it by converting the binary code into appropriate operations:

```
elif mnemonic == 'NOP':  pass                           # NOP does nothing. Just drop to end of loop
elif mnemonic == 'INC': r[rD] = rDval + 1    # Increment: add 1 to destination register
elif mnemonic == 'DEC':                                 # Decrement: subtract 1 from register and update z bit
    z = 0
    r[rD] = rDval - 1
    if r[rD] == 0: z = 1
elif mnemonic == 'BRA':                                 # Unconditional branch
    pc = pc + lit - 1
elif mnemonic == 'BEQ':                                 # Conditional branch on zero
    if z == 1: pc = pc + lit - 1
elif mnemonic == 'BNE':                                 # Conditional branch on not zero
    if z == 0: pc = pc + lit - 1
```

```
    elif mnemonic == 'ADD':  r[rD]=rS1val+rS2val  # Add
    elif mnemonic == 'ADDL': r[rD] = rS1val+lit   # Add literal
    elif mnemonic == 'SUB':                       # Subtract and set/clear z
        r[rD] = rS1val - rS2val
        z = 0
        if r[rD] == 0: z = 1
    elif mnemonic == 'SUBL':                      # Subtract literal
        r[rD] = rS1val - lit
        z = 0
        if r[rD] == 0: z = 1
    elif mnemonic == 'CMPL':                      # Compare literal
        diff = rDval - lit
        z = 0
        if diff == 0 : z = 1
    elif mnemonic == 'CMP':                       # Compare
        diff = rDval - rS1val
        z = 0
        if diff == 0: z = 1
    elif mnemonic == 'MOV':  r[rD] = rS1val       # Move, load, and store operations
    elif mnemonic == 'LDRL': r[rD] = lit
    elif mnemonic == 'LDRI': r[rD] = m[rPntV]
    elif mnemonic == 'STRI': m[rPntV] = rDval
    regs = ' '.join('%02x' % b for b in r)        # Format memory locations hex
    mem  = ' '.join('%02x' % b for b in m)        # Format registers hex
    print('pc =','{:<3}'.format(pcOld), '{:<14}'.format(thisLine), \
          'Regs =',regs, 'Mem =',mem, 'z =', z)
    x = input('>>> ')                             # Request keyboard input before dealing with next instruction
```

Note that the execution loop ends with an input request from the keyboard. In this way, the next cycle is not executed until the *Enter/Return* key is pressed.

The following shows the output of the simulator as the embedded program is executed. Changed registers, memory locations, and flag values are in bold font:

```
pc = 1    LDRL r2,1      Regs = 01 02 01 04 Mem = 00 00 00 00 00 00 00 00 z = 0
pc = 2    LDRL r0,4      Regs = 04 02 01 04 Mem = 00 00 00 00 00 00 00 00 z = 0
pc = 3    NOP            Regs = 04 02 01 04 Mem = 00 00 00 00 00 00 00 00 z = 0
pc = 4    STRI r0,[r2]   Regs = 04 02 01 04 Mem = 00 04 00 00 00 00 00 00 z = 0
pc = 5    LDRI r3,[r2]   Regs = 04 02 01 04 Mem = 00 04 00 00 00 00 00 00 z = 0
pc = 6    INC r3         Regs = 04 02 01 05 Mem = 00 04 00 00 00 00 00 00 z = 0
pc = 7    ADDL r3,r3,2   Regs = 04 02 01 07 Mem = 00 04 00 00 00 00 00 00 z = 0
pc = 8    NOP            Regs = 04 02 01 07 Mem = 00 04 00 00 00 00 00 00 z = 0
pc = 9    DEC r3         Regs = 04 02 01 06 Mem = 00 04 00 00 00 00 00 00 z = 0
pc = 10   BNE -2         Regs = 04 02 01 06 Mem = 00 04 00 00 00 00 00 00 z = 0
```

```
pc = 8     NOP            Regs = 04 02 01 06 Mem = 00 04 00 00 00 00 00 00 z = 0
pc = 9     DEC r3         Regs = 04 02 01 05 Mem = 00 04 00 00 00 00 00 00 z = 0
pc = 10    BNE -2         Regs = 04 02 01 05 Mem = 00 04 00 00 00 00 00 00 z = 0
pc = 8     NOP            Regs = 04 02 01 05 Mem = 00 04 00 00 00 00 00 00 z = 0
pc = 9     DEC r3         Regs = 04 02 01 04 Mem = 00 04 00 00 00 00 00 00 z = 0
pc = 10    BNE -2         Regs = 04 02 01 04 Mem = 00 04 00 00 00 00 00 00 z = 0
pc = 8     NOP            Regs = 04 02 01 04 Mem = 00 04 00 00 00 00 00 00 z = 0
pc = 9     DEC r3         Regs = 04 02 01 03 Mem = 00 04 00 00 00 00 00 00 z = 0
pc = 10    BNE -2         Regs = 04 02 01 03 Mem = 00 04 00 00 00 00 00 00 z = 0
pc = 8     NOP            Regs = 04 02 01 03 Mem = 00 04 00 00 00 00 00 00 z = 0
pc = 9     DEC r3         Regs = 04 02 01 02 Mem = 00 04 00 00 00 00 00 00 z = 0
pc = 10    BNE -2         Regs = 04 02 01 02 Mem = 00 04 00 00 00 00 00 00 z = 0
pc = 8     NOP            Regs = 04 02 01 02 Mem = 00 04 00 00 00 00 00 00 z = 0
pc = 9     DEC r3         Regs = 04 02 01 01 Mem = 00 04 00 00 00 00 00 00 z = 0
pc = 10    BNE -2         Regs = 04 02 01 01 Mem = 00 04 00 00 00 00 00 00 z = 0
pc = 8     NOP            Regs = 04 02 01 01 Mem = 00 04 00 00 00 00 00 00 z = 0
pc = 9     DEC r3         Regs = 04 02 01 00 Mem = 00 04 00 00 00 00 00 00 z = 1
pc = 10    BNE -2         Regs = 04 02 01 00 Mem = 00 04 00 00 00 00 00 00 z = 1
pc = 11    DEC r3         Regs = 04 02 01 -1 Mem = 00 04 00 00 00 00 00 00 z = 0
Program terminated
pc = 12    STOP           Regs = 04 02 01 -1 Mem = 00 04 00 00 00 00 00 00 z = 0
```

We will now look at the program for the TC1 simulator. We will include a short introduction to some of its facilities before providing the code.

The TC1 simulator program

In this section, we provide the full code for the TC1 assembler and simulator. This will enable you to construct and modify a computer assembler and simulator that can execute the code supported by TC1 or your own instruction set (if you modify TC1).

The assembler is the more complicated part because it involves reading text, analyzing it, and formatting it into binary codes. The simulator itself simply reads each binary code and then performs the appropriate action.

The simulator includes features that we haven't covered yet in previous sections (e.g., debugging and trace facilities). In the first draft of this book, TC1 was rather more basic with a minimal subset of features. As the book was edited and the program modified, the set of features was enhanced to make it a more practical tool. We first provide brief notes on some of these features to aid understanding of the program.

Single-stepping

A computer executes instructions sequentially unless a branch or subroutine call is encountered. When testing a simulator, you frequently want to execute a batch of instructions together (i.e., without printing register values), or you may wish to execute instructions one at a time by hitting *Enter/Return* after each instruction has been executed or to execute instructions until you hit a specific instruction.

In this version of TC1, you can execute and display an instruction, skip the display of the next n instructions, or not display instructions until a change-of-flow instruction is encountered. After the program is loaded, the input prompt is displayed. If you enter a return, the simulator executes the next instruction and waits. If you enter an integer (and return), the specified number of instructions is executed without displaying the results. If you enter b followed by a return, the simulator executes instructions without displaying them until the next branch instruction is encountered.

Consider the following example. The code is just a set of random instructions for demonstration. I've used no-operations (nop) as a filler. I've also tested literal address formats (hex and binary) and demonstrated case insensitivity:

```
@ test trace modes
    nop
    nop
    inc r1
    NOP
    dec r2
    ldrl r6,0b10101010
    bra abc
    nop
    inc R7
    nop
abc ldrl r3,$ABCD
    nop
    inc r3
    INC r4
    nop
    nop
    inc r5
    END!
```

I've edited it to remove memory locations as they are not accessed. After the prompt, >>>, you select what is to happen: trace one instruction, execute n instructions without stopping or displaying registers, or execute code to the next branch instruction without displaying it. In each case, the following program counter value is highlighted in the following output. The text in bold is a comment I left on an action on the current line (trace indicates a *Return/Enter* was hit, which executes the next instruction):

```
  >>>  trace
0      NOP            PC= 0 z=0 n=0 c=0 R 0000 0000 0000 0000 0000 0000 0000 0000
>>>3 jump 3 instructions (silent trace)
4      DEC R2         PC= 4 z=0 n=1 c=1 R 0000 0001 ffff 0000 0000 0000 0000 0000
>>>b jump to branch (silent mode up to next branch/rts/jsr)
6      BRA ABC        PC= 6 z=0 n=1 c=1 R 0000 0001 ffff 0000 0000 0000 00aa 0000
```

```
>>>   trace Here's the sample run
10 ABC LDRL R3 $ABCD PC=10 z=0 n=1 c=1 R 0000 0001 ffff abcd 0000 0000 00aa 0000
>>>   trace
11    NOP           PC=11 z=0 n=1 c=1 R 0000 0001 ffff abcd 0000 0000 00aa 0000
>>>4 jump 4
16    INC R5        PC=16 z=0 n=0 c=1 R 0000 0001 ffff abce 0001 0001 00aa 0000
>>>   trace
17    END!          PC=17 z=0 n=0 c=1 R 0000 0001 ffff abce 0001 0001 00aa 0000
```

File input

When we first started writing a simulator, we inputted test programs the easy way by typing the instructions in one by one. This worked for the simplest of tests but soon became tedious. Later, programs were input as a text file. That worked well when the filename was short, such as t.txt, but it got more tedious with long filenames (e.g., when I stored the source code in a specific directory).

We then included the filename in the actual TC1 program. That's convenient when you're going to be running the same program over and over again while you're testing various features of the simulator. What we needed was a means of using my working program (baked into the simulator) most of the time, but to switch to an alternative when required.

One sensible solution would be to generate an input banner prompting you to press *Enter* for the default file, or provide a filename for an alternative source program, say, *Enter return for the default file* or *Enter a filename for an alternative source program*. We decided to use Python's exception mechanism to implement this. In computing, an *exception* (also called a *software interrupt*) is a mechanism designed to deal with unexpected events. In Python, the exception handler uses two reserved words: try and exception.

As their names suggest, try requires Python to run the following block of code, and exception is a block of code that is executed if the try block failed. Essentially, it means, *"If you can't do this, do that."* The difference between if and try is that if returns True or False and performs the specified action if True, whereas try *attempts* to run a block and calls an exception if it fails, that is, if it crashes.

try allows you to attempt to open a file and then gives you a way out if the file doesn't exist (i.e., it avoids a fatal error). Consider the following:

```
myProg = 'testException1.txt'                    # Name of default program
try:                                             # Check whether this file exists
    with open(myProg,'r') as prgN:               # If it's there, open it and read it
        myFile = prgN.readlines()
except:                                          # Call exception if file not there
    altProg = input('Enter source file name: ')  # Request a filename
    with open(altProg,'r') as prgN:              # Open the user file
        myFile = prgN.readlines()
print('File loaded: ', myFile)
```

This code looks for a file called `testException1.txt`. If it's present (as it is in this case), the simulator runs it and we get the following output:

```
>>> %Run testTry.py
File loaded:  ['  @ Test exception file\n', ' nop\n', ' nop\n', ' inc\n', '
end!']
```

In the next case, we've deleted `testException1.txt`. We now get the following output after the prompt:

```
>>> %Run testTry.py
Enter source file name: testException2.txt
File loaded:  ['  @ Test exception file TWO\n', ' dec r1\n', ' nop\n', ' inc
r2\n', ' end!']
```

The line in bold is the alternative filename.

In the TC1 program, I further simplify things by including the file directory in the exception (because I always use the same directory) and I include the file extension, `.txt`. This looks as follows:

```
prgN = 'E://ArchitectureWithPython//' + prgN + '.txt'
```

This expression automatically provides the path for the filename and address of the file type.

Remember that Python lets you use the + operator to concatenate strings.

TC1 program

The first part of the program provides a list of instructions and their encoding. This text is placed between two `'''` markers that indicate it is not part of the program. This avoids having to start each line with #. The triple quote marks is called a docstring comment.

The first part of TC1 is a listing of the instructions. These are provided to make the program easier to follow:

```
### TC1 computer simulator and assembler. Version of 11 September 2022
''' This is the table of instructions for reference and is not part of the program code
00  00000   stop operation              STOP              00  00000 000 000 000 0  0000
00  00001   no operation                NOP               00  00001 000 000 000 0  0000
00  00010   get character from keyboard  GET   r0         00  00010 rrr 000 000 0  1000
00  00011   get character from keyboard  RND   r0         00  00011 rrr 000 000 L  1001
00  00100   swap bytes in register      SWAP r0           00  00100 rrr 000 000 0  1000
00  01000   print hex value in register PRT r0            00  01000 rrr 000 000 0  1000
00  11111   terminate program           END!              00  11111 000 000 000 0  0000
01  00000   load register from register MOVE r0,r1        01  00000 rrr aaa 000 0  1100
01  00001   load register from memory   LDRM r0,L         01  00001 rrr 000 000 L  1001
01  00010   load register with literal  LDRL r0,L         01  00010 rrr 000 000 L  1001
01  00011   load register indirect      LDRI r0,[r1,L]    01  00011 rrr aaa 000 L  1101
01  00100   store register in memory    STRM r0,L         01  00100 rrr 000 000 L  1001
```

01	00101	store register indirect	STRI	r0,[r1,L]	01	00101	rrr	aaa	000 L	1101
10	00000	add register to register	ADD	r0,r1,r2	10	00000	rrr	aaa	bbb 0	1110
10	00001	add literal to register	ADDL	r0,r1,L	10	00001	rrr	aaa	000 L	1101
10	00010	subtract register from register	SUB	r0,r1,r2	10	00010	rrr	aaa	bbb 0	1110
10	00011	subtract literal from register	SUBL	r0,r1,L	10	00011	rrr	aaa	000 L	1101
10	00100	multiply register by register	MUL	r0,r1,r2	10	00100	rrr	aaa	bbb 0	1110
10	00101	multiply literal by register	MULL	r0,r1,L	10	00101	rrr	aaa	000 L	1101
10	00110	divide register by register	DIV	r0,r1,r2	10	00110	rrr	aaa	bbb 0	1110
10	00111	divide register by literal	DIVL	r0,r1,L	10	00111	rrr	aaa	000 L	1101
10	01000	mod register by register	MOD	r0,r1,r2	10	01000	rrr	aaa	bbb 0	1110
10	01001	mod register by literal	MODL	r0,r1,L	10	01001	rrr	aaa	000 L	1101
10	01010	AND register to register	AND	r0,r1,r2	10	01000	rrr	aaa	bbb 0	1110
10	01011	AND register to literal	ANDL	r0,r1,L	10	01001	rrr	aaa	000 L	1101
10	01100	OR register to register	OR	r0,r1,r2	10	01010	rrr	aaa	bbb 0	1110
10	01101	NOR register to literal	ORL	r0,r1,L	10	01011	rrr	aaa	000 L	1101
10	01110	EOR register to register	OR	r0,r1,r2	10	01010	rrr	aaa	bbb 0	1110
10	01111	EOR register to literal	ORL	r0,r1,L	10	01011	rrr	aaa	000 L	1101
10	10000	NOT register	NOT	r0	10	10000	rrr	000	000 0	1000
10	10010	increment register	INC	r0	10	10010	rrr	000	000 0	1000
10	10011	decrement register	DEC	r0	10	10011	rrr	000	000 0	1000
10	10100	compare register with register	CMP	r0,r1	10	10100	rrr	aaa	000 0	1100
10	10101	compare register with literal	CMPL	r0,L	10	10101	rrr	000	000 L	1001
10	10110	add with carry	ADC		10	10110	rrr	aaa	bbb 0	1110
10	10111	subtract with borrow	SBC		10	10111	rrr	aaa	bbb 0	1110
10	11000	logical shift left	LSL	r0,L	10	10000	rrr	000	000 0	1001
10	11001	logical shift left literal	LSLL	r0,L	10	10000	rrr	000	000 L	1001
10	11010	logical shift right	LSR	r0,L	10	10001	rrr	000	000 0	1001
10	11011	logical shift right literal	LSRL	r0,L	10	10001	rrr	000	000 L	1001
10	11100	rotate left	ROL	r0,L	10	10010	rrr	000	000 0	1001
10	11101	rotate left literal	ROLL	r0,L	10	10010	rrr	000	000 L	1001
10	11110	rotate right	ROR	r0,L	10	10010	rrr	000	000 0	1001
10	11111	rotate right literal	RORL	r0,L	10	10010	rrr	000	000 L	1001
11	00000	branch unconditionally	BRA	L	11	00000	000	000	000 L	0001
11	00001	branch on zero	BEQ	L	11	00001	000	000	000 L	0001
11	00010	branch on not zero	BNE	L	11	00010	000	000	000 L	0001
11	00011	branch on minus	BMI	L	11	00011	000	000	000 L	0001
11	00100	branch to subroutine	BSR	L	11	00100	000	000	000 L	0001
11	00101	return from subroutine	RTS		11	00101	000	000	000 0	0000
11	00110	decrement & branch on not zero	DBNE	r0,L	11	00110	rrr	000	000 L	1001
11	00111	decrement & branch on zero	DBEQ	r0,L	11	00111	rrr	000	000 L	1001
11	01000	push register on stack	PUSH	r0	11	01000	rrr	000	000 0	1000
11	01001	pull register off stack	PULL	r0	11	01001	rrr	000	000 0	1000

. . .

```
import random                           # Get library for random number generator
def alu(fun,a,b):                       # Alu defines operation and a and b are inputs
    global c,n,z                        # Status flags are global and are set up here
    if   fun == 'ADD': s = a + b
    elif fun == 'SUB': s = a - b
    elif fun == 'MUL': s = a * b
    elif fun == 'DIV': s = a // b       # Floor division returns an integer result
    elif fun == 'MOD': s = a % b        # Modulus operation gives remainder: 12 % 5 = 2
    elif fun == 'AND': s = a & b        # Logic functions
    elif fun == 'OR':  s = a | b
    elif fun == 'EOR': s = a & b
    elif fun == 'NOT': s = ~a
    elif fun == 'ADC': s = a + b + c    # Add with carry
    elif fun == 'SBC': s = a - b - c    # Subtract with borrow
    c,n,z = 0,0,0                       # Clear flags before recalculating them
    if s & 0xFFFF == 0: z = 1           # Calculate the c, n, and z flags
    if s & 0x8000 != 0: n = 1           # Negative if most sig bit 15 is 1
    if s & 0xFFFF != 0: c = 1           # Carry set if bit 16 is 1
    return (s & 0xFFFF)                 # Return the result constrained to 16 bits
```

Because the `shift` operation is rather complex with left and right shifts, variable-length shifts, plus shifts, and rotates, we have provided a function to implement shifts. This takes the type of shift, direction, and number of places shifted as input parameters, together with the word to be shifted:

```
def shift(dir,mode,p,q):    # Shifter: performs shifts and rotates. dir = left/right, mode = logical/rotate
    global z,n,c                            # Make flag bits global. Note v-bit not implemented
    if dir == 0:                            # dir = 0 for left shift, 1 for right shift
        for i in range (0,q):               # Perform q left shifts on p
            sign = (0x8000 & p) >> 15        # Sign bit
            p = (p << 1) & 0xFFFF            # Shift p left one place
            if mode == 1:p = (p & 0xFFFE) | sign # For rotate left, add in bit shifted out
    else:                                   # dir = 1 for right shift
        for i in range (0,q):               # Perform q right shifts
            bitOut = 0x0001 & p             # Save lsb shifted out
            sign = (0x8000 & p) >> 15        # Get sign-bit for ASR
            p = p >> 1                       # Shift p one place right
            if mode == 1:p = (p&0x7FFF)|(bitOut<<15)  # If mode = 1, insert bit rotated out
            if mode == 2:p = (p&0x7FFF)|(sign << 15)  # If mode = 2, propagate sign bit
    z,c,n = 0,0,0                           # Clear all flags
    if p == 0:          z = 1               # Set z if p is zero
    if p & 0x8000 != 0: n = 1               # Set n-bit if p = 1
    if (dir == 0) and (sign == 1):   c = 1  # Set carry if left shift and sign 1
    if (dir == 1) and (bitOut == 1): c = 1  # Set carry bit if right shift and bit moved out = 1
    return(0xFFFF & p)                      # Ensure output is 16 bits wide
```

```
def listingP():                             # Function to perform listing and formatting of source code
    global listing                          # Listing contains the formatted source code
    listing = [0]*128                       # Create formatted listing file for display
    if debugLevel > 1: print('Source assembly code listing ')
    for i in range (0,len(sFile)):          # Step through the program
        if sFile[i][0] in codes:            # Is first token in opcodes (no label)?
            i2 = (' ').join(sFile[i])       # Convert tokens into string for printing
            i1 = ''                         # Dummy string i1 represents missing label
        else:
            i2 = (' ').join(sFile[i][1:])   # If first token not opcode, it's a label
            i1 = sFile[i][0]                # i1 is the label (first token)
        listing[i] = '{:<3}'.format(i) + '{:<7}'.format(i1) + \
                     '{:<10}'.format(i2)    # Create listing table entry
        if debugLevel  > 1:                 # If debug = 1, don't print source program
            print('{:<3}'.format(i),'{:<7}'.format(i1),'{:<10}'.format(i2)) \
                                            # print: pc, label, opcode
    return()
```

This is the function, getLit, that processes a literal. It can handle literals in a range of possible formats, including decimal, binary, hexadecimal, and symbolic form:

```
def getLit(litV):                              # Extract a literal
    if  litV[0]    == '#': litV = litV[1:]      # Some systems prefix literal with '#
    if  litV in symbolTab:                      # Look in sym tab and get value if there
        literal = symbolTab[litV]               # Read the symbol value as a string
        literal = int(literal)                  # Convert string into integer
    elif  litV[0]   == '%': literal = int(litV[1:],2)
                                                # If first char is %, convert to integer
    elif  litV[0:2] == '0B':literal = int(litV[2:],2)
                                                # If prefix 0B, convert binary to integer
    elif  litV[0:2] == '0X':literal = int(litV[2:],16)
                                                # If 0x, convert hex string to integer
    elif  litV[0:1] == '$': literal = int(litV[1:],16)
                                                # If $, convert hex string to integer
    elif  litV[0]   == '-': literal = (-int(litV[1:]))&0xFFFF
                                                # Convert 2's complement to int
    elif  litV.isnumeric():  literal = int(litV)
                                                # If decimal string, convert to integer
    else:                   literal = 0         # Default value 0 (default value)
    return(literal)
```

`Print` statements can be a little complicated. Consequently, we have created a `print` function that is used to display register and memory contents. We discuss print formatting elsewhere in this book. We generate the data as strings to be printed, m, m1, and m2, and then print them using the appropriate formatting:

```
def printStatus():                                # Display machine status (registers, memory)
    text = '{:<27}'.format(listing[pcOld])        # Format instruction for listing
    m = mem[0:8]                                   # Get the first 8 memory locations
    m1 = ' '.join('%04x' % b for b in m)          # Format memory location's hex
    m2 = ' '.join('%04x' % b for b in r)          # Format register's hex
    print(text, 'PC =', '{:>2}'.format(pcOld) , 'z =',z,'n =',n,'c =',c, m1,\
    'Registers ', m2)
    if debugLevel == 5:
        print('Stack =', ' '.join('%04x' % b for b in stack), \
        'Stack pointer =', sp)
    return()
print('TC1 CPU simulator 11 September 2022 ')    # Print the opening banner
debugLevel = input('Input debug level 1 - 5: ')  # Ask for debugging level
if debugLevel.isnumeric():                        # If debug level is an integer, get it
    debugLevel = int(debugLevel)                  # Convert text to integer
else: debugLevel = 1                              # Else, set default value to level 1
if debugLevel not in range (1,6): debugLevel = 1 # Ensure range 1 to 5
print()                                           # New line
```

The preceding block of code provides a debug functionality and is intended to demonstrate the concept of debugging and provide a facility to check the assembly process by displaying intermediate information during the assembly phase. A variable, `debugLevel`, is read from the keyboard at the start of the program. This determines the level of the debugging facility from 1 (none) to 5 (maximum). Debugging information can include the source code, decoded operations, and other parameters:

```
global c,n,z                                      # Processor flags (global variables)
symbolTab = {'START':0}                           # Create symbol table for labels + equates with dummy entry
c,n,z = 0,0,0                                      # Initialize flags: carry, negative, zero
sFile = ['']* 128                                 # sFile holds the source text
memP  = [0] * 128                                 # Create program memory of 128 locations
mem   = [0] * 128                                 # Create data memory of 128 locations
stack = [0] * 16                                  # Create a stack for return addresses
# codes is a dictionary of instructions {'mnemonic':(x.y)} where x is the instruction operand format, and y the opcode
codes = {                                                                                  \
        'STOP':(0,0),  'NOP' :(0,1),  'GET' :(8,2),  'RND' : (9,3),  \
        'SWAP':(8,4),  'SEC' :(0,5),  'PRT' :(8,8),  'END!':(0,31),  \
        'MOVE':(12,32),'LDRM':(9,33), 'LDRL':(9,34), 'LDRI':(13,35), \
        'STRM':(9,36), 'STRI':(13,37),'ADD' :(14,64),'ADDL':(13,65), \
        'SUB' :(14,66),'SUBL':(13,67),'MUL' :(14,68),'MULL':(13,69), \
        'DIV' :(14,70),'DIVL':(13,71),'MOD' :(14,72),'MODL':(13,73), \
```

```
            'AND' :(14,74),'ANDL':(13,75),'OR'  :(14,76),'ORL' :(13,77), \
            'EOR' :(14,78),'EORL':(13,79),'NOT' :(8,80), 'INC' :(8,82),  \
            'DEC' :(8,83), 'CMP' :(12,84),'CMPL':(9,85), 'LSL' :(12,88), \
            'LSLL':(9,89), 'LSR' :(12,90),'LSRL':(9,91), 'ROL' :(12,92), \
            'ROLL':(9,93), 'ROR' :(12,94),'RORL':(9,95), 'ADC' :(14,102),\
            'SBC':(14,103),'BRA' :(1,96), 'BEQ' :(1,97), 'BNE' :(1,98),  \
            'BMI' :(1,99), 'BSR' :(1,100),'RTS' :(0,101),'DBNE':(9,102), \
            'DBEQ':(9,103),'PUSH':(8,104),'PULL':(8,105)  }

branchGroup = ['BRA', 'BEQ', 'BNE', 'BSR', 'RTS']  # Operations responsible for flow control
```

The following section is responsible for reading the source file to be assembled and executed. This source code should be in the form of a `.txt` file. Note that this code uses Python's `try` and `except` mechanism, which is able to perform an action (in this case, try and load a file from disk) and, if the action fails, perform a new action instead. Here, we use it to test for a default filename and then get one from the terminal if that file does not exist:

```
# Read the input source code text file and format it. This uses a default file and a user file if default is absent
prgN = 'E://ArchitectureWithPython//C_2_test.txt'  # prgN = program name: default test file
try:                                                # Check whether this file exists
    with open(prgN,'r') as prgN:                    # If it's there, open it and read it
        prgN = prgN.readlines()
except:                                             # Call exception program if not there
    prgN = input('Enter source file name: ')        # Request a filename (no extension needed)
    prgN = 'E://ArchitectureWithPython//' + prgN + '.txt' # Build filename
    with open(prgN,'r') as prgN:                    # Open user file
        prgN = prgN.readlines()                      # Read it
for i in range (0,len(prgN)):                       # Scan source prgN and copy it to sFile
    sFile[i] = prgN[i]                              # Copy prgN line to sFile line
    if 'END!' in prgN[i]: break                     # If END! found, then stop copying


            # Format source code
sFile = [i.split('@')[0] for i in sFile]            # But first, remove comments  ###
for i in range(0,len(sFile)):                       # Repeat: scan input file line by line
    sFile[i] = sFile[i].strip()                     # Remove leading/trailing spaces and eol
    sFile[i] = sFile[i].replace(',',' ')            # Allow use of commas or spaces
    sFile[i] = sFile[i].replace('[','')             # Remove left bracket
    sFile[i] = sFile[i].replace(']','')             # Remove right bracket and convert [R4] to R4
    while '  ' in sFile[i]:                         # Remove multiple spaces
        sFile[i] = sFile[i].replace('  ', ' ')
sFile = [i.upper() for i in sFile]                  # Convert to uppercase
sFile = [i.split(' ') for i in sFile if i != '']    # Split the tokens into list items
```

This short section deals with the equate assembler directive and binds values to symbolic names using the EQU directive. These bindings are placed in the symbol table dictionary and the equates are removed from the source code:

```
                                        # Remove assembler directives from source code
for i in range (0,len(sFile)):          # Deal with equates of the form PQR EQU 25
    if len(sFile[i]) > 2 and sFile[i][1] == 'EQU':   # If line is > 2 tokens and second is EQU
        symbolTab[sFile[i][0]] = sFile[i][2]         # Put third token EQU in symbol table
sFile = [i for i in sFile if i.count('EQU') == 0]    # Remove all lines with 'EQU'


                                        # Debug: 1 none, 2 source, 3 symbol tab, 4 Decode i, 5 stack
listingP()                              # List the source code if debug level is 1
```

Here, we perform the instruction decoding; that is, we analyze the text of each instruction to extract the opcode and parameters:

```
                                        # Look for labels and add to symbol table
for i in range(0,len(sFile)):           # Add branch addresses to symbol table
    if sFile[i][0] not in codes:        # If first token not opcode, then it is a label
        symbolTab.update({sFile[i][0]:str(i)})   # Add it to the symbol table

if debugLevel > 2:                      # Display symbol table if debug level 2
    print('\nEquate and branch table\n')         # Display the symbol table
    for x,y in symbolTab.items(): print('{:<8}'.format(x),y) \
                                        # Step through the symbol table dictionary
    print('\n')
              # Assemble source code in sFile
if debugLevel > 3: print('Decoded instructions')  # If debug level 4/5, print decoded ops
for pcA in range(0,len(sFile)):         # ASSEMBLY: pcA = prog counter in assembly
    opCode, label, literal, predicate = [], [], 0, []   # Initialize variables
                                        # Instruction = label + opcode + predicate
    rD, rS1, rS2  = 0, 0, 0             # Clear all register-select fields
    thisOp = sFile[pcA]                 # Get current instruction, thisOPp, in text form
                                        # Instruction: label + opcode or opcode
    if thisOp[0] in codes: opCode = thisOp[0]    # If token opcode, then get token
    else:                               # Otherwise, opcode is second token
        opCode = thisOp[1]              # Read the second token to get opcode
        label = sFile[i][0]             # Read the first token to get the label
    if (thisOp[0] in codes) and (len(thisOp) > 1):  # If first token opcode, rest is predicate
        predicate = thisOp[1:]          # Now get the predicate
    else:                               # Get predicate if the line has a label
        if len(thisOp) > 2: predicate = thisOp[2:]
    form = codes.get(opCode)            # Use opcode to read type (format)
                                        # Now check the bits of the format code
```

```
if form[0] & 0b1000 == 0b1000:                 # Bit 4 selects destination register rD
    if predicate[0] in symbolTab:              # Check if first token in symbol table
        rD = int(symbolTab[predicate[0]][1:])  # If it is, then get its value
    else: rD = int(predicate[0][1:])           # If not label, get register from the predicate
if form[0] & 0b0100 == 0b0100:                 # Bit 3 selects source register 1, rS1
    if predicate[1] in symbolTab:
        rS1 = int(symbolTab[predicate[1]][1:])
    else: rS1 = int(predicate[1][1:])
if form[0] & 0b0010 == 0b0010:                 # Bit 2 of format selects register rS1
    if predicate[2] in symbolTab:
        rS2 = int(symbolTab[predicate[2]][1:])
    else: rS2 = int(predicate[2][1:])
if form[0] & 0b0001 == 0b0001:                 # Bit 1 of format selects the literal field
    litV = predicate[-1]
    literal = getLit(litV)
```

This section was added after the development of TC1. We introduce the concept of a debug level. That is, at the beginning of a simulation run, you can set a parameter in the range of 1 to 3 that determines how much information is displayed during the assembly processing. This allows you to get more information about the instruction encoding when testing the program:

```
if debugLevel > 3:                             # If debug level > 3, print decoded fields
    t0 = '%02d' % pcA                          # Format instruction counter
    t1 = '{:<23}'.format(' '.join(thisOp))     # Format operation to 23 spaces
    t3 = '%04x' % literal                       # Format literal to 4-character hex
    t4 = '{:04b}'.format(form[0])              # Format the 4-bit opcode format field
    print('pc =',t0,'Op =',t1,'literal',t3,'Dest reg =',rD,'rS1 =', \
          'rS1','rS2 =',rS2,'format =',t4)     # Concatenate fields to create 32-bit opcode
binCode = form[1]<<25|(rD)<<22|(rS1)<<19|(rS2)<<16|literal  # Binary pattern
memP[pcA] = binCode                            # Store instruction in program memory
                                               # End of the assembly portion of the program
```

We are about to execute the instructions. Before we do that, it is necessary to initialize several variables concerning the current operation (e.g., tracing):

```
                            # The code is executed here
r = [0] * 8                 # Define registers r[0] to r[7]
pc = 0                      # Set program counter to 0
run = 1                     # run = 1 during execution
sp = 16                     # Initialize the stack pointer (BSR/RTS)
goCount = 0                 # goCount executes n operations with no display
traceMode    = 0            # Set to 1 to execute n instructions without display
skipToBranch = 0            # Used when turning off tracing until a branch
silent = 0                  # silent = 1 to turn off single stepping
```

This is the main loop where we decode instructions to extract the parameters (register numbers and the literal):

```
                                        # Executes instructions when run is 1
while run == 1:                         # Step through instructions: first, decode them!
    binCode = memP[pc]                  # Read binary code of instruction
    pcOld = pc                          # pc in pcOld (for display purposes)
    pc = pc + 1                         # Increment the pc
    binOp = binCode >> 25               # Extract the 7-bit opcode as binOp
    rD    = (binCode >> 22) & 7          # Extract the destination register, rD
    rS1   = (binCode >> 19) & 7          # Extract source register 1, rS1
    rS2   = (binCode >> 16) & 7          # Extract source register 2, rS2
    lit   = binCode & 0xFFFF             # Extract the 16-bit literal
    op0 = r[rD]                         # Get contents of destination register
    op1 = r[rS1]                        # Get contents of source register 1
    op2 = r[rS2]                        # Get contents of source register 2
```

In the next section, we depart from the original version of TC1. The first version of TC1 decoded the opcode as a binary string and then looked it up. However, as we have the source file, it is easier to go directly from the text of the mnemonic and execute it. This makes the code so much easier to read:

```
# Instead of using the binary opcode to determine the instruction, I use the text opcode
# It makes the code more readable if I use 'ADD' rather than its opcode

        mnemonic=next(key for key,value in codes.items() if value[1]==binOp)
                                        # Get mnemonic from dictionary


### INTERPRET INSTRUCTIONS              # Examine the opcode and execute it
    if    mnemonic == 'STOP': run = 0   # STOP ends the simulation
    elif mnemonic == 'END!': run = 0    # END! terminates reading source code and stops
    elif mnemonic == 'NOP':  pass       # NOP is a dummy instruction that does nothing
    elif mnemonic == 'GET':             # Reads integer from the keyboard
        printStatus()
        kbd = (input('Type integer '))  # Get input
        kbd = getLit(kbd)               # Convert string to integer
        r[rD] = kbd                     # Store in register
        continue
    elif mnemonic == 'RND':  r[rD] = random.randint(0,lit)
                                        # Generate random number
    elif mnemonic == 'SWAP': r[rD] = shift(0,1,r[rD],8)
                                        # Swap bytes in a 16-bit word
    elif mnemonic == 'SEC':  c = 1      # Set carry flag
    elif mnemonic == 'LDRL': r[rD] = lit   # LDRL R0,20 loads R0 with literal 20
    elif mnemonic == 'LDRM': r[rD] = mem[lit]
                                        # Load register with memory location (LDRM)
```

```
elif mnemonic == 'LDRI': r[rD] = mem[op1 + lit]
                                                # LDRI r1,[r2,4] memory location [r2]+4
elif mnemonic == 'STRM': mem[lit] = r[rD]       # STRM stores register in memory
elif mnemonic == 'STRI': mem[op1 + lit] = r[rD] # STRI stores rD at location [rS1]+L
elif mnemonic == 'MOVE': r[rD] = op1            # MOVE copies register rS1 to rD
elif mnemonic == 'ADD':  r[rD] = alu('ADD',op1, op2)
                                                # Adds [r2] to [r3] and puts result in r1
elif mnemonic == 'ADDL': r[rD] = alu('ADD',op1,lit) # Adds 12 to [r2] and puts result in r1
elif mnemonic == 'SUB':  r[rD] = alu('SUB',op1,op2) #
elif mnemonic == 'SUBL': r[rD] = alu('SUB',op1,lit)
elif mnemonic == 'MUL':  r[rD] = alu('MUL',op1,op2)
elif mnemonic == 'MULL': r[rD] = alu('MUL',op1,lit)
elif mnemonic == 'DIV':  r[rD] = alu('DIV',op1,op2) # Logical OR
elif mnemonic == 'DIVL': r[rD] = alu('DIV',op1,lit)
elif mnemonic == 'MOD':  r[rD] = alu('MOD',op1,op2) # Modulus
elif mnemonic == 'MODL': r[rD] = alu('MOD',op1,lit)
elif mnemonic == 'AND':  r[rD] = alu('AND',op1,op2) # Logical AND
elif mnemonic == 'ANDL': r[rD] = alu('AND',op1,lit)
elif mnemonic == 'OR':   r[rD] = alu('OR', op1,op2) # Logical OR
elif mnemonic == 'ORL':  r[rD] = alu('OR', op1,lit)
elif mnemonic == 'EOR':  r[rD] = alu('EOR',op1,op2) # Exclusive OR
elif mnemonic == 'EORL': r[rD] = alu('EOR',op1,lit)
elif mnemonic == 'NOT':  r[rD] = alu('NOT',op0,1)   # NOT r1 uses only one operand
elif mnemonic == 'INC':  r[rD] = alu('ADD',op0,1)
elif mnemonic == 'DEC':  r[rD] = alu('SUB',op0,1)
elif mnemonic == 'CMP':  rr     = alu('SUB',op0,op1) # rr is a dummy variable
elif mnemonic == 'CMPL': rr     = alu('SUB',op0,lit)
elif mnemonic == 'ADC':  r[rD] = alu('ADC',op1,op2)
elif mnemonic == 'SBC':  r[rD] = alu('SBC',op1,op2)
elif mnemonic == 'LSL':  r[rD] = shift(0,0,op0,op1)
elif mnemonic == 'LSLL': r[rD] = shift(0,0,op0,lit)
elif mnemonic == 'LSR':  r[rD] = shift(1,0,op0,op1)
elif mnemonic == 'LSRL': r[rD] = shift(1,0,op0,lit)
elif mnemonic == 'ROL':  r[rD] = shift(1,1,op0,op2)
elif mnemonic == 'ROLL': r[rD] = shift(1,1,op0,lit)
elif mnemonic == 'ROR':  r[rD] = shift(0,1,op0,op2)
elif mnemonic == 'RORL': r[rD] = shift(0,1,op0,lit)
elif mnemonic == 'PRT':  print('Reg',rD,'=', '%04x' % r[rD])
elif mnemonic == 'BRA':              pc = lit
elif mnemonic == 'BEQ' and  z == 1: pc = lit
elif mnemonic == 'BNE' and  z == 0: pc = lit
elif mnemonic == 'BMI' and  n == 1: pc = lit
elif mnemonic == 'DBEQ':                        # Decrement register and branch on zero
```

```
        r[rD] = r[rD] - 1
        if r[rD] != 0: pc = lit
    elif mnemonic == 'DBNE':          # Decrement register and branch on not zero
        r[rD] = alu('SUB',op0,1)      # Note the use of the alu function
        if z == 0: pc = lit
    elif mnemonic == 'BSR':           # Stack-based operations. Branch to subroutine
        sp = sp - 1                   # Pre-decrement stack pointer
        stack[sp] = pc                # Push the pc (return address)
        pc = lit                      # Jump to target address
    elif mnemonic == 'RTS':           # Return from subroutine
        pc = stack[sp]                # Pull pc address of the stack
        sp = sp + 1                   # Increment stack pointer
    elif mnemonic == 'PUSH':          # Push register to stack
        sp = sp - 1                   # Move stack pointer up to make space
        stack[sp] = op0               # Push register in op on the stack
    elif mnemonic == 'PULL':          # Pull register off the stack
        r[rD] = stack[sp]             # Transfer stack value to register
        sp = sp + 1                   # Move stack down
```

This section performs a function called tracing and allows us to list the contents of the register or turn off the listing as we execute the code:

```
                                      # Instruction interpretation complete. Deal with display
    if silent == 0:                   # Read keyboard ONLY if not in silent mode
        x = input('>>>')              # Get keyboard input to continue
        if x == 'b': skipToBranch = 1 # Set flag to execute to branch with no display
        if x.isnumeric():             # Is this a trace mode with a number of steps to skip?
            traceMode = 1             # If so, set traceMode
            goCount   = getLit(x) + 1 # Record the number of lines to skip printing

    if skipToBranch == 1:             # Are we in skip-to-branch mode?
        silent = 1                    # If so, turn off printing status
        if mnemonic in branchGroup:   # Have we reached a branch?
            silent = 0                # If branch, turn off silent mode and allow tracing
            skipToBranch = 0          # Turn off skip-to-branch mode

    if traceMode == 1:                # If in silent mode (no display of data)
        silent = 1                    # Set silent flag
        goCount = goCount - 1         # Decrement silent mode count
        if goCount == 0:              # If we've reached zero, turn display on
            traceMode = 0             # Leave trace mode
            silent = 0                # Set silent flag back to zero (off)
    if silent == 0: printStatus()
```

Now that we've explained the TC1 simulator, we'll demonstrate its use.

Example of a TC1 assembly language program

Here, we demonstrate a TC1 program in assembly language. This offers a means of testing the simulator and showing how it works. We would like to test a range of facilities, so we should include looping, conditional testing, and pointer-based memory access. We will write a program to do the following:

1. Fill a region of memory from locations 0 to 4 with random numbers.
2. Reverse the order of the numbers.

Since this problem uses memory and sequential addresses, it involves register indirect addressing, that is, LDRI and STRI instructions. Creating the random numbers and storing them sequentially in memory can be done by doing the following:

```
Set a pointer to the first memory location (i.e.,0)
Set a counter to 5 (we are going to access five locations 0 to 4)
Repeat
   Generate a random number
   Store this number at the pointer address
   Point to next number (i.e., add 1 to the pointer)
   Decrement the counter (i.e., counter 5,4,3,2,1,0)
   Until counter = 0
```

In TC1 code, we can translate this as follows:

```
        LDRL  r0,0        @ Use r0 as a memory pointer and set it to 0
        LDRL  r1,5        @ Use r1 as the loop counter
Loop1   RND   r2          @ Loop: Generate a random number in r2
        STRI  r2,[r0],0   @ Store the random number in memory using pointer r0
        INC   r0          @ Point to the next location (add 1 to the pointer)
        DEC   r1          @ Decrement the loop counter (subtract 1 from the counter)
        BNE   Loop1       @ Repeat until 0 (branch back to Loop1 if the last result was not 0)
```

We've filled a region of memory with random values. We now need to reverse their order. There are many ways of reversing the order of numbers. One is to move the numbers from the source to a temporary location in memory and then write them back in reverse order. Of course, this takes up extra memory for the temporary copy. Consider another solution that does not require a buffer. We will write down the source addresses above the destination addresses:

```
Original (source)        0   1   2   3   4

Swapped (destination)    4   3   2   1   0
```

As you can see, location 0 is swapped with location 4, then location 1 with location 3; then, at location 2, we have reached the middle point and the reversal is complete. To perform this action, we need two pointers, one for each end of the string. We select the two characters at the ends of the string and swap them. Then, we move the pointers inward and do a second swap. The task is complete when the pointers meet in the middle. Note that this assumes an odd number of items to reverse:

```
Set upper pointer to top
Set lower pointer to bottom
Repeat
    Get value at upper pointer
    Get value at lower pointer
    Swap values and store
Until upper pointer and lower pointer are equal
```

In TC1 assembly language, this looks as follows:

```
        LDRL  r0,0          @ Lower pointer points at first entry in table
        LDRL  r1,4          @ Upper pointer points at last entry in table
Loop2   LDRI  r2,[r0],0     @ REPEAT: Get lower value pointed at by r0
        LDRI  r3,[r1],0     @ Get upper value pointed at by r1
        MOVE  r2,r4         @ Save lower value in r4 temporarily
        STRI  r3,[r0],0     @ Store upper value in lower entry position
        STRI  r4,[r1],0     @ Store saved lower value in upper entry position
        INC   r0            @ Increase lower pointer
        DEC   r1            @ Decrease upper pointer
        CMP   r0,r1         @ Compare pointers
        BNE   Loop2         @ UNTIL all characters moved
```

The following shows the output when this program is executed, instruction by instruction. In order to simplify the reading of this data, we've put changes in register and memory values in bold. The branch operations are shaded. Comparison instructions are in italics.

The first block is the source code printed by TC1 before the start of the instruction execution:

```
TC1 CPU simulator 11 September 2022
Input debug level 1 - 5: 4

Source assembly code listing
0               LDRL R0 0
1               LDRL R1 5
2       LOOP1   RND  R2
3               STRI R2 R0 0
4               INC  R0
5               DEC  R1
6               BNE  LOOP1
```

```
 7              NOP
 8              LDRL  R0  0
 9              LDRL  R1  4
10   LOOP2      LDRI  R2  R0  0
11              LDRI  R3  R1  0
12              MOVE  R4  R2
13              STRI  R3  R0  0
14              STRI  R4  R1  0
15              INC   R0
16              DEC   R1
17              CMP   R0  R1
18              BNE   LOOP2
19              NOP
20              STOP
21              END!


Equate and branch table

START     0
LOOP1     2
LOOP2     10
```

The second code block shows the output of the assembler as instructions are decoded. You can see the various registers, the literal, and the format field:

```
Decoded instructions
pc=00 Op =        LDRL R0 0        literal 0000 RD=0 rS1=0 rS2=0 format=1001
pc=01 Op =        LDRL R1 5        literal 0005 RD=1 rS1=0 rS2=0 format=1001
pc=02 Op= LOOP1 RND R2 0XFFFF      literal ffff RD=2 rS1=0 rS2=0 format=1001
pc=03 Op =        STRI R2 R0 0     literal 0000 RD=2 rS1=0 rS2=0 format=1101
pc=04 Op =        INC  R0          literal 0000 RD=0 rS1=0 rS2=0 format=1000
pc=05 Op =        DEC  R1          literal 0000 RD=1 rS1=0 rS2=0 format=1000
pc=06 Op =        BNE  LOOP1       literal 0002 RD=0 rS1=0 rS2=0 format=0001
pc=07 Op =        NOP              literal 0000 RD=0 rS1=0 rS2=0 format=0000
pc=08 Op =        LDRL R0 0        literal 0000 RD=0 rS1=0 rS2=0 format=1001
pc=09 Op =        LDRL R1 4        literal 0004 RD=1 rS1=0 rS2=0 format=1001
pc=10 Op= LOOP2 LDRI R2 R0 0       literal 0000 RD=2 rS1=0 rS2=0 format=1101
pc=11 Op =        LDRI R3 R1 0     literal 0000 RD=3 rS1=1 rS2=0 format=1101
pc=12 Op =        MOVE R4 R2       literal 0000 RD=4 rS1=2 rS2=0 format=1100
pc=13 Op =        STRI R3 R0 0     literal 0000 RD=3 rS1=0 rS2=0 format=1101
pc=14 Op =        STRI R4 R1 0     literal 0000 RD=4 rS1=1 rS2=0 format=1101
pc=15 Op =        INC  R0          literal 0000 RD=0 rS1=0 rS2=0 format=1000
pc=16 Op =        DEC  R1          literal 0000 RD=1 rS1=0 rS2=0 format=1000
pc=17 Op =        CMP  R0 R1       literal 0000 RD=0 rS1=1 rS2=0 format=1100
```

```
pc=18 Op =          BNE   LOOP2      literal 000a RD=0 rS1=0 rS2=0 format=0001
pc=19 Op =          NOP              literal 0000 RD=0 rS1=0 rS2=0 format=0000
pc=20 Op =          STOP             literal 0000 RD=0 rS1=0 rS2=0 format=0000
pc=21 Op =          END!             literal 0000 RD=0 rS1=0 rS2=0 format=0000
```

The following provides the output of a run using this program. We've set the trace level to 4 to show the source code (after text processing), the symbol table, and the decoded instructions.

Then, we've executed the code line by line. In order to make the output more readable and to fit it on the page, we've removed registers and memory locations that don't change, and we've highlighted values (memory, registers, and z-flag) that change as the result of an instruction. You can follow this through and see how memory/registers change with each instruction.

As you can see, we create five random numbers in memory locations 0 to 4 and then reverse their order. This does not match the output of the print status because it's been modified for printing:

```
0             LDRL R0  0      PC =   0 z = 0 0000 0000 0000 0000 0000
                              R   0000 0000 0000 0000 0000


1             LDRL R1  5      PC =   1 z = 0 0000 0000 0000 0000 0000
                              R   0000 0005 0000 0000 0000


2   LOOP1     RND   R2        PC =   2 z = 0 0000 0000 0000 0000 0000
                              R   0000 0005 9eff 0000 0000


3             STRI R2 R0 0    PC =   3 z = 0 9eff 0000 0000 0000 0000
                              R   0000 0005 9eff 0000 0000


4             INC   R0        PC =   4 z = 0 9eff 0000 0000 0000 0000
                              R   0001 0005 9eff 0000 0000


5             DEC   R1        PC =   5 z = 0 9eff 0000 0000 0000 0000
                              R   0001 0004 9eff 0000 0000


6             BNE   LOOP1     PC =   6 z = 0 9eff 0000 0000 0000 0000
                              R   0001 0004 9eff 0000 0000


2   LOOP1     RND   R2        PC =   2 z = 0 9eff 0000 0000 0000 0000
                              R   0001 0004 6d4a 0000 0000


3             STRI R2 R0 0    PC =   3 z = 0 9eff 6d4a 0000 0000 0000
                              R   0001 0004 6d4a 0000 0000
```

```
4            INC   R0        PC =  4 z = 0 9eff 6d4a 0000 0000 0000
                             R  0002 0004 6d4a 0000 0000

5            DEC   R1        PC =  5 z = 0 9eff 6d4a 0000 0000 0000
                             R  0002 0003 6d4a 0000 0000

6            BNE   LOOP1     PC =  6 z = 0 9eff 6d4a 0000 0000 0000
                             R  0002 0003 6d4a 0000 0000

2    LOOP1   RND   R2        PC =  2 z = 0 9eff 6d4a 0000 0000 0000
                             R  0002 0003 a387 0000 0000

3            STRI  R2 R0 0   PC =  3 z = 0 9eff 6d4a a387 0000 0000
                             R  0002 0003 a387 0000 0000

4            INC   R0        PC =  4 z = 0 9eff 6d4a a387 0000 0000
                             R  0003 0003 a387 0000 0000

5            DEC   R1        PC =  5 z = 0 9eff 6d4a a387 0000 0000
                             R  0003 0002 a387 0000 0000

6            BNE   LOOP1     PC =  6 z = 0 9eff 6d4a a387 0000 0000
                             R  0003 0002 a387 0000 0000

2    LOOP1   RND   R2        PC =  2 z = 0 9eff 6d4a a387 0000 0000
                             R  0003 0002 2937 0000 0000

3            STRI  R2 R0 0   PC =  3 z = 0 9eff 6d4a a387 2937 0000
                             R  0003 0002 2937 0000 0000

4            INC   R0        PC =  4 z = 0 9eff 6d4a a387 2937 0000
                             R  0004 0002 2937 0000 0000

5            DEC   R1        PC =  5 z = 0 9eff 6d4a a387 2937 0000
                             R  0004 0001 2937 0000 0000

6            BNE   LOOP1     PC =  6 z = 0 9eff 6d4a a387 2937 0000
                             R  0004 0001 2937 0000 0000

2    LOOP1   RND   R2        PC =  2 z = 0 9eff 6d4a a387 2937 0000
                             R  0004 0001 db95 0000 0000
```

```
3              STRI R2 R0 0        PC =  3  z = 0  9eff 6d4a a387 2937 db95
                                   R  0004 0001 db95 0000 0000

4              INC  R0             PC =  4  z = 0  9eff 6d4a a387 2937 db95
                                   R  0005 0001 db95 0000 0000

5              DEC  R1             PC =  5  z = 1  9eff 6d4a a387 2937 db95
                                   R  0005 0000 db95 0000 0000

6              BNE LOOP1           PC =  6  z = 1  9eff 6d4a a387 2937 db95
                                   R  0005 0000 db95 0000 0000
7              NOP                 PC =  7  z = 1  9eff 6d4a a387 2937 db95
                                   R  0005 0000 db95 0000 0000

8              LDRL R0 0           PC =  8  z = 1  9eff 6d4a a387 2937 db95
                                   R  0000 0000 db95 0000 0000

9              LDRL R1 4           PC =  9  z = 1  9eff 6d4a a387 2937 db95
                                   R  0000 0004 db95 0000 0000

10 LOOP2       LDRI R2 R0 0        PC = 10  z = 1  9eff 6d4a a387 2937 db95
                                   R  0000 0004 9eff 0000 0000

11             LDRI R3 R1 0        PC = 11  z = 1  9eff 6d4a a387 2937 db95
                                   R  0000 0004 9eff db95 0000

12             MOVE R4 R2          PC = 12  z = 1  9eff 6d4a a387 2937 db95
                                   R  0000 0004 9eff db95 9eff

13             STRI R3 R0 0        PC = 13  z = 1  db95 6d4a a387 2937 db95
                                   R  0000 0004 9eff db95 9eff

14             STRI R4 R1 0        PC = 14  z = 1  db95 6d4a a387 2937 9eff
                                   R  0000 0004 9eff db95 9eff

15             INC  R0             PC = 15  z = 0  db95 6d4a a387 2937 9eff
                                   R  0001 0004 9eff db95 9eff

16             DEC  R1             PC = 16  z = 0  db95 6d4a a387 2937 9eff
                                   R  0001 0003 9eff db95 9eff

17             CMP  R0 R1          PC = 17  z = 0  db95 6d4a a387 2937 9eff
                                   R  0001 0003 9eff db95 9eff
```

```
18          BNE   LOOP2        PC = 18 z = 0 db95 6d4a a387 2937 9eff
                               R   0001 0003 9eff db95 9eff

10 LOOP2    LDRI R2 R0 0       PC = 10 z = 0 db95 6d4a a387 2937 9eff
                               R   0001 0003 6d4a db95 9eff

11          LDRI R3 R1 0       PC = 11 z = 0 db95 6d4a a387 2937 9eff
                               R   0001 0003 6d4a 2937 9eff

12          MOVE R4 R2         PC = 12 z = 0 db95 6d4a a387 2937 9eff
                               R   0001 0003 6d4a 2937 6d4a

13          STRI R3 R0 0       PC = 13 z = 0 db95 2937 a387 2937 9eff
                               R   0001 0003 6d4a 2937 6d4a

14          STRI R4 R1 0       PC = 14 z = 0 db95 2937 a387 6d4a 9eff
                               R   0001 0003 6d4a 2937 6d4a

15          INC   R0           PC = 15 z = 0 db95 2937 a387 6d4a 9eff
                               R   0002 0003 6d4a 2937 6d4a

16          DEC   R1           PC = 16 z = 0 db95 2937 a387 6d4a 9eff
                               R   0002 0002 6d4a 2937 6d4a

17          CMP   R0 R1        PC = 17 z = 1 db95 2937 a387 6d4a 9eff
                               R   0002 0002 6d4a 2937 6d4a

18          BNE   LOOP2        PC = 18 z = 1 db95 2937 a387 6d4a 9eff
                               R   0002 0002 6d4a 2937 6d4a

19          NOP                PC = 19 z = 1 db95 2937 a387 6d4a 9eff
                               R   0002 0002 6d4a 2937 6d4a

20          STOP               PC = 20 z = 1 db95 2937 a387 6d4a 9eff
                               R   0002 0002 6d4a 2937 6d4a
```

In the next section, we demonstrate how you might go about testing the operation of TC1. We cover the following:

- Testing the assembler (e.g., the ability to use a free format of code)
- Testing flow control instructions (branches)
- Testing shift operations

Testing the assembler

Since the TC1 assembler can deal with several typographic features (e.g., uppercase or lowercase and multiple spaces), a simple way of testing the assembler is to give it a file to assemble that includes various conditions, such as multiple spaces, equates, and uppercase and lowercase conversion. My initial test source code was as follows:

```
      NOP
 BRA eee
         INC r4
alan inc r5
eee    STOP
aa NOP @comment2

bb NOP       1
       LDRL         r0,    12
       LDRL  r3,0x123  @ comment1

       LDRL  r7,        0xFF
       INC R2
  BRA last
test1      EQU      999
  @comment3
@comment4
  @ qqq EQU 7
www STRI r1,r2,1
abc     equ 25
qwerty  equ     888
last LDRL r5,0xFAAF
  beQ Aa
         STOP 2
```

This is not exactly stylish code; it's just random test code. In the following code, we provide the output of the assembler when operated in debug mode. This includes the formatting of the code (removal of blank lines and lowercase to uppercase conversion). The first listing provides the instructions as an array of lists of tokens:

```
TC1 CPU simulator 11 September 2022
Input debug level 1 - 5: 4

Source assembly code listing
0              NOP
1              BRA EEE
2              INC R4
3    ALAN      INC R5
4    EEE       STOP
5    AA        NOP
```

```
6    BB      NOP 1
7            LDRL R0 12
8            LDRL R3 0X123
9            LDRL R7 0XFF
10           INC R2
11           BRA LAST
12   WWW     STRI R1 R2 1
13   LAST    LDRL R5 0XFAAF
14           BEQ AA
15           STOP 2
```

The second listing is the symbol table that ties symbol names and labels to integer values:

```
Equate and branch table

START      0
TEST1      999
ABC        25
QWERTY     888
ALAN       3
EEE        4
AA         5
BB         6
WWW        12
LAST       13
LOOP1      18
LOOP2      26
```

The next listing was used largely for debugging when an instruction didn't behave as intended. It lets you determine whether an instruction has been correctly decoded:

```
Decoded instructions
pc=0  op=NOP              literal 000 Dest reg=0 rS1-0 rS2=0 format=0000
pc=00 Op=NOP              literal 0000 Dest reg=0 rS1=0 rS2=0 format=0000
pc=01 Op=BRA EEE          literal 0004 Dest reg=0 rS1=0 rS2=0 format=0001
pc=02 Op=INC R4           literal 0000 Dest reg=4 rS1=0 rS2=0 format=1000
pc=03 Op=ALAN INC R5      literal 0000 Dest reg=5 rS1=0 rS2=0 format=1000
pc=04 Op=EEE STOP         literal 0000 Dest reg=0 rS1=0 rS2=0 format=0000
pc=05 Op=AA NOP           literal 0000 Dest reg=0 rS1=0 rS2=0 format=0000
pc=06 Op=BB NOP 1         literal 0000 Dest reg=0 rS1=0 rS2=0 format=0000
pc=07 Op=LDRL R0 12       literal 000c Dest reg=0 rS1=0 rS2=0 format=1001
pc=08 Op=LDRL R3 0X123    literal 0123 Dest reg=3 rS1=0 rS2=0 format=1001
pc=09 Op=LDRL R7 0XFF     literal 00ff Dest reg=7 rS1=0 rS2=0 format=1001
pc=10 Op=INC R2           literal 0000 Dest reg=2 rS1=0 rS2=0 format=1000
pc=11 Op=BRA LAST         literal 000d Dest reg=0 rS1=0 rS2=0 format=0001
pc=12 Op=WWW STRI R1 R2 1 literal 0001 Dest reg=1 rS1=2 rS2=0 format=1101
```

```
pc=13 Op=LAST LDRL R5 0XFAAF   literal faaf Dest reg=5 rS1=0 rS2=0 format=1001
pc=14 Op=BEQ AA                literal 0005 Dest reg=0 rS1=0 rS2=0 format=0001
pc=15 Op=STOP 2                literal 0000 Dest reg=0 rS1=0 rS2=0 format=0000
>>>
```

Testing flow control operations

Here, we demonstrate how to test the computer's most important class of operations, the flow-control instruction, that is, the conditional branch.

One of the most important classes of instructions to test are those that change the flow of control: the branch and subroutine call instructions. The following fragment of code is also meaningless (it serves only to test instruction execution) and is designed only to test loops. One loop is built using a branch on a not-zero operation, and the other uses an automatic loop mechanism that operates by decrementing a register and branching until the register decrements to zero. The **decrement and branch on not zero** (**DBNE**) instruction has the format DBNE r0,loop, where r0 is the counter being decremented and loop is the branch target address.

We first provide the source listing and symbol table:

```
>>> %Run TC1_FinalForBook_V1.2_20220911.py
TC1 CPU simulator 11 September 2022
Input debug level 1 - 5: 4

Source assembly code listing
0               NOP
1               BRA LAB1
2               INC R0
3       LAB1    INC R2
4               NOP
5               BRA LAB6
6               NOP
7       LAB2    LDRL R2 3
8       LAB4    DEC R2
9               NOP
10              BNE LAB4
11              NOP
12              BSR LAB7
13              NOP
14              LDRL R3 4
15      LAB5    NOP
16              INC R7
17              DBNE R3 LAB5
18              NOP
19              STOP
20      LAB6    BRA LAB2
```

```
21              NOP
22  LAB7        DEC R7
23              DEC R7
24              RTS
25              END!
```

Equate and branch table

```
START     0
LAB1      3
LAB2      7
LAB4      8
LAB5      15
LAB6      20
LAB7      22
```

The following provides the output after a debugging session. As you can see, the sequence of branches is faithfully implemented. Note that we've highlighted the branch actions and consequences (i.e., the next instruction):

```
0            NOP              PC= 0  z=0  n=0  c=0
                              R  0000 0000 0000 0000 0000 0000 0000 0000

1            BRA LAB1         PC= 1  z=0  n=0  c=0
                              R  0000 0000 0000 0000 0000 0000 0000 0000

3  LAB1      INC R2           PC= 3  z=0  n=0  c=1
                              R  0000 0000 0001 0000 0000 0000 0000 0000

4            NOP              PC= 4  z=0  n=0  c=1
                              R  0000 0000 0001 0000 0000 0000 0000 0000

5            BRA LAB6         PC= 5  z=0  n=0  c=1
                              R  0000 0000 0001 0000 0000 0000 0000 0000

20 LAB6      BRA LAB2         PC=20  z=0  n=0  c=1
                              R  0000 0000 0001 0000 0000 0000 0000 0000

7  LAB2      LDRL R2 3        PC= 7  z=0  n=0  c=1
                              R  0000 0000 0003 0000 0000 0000 0000 0000

8  LAB4      DEC R2           PC= 8  z=0  n=0  c=1
                              R  0000 0000 0002 0000 0000 0000 0000 0000

9            NOP              PC= 9  z=0  n=0  c=1
                              R  0000 0000 0002 0000 0000 0000 0000 0000
```

```
10           BNE LAB4        PC=10 z=0 n=0 c=1
                            R  0000 0000 0002 0000 0000 0000 0000 0000

8   LAB4     DEC R2          PC= 8 z=0 n=0 c=1
                            R  0000 0000 0001 0000 0000 0000 0000 0000

9            NOP             PC= 9 z=0 n=0 c=1
                            R  0000 0000 0001 0000 0000 0000 0000 0000

10           BNE LAB4        PC=10 z=0 n=0 c=1
                            R  0000 0000 0001 0000 0000 0000 0000 0000

8   LAB4     DEC R2          PC= 8 z=1 n=0 c=0
                            R  0000 0000 0000 0000 0000 0000 0000 0000

9            NOP             PC= 9 z=1 n=0 c=0
                            R  0000 0000 0000 0000 0000 0000 0000 0000

10           BNE LAB4        PC=10 z=1 n=0 c=0
                            R  0000 0000 0000 0000 0000 0000 0000 0000

11           NOP             PC=11 z=1 n=0 c=0
                            R  0000 0000 0000 0000 0000 0000 0000 0000

12           BSR LAB7        PC=12 z=1 n=0 c=0
                            R  0000 0000 0000 0000 0000 0000 0000 0000

22  LAB7     DEC R7          PC=22 z=0 n=1 c=1
                            R  0000 0000 0000 0000 0000 0000 0000 ffff

23           DEC R7          PC=23 z=0 n=1 c=1
                            R  0000 0000 0000 0000 0000 0000 0000 fffe

24           RTS             PC=24 z=0 n=1 c=1
                            R  0000 0000 0000 0000 0000 0000 0000 fffe

13           NOP             PC=13 z=0 n=1 c=1
                            R  0000 0000 0000 0000 0000 0000 0000 fffe

14           LDRL R3 4       PC=14 z=0 n=1 c=1
                            R  0000 0000 0000 0004 0000 0000 0000 fffe

15  LAB5     NOP             PC=15 z=0 n=1 c=1
                            R  0000 0000 0000 0004 0000 0000 0000 fffe
```

| 16 | INC R7 | PC=16 z=0 n=1 c=1 |
| | | R   0000 0000 0000 0004 0000 0000 0000 ffff |

| 17 | **DBNE R3 LAB5** | PC=17 z=0 n=1 c=1 |
| | | R   0000 0000 0000 0003 0000 0000 0000 ffff |

| **15 LAB5** | NOP | PC=15 z=0 n=1 c=1 |
| | | R   0000 0000 0000 0003 0000 0000 0000 ffff |

| 16 | INC R7 | PC=16 z=1 n=0 c=0 |
| | | R   0000 0000 0000 0003 0000 0000 0000 0000 |

| 17 | **DBNE R3 LAB5** | PC=17 z=1 n=0 c=0 |
| | | R   0000 0000 0000 0002 0000 0000 0000 0000 |

| **15 LAB5** | NOP | PC=15 z=1 n=0 c=0 |
| | | R   0000 0000 0000 0002 0000 0000 0000 0000 |

| 16 | INC R7 | PC=16 z=0 n=0 c=1 |
| | | R   0000 0000 0000 0002 0000 0000 0000 0001 |

| 17 | **DBNE R3 LAB5** | PC=17 z=0 n=0 c=1 |
| | | R   0000 0000 0000 0001 0000 0000 0000 0001 |

| **15 LAB5** | NOP | PC=15 z=0 n=0 c=1 |
| | | R   0000 0000 0000 0001 0000 0000 0000 0001 |

| 16 | INC R7 | PC=16 z=0 n=0 c=1 |
| | | R   0000 0000 0000 0001 0000 0000 0000 0002 |

| 17 | **DBNE R3 LAB5** | PC=17 z=0 n=0 c=1 |
| | | R   0000 0000 0000 0000 0000 0000 0000 0002 |

| 18 | NOP | PC=18 z=0 n=0 c=1 |
| | | R   0000 0000 0000 0000 0000 0000 0000 0002 |

| 19 | STOP | PC=19 z=0 n=0 c=1 |
| | | R   0000 0000 0000 0000 0000 0000 0000 0002 |

In the next chapter, we will look at some of the ways in which the TC1 program can be enhanced to add facilities such as error checking, the inclusion of new instructions, and special features such as variable-length operand fields.

Testing shift operations

TC1 supports two shift types: *logical* and *rotate*. A logical shift moves the bits left or right. At one end, vacated bits are replaced by zeros and, at the other end, the bit shifted out is copied to the carry flag. In a rotation, the bit that is shifted out of one end is copied to the other end; that is, the string of bits is treated as a ring. No bit is lost, no matter how many shifts take place. At each bit shift, the bit that was shifted to the other end is also copied to the carry bit.

Most real computers have two other shift variations: an arithmetic shift that preserves the sign of two's complement numbers when shifted right (divide-by-2 operation) and a rotate-through-carry shift where the bit shifted in at one end is the old carry bit and the bit shifted out becomes the new carry bit. Essentially, if the register has m bits, the carry bit is included to create an m+1 bit word. This feature is used for multi-precision arithmetic. We haven't included these modes in TC1.

As well as specifying the shift type, we have to specify the shift direction (left or right). Most computers let you specify the number of shifts. We provide both facilities and the number of shifts can be specified using either a register or a literal. In a multi-length shift, the state of the carry bit is the last bit shifted out into the carry. The shift operations (with examples) are as follows:

Shift Type	Register/Literal	Example
Logical shift left	literal	LSLL r0,r1,2
Logical shift left	register	LSL r3,r1,r4
Logical shift right	literal	LSRL r0,r1,2
Logical shift right	register	LSR r3,r1,r2
Rotate left	literal	ROLL r0,r1,2
Rotate left	register	ROL r3,r1,r0
Rotate right	literal	RORL r0,r3,2
Rotate right	register	ROR r3,r1,r0

Table 6.1 – TC1 shifting modes

When we test these instructions, we have to ensure that the shift direction is correct, the right number of shifts take place, the end bits (those shifted out or in) behave correctly, and the flag bits are set appropriately.

Consider the following fragment of code using the 16-bit value 1000000110000001 in a series of shifts:

```
LDRL  r1,%1000000110000001
LSLL  r0,r1,1
LSLL  r0,r1,2
LSRL  r0,r1,1
LSRL  r0,r1,1
LDRL  r1,%1000000110000001
LDRL  r2,1
```

```
LDRL  r3,2
LSLL  r0,r1,r2
LSLL  r0,r1,r3
LSRL  r0,r1,r2
LSRL  r0,r1,r2
```

The following output from the simulator (edited to show only relevant information) gives the registers and condition codes as the preceding code is executed. The binary value of register r0 is displayed on the right. This allows us to verify whether the operations have been executed correctly by manual inspection:

```
1   LDRL R1 %1000000110000001 z = 0 n = 0 c = 0
    Regs 0 - 3   0000 8181 0000 0000   R0 =  0000000000000000

2   LSLL R0 R1 1              z = 0 n = 0 c = 1
    Regs 0 - 3   0302 8181 0000 0000   R0 =  0000001100000010

3   LSLL R0 R1 2              z = 0 n = 0 c = 0
    Regs 0 - 3   0604 8181 0000 0000   R0 =  0000011000000100

4   LSRL R0 R1 1              z = 0 n = 0 c = 1
    Regs 0 - 3   40c0 8181 0000 0000   R0 =  0100000011000000

5   LSRL R0 R1 1              z = 0 n = 0 c = 1
    Regs 0 - 3   40c0 8181 0000 0000   R0 =  0100000011000000

6   LDRL R1 %1000000110000001 z = 0 n = 0 c = 1
    Regs 0 - 3   40c0 8181 0000 0000   R0 =  0100000011000000

7   LDRL R2 1                z = 0 n = 0 c = 1
    Regs 0 - 3   40c0 8181 0001 0000   R0 =  0100000011000000

8   LDRL R3 2                z = 0 n = 0 c = 1
    Regs 0 - 3   40c0 8181 0001 0002   R0 =  0100000011000000

9   LSL  R0 R1 R2            z = 0 n = 0 c = 1
    Regs 0 - 3   0302 8181 0001 0002   R0 =  0000001100000010

10  LSL  R0 R1 R3            z = 0 n = 0 c = 0
    Regs 0 - 3   0604 8181 0001 0002   R0 =  0000011000000100

11  LSR  R0 R1 R2            z = 0 n = 0 c = 1
    Regs 0 - 3   40c0 8181 0001 0002   R0 =  0100000011000000

12  LSR  R0 R1 R2            z = 0 n = 0 c = 1
    Regs 0 - 3   40c0 8181 0001 0002   R0 =  0100000011000000
```

Note that a load operation does not affect the z-bit. Some computers update the z-bit after almost every operation. Some update the z-bit on demand (e.g., ARM, which we will introduce later), and some update it only after certain operations.

The penultimate section of this chapter covers adding a postscript to TC1 where we provide a simpler example that performs the same basic function but carries out some operations in a different way, such as instruction decoding. The purpose of this is to demonstrate that there are many ways of constructing a simulator.

TC1 postscript

The version of TC1 presented here grew during the development of this book. The current version has more features than the prototype; for example, initially, it didn't include symbolic branch addresses and required users to enter actual line numbers.

Here, we're presenting a cut-down version of TC1, called $TC1_{mini}$, where we do some things differently; for example, by not allowing a free format (mnemonics must be uppercase and registers lowercase, and you can't use spaces and commas as interchangeable delimiters). In this version, a simple function checks that the mnemonic is valid and terminates the program if it isn't. Similarly, we've added a feature that checks whether an address generated by a pointer lies within the bounds of your memory space. The following section provides some comments on this version.

The classDecode function

TC1 associates a 4-bit binary value with each instruction to indicate that parameters are required by the current instruction; for example, 1101 indicates registers rD, rS1, and a literal. The $TC1_{mini}$ version associates a *class number* in the range 0 to 7, with each instruction that describes its type. The classes range from 0 (mnemonic with no parameters) to 7 (mnemonic with an indirect address, such as LDRI r2, [r4]). Unlike TC1, the [ ] brackets are not optional in $TC1_{mini's}$ assembly language.

The difference between the two simulators, TC1 and $TC1_{mini}$, is that the 4-bit binary code provides *pre-decoding*; that is, the simulator doesn't have to calculate what parameters the instruction requires because the code directly tells you that. If you use a class number instead, you have to decode the class number to determine the actual parameters required. However, a class number can be very creative. $TC1_{mini}$ uses seven different instruction formats and requires a minimum of seven classes to be defined. If you had, say, 14 classes, each addressing mode class could be divided into two subclasses to give you greater control over the instruction execution process.

The classDecode function takes in an instruction's predicate and returns the four predicate values, the destination register, source register 1, source register 2, and the literal. Of course, instructions may have from zero to four of these values. Consequently, these parameters are initially set to dummy values, either a null string or zero.

Before continuing, recall that Python's `in` operator is useful for testing whether an element is a member of a set. For example, if an operation is in classes 2, 4, 5, and 9, we can write the following:

```
if thisThing in [2, 4, 5, 9]:              # Test for membership of the set
def classDecode(predicate):
    lit,rD,rS1,rS2 = '',0,0,0              # The literal is a null string initially
    if opClass in [1]:       lit = predicate     # Class 1 is mnemonic plus a literal
    if opClass in [2]:       rD  = reg1[predicate]  # Class 2 is mnemonic plus a literal
    if opClass in [3,4,5,6,7]:             # Classes 3 to 7 have multiple parameters
        predicate = predicate.split(',')   # So, split predicate into tokens
        rD = reg1[predicate[0]]            # Get first token (register number)
```

The current instruction's `opClass` is used to extract the parameters. Instead of using `if` constructs, we've used Python's `if in [list]` construct; for example, `if opClass in [3,4,5,6,7]` returns `True` if the instruction is in classes 3 to 7. If it is, the predicate (a string) is divided into a list using the `split()` function, and the first element is read to extract the destination register, `rD`. Note that we need to split the predicate only once, because all the following cases also fall within this group.

The testLine function

Another limitation of TC1 is the lack of testing and validation; for example, I sometimes type MOVE instead of MOV and the program crashes. Normally, this isn't a problem; you just re-edit the source program. However, when debugging TC1, I often assumed an error was due to a mistake in my new code, only to discover that it was simply a misprint in the assembly language program. So, I added a small amount of testing. The following provides the testing function:

```
def testLine(tokens):                      # Check whether there's a valid instruction in this line
    error = 1                              # error flag = 1 for no error and 0 for an error state
    if len(tokens) == 1:                   # If the line is a single token, it must be a mnemonic
        if tokens[0] in codes: error = 0   # If the token is in codes, there's no error
    else:                                  # Otherwise, we have a multi-token line
        if (tokens[0] in codes) or (tokens[1] in codes): error = 0:
    return(error)                          # Return the error code
```

The only line of interest is the following:

```
if (tokens[0] in codes) or (tokens[1] in codes): error = 0:
```

There are two cases to consider: instructions with a label and those without a label. In the former case, the mnemonic is the second token in the instruction, and in the latter case, the mnemonic is the first token. We can test whether a token is a mnemonic by using Python's `if ... in` construct. Say we have the following construct:

```
if token[0] in codes
```

This returns `True` if the first token is a valid mnemonic. We can combine the two tests with an `or` Boolean to get the preceding expression. In the program, we call `testLine` with the `tokens` parameter and it returns an error. We use the error to print a message and return it to the operating system with the `sys.exit()` function.

The testIndex() function

This simulator provides an instruction in the form `LDRI  r1, [r2]` to provide memory indirect addressing (i.e., pointer-based or indexed addressing).

In this case, register `r1` is loaded with the contents of memory pointed at by register `r2`. If the pointer register contains an invalid value that is outside the range of legal addresses, the program will crash. By testing the index, we can ensure that an out-of-range index is detected. Note that only the first source register, `rS1`, is ever used as a memory pointer:

```
def testIndex():                          # Test for register or memory index out of range
    if (rD > 7) or (rS1 > 7) or (rS2 > 7): # Ensure register numbers are in the range 0 to 7
        print('Register number error')
        sys.exit()                        # Call operating system to leave the Python program
    if mnemonic in ['LDRI', 'STRI']:      # Memory index testing only for memory load and store
        if r[rS1] > len(m) - 1:           # Test rS1 contents are less than memory size
            print(' Memory index error')
            sys.exit()
    return()
```

General comments

The following line demonstrates how we extract the operation class from the mnemonic. The expression looks strange because of the () and [] parentheses. The `codes.get(key)` operation uses `key` to get the associated value from the `codes` dictionary:

```
opClass = codes.get(mnemonic)[0]       # Use mnemonic to read opClass from the codes dictionary
```

In this case, the key is the mnemonic, and the value returned is the operation class; for example, if the mnemonic is `'LDRL'`, the corresponding value is `[3]`. Note that the value returned is not 3! It is a *list* with the single value 3. Consequently, we have to extract the value from the list by specifying the first item, that is, `mnemonic[0]`.

There are many ways to build an instruction. In TC1, we create a binary value, just like a real assembler. In TC1$_{mini}$, we directly execute the instruction from the assembly language form. So, when we compile the instructions, we create a program in text form. To do that, we need to combine the label, mnemonic, registers, and literal into a list.

The code to do that is as follows:

```
thisLine = list((i,label,mnemonic,predicate,opClass))
                                    # Combine the component parts in a list
prog.append(thisLine)               # Add the new line to the existing program
```

In this example, we use the `list()` function to combine items into a list, and then we use `append()` to add this item to an existing list. Note the syntax of `list()`. You might expect it to be `list(a,b,c)`. No. It's `list((a,b,c))`. The `list()` function uses parentheses as normal but the list itself must be in parentheses. That's because the list items constitute a *single* parameter to list.

The TC1$_{tiny}$ code listing

This is the listing of the cut-down version of TC1. Instructions fall into eight classes depending on the number and arrangements of operands. Each instruction is in a dictionary, `codes`, which provides the class number that is used to decode operands. The instruction itself is executed directly from its mnemonic. Unlike TC1, there is no intermediate binary code. Similarly, both register names and indirect register names are in dictionaries to simplify instruction decoding:

```
# Simple CPU instruction interpreter. Direct instruction interpretation. 30 September 2022. V1.0
# Class 0: no operand                NOP
# Class 1: literal                   BEQ  3
# Class 2: register                  INC  r1
# Class 3: register,literal          LDRL r1,5
# Class 4: register,register,        MOV  r1,r2
# Class 5: register,register,literal ADDL r1,r2,5
# Class 6: register,register,register ADD  r1,r2,r3
# Class 7: register,[register]       LDRI r1,[r2]
import sys                           #NEW
codes = {'NOP':[0],'STOP':[0],'END':[0],'ERR':[0], 'BEQ':[1],'BNE':[1], \
         'BRA':[1],'INC':[2],'DEC':[2],'NOT':[2],'CMPL':[3],'LDRL':[3], \
         'DBNE':[3],'MOV':[4],'CMP':[4],'SUBL':[5],'ADDL':[5],'ANDL':[5], \
         'ADD':[6],'SUB':[6],'AND':[6],'OR':[6],'LDRI':[7],'STRI':[7]}

reg1  = {'r0':0,    'r1':1,    'r2':2,   'r3':3,    'r4':4,    'r5':5, \
         'r6':6,    'r7':7}                         # Registers
reg2  = {'[r0]':0, '[r1]':1, '[r2]':2,'[r3]':3, '[r4]':4, \
         '[r5]':5,  '[r6]':6,'[r7]':7}              # Pointer registers
symTab = {}                                         # Symbol table
r = [0] * 8                                         # Register set
m = [0] * 8
prog = [] * 32                                      # Program memory

def equates():                                      # Process directives and delete from source
```

```
global symTab, sFile
for i in range (0,len(sFile)):          # Deal with equates
    tempLine = sFile[i].split()
    if len(tempLine) > 2 and tempLine[1] == 'EQU':
                                        # If line > 2 tokens and second EQU
        print('SYMB' , sFile[i])
        symTab[tempLine[0]] = tempLine[2]  # Put third token EQU in symbol table
sFile = [ i for i in sFile if i.count('EQU') == 0] # Remove all lines with 'EQU'
print('Symbol table ', symTab, '\n')
return()
```

This section deals with decoding instructions into the appropriate task in order to correctly execute them with the appropriate parameters:

```
def classDecode(predicate):
    lit,rD,rS1,rS2 = '',0,0,0                          # Initialize variables
    if opClass in [1]:      lit =  predicate
    if opClass in [2]:      rD  = reg1[predicate]
    if opClass in [3,4,5,6,7]:
        predicate = predicate.split(',')
        rD = reg1[predicate[0]]
    if opClass in [4,5,6]:  rS1 = reg1[predicate[1]] \
                                            # Get source reg 1 for classes 4, 5, and 6
    if opClass in [3,5]:    lit = (predicate[-1])      # Get literal for classes 3 and 5
    if opClass in [6]:      rS2 = reg1[predicate[2]]   # Get source reg 2 for class 6
    if opClass in [7]:      rS1 = reg2[predicate[1]]   # Get source pointer reg for class 7
    return(lit,rD,rS1,rS2)
```

Unlike TC1, we perform a little testing on the input, for example, whether the memory or register index is out of range. This is simply an illustrative example of data validation:

```
def testLine(tokens):     # Check there's a valid instruction in this line
    error = 1
    if len(tokens) == 1:
        if tokens[0] in codes: error = 0
    else:
        if (tokens[0] in codes) or (tokens[1] in codes): error = 0
    return(error)
    def testIndex():                        # Test for reg or memory index out of range
    print('rD,rS1 =', rD,rS1, 'r[rS1] =', r[rS1], 'len(m)', len(m),\
    'mnemonic =', mnemonic)
    if rD > 7 or rS1 > 7 or rS2 > 7:
        print('Register number error')
        sys.exit()                          # Exit program on register error
```

```
    if mnemonic in ['LDRI', 'STRI']:
        if r[rS1] > len(m) - 1:
            print(' Memory index error')
            sys.exit()                                        # Exit program on pointer error
    return()


def getLit(litV):                                             # Extract a literal (convert formats)
    if litV == '': return(0)                                  # Return 0 if literal field empty
    if  litV in symTab:                        # Look in symbol table and get value if there
        litV = symTab[litV]                                   # Read the symbol value as a string
        lit = int(litV)                                       # Convert string to integer
    elif  litV[0]    == '%': lit = int(litV[1:],2)    # If % convert binary to int
    elif  litV[0:1]  == '$': lit = int(litV[1:],16)   # If first symbol $, convert hex to int
    elif  litV[0]    == '-':
        lit = (-int(litV[1:]))&0xFFFF                         # Deal with negative values
    elif  litV.isnumeric():  lit = int(litV)                  # Convert decimal string to integer
    else:                    lit = 0                          # Default value 0 (if all else fails)
    return(lit)


prgN = 'E://ArchitectureWithPython//NewIdeas_1.txt'  # prgN = program name: test file
sFile = [ ]                                          # sFile source data
with open(prgN,'r') as prgN:                         # Open it and read it
    prgN = prgN.readlines()
for i in range(0,len(prgN)):                         # First level of text-processing
    prgN[i] = prgN[i].replace('\n','')               # Remove newline code in source
    prgN[i] = ' '.join(prgN[i].split())              # Remove multiple spaces
    prgN[i] = prgN[i].strip()                         # First strip spaces
prgN = [i.split('@')[0] for i in prgN]               # Remove comment fields
while '' in prgN: prgN.remove('')                    # Remove blank lines
for i in range(0,len(prgN)):                         # Copy source to sFile: stop on END
    sFile.append(prgN[i])                            # Build new source text file sFile
    if 'END' in sFile[i]: break           # Leave on 'END' and ignore any more source text


for i in range(0,len(sFile)): print(sFile[i])
print()


equates()                                            # Deal with equates
for i in range(0,len(sFile)): print(sFile[i])
print()


for i in range(0,len(sFile)):             # We need to compile a list of labels
    label = ''                            # Give each line a default empty label
    predicate = ''                        # Create default predicate (label + mnemonic + predicate)
```

```
    tokens = sFile[i].split(' ')          # Split into separate groups

    error = testLine(tokens)              # Test for an invalid instruction
    if error == 1:                        # If error found
        print('Illegal instruction', tokens, 'at',i)
        sys.exit()                        # Exit program

    numTokens = len(tokens)               # Process this line
    if numTokens == 1: mnemonic = tokens[0]
    if numTokens > 1:
        if tokens[0][-1] == ':':
            symTab.update({tokens[0][0:-1]:i})      # Insert new value and line number
            label = tokens[0][0:-1]
            mnemonic = tokens[1]
        else: mnemonic = tokens[0]
        predicate = tokens[-1]
    opClass = codes.get(mnemonic)[0]  # Use the mnemonic to read opClass from codes dictionary
    thisLine = list((i,label,mnemonic,predicate,opClass))
    prog.append(thisLine)                 # Program line + label + mnemonic + predicate + opClass
print('Symbol table ', symTab, '\n')  # Display symbol table for equates and line labels
```

The following is the actual instruction execution loop. As you can see, it is remarkably compact:

```
                                      # Instruction execution
run = 1
z = 0
pc = 0
while run == 1:
    thisOp = prog[pc]
    if thisOp[2] in ['STOP', 'END']: run = 0 # Terminate on STOP or END (comment on this)
    pcOld = pc
    pc = pc + 1
    mnemonic  = thisOp[2]
    predicate = thisOp[3]
    opClass   = thisOp[4]
    lit,rD,rS1,rS2 = classDecode(predicate)
    lit = getLit(lit)

    if    mnemonic == 'NOP': pass
    elif mnemonic == 'BRA': pc = lit
    elif mnemonic == 'BEQ':
        if z == 1: pc = lit
    elif mnemonic == 'BNE':
        if z == 0: pc = lit
```

```
elif mnemonic == 'INC': r[rD] = r[rD] + 1
elif mnemonic == 'DEC':
    z = 0
    r[rD] = r[rD] - 1
    if r[rD] == 0: z = 1
elif mnemonic == 'NOT': r[rD] = (~r[rD])&0xFFFF   # Logical NOT
elif mnemonic == 'CMPL':
    z = 0
    diff = r[rD] - lit
    if diff == 0: z = 1
elif mnemonic == 'LDRL': r[rD] = lit

elif mnemonic == 'DBNE':
    r[rD] = r[rD] - 1
    if r[rD] != 0: pc = lit
elif mnemonic == 'MOV':  r[rD] = r[rS1]
elif mnemonic == 'CMP':
    z = 0
    diff = r[rD] - r[rS1]
    if diff == 0: z = 1
elif mnemonic == 'ADDL': r[rD] = r[rS1] + lit
elif mnemonic == 'SUBL': r[rD] = r[rS1] - lit
elif mnemonic == 'ADD':  r[rD] = r[rS1] + r[rS2]
elif mnemonic == 'SUB':  r[rD] = r[rS1] - r[rS2]
elif mnemonic == 'AND':  r[rD] = r[rS1] & r[rS2]
elif mnemonic == 'OR':   r[rD] = r[rS1] | r[rS2]
elif mnemonic == 'LDRI':
    testIndex()
    r[rD] = m[r[rS1]]
elif mnemonic == 'STRI':
    testIndex()
    m[r[rS1]] = r[rD]

regs = ' '.join('%04x' % b for b in r)          # Format memory location's hex
mem  = ' '.join('%04x' % b for b in m)          # Format register's hex
print('pc =','{:<3}'.format(pcOld),'{:<18}'.format(sFile[pcOld]),\
      'regs =',regs,'Mem =',mem,'z =',z)
```

The code execution loop, like most of the simulators we discuss, is remarkably straightforward. The current instruction is fetched and decoded into mnemonic, class, and register numbers. The program counter is advanced and the mnemonic is presented to a series of then...elif statements.

Many of the instructions are executed in only one line of code; for example, ADD is implemented by adding two registers together: r[rD] = r[rS1] + r[rS2]. Some instructions, such as compare, require two registers to be subtracted and then the status bits to be set accordingly.

We included one relatively complex instruction, decrement and branch on not zero, which decrements a register and then branches to a target address if the register has not counted down to 0.

In the final section, we will look at yet another variation of TC1.

TC1 postscript mark II

If one postscript is good, two are even better. We've added this second variation on a theme to demonstrate some different ways of doing things. Much of the program's structure is the same as before. The features are as follows:

- Direct execution (revisited)
- The ability to avoid different mnemonics (e.g., ADD and ADDL) for the same basic operation

The principal enhancement is the way to handle instructions and decode them. In TC1, we use a 4-bit code to define the structure of each instruction in terms of its parameters. When a mnemonic is looked up in the dictionary, it returns a code giving the required parameters.

One feature (problem?) with TC1 is that we have different mnemonics for variations on an instruction, for example, ADD and ADDL. The suffix L tells the assembler that a literal operand (rather than a register number) is required. In this example, we avoid different instruction formats and use a single mnemonic by putting instructions into classes. Each class defines an instruction format, ranging from class 0 (instruction with no parameters) to class 9 (instruction with *four* registers).

This example uses the direct execution of an instruction. That is, we don't compile an instruction into binary and then execute the binary. We execute an instruction directly from its mnemonic.

A consequence of this arrangement is that an instruction may fall into multiple classes; for example, LDR is in *three* classes, rather than having the LDR, LDRL, and LDRI variants. When an instruction is encountered, it is checked against each class. If the mnemonic is in a class, the attributes of the instruction are checked before deciding whether we've found the correct class.

Consider ADD. We can write ADD r1,r2,5 or ADD r1,r2,r3; that is, the second number added to a register may be a literal or a register. Consequently, ADD is in class 5 and class 6. To resolve the ambiguity, we look at the final operand; if it's a literal, then it's class 5, and if it's a register, it's class 6.

Testing for a register is easy because we've put registers in a dictionary, so it's necessary only to check whether the final operand is in the dictionary or not. Consider class 3:

```
if (mnemonic in class3) and (predLen == 2) and (predicate[1] not in regList)
```

Here, we do a triple test. First, we check whether the mnemonic is in class 3. Then, we test the predicate length (it's 2 for two operands, such as CMP r1,5). Finally, we test for a numeric second operand by ensuring that the operand is not in the list of registers.

The Python program for this experiment is as follows.

```
# Instruction formats
# NOP                  # class 0
# BRA  4               # Class 1
# INC  r1              # class 2
# LDR  r1,#4           # class 3
# MOV  r1,r2           # class 4
# ADD  r1,r2,5         # class 5
# ADD  r1,r2,r3        # class 6
# LDR  r1,[r2]         # class 7
# LDR  r1,[r2],4       # class 8
# MLA  r1,r2,r3,r4 # class 9 [r1] = [r2] + [r3] * [r3]

def getLit(lit):                              # Extract a literal
    if     lit in symTab:    literal = symTab[lit] \
                                  # Look in symbol table and get if there
        elif   lit        == '%': literal = iint(lit[1:],2) \
                                  # If first symbol is %, convert binary to integer
        elif   lit[0:1]   == '$': literal = int(lit[1:],16) \
                                  # If first symbol is $, convert hex to integer
        elif   lit[0]     == '-': literal = i(-int(lit[1:]))&0xFFFF \
                                  # Deal with negative values
        elif   lit.isnumeric(): literal = iint(lit) \
                                  # If number is a decimal string, then convert to integer
        else:                    literal = 0 # Default value 0 if all else fails
        return(literal)

regList = {'r0':0,'r1':1,'r2':2,'r3':3,'r4':4,'r5':5,'r6':6,'r7':7}
iRegList = {'[r0]':0,'[r1]':1,'[r2]':2,'[r3]':3,'[r4]':4,'[r5]':5, \
            '[r6]':6,'[r7]':7}
class0 = ['NOP','STOP','RTS']                 # none
class1 = ['BRA','BEQ', 'BSR']                 # register
class2 = ['INC', 'DEC']                       # register
class3 = ['LDR', 'STR','CMP','DBNE','LSL','LSR','ROR']   # register, literal
class4 = ['MOV','CMP','ADD']                  # register, register Note ADD r1,r2
class5 = ['ADD','SUB']                        # register, register, literal
class6 = ['ADD', 'SUB']                       # register, register, register
class7 = ['LDR','STR']                        # register, pointer
class8 = ['LDR','STR']                        # register, pointer, literal
class9 = ['MLA']                              # register, register, register, register

inputSource = 0                               # Manual (keyboard) input if 0; file input if 1
singleStep  = 0                               # Select single-step mode or execute all-to-end mode
```

```
x = input('file input? type y or n ')       # Ask for file input (y) or keyboard input (any key)
if x == 'y':
    inputSource = 1
    x = input('Single step type y ')         # Type 'y' for single-step mode
    if x == 'y': singleStep = 1
    with open('C:/Users/AlanClements/Desktop/c.txt','r') as fileData:
        fileData = fileData.readlines()
    for i in range (0,len(fileData)):         # Remove leading and trailing spaces
        fileData[i] = fileData[i].strip()

r =      [0] * 8                              # Eight registers
m =      [0] * 16                             # 16 memory locations
stack = [0] * 8                               # Stack for return addresses (BSR/RTS)
prog =   []  * 64                             # Program memory
progDisp = [] * 64                            # Program for display
symTab = {}                                   # Symbol table for symbolic name to value binding
run = True
pc = 0                                        # Clear program counter
sp = 7                                        # Set stack pointer to bottom of stack
while run == True:                            # Program processing loop
    predicate = []                            # Dummy
    if inputSource == 1:                      # Get instruction from file
        line = fileData[pc]
    else: line = input('>> > ')               # Or input instruction from keyboard
    if line == '':
        run = False
        break
    line = ' '.join(line.split())             # Remove multiple spaces. Uses join and split
    progDisp.append(line)                     # Make a copy of this line for later display
    line = line.replace(',',' ')
    line = line.split(' ')                    # Split instruction into tokens
    if (len(line) > 1) and (line[0][-1] == ':'): # Look for a label (token 0 ending in :)
        label = line[0]
        symTab[line[0]] = pc                  # Put a label in symTab alongside the pc
    else:
        line.insert(0,'    :')                # If no label+, insert a dummy one (for pretty printing)
    mnemonic  = line[1]                       # Get the mnemonic, second token
    predicate = line[2:]                      # What's left is the predicate (registers and literal)

    prog.append(line)                         # Append the line to the program
    pc = pc + 1                               # And bump up the program counter
    progLength = pc - 1                       # Record the total number of instructions
for i in range (0,pc-1):
```

```
    print('pc =', f'{i:3}', (' ').join(prog[i]))  # Print the program
print('Symbol table =', symTab, '\n')      # Display the symbol table
pc = 0
run = True
z = 0
c = 0
classNim = 10
while run == True:                         # Program execution loop
    instruction = prog[pc]
    pcOld = pc
    pc = pc + 1
    if instruction[1] == 'STOP':           # Halt on STOP instruction
        print('End of program exit')
        break
    mnemonic  = instruction[1]
    predicate = instruction[2:]

    predLen   = len(predicate)
    if (predLen > 0) and (mnemonic not in class1): rD = regList[predicate[0]]
                                    # Get rD for classes 2 to 8
```

In this simulator, we deal with instructions by class rather than by mnemonic. This feature means that the same mnemonic can have different addressing modes, such as literal, register, or even memory. The first class, 0, is reserved for mnemonics with no operands, such as NOP. Of course, this mechanism would make it possible to invent a new operation, such as, say, NOP 4, that acts in a different way:

```
    if mnemonic in class0:               # Deal with instructions by their group (class)
        classNum = 0
        if mnemonic == 'NOP': pass
        if mnemonic == 'RTS':            # Return from subroutine pull address off the stack
            pc = stack[sp]
            sp = sp + 1

    if mnemonic in class1:               # Class deals with branch operations so get literal
        classNum = 1
        literal = getLit(predicate[0])
        if   mnemonic == 'BRA': pc = literal
        elif mnemonic == 'BEQ':
            if z == 1: pc = literal
        elif mnemonic == 'BSR':          # Deal with subroutine call
            sp = sp - 1                  # Push return address on the stack
            stack[sp] = pc
            pc = literal
```

```
if mnemonic in class2:                      # Class 2 increment and decrement so get register
    classNum = 2
    if mnemonic == 'INC': r[rD] = r[rD] + 1
    if mnemonic == 'DEC':
        r[rD] = r[rD] - 1
        if r[rD] == 0: z = 1                 # Decrement sets z flag
        else: z = 0


if (mnemonic in class3) and (predLen == 2) and \
(predicate[1] not in regList):
    classNum = 3
    literal = getLit(predicate[-1])
    if mnemonic == 'CMP':
        diff = r[rD] - literal
        if diff == 0: z = 1
        else:         z = 0
    elif mnemonic == 'LDR': r[rD] = literal
    elif mnemonic == 'STR': m[literal] = r[rD]
    elif mnemonic == 'DBNE':
        r[rD] = r[rD] - 1
        if r[rD] != 0: pc = literal          # Note we don't use z flag
    elif mnemonic == 'LSL':
        for i in range(0,literal):
            c = ((0x8000) & r[rD]) >> 16
            r[rD] = (r[rD] << 1) & 0xFFFF    # Shift left and constrain to 16 bits
    elif mnemonic == 'LSR':
        for i in range(0,literal):
            c = ((0x0001) & r[rD])
            r[rD] = r[rD] >> 1
    elif mnemonic == 'ROR':
        for i in range(0,literal):
            c = ((0x0001) & r[rD])
            r[rD] = r[rD] >> 1
            r[rD] = r[rD] | (c << 15)


if (mnemonic in class4) and (predLen == 2) and (predicate[1]\
in regList):                                 #
    classNum = 4
    rS1 = regList[predicate[1]]              # Get second register
    if mnemonic == 'MOV':                    # Move source register to destination register
        r[rD] = r[rS1]
    elif mnemonic == 'CMP':
        diff = r[rD] -  r[rS1]
```

```
            if diff == 0: z = 1
            else:         z = 0
        elif mnemonic == 'ADD':                    # Add source to destination register
            r[rD] = r[rD] + r[rS1]


if (mnemonic in class5) and (predLen == 3) and (predicate[2] not\
in regList):
        classNum = 5                               # Class 5 is register with literal operand
        literal = getLit(predicate[2])
        rS1 = regList[predicate[1]]
        if   mnemonic == 'ADD': r[rD] = r[rS1] + literal
        elif mnemonic == 'SUB': r[rD] = r[rS1] - literal


if (mnemonic in class6) and (predLen == 3) and (predicate[-1]\
in regList):
        classNum = 6                               # Class 6 uses three registers
        rS1 = regList[predicate[1]]
        rS2 = regList[predicate[2]]
        if   mnemonic == 'ADD': r[rD] = r[rS1] + r[rS2]
        elif mnemonic == 'SUB': r[rD] = r[rS1] - r[rS2]


if (mnemonic in class7) and (predLen == 2) and (predicate[1]\
in iRegList):
        classNum = 7                               # Class 7 uses a pointer register with load and store
        pReg  = predicate[1]
        pReg1 = iRegList[pReg]
        pReg2 = r[pReg1]
        if   mnemonic == 'LDR': r[rD] = m[pReg2]
        elif mnemonic == 'STR': m[pReg2] = r[rD]


if (mnemonic in class8) and (predLen == 3):
        classNum = 8                               # Class 8 uses a pointer register and a literal offset
        pReg  = predicate[1]
        pReg1 = iRegList[pReg]
        pReg2 = r[pReg1]
        literal = getLit(predicate[2])
        if   mnemonic == 'LDR': r[rD] = m[pReg2 + literal]
        elif mnemonic == 'STR': m[pReg2 + literal] = r[rD]


if mnemonic in class9:                             # Class 9 demonstrates a 4-operand instruction
        classNum = 9
        if mnemonic == 'MLA':
            rS1 = regList[predicate[1]]
```

```
            rS2 = regList[predicate[2]]
            rS3 = regList[predicate[3]]
            r[rD] = r[rS1] * r[rS2] + r[rS3]

    pInst = ' '.join(instruction)           ##############
    Regs = ' '.join('%04x' % i for i in r)


    print('pc {:<2}'.format(pcOld),'Class =', classNum,      \
          '{:<20}'.format(pInst),'Regs: ', regs, 'Mem', m,   \
          'r[0] =', '{:016b}'.format(r[0]),                   \
          'c =', c, 'z =', z, '\n')
    print(progDisp[pcOld])
    if singleStep == 1: input(' >>> ')
```

The purpose of the previous program is to demonstrate another way of categorizing instructions and using the number of operands to distinguish between instruction types, such as ADD r1,r2 and ADD r1,r2,r3.

Summary

In this chapter, we presented the TC1 simulator, which can take a text file in TC1 assembly language, convert it into machine code, and then execute it. TC1's instruction set architecture is close to the classic RISC architecture with a register-to-register architecture (i.e., data operations take place on the contents of registers). The only memory operations permitted are loading a register from memory (or a literal) and storing a register in memory.

The simulator has two basic components: an assembler that translates a mnemonic such as ADD r1,r2,r3 into a 32-bit binary instruction, and an interpreter that reads the instruction, extracts the necessary information, and then executes the instruction.

Some of the elements of TC1 are rather unusual. A free-format structure for the source code is provided; for example, you can write ADD r1,r2,r3 or adD R1 r2 r3 and both instructions will be happily accepted. Why? First, it was done to demonstrate the use of string processing in Python. Second, it makes it easier for the user to enter input in their chosen case. All input is automatically converted into uppercase to make the language case-free. Similarly, a comma or space is allowed as a separator between parameters. Finally, the need for [] brackets to indicate indirect addressing was removed. Users may enter LDRI r0, [r1] or LDRI r0,r1.

Similarly, numbers can be entered in different forms (decimal, binary, or hexadecimal); for example, number bases can be indicated in *Motorola format* or *Python format*. Most real assemblers don't permit such luxury.

The first versions of TC1 required all addresses to be numeric; if you wanted to branch to line 30, you had to write BRA 30. It was the remarkable power and ease of use of Python's dictionary structure that made it so easy to include labels. All you have to do is recognize a label, pop it in the dictionary together with its value, and then, whenever you encounter that label, just look up its value in the dictionary.

We also provided an example assembly language program to test TC1 and a short discussion of how we go about testing various instructions.

Having designed TC1, we created a rather simplified version and called it TC1$_{mini}$. This simulator does not provide the same flexibility in writing instructions, and it does not have a large instruction set. It also does not encode the instruction into a binary form and then decode it again and execute it. It executes the assembly instruction directly (thanks one more to Python's dictionary mechanism).

At the end of this chapter, we provided yet another simplified computer simulator to both emphasize the structure of a computer simulator and provide an example of the way in which you can modify the basic design.

In this key chapter, we introduced the TC1 computer simulator and presented its design. We also looked at variations of TC1 to help create a more complete picture of the simulator and assembler. In the next chapter, we will take things a step further and look at some more aspects of the simulator. We will describe several simulators that have different architectures.

7
Extending the TC1

In this chapter, you will learn how to expand the functionality of the TC1 simulator that we designed in *Chapter 6*. We also look at some of the elements of the design of a simulator, including input/output techniques and data validation, and describe how the simulator can display the state of a processor as it executes instructions.

TC1 is a compromise. Initially, it was designed to support teaching the basics of computer architecture. It is an aid to understanding instruction encoding, instruction format trade-offs, the execution of an instruction, addressing modes, and the ability to design and implement an instruction set.

Here, we look at ways of expanding TC1 by, for example, discussing how new instructions can be added. Finally, we deal with a topic that we have omitted so far: how to create a computer architecture with variable-length instructions. That is, individual instructions can be an integer multiple of the basic word length.

The TC1 CPU simulator executes instructions one by one and prints the contents of the registers, program counter, and status flags after each instruction is executed. You can use this information to debug assembly-level programs. Often, when you look at the data, you find that the results are not what was expected; for example, you might want to execute a loop 9 times but execute it 10 times because you made an error in testing for the end of the loop.

We have three issues to deal with. The first is displaying the data. How do we display the data and how do we format it? Should the contents of a register be displayed as a decimal value, a binary string of 1s and 0s, or as hexadecimal characters?

Another design issue is whether to store historic data. That is, do we store the registers and flags after each instruction has been executed in an array so that we can look at values in previous operations?

Finally, how do we proceed? The TC1 simulator executes an instruction every time the *Enter* key is pressed. This provides a great way of stepping through a program but becomes infeasible when a loop requires 1,000 instructions to be executed before you get to the part of the program of interest. We will demonstrate how you can leave the single-step mode, execute a batch of instructions, and return to the single-step mode.

Technical requirements

You can find the programs used in this chapter on GitHub at https://github.com/PacktPublishing/Computer-Architecture-with-Python-and-ARM/tree/main/Chapter07.

Another look at python's input and output

Here, we go into a little more detail about data input and output mechanisms, as these topics are so important in the design of a simulator because formatting data is all-important to the interpretation of the data.

Let's have another look at input in Python. Inputting data from the keyboard is very easy. To input text, you write x = input() and that's it. When this statement is encountered, Python waits for your input. You enter the text and terminate it with a return (*Enter* key). If you just enter a return without text, the value of x will be a null string – that is, ''. The data you input is stored in text form.

Python lets you display a prompt before receiving the input; for example, you can write the following:

```
x = input('Please enter your age')
```

Because the input is in character form, you must convert numeric values into integer form before using them. It's easy to perform conversions into decimal, binary, or hexadecimal, as the following examples show. You just add the number base as a second parameter to the int() function:

```
x = input('Enter the constant ')
y = int(x)                          # For a decimal constant
y = int(x,2)                        # For a binary constant
y = int(x,16)                       # For a hexadecimal constant
```

Let's consider a more sophisticated example. We'll input an instruction such as ADD R3,R7,$12FA and extract the three integers 3, 7, and 0x12FA. In this example, a $ prefix indicates a hexadecimal value (a convention used by Motorola).

The following code performs this operation. The input uses a replace function to convert all commas into spaces. We combine the replace operation with the input operation to create compact code. The input is followed by a split function to convert the string into tokens:

```
inst        = input('Enter operation: >>').replace(',',' ')
p           = inst.split(' ')
t1,t2,t3,t4 = p[0],int(p[1][1:]),int(p[2][1:]),int(p[3][1:],16)
```

Finally, we examine each of the four tokens in turn and extract the parameter as an integer (t1, t2, t3, and t4). Consider t4. The p[3] expression extracts the "$12FA" string. The second index, [1:], extracts all characters after the first one to give "12FA". This is still a character string. The final operation, int(p[3][1:],16), converts the parameter string in hexadecimal form into the integer 4858. The output produced by a second example, ADD r3,r7,$1102, was ADD 3 7 4354.

As we've already seen, Python lets you put several equates on a line – for example, a,b,c = p,q,r. This results in the following:

```
a = p
b = q
c = r
```

This shorthand is useful when dealing with simple equates (usually during an initialization process). Some programmers prefer not to use this technique as it can reduce program readability. Let's test the preceding fragment of code. We've added some `print` statements between the operations so that we can follow what's going on as the code is executed:

```
inst = input('Enter operation: >>').replace(',',' ')
print('inst',inst)
p = inst.split(' ')
print ('p',p)
t1,t2,t3,t4 = p[0],int(p[1][1:]),int(p[2][1:]),int(p[3][1:],16)
print(,t1,t2,t3,t4',t1,t2,t3,t4)
```

The output is next. Note that when we print `t1` to `t4`, the numeric value of the hexadecimal operand is given in its decimal form:

```
Enter operation: >>add r1,r2,$FACE
inst add r1 r2 $FACE
p ['add', 'r1', 'r2', '$FACE']
t1,t2,t3,t4 add 1 2 64206
```

The next section looks at how we format data such as numbers so that they can be made much easier for the reader to understand; for example, sometimes you might wish to represent the decimal 42 as `101010` and sometimes as `00101010` or `002A`.

Displaying data

We now look more deeply at the ways in which data can be displayed in Python. When you are observing the execution of a program, you want to see what has changed after each instruction has been executed. A computer's state is determined by the contents of its registers and memory, the program counter, and its status bits, plus its memory.

How do we display data? Since data can represent anything you want it to, the data in a register has no intrinsic meaning. By convention, CPU simulators represent data in hexadecimal form. This is partially because each 16-bit register holds 4 hexadecimal characters and that provides a rather convenient way for humans to handle data (try remembering 16-bit strings of 1s and 0s). Some simulators permit binary, hex, or decimal displays, and others allow data to be displayed as characters (i.e., the data is assumed to be ASCII-encoded).

As well as choosing the base in which we display numbers, we must choose the formatting in order to make it easy to read (e.g., aligning groups of characters). Like all high-level computer languages, Python provides ways of formatting printed data. And like formatting in most other languages, I am tempted to describe Python's formatting as a bit inelegant.

We do not have the space to do justice to Python's formatting here. We simply provide some examples and enough information for you to modify them.

One thing we need to print in a simulator is the instruction. That could not be simpler because it's a string. So, we can write the following:

```
print(listing[pcOld])          # Listing contains a list of string instructions
```

This looks up the string item (instruction) at the pcOld address and prints it. Since pc is modified during an instruction cycle, we print the old value at the start of the current cycle.

But each instruction is going to be of a different length (depending on the number of operands), and that means the next item printed on the same line will not be vertically aligned. We often need to print the instruction within a predefined frame. We can do this with the following:

```
print("{:<23}".format(listing[pcOld]))
```

We are using the .format() method. The "{:<23}" expression controls the format. The integer 23 is the width of the text in characters. The < symbol indicates that the string is left-justified. If we'd wanted it right-justified, we would have used >. The value following format() is the string to be printed.

Suppose we want to display the eight registers on the same line, each as a six-character hexadecimal value. First, consider the following Python code:

```
z = 0x4ace             # The hex data to print
print("%06x" %z)       # Printing it in 6 chars with leading zeros
```

When executed, this code prints the following:

```
004ace
```

We set up a variable, z, for the 0x4ace hexadecimal value and use print("%06x" %z) to display it as hex characters. The printed value is 004ace because two leading zeros have been inserted. The formatting mechanism is "%06x" %z. The first component, "%06x", specifies the format of the six-digit hex value that follows. It's the first % that indicates the formatting. %z indicates the value to be printed.

The escape character

Python's print mechanism is easy to use; for example, print('Answer =', a) displays anything in quotes as a literal, and the value of any variables that appear in the print statement. You can have as many quoted items and variables as you want.

The print statement also allows formatting by using an *escape character* that gives the following character a special meaning. In Python, the escape character is ' \ '. If the escape is followed by 'n', it is equivalent to a new line; if the escape is followed by 't', it is equivalent to a tab. Consider the following:

```
a = 42
b = 'Test'
print('a is the integer\t',a,'\nb is the string','\t',b)
```

The output from this code is as follows:

```
a is the integer         42
b is the string          Test
```

Note how this has been printed on two lines due to `'\n'` and the two values tabbed by `'\t'`. You can control the size of the tab, as the following example shows. The `expandtabs()` method sets the tab width (number of spaces) to the parameter provided. In this case, we have embedded the tab into a string and set the tab width to 6:

```
print('This is a\ttab\ttest'.expandtabs(6))
This is a    tab   test
```

Some of the other escape sequences are as follows:

- `\'`   Single quote
- `\\`   Backslash
- `\r`   Enter (return)
- `\b`   Backspace
- `\f`   Form feed (move to the same spot on the line below)
- `\xhh`   Hexadecimal character value (e.g., `\x41` would print A because `0x41` is the ASCII value for A)

Escaping the escape

There are occasions when you wish to escape the escape character and use the backslash as a printable character. In that case, you precede the string to be printed with either r or R. Note the r letter goes outside the string quotation marks, as in this example:

```
print(R'test\n one', 'test\n two')
```

This results in the following:

```
test\n one test
 two
```

In this example, we use R to suppress `\n` as a newline command and print the actual `\n`. The second `\n` is not preceded by R and therefore acts as the newline command.

To and from ASCII

I was lucky enough to be around at the birth of the microprocessor and I built a Motorola 6000 microprocessor system from the individual chips (including the display). At that time, I did not have any commercial software and I had to convert between ASCII characters and their numeric values myself. Life is easier today. Python provides two functions that allow you to convert between numeric and ASCII values. These are `ord()` and `chr()`. If you write `x = ord('B')`, the value of x would be its ASCII equivalent, `0x42` or `01000010` in binary. Similarly, if you write `y = chr(0x41)`, the value of y would be `'A'`.

Binary and hexadecimal strings

Before we look at formatted strings in detail, consider the following simple example of console input using the Python interpreter. The text in bold is the output:

```
>>> x = 12345
>>> y = hex(x)
>>> print(y)
0x3039
>>> z = y + 1
TypeError: can only concatenate str (not "int") to str
>>> z = int(y,16) + 1
>>> print(z)
12346
>>> print(hex(z))
0x303a
```

We create an x variable equal to 12345 and create a new y value that is the hex version of x. Then, we print it and get the expected result of 0x3039. Next, we create a new variable, z, where z = y + 1. This generates an error message because y is a text string and we cannot add the integer 1 to it. In the next line, we perform the addition again, but this time, we convert the hex string into integer form with int(y,16). Now, we can print z as a decimal integer or as a hexadecimal string using print(hex(z)). In short, Python makes it easy to handle decimal, hexadecimal, and binary values, but you must be very careful to remember to ensure that you convert between string and integer forms where necessary.

Because we are dealing with binary numbers, it makes sense to display the output of TC1 in binary or hexadecimal formats. Suppose we wish to convert a decimal integer value into a *binary* string. Consider the following where we convert an integer, p, into a binary string and then print it:

```
p = 1022
q = "{0:b}".format(p)
print('p in decimal is',p, "and in binary, it's",q)
```

The "{0:b}" expression is the key to the formatting. It is a string enclosed in curly brackets. 0 tells it to print from the first character of the string and b signifies binary. This produces the following output:

p in decimal is 1022 and in binary, it's 1111111110

So far, so good. But what if we want the output to be justified with a fixed number of characters – for example, 16? The following demonstrates such formatting when we convert 26 and 2033 into binary format:

```
p1, p2 = 26, 2033
q1 = "{0:16b}".format(p1)
q2 = "{0:16b}".format(p2)
print('p1 is',q1, '\nand p2 is',q2)
```

The only change to the format string is from "{0:b}" to "{0:16b}". That is, we have inserted the field-width of 16 characters before b. The effect of 16 is to define a 16-bit width for the string. The string is padded with spaces on the left. The output of this code is as follows:

```
p1 is            11010
p2 is      11111110001
```

In a lot of computer texts, it is normal to pad binary and decimal values with leading zeros on the left, rather than spaces. We can do this with a small change in the format. We insert 0 before the field width – that is, "{0:016b}". Now consider the following:

```
p1, p2 = 26, 2033
q1 = "{0:016b}".format(p1)
q2 = "{0:016b}".format(p2)
print('p1 is',q1, '\nand p2 is',q2)
```

This gives an output where the numbers are displayed in 16 bits and padded with leading zeros, as follows:

```
p1 is 0000000000011010
p2 is 0000011111110001
```

Hexadecimal values are treated in the same way by substituting x for b in the format statement:

```
p1, p2 = 30, 64123
q1 = "{0:8x}".format(p1)
q2 = "{0:8x}".format(p2)
q3 = "{0:08x}".format(p1)
q4 = "{0:08x}".format(p2)
print('\n', q1, '\n', q3, '\n', q2, '\n', q4)
```

This gives the following output. As you can see, it's analogous to the binary version:

```
      1e
0000001e
    fa7b
0000fa7b
```

Of course, we can combine both print formats (i.e., binary and hexadecimal), as in this example:

```
x, y = 1037, 325
xBin = "{0:016b}".format(x)
yHex = "{0:04x}".format(y)
print("x is",xBin,"y is",yHex)
print("x is","0b" + xBin,"y is","0x" + yHex)
```

We print two numbers, one in a binary format and one in a hexadecimal format. In the first case, the number is padded to 16 bits with leading zeros, and in the second case, it's padded to 4 characters with leading zeros.

We print the result twice. In the second case, prefixes are added to the values to indicate the base. If the first number, xBin, is binary, we can concatenate "0b" simply by using a "+" symbol to add 0b immediately before the binary string. The output from this code is as follows:

```
x is 0000010000001101 y is 0145
x is 0b0000010000001101 y is 0x0145
```

We can generalize the string method format as "someString".format(<parameter list>. This string method takes the string and inserts parameters into it that appear in the parameter list. You have to insert *placeholders* in the form of {a:b} into the string, which will receive the parameters when the string is printed.

Suppose you were printing a table of the powers of integers in the form x, x^2, x^3, x^4. We could write the following:

```
for x in range (1,7):
    print("Table of powers {0:2d}{1:3d}{2:4d}{3:6d}".format(x,x**2,x**3,x**4))
```

Each parameter placeholder is of the form {a:b} where the first element, a, is the position of the parameter in the list of parameters in the format. The second element, b, determines how the parameter is printed. In this case, it is a number and the letter d. The number defines the parameter's width, and d indicates that it's decimal; for example, the last parameter is specified as {3:6d}, which indicates the fourth parameter is a decimal integer taking six places. The following demonstrates the output from this fragment of code:

```
Table of powers  1   1    1      1
Table of powers  2   4    8     16
Table of powers  3   9   27     81
Table of powers  4  16   64    256
Table of powers  5  25  125    625
Table of powers  6  36  216   1296
```

In order to demonstrate the versatility of this approach, the next example prints the same table of powers but using a different format. As well as decimal, we also use binary and hexadecimal. Note that you only have to change b in {a:b} to change the base; for example, {6:x} tells the print statement to print the seventh parameter in hexadecimal format:

```
for x in range (1,10):
    print('Table of powers {0:2d} binary {1:10b} {2:4d} \
    hex {3:6x}'.format(x, x*x, x*x*x, x*x*x*x))
```

Note you can write x*x*x, or x**3.

The following output demonstrates the results of this formatting technique:

```
Table of powers 1 binary          1    1 hex      1
Table of powers 2 binary        100    8 hex     10
Table of powers 3 binary       1001   27 hex     51
Table of powers 4 binary      10000   64 hex    100
Table of powers 5 binary      11001  125 hex    271
Table of powers 6 binary     100100  216 hex    510
Table of powers 7 binary     110001  343 hex    961
Table of powers 8 binary    1000000  512 hex   1000
Table of powers 9 binary    1010001  729 hex   19a1
```

We have repeated the example with a few modifications. It is not necessary to give the order of the parameters if they are to be printed sequentially; for example, the first parameter specification can be written as {:2d} instead of {0:2d}. We've also changed the spacing to demonstrate how the width parameters operate:

```
for x in range (1,10):
    print('Powers {:2d} binary {:8b}{:4d} hex{:6x}'.format(x,x**2, x**3, x**4))
Powers  1 binary        1    1 hex      1
Powers  2 binary      100    8 hex     10
Powers  3 binary     1001   27 hex     51
Powers  4 binary    10000   64 hex    100
Powers  5 binary    11001  125 hex    271
Powers  6 binary   100100  216 hex    510
Powers  7 binary   110001  343 hex    961
Powers  8 binary  1000000  512 hex   1000
Powers  9 binary  1010001  729 hex   19a1
```

Consider the following examples of the format mechanism. Here, we use the symbols "<, >, ^" to control formatting. In order, these symbols force left justification, right justification, and centering within the stated width.

The following code prints the decimal integer 123 first in decimal form, using the three modifiers, and then in binary form using the same three modifiers. In each case, we have specified a width of 10 characters:

```
x = 123
print('{:<10d}'.format(x))
print('{:>10d}'.format(x))
print('{:^10d}'.format(x))
print('{:<10b}'.format(x))
print('{:>10b}'.format(x))
print('{:^10b}'.format(x))
```

The output generated by this code is as follows:

```
123                              Left-justified
           123                   Right-justified
    123                          Centered

1111011                          Left-justified
       1111011                   Right-justified
    1111011                      Centered
```

We are now going to provide three examples of how strings representing numbers can be printed. The first demonstrates the formatting of individual numbers in integer, hexadecimal, binary, and real forms. The second example shows how we can take a list of registers, join them as a single string, and print their values. This is very useful in displaying data when stepping through instructions during a simulation. The third example demonstrates the successive steps in processing a hexadecimal value into the desired format.

Example 1 – Formatting numbers

The following demonstrates this formatting mechanism, where we print several variables and a string. This uses a format specifier such as %05d, which means five decimal digits with leading zeros, and a placeholder such as %x, which means print the value of x in the format specified by %05d:

```
x = 123
y = 0xABCD
p = 13.141592
q ='This is a test'
print("Hex example: %03x" %y, "%05d" %x, 'Alan', "%12.3f" %p, '%-20.14s' %q)
```

This print statement displays the following (note hexadecimal appears in lowercase):

Hex example: abcd 00123 Alan   13.142 This is a test

Example 2 – Printing a list of register values in hexadecimal form

Consider the following expression with an 8-register array filled with data in various formats:

```
R = [0xabcd,2,3,0x123,5,0x11010,7,124]
print('Registers ='," ".join("%04x" % b for b in R))
```

This expression prints the string 'Registers =', followed by a second string that contains eight four-character hexadecimal values. To create the second string, we use the string join() method. The string comprehension iterates over the registers applying the formatting structure to each element. That is, it reads r[0], converts it into a string format, and then joins it to its left-hand neighbor (which is initially an empty string). This is repeated eight times and then that string is printed as follows:

Registers = abcd 0002 0003 0123 0005 11010 0007 007c

Example 3 – Successively processing a decimal value into the desired hex format

Consider the following sequence where we successively process the decimal value 44,350 until it is displayed in hexadecimal format in uppercase without the `0x` indicator prefix:

```
>>> x = 44350                        Here's a decimal number
>>> print(hex(x))                    Can I see that in hex?
0xad3e                               Thanks. But I like uppercase hex
>>> print(hex(x).upper())            OK. We just use the .upper() method on the string.
0XAD3E                               Nice one. But I don't like 0X at the front.
>>> print(hex(x).upper()[2:])        OK, OK, just use slice notation [2:] to strip 0X.
AD3E                                 Great. Can I have that with fries?
```

We have described, briefly, how numbers can be formatted. Formatting is necessary if the printed output is to be read by humans, especially if you are simulating a computer where patterns of 1s and 0s are important. There are several ways of formatting data, and this section provided only an introduction to this topic.

Input validation

In this section, I will introduce the notion of data validation. Historically, some of the major errors involving computers have been caused by a failure to check input data. TC1 doesn't perform source data checking; you can write ADDL R1,R2,10 or ADDL z1,z2,10 with the same result. Why? Because when the assembler sees ADDL, it looks for three parameters. It takes the first parameter, let's call this p1, and reads the register number by regnum = int(p1[1:]). Only the second and successive characters of p1 are recorded, and the "R" is ignored. You can write R1 or even ?1. This makes programming in assembly language easier; you can use any letter you want to represent a register. On the other hand, it encourages poor programming techniques and increases the dangers associated with mistyped input.

Validating data

Since the TC1 assembler doesn't perform error-checking on the input, if you make an error, it's likely that the program will crash, leaving you to do your own debugging. Good software performs error-checking, which ranges from the simple detection of invalid instructions to the exact pinpointing of all errors.

Here, we demonstrate how you can read a line of code and check for several types of common errors – for example, invalid opcodes, invalid instruction formats (too many or two few operands), typos (typing T6 instead of R6), and registers out of range (entering R9).

The purpose of this section is to show how you can add your own modifications to TC1. A formal way of dealing with the problem would be to construct a grammar for the assembly language and then build a parser to determine whether the input conforms to that grammar. We are going to take a simpler and more ad hoc approach.

If the current instruction is x = 'ADD r1 r2 r3', the y = x.split(' ') operation converts it into a list of tokens: y = ['ADD', 'R1', 'R2', 'R3']. We can extract the first token with jj = y[0], which should be a valid mnemonic (in this example, we are forgetting about any labels).

The first test to perform is on the validity of the instruction. Assume that all mnemonics have been defined in a list or directory called codes. All we have to do is to look it up in the codes directory using the following:

```
if jj not in codes: error = 1
```

Python keywords are shaded. This expression sets the error variable to 1 if this instruction is not in the dictionary. Then, we can test error and take whatever action is necessary.

The next step is to use the name of the instruction to look up its details, and then check whether that instruction requires parameters. Remember that our dictionary entries have a two-component tuple, with the first component being the instruction's format (i.e., the number of operands required) and the second being the actual operation code:

```
form = codes.get(y[0])     # Read the 4-bit format code
```

It looks up the instruction (i.e., y[0]) in the dictionary and returns its value, which is a tuple, such as (8:12). The first element of the tuple, form[0], describes the instruction's operands and the second is the opcode (which is not of interest here). The parameters required by the instruction are determined by form[0]. Consider the following code:

```
opType = form[0]                                            # Get operand info
if    opType == 0:                     totalOperands = 1    # Just a mnemonic
elif opType == 8  or opType == 1:      totalOperands = 2    # Mnemonic + 1 operand
elif opType == 12 or opType == 9:      totalOperands = 3    # Mnemonic + 2 operands
elif opType == 14 or opType == 13:     totalOperands = 4    # Mnemonic + 3
elif opType == 15:                     totalOperands = 5    # Mnemonic + 4 (not used)
```

The four bits of the format code represent rD, rS1, rs2, and a literal. TC1 instructions have several valid formats; for example, if opType = 0b1001 = 9, then the format defines an instruction with a destination register and a literal such as LDRL **R3 25**. We've used bold and shading to demonstrate the relationship between the bits of the format code and the actual instruction.

The preceding code uses an if...else to get the length (the number of tokens including the opcode) of each instruction. All we then have to do is to count the number of tokens in the current instruction and see whether it's the same as the expected value (i.e., the total length). The following code performs this check:

```
totalTokens = len(y)                   # Get the number of tokens in this instruction y
if totalTokens < totalOperands:        # Are there enough tokens?
    error = 2                          # Error 2: Too few operands
    continue
if totalTokens > totalOperands:        # Are there too many tokens?
    error = 3                          # Error 3: Too many operands
    continue
```

We set the error number to 2 or 3 if the number of tokens doesn't match the expected value. After both tests, there is a `continue` statement. The effect of `continue` is to drop to the end of the current block and abandon further error-testing (because we know this current instruction is in error).

Once we have established a valid instruction and the correct number of operands, the next step is to check each operand. An operand must be of the form R0 to R7 (or a literal).

We use the format information to test for each operand in turn. Here, we just deal with the first operand, rD (the destination register):

```
if opType & 0b1000 == 0b1000:          # If the destination register bit is set
    rDname = y[1]                       # Get the register name (second item in string)
    error,q = syntaxTest(rDname)        # Call syntax test to look for errors
```

The first line of this code tests whether the leftmost bit of `format` is 1 or 0 by ANDing the format code with `0b1000` and testing for `0b1000`. If the result is `true`, then we need to check for the first register operand, which is the second token – that is, `y[1]`.

Because we are going to test for three operands, we have created a `syntaxText` function that takes the token as a parameter and returns two parameters: `error` and `q`. The value of `error` is the error code returned (0 for no error, and q is the number of the register). The Python code for the `syntaxTest` function is as follows:

```
def syntaxTest(token):                           # Test register for validity (R0 to R7)
    if token[0] != 'R': return(4,0)              # Fail on missing initial R. Return error 4
    if not token[1:].isnumeric(): return(5,0)    # Fail on missing register number. Return 5
    if int(token[1:]) > 7: return(6,0)           # Fail on register number not in 0-7. Return 6
    return(0,int(token[1:]))                     # OK so return with error 0 and reg number
```

Three tests are performed, one for each type of error that we are looking for. The first test is to check whether the first character of the token is `'R'`. If it is not `'R'`, a return is made with the error code 4, and the dummy or default register number is set to 0. The second test looks for a numeric value for the register (the characters following the `'R'`, which is `token[1:]`). The third test checks whether the number is greater than 7 and returns an error code if it is. Finally, when the last line is reached, a return is made with the error code 0 and the appropriate register number. Note that we don't need to use an `elif` because if an `if` yields `True`, the code is exited via `return()`.

This routine is called up to three times in the event of an instruction having a format code of `0b1110` corresponding to a register-to-register operation such as ADD R1 R2 R3. In this exercise, we do not check the literal. If you wish to add that check, it would be necessary to check for an integer in the range 0 to 65,535 or -32,766 to 32,755 (plus a number beginning with % if it's binary or 0x if it's hexadecimal).

Using the `continue` statement

When testing for errors, do you test for each error in a statement or do you stop once you have found an error?

The code uses a `continue` statement whenever an error is found to bypass further testing. An unfortunate side effect is that `continue` takes you past the end of the loop and begins the next iteration; that is, you can't print the nature of the error. The solution is to print any errors found in the previous iteration at the start of the loop. Of course, this causes a problem on the first iteration because there is no previous error value. That is easily fixed by setting `error` to zero before beginning the loop. The following code demonstrates this approach:

```
run = 1
error = 0
while run == 1:
    if error != 0: printError(error)

        .

        .
    <test for error 1>
    if error != 0: continue
        <test for error 2>
    if error != 0: continue

        .
    <test for error n>
    if error != 0: continue
```

In this fragment of code, `error` is tested to determine whether an error occurred in the previous cycle. If `error` is not 0, the `printError` function is called to print the error number and type. Using a function code to do the printing enhances the readability of the program.

The code for an error-testing routine is given next. This is not intended to be a complete program, but a demonstration of the way in which you can extend a program to include error-testing on the input data:

```
# Testing Python parsing # 22 Aug 2020 Version of 29 July 2021
import sys                                      # System library used to exit program
codes = {'NOP':(0,0), 'STOP': (0,1),'BEQ':(1,4), 'INC':(8,2), \
         'MOVE':(12,23), 'LDRL':(9,13), 'ADD':(14,12),'ADDL':(13,12)}
def syntaxTest(token):                 # Test the format of a register operand for validity (R0 to R7)
    if token[0] != 'R': return(4,0)            # Fail on missing initial R. Return error 2
    if not token[1:].isnumeric(): return(5,0)  # Fail on missing register number. Return error 3
    if int(token[1:]) > 7: return(6,0)    # Fail on register number not in range 0-7. Return error 4
    return(0,int(token[1:]))               # Success return with error code 0 and register number
def printError(error):
    if error != 0:
        if error == 1: print("Error 1: Non-valid operation")
        if error == 2: print("Error 2: Too few operands")
        if error == 3: print("Error 3: Too many operands")
        if error == 4: print("Error 4: Register operand error- no 'R'")
        if error == 5: print("Error 5: Register operand error - no valid num")
        if error == 6: print("Error 6: Register operand error - not in range")
```

```
run = 1
error = 0
while run == 1:
    if error != 0: printError(error)    # if error not zero, print message
    x = input("\nEnter instruction >> ") # Type an instruction (for testing)
    x = x.upper()                        # Convert lowercase into uppercase
    x = x.replace(',',' ')               # Replace comma with space to allow add r1,r2 or add r1 r2
    y = x.split(' ')                     # Split into tokens. y is the tokenized instruction
    if len(y) > 0:                       # z is the predicate (or null if no operands)
        z = y[1:]
    else: z  = ''

    print("Inst =",y, 'First token',y[0])
    if y[0] not in codes:                # Check for valid opcode
        error = 1                        # Error 1: instruction not valid
        print("Illegal instruction", y[0])
        continue
    form = codes.get(y[0])               # Get the code's format information
    print('Format', form)
    if form[1] == 1:                     # Detect STOP, opcode value 1,and terminate
        print("\nProgram terminated on STOP")  # Say "Goodbye"
        sys.exit()                       # Call OS function to leave
    opType = form[0]
    if   opType == 0:                                          totalOperands = 1
    elif opType == 8  or opType == 4  or opType == 1:  totalOperands = 2
    elif opType == 12 or opType == 9:                  totalOperands = 3
    elif opType == 14 or opType == 13:                 totalOperands = 4
    totalTokens = len(y)                 # Compare tokens we have with those we need
    if totalTokens < totalOperands:
        error = 2                        # Error 2: Too few operands
        continue
    if totalTokens > totalOperands:
        error = 3                        # Error 3: Too many operands
        continue
    if opType & 0b1000 == 0b1000:
        rDname = y[1]
        error,q = syntaxTest(rDname)
        if error != 0: continue
    if opType & 0b0100 == 0b0100:
        rS1name = y[2]
        error,q = syntaxTest(rS1name)
        if error != 0: continue
    if opType & 0b0010 == 0b0010:
```

```
            rS2name = y[3]
            error,q = syntaxTest(rS2name)
            if error != 0: continue
    if opType & 0b0001 == 0b0001:
        if not y[-1].isnumeric():
            error == 7
            print("Error 7: Literal error")
    if error == 0:
        print("Instruction", x, "Total operands", totalOperands,"Predicate", z)
```

Checking parameters – using dictionaries

The next example provides another look at parameter checking. It examines the mnemonic and predicate of each instruction and checks whether it represents a valid operation. It stops after finding an error. In other words, it will detect only one error in INC R9,R2 even though there are two errors (i.e., too many operands and the first operand is out of range).

We also expand the use of the Python dictionary. Previously, we tested for a valid register operand by checking that the initial character was 'R' and that this was followed by a number in the range of 0 to 7. Since there are only eight register names (R0 to R7), it's easy to employ a dictionary in error checking:

```
 regSet = {'R0':0, 'R1':1, 'R2':2, 'R3':3, 'R4':4, 'R5':5, 'R6':6, 'R7':7}
```

The dictionary, regSet, contains the register names (the keys) and the corresponding value. Because we do so much register checking, it's convenient to create a function, regTest, to perform the check. This function takes two parameters. The first is a string, tokNam, that gives the register a name, and the second parameter is the token being tested – for example, regTest('rD',predicate[0]). The reason for passing a name to the function is so that the function can print the name of the operand in error.

The function returns two values: an error code and the number of the register. If an error is detected, the register value of 0 is returned as a default. The function is given here:

```
def regTest(tokNam,token):          # Test format of a register operand for validity (R0 to R7)
    if token in regSet:             # Is it in the register set?
        return (0,regSet.get(token)) # If it's there, return 0 and token value
    else:                           # If not there, return error code 4 and the token's name
        print("Error in register ",tokNam)
        return (4,0)
```

Testing for validity is easy. The if token in regSet: condition checks whether this parameter is in the register set. If it is, we read the value of the register from the dictionary and return its value. If the token is not in the register set, an error message is printed (using tokNam to display the faulty value), and an error message number 4 is reported back.

Using `regSet.get(token)` is a little heavy-handed. We do not actually need to read the register value. If it is in the set of valid registers, we can use `int(token[1])` to extract the register number from the name. The advantage of using the dictionary mechanism is that we can amend the code to add new registers such as `SP`, `PC`, and so on if we want. We can rename registers or even use aliases; for example, if we use the R7 register as a temporary register, we could enter , `{ . . . 'R6':6, 'R7':7, 'T':7}` and then write either `INC R7` or `INC T`.

We have also experimented with a new instruction dictionary. Some of the information in the dictionary is redundant because it can be derived from other information (e.g., the length can be derived from the format). However, we adopted the following system because we may change the program at a later date.

In the previous version of the assembler, we used a dictionary in which each entry had a key that was a mnemonic and a two-element tuple – for example, `'INC':(8,12)`. The first element of the tuple was a format code that expressed the operands required by the mnemonic, and the second element was the instruction's opcode.

In this example, we are using a four-element tuple to provide the following information:

- **Format**: The format is a decimal number in the range 0 to 15, representing a 4-bit binary value. The 1s in the binary format indicate the operands required by the instruction in the order: `rD, rS1, rS2, literal` (as before).

- **Style**: The style describes the class of instruction – for example, mnemonic only, mnemonic plus literal, mnemonic plus register plus literal, and so on. There is a direct relationship between format and style.

- **Length**: The length gives the number of tokens in the instruction – that is, the mnemonic plus its operands. This is equivalent to the number of 1s in the format plus 1.

- The instruction's opcode.

The initial processing of an instruction is given by the following code. In section 1 (light shading), the mnemonic is read from the input token string (i.e., the first element). That may or may not be followed by additional parameters.

The mnemonic is used to access the `codes` dictionary to check whether it's valid. The error code is set to `1` (invalid operation) and a `continue` statement forces a drop to the end of the loop (further input testing is not necessary as the instruction is not valid).

The code with the light gray background reads the tuple with the four data elements associated with the mnemonic and extracts the individual parameters.

The three lines beginning with "`if opCode == 1:`" read the operation to determine whether the instruction was "STOP". If it was STOP, the `sys.exit()` operation terminates the program. Note that we have to use `import sys` at the start of the program to import the library of system functions:

```
mnemonic = y[0]                  # Get the mnemonic
if mnemonic not in codes:        # Check for a valid opcode
    error = 1                    # If none found, set error code
    continue                     # and jump to the end of the loop
```

```
    opData  = codes.get(mnemonic)      # Read codes to get the data for this instruction
    opForm  =  opData[0]               # Get each of this instruction's parameters
    opStyle =  opData[1]
    opCode  =  opData[2]
    opLen   =  opData[3]

    if opCode == 1:                    # If the op_Code is 1, then it's "STOP", so exit the program
        print("\nProgram terminated on STOP")
        sys.exit()
    totalTokens = len(y)               # How many tokens do we have?
    if totalTokens < opLen:            # Compare with the expected number
        error = 2                      # Error 2: Too few operands
        continue

    if totalTokens > opLen:
        error = 3                      # Error 3: Too many operands
        continue
```

The final two blocks in the preceding code fragment with a dark gray background perform error-detecting operations. They both get the number of tokens from the instruction and then compare that number to the value for this instruction. In the first case, an error of 2 indicates too few tokens, and in the second case, an error of 3 indicates too many tokens.

At this stage, we have determined that the instruction is valid and has the correct number of operands. The next stage is to check the operands. The check is performed according to the style of the instruction. There are seven styles. Style 1 has no further checking because there is no operand (e.g., for NOP). We will just look at the checking for style 6, which corresponds to instructions with a mnemonic, rD1, rS1, and a literal such as ADD R1,R2,25.

We call the `regTest` function first with the 'rD' parameter to tell it we are testing for the destination register and the `predicate[0]` token, which is the first parameter. This returns an error flag and the value of the register.

Because we perform two tests (register rD and rS1), we must use two error names: e1 for the first and e2 for the second test. If we used `error` as the variable in both cases, a non-error second result would clear the first error. The line if (e1 != 0) or (e2 != 0): error = 4 returns `error` with the appropriate error status independent of which register was in error. `continue` at the end of this block skips further error checking for this instruction:

```
# Input error checking - using dictionaries Modified 30 July 2021
# Instruction dictionary 'mnemonic':(format, style, op_code, length)
# Style definition and example of the instruction format
# 0 NOP            mnemonic only
# 1 BEQ L          mnemonic + literal
# 2 INC R1         mnemonic + rD
# 3 MOVE R1,R2     mnemonic + rD1 + rS1
```

```
# 4 LDRL R1,L        mnemonic + rD1 + literal
# 5 ADD R1 R2 R3     mnemonic + rD + rS1 + rS2
# 6 ADDL R1 R2 L     mnemonic + rD + rS1 + literal
# 7 LDRI R1 (R2 L)   mnemonic + rD + rS1 + literal (same as 6)


import sys                                       # System library used to exit program
              # Dictionary of instructions (format, style, op_code, length)
codes = {'NOP': (0b0000,0,0,1),'STOP':(0b0000,0,1,1),'BEQ': (0b0001,1,2,2), \
         'INC': (0b1000,2,3,2),'MOVE':(0b1100,3,4,3),'LDRL':(0b1001,4,6,3), \
         'LDRI':(0b1101,7,7,4),'ADD': (0b1110,5,8,4),'ADDL':(0b1101,6,9,4)}
regSet = {'R0':0,'R1':1,'R2':2,'R3':3,'R4':4,'R5':5,'R6':6,'R7':7}  # Registers
def regTest(token):                              # Test register operand for R0 to R7
    if token in regSet: return (0)               # Return with error 0 if legal name
    else:               return (4)               # Return with error 4 if illegal register name
def printError(error):                           # This function prints the error message
    if error != 0:
        if error == 1: print("Error 1: Non-valid operation")
        if error == 2: print("Error 2: Too few operands")
        if error == 3: print("Error 3: Too many operands")
        if error == 4: print("Error 4: Register name error")
        if error == 5: print("Error 5: Failure in pointer-based expression")
        if error == 6: print("Error 6: Invalid literal")
def litCheck(n):                                 # Check for invalid literal format (this is just a demo)
    if n.isnumeric():     error = 0              # Decimal numeric OK
    elif n[0] == '-':     error = 0              # Negative number OK
    elif n[0] == '%':     error = 0              # Binary number OK
    elif n[0:2] == '0X':  error = 0              # Hex number OK
    else:                 error = 6              # Anything else is an error
    return (error)                               # Return with error number
```

This is the main loop. An instruction is input and then checked for errors. As in earlier examples, the instruction is processed for validity first and the mnemonic is checked to see whether it is in codes:

```
error = 0
while True:              # Infinite loop
    if error != 0: printError(error)
    error = 0
    x = input(">> ").upper()                     # Read instruction and provide limited processing
    if len(x) == 0: continue                     # Ignore empty lines and continue
    x = x.replace(',',' ')                       # remove commas
    x = x.replace('(','')                        # remove (
    x = x.replace(')','')                        # remove )
    y = x.split(' ')                             # Create list of tokens (mnemonic + predicate)
    mnemonic = y[0]                              # Get the mnemonic (first token)
    if mnemonic not in codes:                    # Check for validity
```

```
        error = 1                          # If not valid, set error code and drop out
        continue
opData = codes.get(mnemonic)               # Read the four parameters for this instruction
opForm  =  opData[0]                       # opcode format (rDS,rS1,rS2,L)
opStyle =  opData[1]                       # Instruction style (0 to 7)
opCode  =  opData[2]                       # Numeric opcode
opLen   =  opData[3]                       # Length (total mnemonic + operands in range 1 to 4)
if opLen > 1: predicate = y[1:]            # Get predicate if this is one
else:             predicate = ''           # If single token, return null
print("Mnemonic =",mnemonic, "Predicate", predicate, \
      "Format =", bin(opForm),"Style =",opStyle,"Code =",opCode, \
      "Length =",opLen)
if opCode == 1:                            # Used to terminate this program
    print("\nProgram ends on STOP")
    sys.exit()
totalTokens = len(y)
if totalTokens < opLen:
    error = 2                              # Error 2: Too few operands
    continue
if totalTokens > opLen:
    error = 3                              # Error 3: Too many operands
    continue
if opStyle == 0:                           # e.g., NOP or STOP so nothing else to do
    continue
elif opStyle == 1:                         # e.g., BEQ 5 just check for literal
    literal = predicate[0]
    error = litCheck(literal)
    continue
elif opStyle == 2:                         # e.g., INC r6 check for single register
    error = regTest(predicate[0])
    continue
elif opStyle == 3:                         # e.g., MOVE r1,r2 check for two registers
    e1 = regTest(predicate[0])
    e2 = regTest(predicate[1])
    if e1 != 0 or e2 != 0:
        error = 4
    continue
elif opStyle == 4:                         # e.g., LDRL r1,12 Check register then literal
    error = regTest(predicate[0])
    if error != 0: continue
    literal = predicate[1]
    error = litCheck(literal)
    continue
```

```
      elif opStyle == 5:                   # e.g., ADD r1,r2,r3 Check for three register names
          e1 = regTest(predicate[0])
          e2 = regTest(predicate[1])
          e3 = regTest(predicate[2])
          if e1 != 0 or e2 != 0 or e3 !=0:
              error = 4
          continue
      elif opStyle == 6:                   # e.g., ADDL R1,R2,4 Check for two registers and literal
          e1 = regTest(predicate[0])
          e2 = regTest(predicate[1])
          literal = predicate[2]
          e3 = litCheck(literal)
          if e1 != 0 or e2 != 0:
              error = 4
          if e1==0 and e2==0 and e3 !=0:   # If registers are OK but not literal
              error = 6                     # report literal error
          continue
      elif opStyle == 7:                   # e.g., LDRI r4,r0,23 or LDRI r4,(r0,23)
          e1 = regTest(predicate[0])
          e2 = regTest(predicate[1])
          literal = predicate[2]
          e3 = litCheck(literal)
          if e1 != 0 or e2 != 0:
              error = 4
          if e1==0 and e2==0 and e3 !=0:   # If registers are OK but not literal
              error = 6                     # report literal error
          continue
```

Having looked at input validation, we now look at how we can control the display of *useful* information during a simulation.

Tracing and breakpoints

When you simulate a computer, you have to show what is happening during the simulation. Consequently, you have to answer the following three questions:

- When do you display data?
- How do you display the data?
- What do you display?

When you have completed this section, you will be able to construct your own instruction tracing facilities.

CPU simulators execute one instruction at a time. At the end of an instruction, the state of the computer (i.e., its registers, status flags, and memory) can be displayed. This mode is called *single-stepping*. Every time you hit *Enter*, an instruction is executed and the machine's status is displayed on the screen.

Stepping through instructions sequentially, one by one, has limitations. What if there's a 3-instruction loop that clears, say, 1,000 locations in an array? Do you expect someone to hit the *Enter* key 3,000 times to trace past this operation? We need a means of stepping past the boring bits of a program and jumping to the interesting bits – that is, a mechanism that lets us execute some instructions as a batch, without having to hit *return* after each instruction has been executed or printing the results of that execution.

Suppose we create a variable, `trace`, and then, at the end of the `execute` loop, print the appropriate data if `trace` is 1 and jump to the next instruction without printing data if `trace = 0`:

```
trace = 1                           # Trace mode active when trace = 1
run = 1                             # run = 1 to execute program
pc = 0                              # Initialize program counter
while run == 1:                     # Main program loop
    read instruction
    execute instruction
    if trace == 1: displayData()    # When in trace mode, print results
```

The CPU state is printed after each instruction only if `trace = 1`. How do we turn `trace` on and off? Turning `trace` off is easy; all you need do is read the keyboard input when single-stepping, and turn `trace` off if a particular character or string is entered. However, once `trace` is 0, we've lost control, and instructions are executed until the program is terminated.

One solution is to set up a trace count, with the number of instructions to be executed before `trace` is turned on again; for example, entering `T 10`, would turn off tracing, execute 10 instructions without displaying anything, and then turn tracing on again. Defining a fixed number of instructions to execute is not always helpful, as it requires the programmer to count the number of instructions to be executed before a point of interest is reached. The programmer may not always know that.

A better solution is to turn tracing on when a specific point in the assembly language program, called a *breakpoint,* is reached. A breakpoint can be the value of the program counter, a label, or a specific instruction. Typically, the value of the program counter at which you wish to display machine status is stored in a table of breakpoints. Execution continues (without any display) until a breakpoint is encountered and the CPU state is displayed.

The following fragment of Python demonstrates this approach. It is not a computer simulator and has only three instructions (`nop`, `test`, and `test1`), which do nothing, plus `stop`. The program is intended to demonstrate a possible approach to the implementation of single-stepping and breakpoints. At the end of each instruction cycle, several choices are possible:

- Show the machine status after the execution of this instruction

- Wait for keyboard input before executing the next cycle

- Print the machine status at a specific breakpoint (address or instruction)

The following code uses different fonts and background shading to highlight the various functional parts of the code. The first two sections are the setting up and initialization of variables, and (shaded) the main program execution loop. This loop does nothing other than step through instructions that are nop (no operation); test and test1 are just used as markers. The stop instruction serves to terminate execution.

Note that, when tracing, we require a second program counter, pcOld, because pc gets incremented during the fetch cycle and we need to display it before it was modified:

```
def display():                                          # Display processor status
    if oldPC in breakTab: print('Breakpoint at %03x' %oldPC)      # if pc in the table
    print("PC = %03x" %oldPC,   ' Op-code = %s' %instruction)
    return()
opCodes = ['nop', 'test', 'test1', 'stop']              # Op-code set
traceCodes = []                                         # List of codes to be traced (initially empty)
mem = ['nop'] * 32                                      # Initialize memory to NOPs
mem[10] = 'test'                                        # Dummy operation at 10
mem[20] = 'test'                                        # Dummy operation at 20
mem[25] = 'test1'                                       # Dummy operation at 25
r = [0] * 4                                             # Set up 4 registers (not used)
pc = 0                                                  # Initialize program counter
oldPC = 0                                               # Initialize previous program counter
run = 1                                                 # Set run to 1 to go
trace = 1                                               # Set trace to 1 to single-step
count = 0                                       # Count is the number of cycles not displayed
breakTab = []                                           # Create table for breakpoints

while run == 1:                                         # PROGRAM LOOP
    instruction = mem[pc]                               # read instruction
    oldPC = pc                                          # Save current PC for display
    pc = pc + 1                                         # Increment PC
    # Do processing here                                # For experimentation (add stuff here)
    if pc == 32 or instruction == 'stop': run = 0  # End on stop instruction or max PC

    if trace == 0 and count != 0:                      # Test for single-step mode
        count = count - 1                              # If not single-step, decrement counter
        if count == 0:                                 # If count zero, return to single step mode
            trace = 1                                  # Exit silent mode
            continue                                   # Now drop to bottom of the loop
    if trace == 0 and pc in breakTab:                  # If not single-step, check for breakpoint
        print('Breakpoint\n')                          # Print status at the breakpoint
        display()

    if trace == 0 and instruction in traceCodes:  # If not single-step and opcode in table
```

```
         print('Trace Code')                              # Print status info
         display()
   if trace == 1:                                         # If single-step with trace on
         display()                                        # Display the status
         c = input('>> ')                                 # Wait for keyboard input
         if c == '': continue                             # If it's just a return, continue
         elif c[0]== 't' and len(c) > 2 and c[2:].isdigit():
                                                          # Test for 't' and number
             count = int(c[2:])                           # Set the count for silent mode
             trace = 0                                    # Turn off single-step
         elif c[0] == 'b' and len(c) > 2 and c[2:].isdigit():
                                                          # Test for b (set breakpoint)
             breakPoint = int(c[2:])                      # Get breakpoint address and add to table
             breakTab.append(breakPoint)
         elif c == 'd':                                   # Test for d to display breakpoint info
             print('Display status: breakpoints =', breakTab, \
                     'traced codes =',traceCodes)
         elif c in opCodes: traceCodes.append(c)          # Test for a valid opcode and add to list
print('\nProgram terminated')
```

Initially, trace is set to 1, indicating that we are in a *single-step* mode. After displaying the program counter and instruction, the program waits for keyboard input. The code that does this is as follows:

```
   if trace == 1:                                         # If single-step with trace on
         display()                                        # Display the status
         c = input('>> ')                                 # Wait for input from user
         if c == '': continue                             # If it's just a return, continue
```

If the input is a return (i.e., enter), the loop is terminated by continue and the next instruction cycle is executed. If you enter t followed by an integer (e.g., t 13), the integer is transferred to the count variable and t is set to 0. Setting t to 0 turns off the single-step mechanism, and instructions are executed without printing the machine status or waiting for a keyboard input at the end of each cycle. At the end of each cycle, the count variable is decremented. When count becomes 0, trace is set to 1 and the single-step mode is re-entered.

If you enter b followed by an integer (e.g., b 21), a breakpoint at address 21 is recorded in the breakpoint table (a dictionary). You can enter more than one breakpoint and it will be saved in the dictionary. Each breakpoint is an address in the program being executed. When the program counter reaches that address, the system status is displayed. For example, if you were to enter the sequence b 12, b 30, t 50 (each on a separate line), the simulator would set breakpoints at addresses 12 and 30, and then execute 50 cycles without displaying any data. However, if the program counter becomes either 12 or 30 during this period, the machine status will be printed.

Similarly, you can enter an instruction that will be loaded into the `traceCodes` table. This behaves exactly like the PC breakpoint. When an instruction that's in the `traceCodes` table is encountered, the machine status is displayed. Thus, the simulator provides four modes:

- Execute instruction step by step
- Execute *n* instructions without displaying system status (the silent mode)
- Execute instructions in silent mode but stop and display if a breakpoint address is encountered
- Execute instructions in silent mode but stop and display if a specific opcode is encountered

Of course, the program can be extended to more exotic forms of breakpoints that take account of register data, memory data, or any combination of events. For example, you could permit breakpoints of the following form:

```
If PC > 200 or PC < 300 and instruction = 'ADD'
```

Some simulators let you set a breakpoint on a change of instruction flow – that is, after any jump, branch, or subroutine call. That's very useful for tracing the execution of a complex program.

The following is the output of a short session with this fragment program. Remember that it is intended to be a demonstration of the principles involved, rather than an actual working system:

```
PC = 000   Op-code = nop            # Hit enter key and trace first instruction
>>
PC = 001   Op-code = nop
>>
PC = 002   Op-code = nop
>> t 4                              # Type t 4 to execute but skip printing 4 instructions
PC = 007   Op-code = nop            # Note how PC jumps from 2 to 7
>>
PC = 008   Op-code = nop
>>
PC = 009   Op-code = nop
>> b 12                             # Type b 12 to insert breakpoint at PC = 12
PC = 00a   Op-code = nop
>> t 6                              # Type t 6 to execute 6 instructions without display
Breakpoint

Breakpoint at 00c                   # No display continues until PC = 12 (0xC)
PC = 00c   Op-code = nop            # Processor printed for PC = 12
PC = 011   Op-code = nop            # Execution continues until PC = 17 (0x11)
>> test1                            # Type 'test1' to make instruction test1 a breakpoint
PC = 012   Op-code = nop
>> t 15                             # Type t 15 to execute but skip printing 15 instructions
```

```
Trace Code
PC = 019  Op-code = test1          # Execution continues until 'test1' encountered at PC = 25 (0x19)

Program terminated
```

The next step is to demonstrate how the simulated computer can be extended by adding new instructions. We demonstrate what parts of the code have to be modified and how you can create new instructions of arbitrary complexity. For example, if you were developing a computer to be used primarily for playing chess, you could create an instruction, ROOK R1, R2, that takes the position of a rook in register R2 and calculates the legal positions it could move to and put them in R1.

Adding new instructions

So far, we have provided a modest set of instructions for TC1. In this section, we show how to add a new instruction to the TC1's repertoire in order to see what's involved in extending an instruction set. In fact, this is a remarkably straightforward task.

The first step is to choose a mnemonic and unique opcode and insert them into the table of code. We've arranged the instruction set to leave some unallocated code (e.g., code beginning with 11). The second step is to write the code to interpret the new instruction.

First example – putting two memory locations in ascending order

Let's create an instruction that takes the contents of two consecutive locations in memory and puts the largest number in the first location at the lower address (i.e., it orders them). This instruction takes a single parameter, a pointer register, and reads the numeric value pointed at by the register. We'll assume that the register is r[i]. The instruction compares this number with the value stored at address r[i] + 1, and swaps them if the second number is higher than the one at the r[i] location. In pseudocode, this is as follows:

```
temp ← mem[r[i]]                   # Save first number. Assume ri is the pointer register
if mem[r[i] + 1] > temp            # If the second number is greater than the first
    mem[r[i]]    ← mem[r[i]+1]     # then put the second number in the first location
    mem[r[i]+1] ← temp            # and the first number in the second location
```

We will call the instruction ORD (order numbers) and write it as ORD r0. The binary code is 1110000 rrr 00...0 (where rrr is the 3-bit register field) and is assigned to this instruction. 'ORD':(8,112) is entered in the Python dictionary of instructions. The opcode is 112 and the parameter allocation code in binary is 1000 (i.e., 8), because the only parameter required is Rd.

The new instruction is detected in the execution part of the program:

```
elif opCode == 0b1110000:          # Test for 'ORD' ( 112 in decimal and in 1110000 binary)
```

This is followed by the Python version of the preceding pseudocode. We can write the following:

```
temp = mem[r[dest]]                          # dest is the destination register
if mem[r[dest] + 1] > temp:
    mem[r[dest]] = mem[r[dest]+1]
    mem[r[dest] + 1] = temp
```

What could be simpler? The following code provides a testbed for the instruction. We fill memory with random numbers and then request a memory address. The data at that address is exchanged with the data at the next address to create an ordered pair. Note that this example does not use global variables: the registers and memory are passed to the function as parameters. To simplify testing, it is assumed that the memory address is in the r[0] register:

```
import random                                # System library to generate random numbers
mem = [0] * 32                               # Set up memory
r   = [0] * 8                                # Set up registers
for i in range(32): mem[i] = random.randint(0,256)  # Fill memory with random numbers
for i in range(32): print(i, mem[i])

def ord(reg,rD,memory):                      # Pass registers, memory, and register number
    temp = memory[reg[rD]]                   # rD is the destination register
    if memory[reg[rD] + 1] > temp:
        memory[reg[rD]] = memory[reg[rD]+1]
        memory[reg[rD] + 1] = temp
    return()

go = True
r  = [0] * 8
rD = 0
while go:
    x = input('Type address of first: ')
    r[rD] = int(x)
    if r[rD] > 30:                           # Exit on memory address 31 or higher
        print('End of run')
        break
    else:
        print('Before: mem[x] = ',mem[r[rD]], 'next = ',mem[r[rD] + 1])
        ord(r,0,mem)
        print('After:  mem[x] = ',mem[r[rD]], 'next = ',mem[r[rD] + 1])
```

Second example – adding a bit-reversal instruction

Let's add a more complicated instruction to the TC1 instruction set. Suppose you want to reverse the order of bits in a register so that the binary code 1100111000101001 in r0 becomes 1001010001110011. Assume that the new instruction is REV r0, which reverses the 16 bits in r0 and returns the result in r0.

How do we reverse bits? Consider the four bits 1101 and assume they are in T1 (*see Fig 7.1*). Suppose we shift the bits one place left so that the bit that leaves the left-hand end of T1 goes into the right-hand end of T2, and then we shift T2 one place to the right. We repeat that operation four times. *Figure 7.1* shows what we get:

Step	T1 Shift left	Bit shifted out of T1	T2 Shift right
Initially	1101	1	0000
Shift 1	1010	1	1000
Shift 2	0100	0	1100
Shift 3	1000	1	0110
Shift 4	0000	0	1011

Figure 7.1 – Shifting one register's output into a second register's input to reverse a string

We have reversed the order of the bits. If the register to be shifted is op1, then we can write the Python code as follows. This code is in the form of a function that can be called from the instruction interpreter:

```
def reverseBits(op1):              # Reverse the bits of register op1
    reversed = 0                   # The reversed value is initialized
    toShift  = r[op1]              # Read the register contents
    for i in range(0,16):          # Repeat for all 16 bits
        bitOut   = toShift & 0x8000  # Get msb of word to reverse
        toShift  = toShift << 1      # Shift source word one place left
        reversed = reversed >> 1     # Shift result one place right
        reversed = reversed | bitOut # Use OR to insert bit in lsb of result
    return(reversed)
```

We can now change the code of TC1 to incorporate this. There are three steps:

1. **Step 1**: Insert the new instruction, 'REV' : (8,113), into the codes dictionary. 8 indicates 1000 in binary and informs the computer that the reverse instruction requires the destination rD register to be specified by the instruction. 113 is the opcode, which is 0b1110001 in binary.

2. **Step 2**: In the opcode interpretation list, insert the new entry:

   ```
   elif 'code ' == 0b1110001: r[op0] = reverseBits(op0)
   ```

   This checks whether the current instruction is 0b1110001 (i.e., 161 decimal) and calls the reverseBits() function to perform the required operation.

3. **Step 3**: Insert the `reverseBits` function into the Python code. This instruction replaces the data in the rD register with the bits reversed.

    Suppose that we wanted a non-destructive instruction that did not overwrite the register containing the bits to be reversed – that is REV r0, r1. What changes would we need?

First, we would need a new instruction format code. We have to specify two registers: the source and destination register. The code in the directory would now be `'REV': (12,113)` because the opcode parameter value would be 1100 in binary or 12 in decimal. The other change would be to the instruction interpreter:

```
elif 'code' == 0b1110010: R[dest] = reverseBits(op1)
```

Note that we have changed the instruction format for minimal changes to the code (in this case, it's just the change of source register from op0 to op1).

A new comparison operation

Suppose you are performing an operation on a string where you have to find the *middle* of the string. You can do this by stepping in from both ends until you get to the middle. But there are *two* types of middle. A string with an odd number of characters has a character in its middle. A string with an even number of characters has no middle character; it has two characters next to each other. Consider these two examples:

String 1: 1234567   Odd number of characters

String 2: 12345678   Even number of characters

String 1 has an odd number of characters and 4 is the center. String 2 has an even number of characters, and 4 and 5 are on either side of the middle.

Suppose we are stepping through a string using two pointers, one at each end. As we step in from both sides, one pointer goes up and the other goes down. When we get to the middle, either the pointers are the same (odd length) or the pointers differ by one (even length).

It would be nice to have a compare operation that compares two values and returns equality if either they are the same or if the second one differs from the first by +1. The new instruction, CMPT (*compare together*), does this. For example, CMPT r4, r6 sets the z bit to 1 if the contents of r4 and r6 are the same, or if the contents of r4 are one less than the contents of r6. The code to do this is as follows:

```
if mnemonic == "CMPT":
    z = 0
    if (r[rD] == r[rS1]) or (r[rD] == r[rS1] + 1): z = 1
```

As you can see, this performs two tests on the pointers, one for equality and one for higher by 1, and combines the test results using a Boolean or operator; that is, if the pointers are x and y, then the test is true if x = y is true or if x + 1 = y is true.

This instruction is not implemented in a real processor. Why not if it's a great idea? Well, first, it would be used in only a small number of programs requiring this particular operation. It takes up silicon real estate on the chip that is hardly ever used. That's a waste of precious resources. Second, machine code is mostly generated by compilers, and it's not easy to design compilers that use special-purpose operations such as this effectively. Third, this instruction performs three operations: comparing p and q, adding 1 to q, comparing p and q+1. Consequently, it takes longer to execute than single-operation instructions. That reduces the efficiency of the computer.

In the next section, you will be introduced to the notion of instructions with fields that have variable lengths. Real machines do not have this facility. The reason for including this section is to demonstrate instruction decoding and bit processing.

Variable-length instructions

This short section provides ideas for experimentation with instructions and their formats and extends your understanding of instructions, their structure, and the trade-off involved in creating instruction sets. It is not designed to illustrate a real computer.

Like many computers, TC1 has *fixed-length fields* in its opcode; that is, the number of bits dedicated to each field is fixed and does not vary from instruction to instruction. There are always 16 bits in the literal field, even if the current instruction does not require a literal. Wasteful indeed. Since the purpose of TC1 is experimentation, we demonstrate how you might make the number of registers variable (i.e., user-definable). Adding more registers speeds up computation by requiring fewer memory accesses. However, there is a price; where do you get the extra bits that would be needed to specify the registers? Do you take the extra register bits from the opcode field (reducing the number of different instructions), or do you take them from the literal field (reducing the maximum size of a literal that can be loaded in a single instruction)? Or do you implement multiple banks of registers and switch in a new set of registers (called *windowing*) as a temporary measure?

Here, we provide some code that we used to experiment with variable register sizes. This is not a complete program. All it does is let you enter the size of register fields and then run a test by creating a *dummy* instruction. It's a dummy instruction because the opcode is set to 1111110 and the literal field is all zeros. It just tests the ability to place the register fields at appropriate points in an instruction and automatically adjust the length of the literal field.

Figure 7.2 provides the output of a single run of this program. The inputs are in bold. You can see that the register fields have been selected as 3, 3, and 5 bits wide. The instruction is ADD R7, R2, R31 (note that the only data extracted is 7, 2, and 31, as we are not interested in the actual instruction):

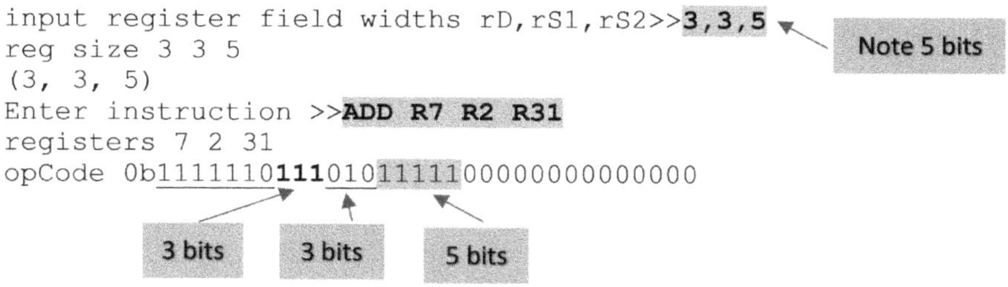

```
input register field widths rD,rS1,rS2>>3,3,5
reg size 3 3 5
(3, 3, 5)
Enter instruction >>ADD R7 R2 R31
registers 7 2 31
opCode 0b1111110111010101111100000000000000000
```

Note 5 bits

3 bits   3 bits   5 bits

Figure 7.2 – Demonstration of variable-length fields

The final binary instruction is given with each of its fields in a different style for clarity. You can see that the register fields have been placed in the correct positions in the instruction and the remaining bits (the literal field) are padded with zeros.

It may seem strange to have register fields of different widths. That means that some parameters in an instruction can access more registers than others. Such a facility can be useful; for example, you could use some of the registers as special-purpose registers (e.g., a stack pointer), or they could be used to hold frequently accessed constants (such as 0, 1, or 2):

```
# 31 Aug 2020 TESTING a variable format instruction set V1
x = input("Enter three width for: rD,rS1,rS2 (e.g., 2,2,3) >> ")
x = x.replace(' ',',')
x = x.split(",")                        # Get register sizes and convert list into tokens
x1 = int(x[0])                          # First register size rD
x2 = int(x[1])                          # Second register size rS1
x3 = int(x[2])                          # Third register size rS2
y = (x1,x2,x3)                          # Convert data size elements into a tuple

z = input("Enter three register operands for: rD,rS1,rS2 (e.g. R1,R3,R2)>> ")
opCode = 0b1111110                      # Dummy 7-bit binary opcode

z = z.replace(' ',',')
z = z.split(",")

t1,t2,t3 = 0,0,0                        # t1,t2,t3 are up to three tokens in the predicate
t1 = int(z[0][1:])                      # Extract three parameters
t2 = int(z[1][1:])
t3 = int(z[2][1:])
print ('Register widths: rD = ',t1, 'rS1 = ',t2,'rS2 = ',t3)    # Print the registers
opCode = opCode << x1 | t1             # Insert the rD field
opCode = opCode << x2 | t2             # Insert the rS1 field
opCode = opCode << x3 | t3             # Insert the rS2 field
intLen = 32 - 7 - x1 - x2 - x3        # Calculate the length of the literal field
opCode = opCode << intLen              # Shift left by literal size to create 16-bit instruction
print("opCode",bin(opCode))           # Print the result
```

Running this code with some sample values gives the following output (*Figure 7.3*). As you can see, the register files have been inserted into the opcode:

```
Enter three width for: rD,rS1,rS2 (e.g., 2,2,3) >> 3,4,5
Enter register operands for: rD,rS1,rS2 (e.g.,R1,R3,R2)>> R4,R6,R30
Register widths: rD =  4 rS1 =  6 rS2 =  30

opCode 0b1111110 100 0110 11110 0000000000000

opCode 0b1111110111010111100000000000000
```

3 bits   3 bits   5 bits

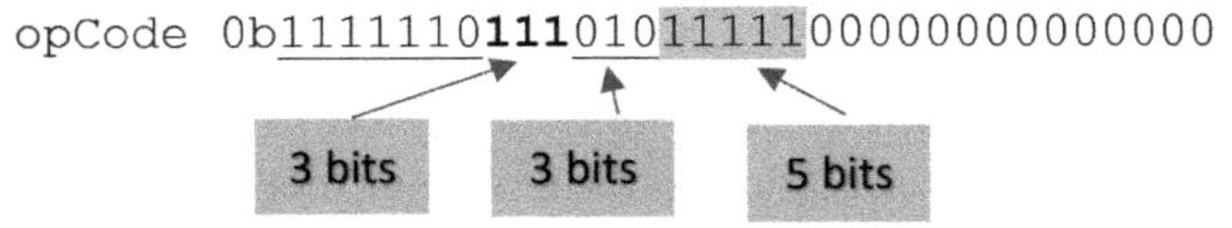

Figure 7.3 – Demonstration of variable-length operand fields

A variable-length instruction machine

Throughout this text, we have demonstrated machines with fixed-length instruction words. Computers based on this paradigm frequently fall into the RISC category. However, classic CISC machines (from the humble 8080 and 6800 to the less humble 8086 and 68000 microprocessors) had variable-length instructions, as we've already pointed out. Consider the following example of a stream of variable-length instructions, where 1 represents a 1-word instruction, 2 represents a 2-word instruction, and so on (*Figure 7.4*):

Instruction stream = **2,2**,1,**2,2**,3,3,3, **2,2**,4,4,4,4,1,**2,2**,1,1,3,3,3

Figure 7.4 – Instruction stream with variable-length opcodes

As instructions are executed, they must be decoded and the appropriate number of bytes appended to the current instruction. A problem with this approach is that it makes look-ahead processing difficult because you do not know where future instructions begin and end until you've decoded the current instruction.

Here, we're going to demonstrate a very simple variable-length machine that uses 8-bit words and an instruction can be 8, 16, 24, or 32 bits long. An operation like nop is 8 bits, branch is 16 bits, move is 24 bits, and add is 32 bits. The instruction itself is 8 bits (in the demonstration, we use only 5 bits for simplicity). An instruction is read and the two most-significant bits determine the total number of bytes required by this instruction.

The number of registers used by this machine is … none! For the sake of simplicity, and fun, we decided to make all instructions memory-based.

Consequently, we need two counters: one that counts the instructions and one that counts the bytes. For example, the instruction sequence in *Table 7.1* demonstrates the *instruction address* (sequential) and the *memory address* of the first byte of an instruction. Here, instructions vary from 1 byte (stop) to 4 bytes (add):

Code	Instruction address	Memory address
`ld 28,7`	0	0
`ld 27,2`	1	3
`ld 26,1`	2	6
`add 28,28,26`	3	9
`dec 26`	4	13
`bne 3`	5	15
`stop`	6	17
Next free space	7	18

Table 7.1 – Instruction and memory addresses for variable-length code

Here, we have used simple numeric addresses. Some addresses are literal bytes; for example, `ld 28,7` means load memory location `28` with the number `7`.

The following code provides a program to implement such a computer. Note that the actual program is supplied as a list. This program does not have the textual flexibility of TC1; it's a simple demonstration. An instruction is entered in lowercase text with commas separating the parameters. All values are in decimal. However, limited symbolic names are permitted; for example, `abc: equ 12` binds the number `12` to the symbolic name `abc:`. Note the need for a colon after the name.

All data is either a number or a memory address; for example, `add 12,13,20` adds the contents of memory location `13` to the contents of memory location `20` and puts the sum in memory location `12`.

A branch requires an actual address. Branching is absolute (direct) and not program counter-relative. To branch to the instruction beginning at address `16`, you write `bra 16`. However, symbolic names are supported and you can write `bra abc:`, provided that the target is labeled with `abc:`.

In this simulator, the instruction counter is incremented by one every time a new instruction is read. However, the memory counter is incremented every time a new byte is added to this instruction. The added bytes may be 1, 2, 3, or 4.

Since you have to give a byte branch address, you not only have to count the number of instructions branched but also the number of bytes branched. To do this, we create a mapping table that maps the instruction address to the byte address. This table is called `map[]`:

```
print ('Demonstrating multiple length instructions.
Version 3 December 8 2022 \n')
mem     = [0] * 128
```

The `lookUp{}` dictionary describes each instruction with a binary key and a value consisting of a mnemonic. The `allOps{}` dictionary consists of a key (the mnemonic) and a tuple containing the instruction length and opcode:

```
lookUp  = {0b00001:'nop',0b00010:'stop',0b01000:'inc',0b01001:'dec',   \
           0b01010:'bra',0b01011:'beq',0b01100:'bne',0b10000:'mov',     \
           0b10001:'cmpl',0b10010:'cmp',0b10011:'ld',0b10100:'st',      \
           0b11000:'add',0b11001:'sub'}
allOps  = {'nop':(1,1),'stop':(1,2),'inc':(2,8),'dec':(2,9),'bra':(2,10),   \
           'beq':(2,11),'bne':(2,12),'mov':(3,16),'ld':(3,19),             \
           'cmpl':(3,17),'cmp':(3,18),'add':(4,24),'sub':(4,25),'test':(0,0)}
# NOTE that progS is the actual program to be executed. It is embedded into the program
progS   = ['this: equ 26','ld this:,7','that: equ 28','ld 27,2', \
           'ld that:,1','loop: add 28,28,26', 'dec 26','bne loop:','stop']
symTab  = {}                                    # Label symbol table
prog    = []                                    # progS is prog without equates
for i in range (0,len(progS)):                  # Process source code for equates
    thisLine = progS[i].split()                 # Split source code on spaces
    if len(thisLine) > 1 and thisLine[1] == 'equ':  # Is this line an equate?
        symTab.update({thisLine[0][0:]:thisLine[2]})  # Store label in symbol table.
    else: prog.append(progS[i])                 # Append line to prog unless it's an equate
```

The next step after removing equates is to clean up the source code and deal with labels:

```
for i in range (0,len(prog)):                   # Process source code (now without equates)
    prog[i] = prog[i].replace(',',' ')          # Remove commas
    prog[i] = prog[i].split(' ')                # Tokenize
    token1 = prog[i][0]                         # Get first token of instruction
    if token1[-1] == ':':                       # If it ends in :, it's a label
        j = str(i)                              # Note: we have to store i as a string not an integer
        symTab.update({token1:j})               # Add label and instruction number to symbol table
        prog[i].pop(0)                          # Remove label from this line. NOTE "pop"
print('Symbol table: ', symTab)
map = [0] * 64                                  # Map instruction number to byte address
```

We now go through the code, but not in execution mode. We create a memory counter, mc, that acts rather like a program counter but serves to keep track of the instructions in memory:

```
mC  = 0                                         # Memory counter (store code from 0)
for iC in range (0,len(prog)):                  # Step through the program
    instruction = prog[iC]                      # Read an instruction. iC = instruction counter
    mCold = mC                                  # Remember old memory counter (address of first byte)
    map[iC] = mC                                # Map byte address to instruction address
    mnemonic = instruction[0]                   # The first token is the mnemonic
    mem[mC] = allOps[mnemonic][1]               # Store opcode in memory
    mC = mC + 1                                 # Point to next free memory location
```

```
    numOperands = allOps[mnemonic][0] - 1      # Get the number of operands from dictionary
    if numOperands > 0:                        # If one or more operands
        if instruction[1] in symTab:      # See if operand is in symbol table
            instruction[1] = symTab[instruction[1]]    # If it is, convert into as string
        mem[mC] = int(instruction[1])     # Store address in memory as integer
        mC = mC + 1                       # Bump up byte counter
    if numOperands > 1:                        # Do the same for two operands
        if instruction[2] in symTab:      # See if operand is in symbol table
            instruction[2] = symTab[instruction[2]]    # Convert to address as string
        mem[mC] = int(instruction[2])
        mC = mC + 1
    if numOperands > 2:                        # Now deal with 3-operand instructions
        if instruction[3] in symTab:      # See if operand is in symbol table
            instruction[3] = symTab[instruction[3]]    # If it is, convert to string
        mem[mC] = int(instruction[3])
        mC = mC + 1
    instPrint =  ' {0:<15}'.format( (' ').join(instruction))  # reformat instruction
    print('iC=', iC,'\t', 'Op =', mnemonic, '\tNumber of operands =',  \
          numOperands, '\t mC =', mCold, '\tInstruction =',              \
          instPrint, 'memory =', mem[mCold:mC])
print('Memory (in bytes) =', mem[0:40], '\n')
                                               # EXECUTE THE CODE
print('\nCode execution: press enter \n')
pc, iC, z = 0, 0, 0                            # Initialize program and instruction counters
```

Now we can execute the code by stepping through the instructions in memory using a program counter. However, the program counter is incremented by the length of each instruction after the current instruction has been read:

```
run = True
while run:                                     # Instruction execution loop
    pcOld  = pc                                # Remember pc at start of this cycle
    opCode = mem[pc]                           # Read opcode
    opLen  = (opCode >> 3) + 1                 # Get instruction length from opcode
    if opCode == 0b00010:                      # Test for stop
        run = False                            # Terminate on stop instruction
        print('Execution terminated on stop') # Say 'Goodbye'
        break                                  # and exit the loop
    operand1, operand2, operand3 = '', '', ''  # Dummy operands (null strings)
    if opLen > 1: operand1 = mem[pc + 1]
    if opLen > 2: operand2 = mem[pc + 2]
    if opLen > 3: operand3 = mem[pc + 3]
    pc = pc + opLen
    iC = iC + 1
    mnemonic = lookUp[opCode]
```

After looking up the opcode, we use an `if`...`elif` construct to examine successive mnemonics to determine the current operation. Note the dummy no-operation is implemented by Python's pass, which does nothing:

```
if   mnemonic == 'nop': pass
elif mnemonic == 'inc': mem[operand1] = mem[operand1] + 1
elif mnemonic == 'dec':
    z = 0
    mem[operand1] = mem[operand1] - 1
    if mem[operand1] == 0: z = 1
elif mnemonic == 'bra':  pc = map[operand1] # Map instruction address to byte address
elif mnemonic == 'beq' and z == 1: pc = map[operand1]
                                   # Map instruction address to byte address
elif mnemonic == 'bne' and z == 0: pc = map[operand1]
                                   # Map instruction address to byte address
elif mnemonic == 'ld':   mem[operand1] = operand2
elif mnemonic == 'mov':  mem[operand1] = mem[operand2]
```

The `cmp` compare operation subtracts two operands and sets the z-bit to 1 if the result is zero. Otherwise, z is set to 0:

```
elif mnemonic == 'cmp':
    diff = mem[operand1] - mem[operand2]
    z = 0
    if diff == 0: z = 1
elif mnemonic == 'cmpl':
    diff = mem[operand1] - operand2
    z = 0
    if diff == 0: z = 1
elif mnemonic == 'add': mem[operand1] = mem[operand2] + mem[operand3]
elif mnemonic == 'sub':
    mem[operand1] = mem[operand2] - mem[operand3]
    z = 0
    if mem[operand1] == 0: z = 1
```

At the end of the `execute` loop, we get input from the keyboard. This simply introduces a wait until the *Enter/return* key is hit before the next instruction is executed. The remaining Python code formats the output:

```
x = input('... ')
xxxx =  mnemonic + ' ' + str(operand1) + ' ' + str(operand2) \
+ ' ' + str(operand3)
instPrint =  ' {0:<15}'.format(xxxx)                        # re-format the instruction
print ('iC=',iC-1,'\tpc=',pcOld,'\tOp=',mnemonic,'z=',z,      \
       '\tmem 24-35=',mem[24:36],'\tInstruction = ', instPrint)
```

We have only briefly touched on the topic of variable-length instructions. In principle, it's a very simple idea. An instruction is read, decoded, and executed. As each instruction is fetched into the computer, it has to be decoded and the program counter advanced by the number of words taken up by the current instruction. In practice, this creates problems because branch addresses are no longer just the number of instructions from the branch but also the number of memory locations taken up by those instructions.

Summary

The previous chapter introduced TC1, a Python-based computer simulator that could be used to develop and test instruction set architectures. In this chapter, we explored aspects of simulator design in more depth.

We looked at how you can create new instructions and add them to TC1's instruction set. Advanced instructions that perform a lot of special-purpose computation were once the province of the classic CISC processor, such as the Motorola 68K family. Then, with the rise of the RISC architecture and its stress on simplicity and single-cycle instructions, the CISC processor seemed about to go out of fashion. However, many modern computers have incorporated complex instructions for special applications such as data encoding, image processing, and AI applications.

We looked a little more deeply at how you can check the input of a simulator and ensure that errors in data and instructions can be detected.

We also looked at various topics in Python programming, such as data formatting. In principle, printing data the way you want it to look is easy. In practice, it is a little more complicated (not least because there are several methods of formatting data).

This chapter expanded on the notion of tracing a program while it is being executed and demonstrated some of the techniques involved in printing the data you want to see during a simulator run.

As well as looking at new instructions, we explored the concept of variable-length instructions. We started with a demonstration of how you could change the number of bits in each register address field at runtime to change the number of addressable registers. This is not a realistic factor in instruction set design (at the moment), but there was a period when register windows became popular and you could, indeed, expand the number of registers.

We introduced the notion of variable-length instructions when each instruction can be an integer number of multiples of the computer's word length. This approach allows instructions with an unlimited level of complexity at the price of more complicated decoding mechanisms. We demonstrated the design of a primitive variable instruction length machine that could easily be expanded to a simulator with the full complexity of TC1.

The next chapter returns to the simulator and looks at several simulators for different types of architecture.

8

Simulators for Other Architectures

In this chapter, you will learn how to create simulators for different instruction set architectures, for example, the stack-based computer and the classic CISC.

After describing a simple stack-based calculator, TC0, we will introduce a simulator for a one-address format. Most operations take place between an accumulator (i.e., register) and the contents of a memory location; for example, ADD Y means *add the contents of memory location Y to the accumulator*. The term *accumulator* indicates the location where the result of an addition is *accumulated*. Early microprocessors lacked room on the silicon chip for multiple registers, and all data had to pass through one or two accumulators.

After that, we will simulate a CISC architecture, which is an extension of the accumulator-based machine, where you can perform an operation on the contents of memory and on-chip registers.

Finally, we will present the code of TC4. This is a simulator for a non-von Neumann machine with separate address and data memories and where the address and data word lengths differ.

We will cover the following topics in this chapter:

- TC0: A Stack-Based Calculator
- TC2: A One-Address Accumulator Machine
- TC3: A CISC Machine with a Register-to-Memory Architecture
- The Complete TC3 Code
- Arithmetic and Logic Unit (ALU)
- A Final Example: TC4

Technical requirements

You can find the programs used in this chapter on GitHub at https://github.com/PacktPublishing/Computer-Architecture-with-Python-and-ARM/tree/main/Chapter08.

TC0: A stack-based calculator

We'll begin with a very simple *stack-based calculator*. Here, we'll introduce a zero-address machine that avoids explicit operand addresses by storing data on a stack. We have included the notion of a stack-based computer for two reasons. First, it forms the basis of many classic calculators, a programming language (FORTH) and the design of a classic computer (Burroughs B5000). Second, constructing a stack-based computer is very easy and you can experiment with this class of computer. Indeed, elements of a stack-based processor can easily be incorporated into any computer. In a conventional computer, two elements are added with an operation such as ADD A, B, C. In a stack-based computer, two elements are added with ADD. There is no need for operand addresses because the elements to be added are the top two in a stack.

The computer we describe here is called TC0 to indicate that it is a proto-simulator, rather than a full simulator (it cannot execute conditional operations).

The stack is a data structure in the form of a queue. Items enter the queue at the top and leave the queue in the reverse order to that in which they entered. It's called a *stack* because it behaves exactly like a stack of papers.

A stack provides two operations: *push*, in which an item is added to the stack, and *pull* (or *pop*), in which an item is removed from the stack.

An operation on a single element (e.g., negate) is applied to the *top* element of the stack. An operation with two operands is applied to the two elements at the **Top of the Stack (TOS)**; for example, an addition is performed by pulling two operands off the stack, performing the addition, and then pushing the result back on the stack. *Figure 8.1* demonstrates the behavior of the stack as we evaluate P = (A + B)×(C − B − D).

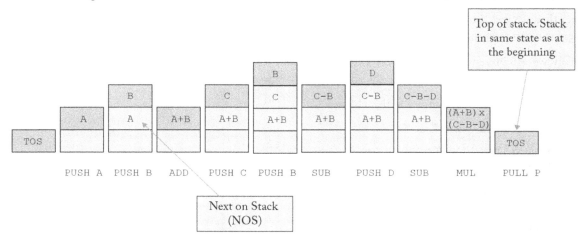

Figure 8.1 – The sequence of actions taking place during the evaluation of (A + B)×(C – B – D)

Table 8.1 shows how we perform the P = (A + B)×(C – B – D) calculation using the PUSH, PULL, ADD, SUB, and MUL stack operations. As well as arithmetic operations, two other common stack operations are DUP (duplicate) and SWAP. The DUP operation makes a copy of the item at the TOS and pushes it on the stack (i.e., the top of the stack is duplicated). The SWAP operation exchanges the TOS and **Next on Stack (NOS)** values.

Operation	The stack as a Python list (bold is top of stack)
PUSH A	stack = [x,x,x,x,x,x,x,**A**]
PUSH B	stack = [x,x,x,x,x,x,**B**,A]
ADD	stack = [x,x,x,x,x,x,x,**A+B**]
PUSH C	stack = [x,x,x,x,x,x,**C**,A+B]
PUSH B	stack = [x,x,x,x,x,**B**,C,A+B]
SUBTRACT	stack = [x,x,x,x,x,x,**C-B**,A+B]
PUSH D	stack = [x,x,x,x,x,**D**,C-B,A+B]
SUBTRACT	stack = [x,x,x,x,x,x,**D-C-B**,A+B]
MULTIPLY	stack = [x,x,x,x,x,x,x,**(D-C-B)(A+B)**]
PULL result	stack = [x,x,x,x,x,x,x,x]

Table 8.1 – The code to evaluate (A + B)×(C – B – D)

To simplify the simulator, each instruction is stored in a Python list consisting of the operation and memory address (for PUSH and PULL). This is not intended to be a practical simulator; it's a demonstration of the use of the stack to handle arithmetic operations and an introduction to the stack for later chapters.

A register called a **Stack Pointer (SP)** points to the TOS. That is, the stack pointer contains the address of the item at the top of the stack. By convention, the stack pointer grows *upward* as items are added and shrinks downward as items are removed. Since we draw memory diagrams with low addresses at the top of the page, the stack grows up toward low addresses. In other words, if the top of a stack is at the location 1231, pushing an element on the stack stores it at address 1230, since the stack grows toward low addresses.

In some implementations, the stack pointer points at the *next free location* above the top of the stack. We will represent the stack in Python by the list stack[]. The stack pointer is sp and the operation to push item A on the stack is as follows:

```
sp = sp - 1       # Decrement the stack pointer. Point to the next free location above TOS
stack[sp] = A     # Load the new value, A, on the stack in this location
```

Remember that the stack pointer is decremented because the stack grows toward lower addresses. If an item is popped off the stack, the inverse operation is as follows:

```
A = stack[sp]     # Retrieve the item at the top of the stack
sp = sp + 1       # Move the stack pointer down
```

These are complementary operations. A pull operation cancels a push. Consider evaluating an expression. *Figure 8.2* shows the state of the stack during the evaluation of $X = (A + B) \times (C - D)$.

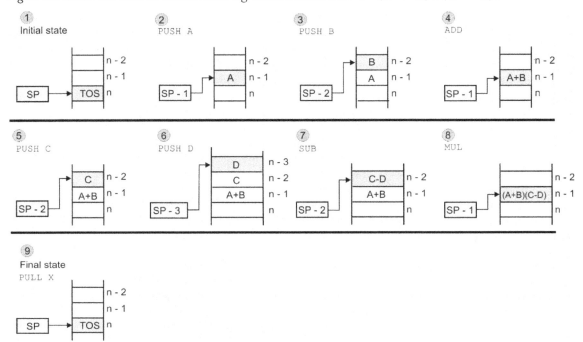

Figure 8.2 – The sequence of actions taking place during the evaluation of X = (A + B)×(C – D)

The next step is to demonstrate how we can implement a simple calculator, TC0, based on a stack.

TC0: A python stack machine

We can represent the addition `y3 = y1 + y2` on a stack machine in Python as follows:

```
y1 = stack[sp]       # Retrieve the item at the top of the stack (y1 and y2 are on the stack)
sp = sp + 1          # Move the stack pointer down
y2 = stack[sp]       # Retrieve the item at the top of the stack
y3 = y1 + y2         # Add the two values
stack[sp] = y3       # Store the result on the stack
```

We've taken a shortcut. We could have pulled two elements off the stack, added them, and pushed the result. Instead, we put the result back where the second operand was and saved two stack pointer movements. The following Python code illustrates a very simple stack machine interpreter. It does not implement branch operations, so it is not a realistic computation machine. Because a stack machine often operates on the top of the stack and the element below it, the second element is frequently called NOS. Note that the program is stored as a list of lists, with each instruction consisting of either a two-element list (e.g., ['push', '2']) or a single-element list (e.g., ['mul']):

```
                                           # Stack machine simulator
prog = [['push',0],['push',1],['add'],    ['push',2],['push',1],          \
        ['sub'],    ['push',3],['sub'],    ['mul'],    ['push',4],         \
        ['swap'],   ['dup'],['pull',4],    ['stop']]

stack = [0] * 8                # 8-location stack. Stack grows to lower addresses
mem   = [3,2,7,4,6,0]          # Data memory (first locations are preloaded 3, 2, 7, 4, 6)
run = True                     # Execution continues while run is true
pc = 0                         # Program counter - initialize
sp = 8                         # Initialize stack pointer to 1 past end of stack
while run:                     # Execute MAIN LOOP until run is false (STOP command)
    inst = prog[pc]            # Read the next instruction
    pc = pc + 1                # Increment program counter
    if    inst[0] == 'push':   # Test for push operation
        sp = sp - 1            # Pre-decrement stack pointer
        address = int(inst[1]) # Get data from memory
        stack[sp] = mem[address]  # Store it on the stack

    elif inst[0] == 'pull':    # Test for a pull instruction
        address = int(inst[1]) # Get destination address
        mem[address] = stack[sp]  # Store the item in memory
        sp = sp + 1            # Increment stack pointer

    elif inst[0] == 'add':     # If operation add TOS to NOS and push result
        p = stack[sp]
        sp = sp + 1
        q = stack[sp]
        stack[sp] = p + q

    elif inst[0] == 'sub':     # sub
        p = stack[sp]
        sp = sp + 1
        q = stack[sp]
        stack[sp] = q - p

    elif inst[0] == 'mul':     # mul
        p = stack[sp]
        sp = sp + 1
        q = stack[sp]
        stack[sp] = p * q
```

```
    elif inst[0] == 'div':              # div (note floor division with integer result)
        p = stack[sp]
        sp = sp + 1
        q = stack[sp]
        stack[sp] = p//q

    elif inst[0] == 'dup':              # dup (duplicate top item on stack)
        p = stack[sp]                   # get current TOS
        sp = sp - 1                     # and push it on the stack to duplicate
        stack[sp] = p

    elif inst[0] == 'swap':             # swap (exchange top of stack and next on stack)
        p = stack[sp]
        q = stack[sp+1]
        stack[sp] = q
        stack[sp+1] =p

    elif inst[0] == 'stop':             # stop
        run = False

    if sp == 8: TOS = 'empty'           # Stack elements 0 to 7. Element 8 is before the TOS
    else: TOS = stack[sp]
    print('pc =', pc-1,'sp =',sp,'TOS =',TOS,'Stack',stack,'Mem',mem,'op',inst)
```

The following is the output from this program, which shows the program counter, the top of the stack, NOS, the stack itself, the data, and the opcode being executed. Values that change between cycles are in bold:

```
pc=0  sp=7  TOS=3 Stack [0,0,0,0,0,0,0,3] Mem [3,2,7,4,6,0] op ['push',0]
pc=1  sp=6  TOS=2 Stack [0,0,0,0,0,0,2,3] Mem [3,2,7,4,6,0] op ['push',1]
pc=2  sp=7  TOS=5 Stack [0,0,0,0,0,0,2,5] Mem [3,2,7,4,6,0] op ['add']
pc=3  sp=6  TOS=7 Stack [0,0,0,0,0,0,7,5] Mem [3,2,7,4,6,0] op ['push',2]
pc=4  sp=5  TOS=2 Stack [0,0,0,0,0,2,7,5] Mem [3,2,7,4,6,0] op ['push',1]
pc=5  sp=6  TOS=5 Stack [0,0,0,0,0,2,5,5] Mem [3,2,7,4,6,0] op ['sub']
pc=6  sp=5  TOS=4 Stack [0,0,0,0,0,4,5,5] Mem [3,2,7,4,6,0] op ['push',3]
pc=7  sp=6  TOS=1 Stack [0,0,0,0,0,4,1,5] Mem [3,2,7,4,6,0] op ['sub']
pc=8  sp=7  TOS=5 Stack [0,0,0,0,0,4,1,5] Mem [3,2,7,4,6,0] op ['mul']
pc=9  sp=6  TOS=6 Stack [0,0,0,0,0,4,6,5] Mem [3,2,7,4,6,0] op ['push',4]
pc=10 sp=6  TOS=5 Stack [0,0,0,0,0,4,5,6] Mem [3,2,7,4,6,0] op ['swap']
pc=11 sp=5  TOS=5 Stack [0,0,0,0,0,5,5,6] Mem [3,2,7,4,6,0] op ['dup']
pc=12 sp=6  TOS=5 Stack [0,0,0,0,0,5,5,6] Mem [3,2,7,4,6,5] op ['pull',5]
pc=13 sp=6  TOS=5 Stack [0,0,0,0,0,5,5,6] Mem [3,2,7,4,6,5] op ['stop']
```

In the next section, we will look at a more realistic machine that implements a simple accumulator machine of the early 8-bit microprocessor era.

TC2: A one-address accumulator machine

In this section, you will learn about a computer that implements a memory-to-register architecture. This is a very simple machine that implements a one-address instruction format (like an 8-bit CISC microprocessor from the 1970s).

The TC2 model can be used to simulate classic 8-bit microprocessors that are found in low-cost computer systems (e.g., controllers in mechanical devices). It also teaches you about the trade-off between simplicity (of the computer) and complexity (of the software that is constrained by the primitive architecture).

Unlike modern RISC architectures with data-processing operations between two registers, this computer implements a dyadic operation between one operand in the accumulator and the other operand, which is either a literal or the contents of memory; for example, ADD M adds the contents of memory location M to the accumulator, and ADD #5 adds a literal to the contents of the accumulator. This computer does not have a large set of general-purpose registers.

The one-address machine permits operations between data in the accumulator and in memory. This contrasts with RISC architectures that permit data-processing operations only between registers. Load and store are the only memory operations permitted by a RISC architecture. This computer, TC2, implements a minimal instruction set that demonstrates its operation. Table 8.2 describes the instruction set:

Mnemonic	Action	Memory form	Literal form	Opcode
LDA	Load accumulator	[A] ← [M]	[A] ← L	0
STA	Store accumulator	[M] ← [A]	[M] ← L	0
ADD	Add to accumulator	[A] ← [A] + [M]	[A] ← [A] + L	1
SUB	Subtract from accumulator	[A] ← [A] - [M]	[A] ← [A] - L	2
CLR	Load accumulator/memory with zero	[A] ← 0	[M] ← 0	3
BRA	Branch unconditionally to L	[PC] ← L		4
BEQ	Branch on zero to L	if Z = 1 then[PC] ← L		5
BNE	Branch on not zero to L	if Z = 0 then[PC] ← L		6
STOP	Stop			7

Table 8.2 – Typical operations of a register-to-memory computer

Here, [A] is the contents of the accumulator, [M] is the contents of memory location M, L is a literal, and the Z-bit is set if the result of a subtraction is zero. M and L represent the literal field of an instruction and are mutually exclusive. You can't have an instruction with both an M and L operand.

Simulating a computer teaches us a lot about partitioning an instruction into various fields and how to implement instructions. In this example, we use a 3-bit opcode, a 1-bit *direction* flag (for LDA and STA) that defines the direction of data movement (to or from memory), and a 1-bit *mode* flag that selects either a literal or a direct memory access. A 5-bit numeric field provides an integer in the range 0 to 31, or a memory address. The instruction size is 10 bits with the format CCC D M LLLLL, where *CCC* is the opcode field, *D* is the direction bit, *M* is the mode bit, and *LLLLL* is the literal or memory address (*Figure 8.3*). The extreme simplicity of this makes it easy to write a tiny simulator and leaves the user with a lot of opportunities to expand the code into a more realistic machine.

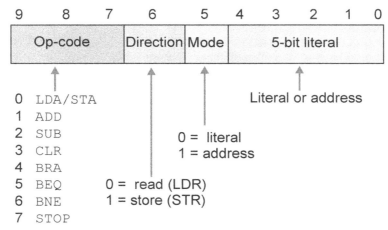

Figure 8.3 – TC2 instruction format

TC2 simulates a stored program computer with a single memory that holds both the program and data. The 32-bit location memory is initialized by memory = [0]*32.

The TC2 code has a setup section and a while loop that includes a fetch instruction and an execute instruction part. The structure of the while loop part of the code (instruction fetch/execute cycle) consists of the following:

```
while run == True:
    operation          # Body of while loop operation
    .
    .
statement              # Next operation after the while loop
```

Within the while loop, we have a fetch phase followed by an execution phase. The fetch phase is identical to the CPUs we have already described. Instruction decoding is included in this phase. Instruction decoding separates OpCode, Dir (i.e., direction to or from memory), Mode, and Literal by using shifting and bit-masking operations:

```
MAR = PC               # PC to Memory Address Register
PC = PC + 1            # Increment PC
```

```
MBR = Memory[MAR]        # Read instruction, copy to Memory Buffer register
IR  = MBR                # Copy instruction to Instruction Register
OpCode = IR >> 7         # Extract Op-Code frominstruction (bits 7 to 10)
Dir  = (IR >> 6) & 1     # Extract data direction from instruction (0 = read, 1 = write)
Mode = (IR >> 5) & 1     # Extract address mode from instruction (0 = literal, 1 = memory)
Lit  = IR & 0x1F         # Extract the literal/address field from the instruction
```

Right shifts and ANDs extract fields from the instruction; for example, the 3-bit opcode is extracted from the 10-bit CCCDMLLLLL instruction by shifting seven places left to get 0000000CCC. The direction bit, Dir, is extracted by performing six left shifts to get 000000CCCD and then ANDing the result with 1 to get 000000000D. These two operations can be combined and written as follows:

```
(IR >> 6) & 1     # 6-bit shift right with >> and AND with 1 using the AND operator, &
```

Similarly, we extract the mode bit by performing Mode = (IR >> 5) & 1. Finally, the literal is in place, so all we have to do is to clear the other bits by ANDing it with 0b0000011111, that is, IR & 0x1F.

In the execute phase, the three op-code bits, OpCode, select one of the eight possible instructions. Of course, the use of if … elif would have been more appropriate:

```
if   OpCode == 0:
     Code for case 0
elif OpCode == 1:
     Code for case 1


 .

 .

elif OpCode == 7:
     Code for case 7
```

Each op-code is guarded by an if statement. Here's the code for the load and store accumulator instruction. We treat this as one operation and use the direction flag, Dir, to select between LDA (direction memory to accumulator) and STA (direction accumulator to memory):

```
if OpCode == 0:                  # Test for Load A or Store A instruction
    if Dir == 0:                 # If direction bit is 0, then it's a load accumulator
        if Mode == 0:            # Test for literal or direct memory operand
            Acc = Lit            # If mode is 0, then it's a literal operand
        else:                    #If mode is 1, then it's a memory access
            MAR = Lit            #Copy field (address) to MAR
            MBR = Memory[MAR]    #Do a read to get the operand in MBR
            Acc = MBR            #and send it to the accumulator
    else:
        MAR = Lit                # If direction is 1 then it's a store accumulator
        MBR = Acc                # Copy accumulator to MBR
        Memory[MAR] = MBR        # and write MBR to memory
```

To make it easier to read the code, we've divided it into two blocks (one shaded in dark gray and one in light gray) guarded by the if Dir == 0 statement. When the direction flag is 0, the instruction is *load accumulator* and the address is copied to the MAR, a read is performed, and the data is copied to the MBR and then the accumulator. If the direction flag is 1, the instruction is a *store accumulator* and the accumulator is copied to the MBR and a write operation is carried out.

Note the use of the Mode flag. When loading the accumulator from memory, LDA, the mode flag is used to ·load the accumulator with either a literal or the contents of memory. When executing a STA, which refers to the store accumulator, the mode flag is ignored because only a memory store is possible.

We don't need to describe the ADD and SUB operations because they are simply extensions of the load and store operations. We've included a clear operation, CLR, which sets either the accumulator to 0 or the contents of memory to 0 depending only on the Mode flag.

We'll now present the full simulator code. The Memory[MAR] notation means the contents of memory whose address is in the MAR and is conveniently identical to the RTL we've been using. In the execute instruction block, alternate opcodes are shaded gray and blue to facilitate reading.

We've included a small program in memory, complete with data that tests several of the instructions, including load and store, add, subtract, and branch.

TC2 has a clear operation, CLR, that sets either the accumulator or the contents of memory to 0 depending on the Mode flag. This simplified computer has only a Z-bit (no N and C bits).

The branch group of instructions (BRA, BEQ, and BNE) load the program counter with a literal to force a jump. BRA performs an unconditional branch, and BEQ/BNE depending on the state of the Z-bit, which is set/cleared by add and subtract operations. The branch target address is an absolute address provided by the literal field.

We have reserved the last instruction opcode, 111, as a stop (halt) instruction that breaks out of the while loop and terminates execution. In general, a real CPU does not need a halt instruction, although a halt instruction can be used to force it into a power-down mode until it is awakened by an external event, such as a keyboard/mouse input or a screen touch:

```
                                    # The TC2: A primitive accumulator machine
mnemonics = {0:'LDA/STR', 1:'ADD', 2:'SUB', 3:'CLR', 4:'BRA', 5: \
             'BEQ', 6:'BNE', 7:'STOP'}
def progSet():
    global mem
    mem = [0] * 32               # The memory holds both instructions and data
  # Format   CCCDMLLLLL           # 000 LDA/STR, 001 ADD, 010 SUB, 011 CLR, 100 BRA, \
                                    101 BEQ, 110 BNE, 111 STOP
    mem[0]  =  0b0000110000       # LDA 16  [A]    = M[16]
    mem[1]  =  0b0010110001       # ADD 17  [A]    = [A] + M[17]
    mem[2]  =  0b0001110010       # STA 18  M[18] = [A]
    mem[3]  =  0b0100000011       # SUB #3  [A]    = [A] - 3
    mem[4]  =  0b1010001000       # BEQ 8
    mem[5]  =  0b0000010010       # LDA #18 [A]    = 18
```

```
    mem[6]   =  0b0001110010    # STA 18   M[18] = [A]
    mem[7]   =  0b0110000000    # CLR      [A]   = 0
    mem[8]   =  0b0000000010    # LDA #2   [A]   = 2
    mem[9]   =  0b0100000010    # SUB #2   [A]   = [A] - 3
    mem[10]  =  0b1010001101    # BEQ 12
    mem[11]  =  0b0000001111    # LDA #15 LDA #18 [A] = 18 Dummy not executed
    mem[12]  =  0b1110000000    # STOP
    mem[16]  =  0b0000000100    # 4 Data for test
    mem[17]  =  0b0000000101    # 5 Data for test
    mem[31]  =  0b1110000000    # Ensure STOP operation
    return(mem)
```

```
run = True       # run is True for code execution. Setting run to False stops the computer
PC  = 0          # The program counter points to the next instruction to execute. Initially 0
z = 0            # Initialize z-bit (note no n and c bits implemented)
mem = progSet()
```

Now that we've loaded memory with the program and set up some variables, we can enter the `fetch execute` loop:

```
                                  # MAIN LOOP – FETCH/EXECUTE
while run:                        # This is the fetch/execute cycle loop that continues until run is False
    MAR    = PC                   # FETCH PC to mem Address Register
    pcOld  = PC                   # Keep a copy of the PC for display
    PC     = PC + 1               # Increment PC
    MBR    = mem[MAR]             # Read the instruction, copy it to the mem Buffer Register
    IR     = MBR                  # Copy instruction to Instruction Register – prior to decoding it
    OpCode = (IR >> 7) & 0x7      # Extract Op-Code from instruction bits 7 to 10 by shifting masking
    Dir    = (IR >> 6) & 1        # Extract data direction from instruction (0 = read, 1 = write)
    Mode   = (IR >> 5) & 1        # Extract address mode from instruction (0 = literal, 1 = mem)
    Lit    = IR & 0x1F            # Extract literal/address field (0 = address, 1= literal)
```

```
                                  # EXECUTE The EXECUTE block is an if statement, one for each opcode
    if OpCode == 0:               # Test for LDA and STA (Dir is 0 for load acc and 1 for store in mem)
        if Dir == 0:              # If Direction is 0, then it's a load accumulator, LDA
            if Mode == 0:         #  Test for Mode bit to select literal or direct mem operand
                Acc = Lit         #  If mode is 0, then the accumulator is loaded with L
            else:                 # If mode is 1, then read mem to get operand
                MAR = Lit         # Literal (address) to MAR
                MBR = mem[MAR]    # Do a read to get operand in MBR
                Acc = MBR         # and send it to the accumulator
        else:
            MAR = Lit             # If Direction is 1, then it's a store accumulator
            MBR = Acc             # Copy accumulator to MBR
            mem[MAR] = MBR        # and write MBR to mem
```

```
elif OpCode == 1:              # Test for ADD to accumulator
    if Mode == 0:              # Test for literal or direct mem operand
        total = Acc + Lit      # If mode is 0, then it's a literal operand
        if total == 0: z = 1   # Deal with z flag
        else: z = 0
```

```
    else:                      # If mode is 1, then it's a direct mem access
        MAR = Lit              # Literal (address) to MAR
        MBR = mem[MAR]         # Do a read to get operand in MBR
        total = MBR + Acc      # And send it to the accumulator
    if Dir == 0: Acc = total   # Test for destination (accumulator)
    else: mem[MAR] = total     # Or mem
```

```
elif OpCode == 2:              # Test for SUB from accumulator
    if Mode == 0:              # Test for literal or direct mem operand
        total = Acc - Lit      # If mode is 0 then it's a literal operand
    else:                      # If mode is 1 then it's a direct mem access
        MAR = Lit              #  Literal (address) to MAR
        MBR = mem[MAR]         # Do a read to get operand in MBR
        total = Lit - MBR      # and send it to the accumulator
    if total == 0: z = 1       # Now update z bit (in all cases)
    if Dir == 0: Acc = total   # Test for destination (accumulator)
    else: mem[MAR] = total     # Or mem
```

The following block (dark shading) implements a clear operation. This instruction is not strictly necessary, because you can always load a zero or subtract x from X. For this reason, some computers do not incorporate a clear instruction. Some computers allow you to write CLR and then substitute an operation such as SUB X, X:

```
elif OpCode == 3:              # Test for CLR (clear Accumulator or clear mem location)
    if Mode == 0:              # If Mode = 0 Then clear accumulator
        Acc = 0
    else:
        MAR = Lit              # If Mode = 1
        mem[MAR] = 0           # Then clear mem location mem[Literal]
```

```
elif OpCode == 4:              # Test for BRA Branch unconditionally
    PC = Lit - 1               # Calculate new branch target address (-1 because PC auto increment)
```

```
elif OpCode == 5:              # Test for BEQ Branch on zero
    if z == 1: PC = Lit - 1    # If z bit = 1 then calculate new branch target address
```

```
elif OpCode == 6:              # Test for BNE Branch on not zero
    if z == 0: PC = Lit - 1    # If z bit = 0 calculate new branch target address
```

```
    elif OpCode == 7:                # Test for STOP
        run = False                  # If STOP then clear run flag to exit while loop and stop
```

You could argue that we should have inserted a break or exit here because if we haven't encountered a valid op-code by the end of the execute loop, the source code must be invalid:

```
# End of main fetch-execute loop
    mnemon = mnemonics.get(OpCode)    # Get the mnemonic for printing

    print('PC',pcOld, 'Op ',OpCode, 'Mode = ', Mode, 'Dir = ',Dir, \
          'mem', mem[16:19], 'z',z, 'Acc', Acc, mnemon)
```

We now run this program. The output when running this program is as follows:

```
PC 0   OpCode  0 Mode =  1 Dir =  0 mem [4, 5, 0]  z 0 Acc 4  LDA/STR
PC 1   OpCode  1 Mode =  1 Dir =  0 mem [4, 5, 0]  z 0 Acc 9  ADD
PC 2   OpCode  0 Mode =  1 Dir =  1 mem [4, 5, 9]  z 0 Acc 9  LDA/STR
PC 3   OpCode  2 Mode =  0 Dir =  0 mem [4, 5, 9]  z 0 Acc 6  SUB
PC 4   OpCode  5 Mode =  0 Dir =  0 mem [4, 5, 9]  z 0 Acc 6  BEQ
PC 5   OpCode  0 Mode =  0 Dir =  0 mem [4, 5, 9]  z 0 Acc 18 LDA/STR
PC 6   OpCode  0 Mode =  1 Dir =  1 mem [4, 5, 18] z 0 Acc 18 LDA/STR
PC 7   OpCode  3 Mode =  0 Dir =  0 mem [4, 5, 18] z 0 Acc 0  CLR
PC 8   OpCode  0 Mode =  0 Dir =  0 mem [4, 5, 18] z 0 Acc 2  LDA/STR
PC 9   OpCode  2 Mode =  0 Dir =  0 mem [4, 5, 18] z 1 Acc 0  SUB
PC 10  OpCode  5 Mode =  0 Dir =  0 mem [4, 5, 18] z 1 Acc 0  BEQ
PC 12  OpCode  7 Mode =  0 Dir =  0 mem [4, 5, 18] z 1 Acc 0  STOP
```

Enhancing the TC2 Simulator

The simple example of an accumulator-based machine illustrates several aspects of the implementation of instructions, the design of the instruction set, and the allocation of bits. The TC2 has a 3-bit opcode giving us eight operations. Or does it?

The direction bit, Dir, is employed only by the LDA/STA instruction. If we removed this bit from the opcode field, we would have a 4-bit opcode giving 16 instructions. Since LDA and STA would now be separate instructions, our eight-instruction computer would have nine instructions, leaving $16 - 9 = 7$ new (i.e., unallocated) opcodes. We could have also used the direction flag with ADD and SUB instructions allowing the destination to be either the accumulator or memory. Consider the following example. The current TC2 simulator can increment variables x and y using the following code:

```
    LDA   x
    ADD   #1
    STA   x
    LDA   y
```

```
ADD  #1
STA  y
```

By extending the addition operation (ADDA to add to the accumulator and ADDM to add to memory), we can now write the following:

```
LDAA #1    ; Load accumulator with 1
ADDM x     ; Add accumulator to memory location x
ADDM y     ; Add accumulator to memory location y
```

This enhancement halves the number of instructions, because we load the accumulator with the literal once and then add it to two different memory locations. The new code for the ADD operation is as follows:

```
if OpCode == 1:                   # Test for ADDA or ADDM instruction
    if Dir == 0:                  # Test for add to accumulator (Dir=0) or add to memory (Dir =1)
        if Mode == 0:             # Test for ADDA literal or direct memory operand
            Acc = Acc + Lit       # If mode is 0, then it's a literal operand
        else:                     # If mode is 1, then it's a direct memory access
            MAR = Lit             # Literal (address) to MAR
            MBR = Memory[MAR]     # Do a read to get operand in MBR
            Acc = MBR + Acc       # and send it to the accumulator
    if Dir == 1:                  #  ADDM: add to memory version of ADD
        MAR = Lit                 #  Set up the memory address
        MBR = Memory[MAR]         #  Read memory contents
        MBR = MBR + Acc           #  Add accumulator to memory
        Memory[MAR] = MBR         #  And write back the result
```

What else can we do to extend the instruction set? We allocated *three* opcodes to the branch group. That was very wasteful. Since each of these branch instructions has a direction and a mode bit that is unused, we can press these bits into service (i.e., redefine their meaning). Consider the arrangement of *Table 8.3*:

Operation	Direction	Mode
BRA	0	0
Undefined	0	1
BEQ	1	0
BNE	1	1

Table 8.3 – Re-purposing the direction and mode bits

We have used the `Dir` and `Mode` instruction bits to select the branch type. As a bonus, we have a spare operation that is marked *undefined*. The code for the branch group is as follows. We've used shading to help identify the blocks. Note that in this example, we demonstrate how branches can be made program counter relative:

```
if OpCode == 3:                              # Test for the branch group
    if Dir == 0:                             # Direction 0 for unconditional
        if Mode == 0: PC = PC + Lit - 1      # If Mode is zero then unconditional branch
        else: run = 0                        # If Mode is 1 then this is undefined so stop
    else:
        if Dir == 1:                         # If direction is 1, it's a conditional branch
            if Mode == 0:                    # If mode is 0 then we have a BNE
                if Z == 0: PC = PC + Lit - 1 # Branch on Z = 0 (not zero)
            else:                            # If Mode is 1 we have a BEQ
                if Z == 1: PC = PC + Lit - 1 # Branch on Z = 1 (zero)
```

This code looks a little more complex than it is, because we have `if` statements nested four deep when we test for op-code, direction, mode, and then Z-bit. However, this example demonstrates how instruction bits can be reused to increase the number of instructions at the cost of decoding complexity.

There's still room to maneuver and squeeze more functionality out of the instruction set. Look at the `CLR` instruction. We use the mode bit to clear memory or the accumulator. How about being a little creative and using the *direction* bit to provide another operation? Incrementing a register or memory is a common operation, so let's provide that. We can use `Dir == 0` for CLR and `Dir == 1` for INC Memory/accumulator. The block shaded in gray is the original clear and the block shaded in blue is the new increment operation:

```
if OpCode == 6:                     # Test for clear mem/Acc or increment mem/Acc
    if Dir == 0:                    # Direction = 0 for clear operation
        if Mode == 0:               # If Mode = 0
            Acc = 0                 # Then clear accumulator
        else:                       # If Mode = 1
            MAR = Lit
            Memory[MAR] = 0         # Then clear memory location
    else:                           # Direction = 1 for increment
        if Mode == 0:               # If Mode = 0
            Acc = Acc + 1           # Then increment accumulator
        else:                       # If Mode = 1
            MAR = Lit
            MBR = Memory[MAR]       # Then increment memory location
            MBR = MBR + 1           # Increment memory in MBR
            Memory[MAR] = MBR       # Write back incremented memory value
```

Finally, consider the STOP (halt) instruction with the 111DMLLLLL opcode. Here, we have 7 bits doing nothing. That is 2^7 = 128 combinations. If we were to reserve one code for halt, say, 1110000000, we could allocate codes 1110000001 to 1111111111 to new instructions. The next section extends this architecture to create a more realistic simulator.

TC3: A CISC machine with a register-to-memory architecture

In this section, you will learn about the design of a simulator that implements a CISC-style instruction set architecture, providing both register-to-register and register-to-memory operations. TC3 is a more sophisticated version of TC2 with a more practical architecture.

TC3 supports register direct, register indirect, memory direct, and literal addressing modes. For example, AND [R2], #129 performs a logical AND between the contents of the memory location pointed at by register R2 and the binary value 10000001.

We have included memory direct operations. These are intended to illustrate the features of a computer, rather than being practical. Early 8-bit microprocessors like the Motorola 6800 let you operate on memory directly. Most modern processors don't. TC3 can access, say, memory at location 12 with MOV R2,M:12. This instruction loads register 2 with the contents of memory location 12. Note the syntax. A TC3 instruction provides a single literal field that can serve as a literal or a memory address, but not both at the same time. I've used # to indicate a literal and M: to indicate a memory address; consider MOV R2,M:12 and MOV R2,#12. The former loads register R2 with the contents of memory location 12, and the latter loads R2 with the integer 12. With a single literal field in the instruction, TC3 can't support an instruction like MOV M:12,#127.

The TC3 instruction set architecture

The TC3 simulator is a one-and-a-half address CISC processor with a 24-bit instruction and an 8-bit data word length. This makes it a Harvard machine, because it has separate data and program memory. We have taken this approach for two reasons. First, an 8-bit data word is easy to work with from an educational point of view. Second, a 24-bit instruction provides functionality, without either using a large 32-bit word or employing variable-length instructions like some CISC processors.

Figure 8.4 describes the TC3's instruction format, which has an instruction class and an op-code field, an addressing mode field, two register fields, and a literal field. The format is the same for all instructions.

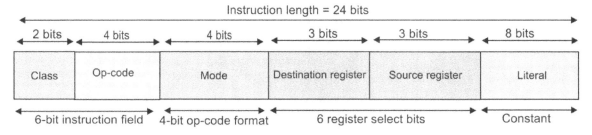

Figure 8.4 – Instruction format of the TC3

We use 8-bit registers, an 8-bit address, and an 8-bit literal to simplify the design. The data space is restricted to $2^8 = 256$ locations, since the literal can access only 256 locations. Changing the instruction width to 32 bits and expanding the literal to 16 bits would provide a data space of 65,536 locations.

The TC3 has eight general-purpose registers, R0 to R7. It requires 6 bits to provide source and destination register fields The instruction field is 6 bits wide and is divided into a 2-bit instruction-class field and a 4-bit op-code field. This allows up to 64 instructions with a maximum of 16 in each class. We took this approach (instruction class and op-code) to simplify the design. This is a rather inefficient approach in terms of instruction-space usage, because most instructions fall within one class and other classes are nearly empty.

The 4-bit mode field defines an instruction's attributes (e.g., addressing modes). The TC3 supports the addressing modes defined by *Table 8.4*, that is, no-operand instructions, one-register instructions, instructions with a literal, and two-operand instructions. Although the TC3 supports only two operands (register + register and register + literal), there are three fields in the instruction. Consequently, the computer could be easily modified to provide three-operand instructions. We chose this approach to simplify instruction encoding and decoding. An alternative approach would be to provide two operand fields – a register field and a register or literal field:

Mode	Address	Example	RTL	Class
0	No operand	STOP		0
1	Single register	INC R1	[R1] ← [R1] + 1	1
2	Literal offset	BEQ 123	[pc] ← 123	2
3	Reserved			
4	Literal to register	MOV R1,#M	[R1] ← M	3
5	Register to register	MOV R1,R2	[R1] ← [R2]	3
6	Register indirect to register	MOV R1,[R2]	[R1] ← [[R2]]	3
7	Register to register indirect	MOV [R1],R2	[[R1]] ← [R2]	3
8	Register indirect to register indirect	MOV [R1],[R2]	[[R1]] ← [[R2]]	3
9	Register to memory	MOV M:123,R2	M[123] ← [R2]	3
10	Register indirect to memory	MOV M:123,[R2]	M[123] ← [[R2]]	3
11	Memory to register	MOV R1,M:123	[R1] ← M[123]	3
12	Memory to register indirect	MOV [R1],M:123	[[R1]] ← M[123]	3
13-15	Reserved			

Table 8.4 – TC3 processor addressing modes

Consider the following assembly language program that runs on this computer. We wish to add together two vectors plus an integer, that is, $z_{i = xi + yi + 5}$ for $i = 0$ to 3. The following code should be largely self-explanatory. Literals are prefixed with #, and a label in an instruction is terminated with a colon. The first part of the code uses the RND R5 instruction to fill vectors X and Y with random numbers to aid testing.

	Code		@ Comment	Instruction encoding
	MOV	R0,#	@ Point to memory location 8	
Next:	RND	R5	@ REPEAT: generate random value in r5	
	MOV	[R0],R5	@ store r5 at location pointed at by r0	
	DEC	R0	@ decrement r0 pointer	
	BNE	Next	@ UNTIL zero	
	EQU	X,#1	@ Vector X memory 1 to 4	
	EQU	Y,#5	@ Vector Y memory 5 to 8	
	EQU	Z,#9	@ Vector Z memory 9 to 12	
	MOV	R0,#X	@ r0 points to array X	00 0000 0010 000 000 00000001
	MOV	R1,#Y	@ r1 points to array Y	00 0000 0010 001 000 00000101
	MOV	R2,#Z	@ r2 points to array Z	00 0000 0010 010 000 00001001
	MOV	R3,#4	@ r3 number of elements to add in r3	00 0000 0010 011 000 00000100
Loop:	MOV	R4,[R0]	@ Get xi	00 0000 0000 100 000 00000000
	ADD	R4,#5	@ Add 5 to xi	00 0001 0010 100 000 00000101
	ADD	R4,[R1]	@ Add xi + 5 to yi Memory to reg operation	00 0001 0001 100 001 00000000
	MOV	[R2],R4	@ Store result in array Z	00 0000 0100 010 100 00000000
	INC	R0	@ Increment pointer to array X	00 1100 0000 000 000 00000000
	INC	R1	@ Increment pointer to array Y	00 1100 0000 001 000 00000000
	INC	R2	@ Increment pointer to array Z	00 1100 0000 010 000 00000000
	DEC	R3	@ Decrement loop counter	00 1101 0000 011 000 00000000
	BNE	Loop	@ Continue until counter 0	01 0011 0000 000 000 00000100

This example uses literal, register direct, and register indirect (pointer-based) addressing. We have provided the binary code of each instruction with the class, op-code, addressing mode, registers, and literal fields.

Initially, we didn't construct an assembler for this simulator. However, it was such a pain to hand-code the instructions that an assembler was incorporated. The key to both the assembler and simulator is the mode field of the instruction, which indicates the addressing mode.

When an instruction in mnemonic form is read, it is examined, and its addressing modes and operands are used to determine the four mode bits required by the instruction. The reverse action is carried out when the instruction is executed, and the mode bits are used to implement the appropriate addressing modes. For example, if the instruction is LDR R6,#5, the mode is 4 and the assembler stores 6 in the first register field and 5 in the literal field. When the instruction is executed, the simulator uses the mode bits, 0100, to determine that the destination register is 110 and the literal is 00000101.

The first part of the TC3 simulator is given as follows. We create two lists: one for the program memory and one for the data memory (pMem and dMem). The instructions in program memory are imported from a file. The data memory is set up as 16 locations that are initialized to 0. The text file containing the source program is src and is processed to reformat instructions and remove assembler directives.

The shaded section of the code was added to detect the 'END' directive in the source code, which terminates the assembly processing and acts as a STOP when the code is executed. I added it for convenience. I sometimes want to test one or two instructions but don't want to write a new source code program. I can put the code under test at the top of an existing program, followed by END. All code after END is ignored. Later, I can delete the new code and END.

```
sTab = {}                                # Symbol table for equates and labels name:integerValue
pMem = []                                # Program memory (initially empty)
dMem = [0]*16                            # Data memory. Initialized and 16 locations
reg  = [0]*8                             # Register set
z,c,n = 0,0,0                            # Define and status flags: zero, carry, negative

testCode = "E:\\AwPW\\TC3_NEW_1.txt"     # Source filename on my computer
with open(testCode) as src:              # Open the source file containing the assembly program
    lines = src.readlines()              # Read the program into lines
src = [i[0:-1].lstrip() for i in lines ]
                                         # Remove the /n newline from each line of the source code
src = [i.split("@")[0] for i in src]     # Remove comments in the code
src = [i for i in src if i != '']        # Remove empty lines
for i in range(0,len(src)):              # Scan source code line-by-line
    src[i] = src[i].replace(',',' ')     # Replace commas by a space
    src[i] = src[i].upper()              # Convert to upper-case
    src[i] = src[i].split()              # Split into tokens (label, mnemonic, operands)

src1 = []                                # Set up dummy source file, initially empty
for i in range (0,len(src)):             # Read source and stop on first END instruction
    src1.append(src[i])                  # Append each line to dummy source file
    if src[i][0] == 'END': break         # Stop on 'END' token
src = src1                               # Copy dummy file to source (having stopped on 'END')

for i in range (0,len(src)):             # Deal with equates of the form EQU PQR 25
    if src[i][0] == 'EQU':               # If the line is 3 or more tokens and first token is EQU
        sTab[src[i][1]] = getL(src[i][2])    # Put token in symbol table as integer
src = [i for i in src if i.count('EQU') == 0]   # Remove lines with "EQU" from source code
```

The following code takes an instruction in assembly language form, tokenizes it, and converts it into the bit pattern of an instruction. In the following code, we use ic as the instruction counter, which steps through the source program line by line.

One issue we must deal with is the label. Some instructions have one and some don't. That means that the mnemonic is token 0 for an instruction without a label, and token 1 if there is a label. The Python code checks for a label (which ends in a colon). If a label is found, j is set to 1, and, if not found, j is set to 0. We then use j to calculate the location of tokens in the instruction. The tLen variable is the number of tokens in an instruction:

```
for ic in range(0,len(src)):            # ASSEMBLY LOOP (ic = instruction counter)
    t0,t1,t2 = '', '', ''               # Prepare to assign tokens. Initialize to null string
    if src[ic][0][-1] != ':':           # If the first token doesn't end in colon, it's an instruction
        j = 0                           # j = 0 forline starting with mnemonic
    else:                               # If the first token ends in a colon it's a label
        j = 1                           # j = 1 if mnemonic is second token
    t0 = src[ic][j]                     # Set t0 to mnemonic j selects first or second token
    if len(src[ic]) > 1+j: t1 = src[ic][j+1]   # Set t1 to ingle operand
    if len(src[ic]) > 2+j: t2 = src[ic][j+2]   # Set t2 to second operand
    tLen = len(src[ic]) - j - 1              # tLen is the number of tokens (adjusted for any label)
```

The next section of the assembler does all the work. Here, we generate the binary code. Unlike other simulators we've developed, we use directories and lists to detect registers, as the following (partial) code shows:

```
rName   = {'R0':0,'R1':1,'R2':2,'R3':3}   # Relate register name to numeric value (lookup table)
rNamInd = {'[R0]':0,'[R1]':1,'[R2]':2,'[R3]':3}
                                           # Look for register indirect addressing (lookup table)
iClass0 = ['STOP', 'NOP', 'END']          # Instruction class 00 mnemonic with no operands
iClass1 = ['BRA',  'BEQ', 'BNE','CZN' ]   # Instruction class 01 mnemonic with literal operand
```

Now, we can take a token and ask whether it's in rName to detect R0 to R7, or whether it's in rNamInd to detect whether it's [R0] to [R7]. Moreover, we can use the mnemonic from an instruction and ask whether it's in each class in turn in order to determine the two class bits of the instruction; for example, if t0 is the first token (corresponding to the mnemonic), we can write the following:

```
if t0 in iClass0: mode = 0.
```

Similarly, we can use if t1 in rNamInd to determine whether the second token is a register used as a pointer (e.g., [R4]).

The most complex class of instructions is iClass3, which deals with two-operand instructions, such as ADD [R3],R4. In this case, token t0 would be 'ADD', token t1 would be '[r3]', and token t2 would be 'R4'. To identify the class of this instruction, we look for a first operand, which is an indirect register, and a second operand, which is a register, as follows:

```
  if (t1 in rNamInd) and (t2 in rName): mode = 7
```

The code that determines the mode of an instruction is as follows:

```
binC = 0                                       # Initialize binary code for this instruction to all zeros
opCode = mnemon[t0]                            # Look up op-code in table mnemon using token t0
iClass = opCode >> 4                           # Get two most significant bits of op-code (i.e., class)
if   t0 in iClass0:                            # If in iClass0 it's a single instruction, no operands
    mode = 0                                   # The mode is 0 for everything in this class
    binC = (mnemon[t0] << 18)                  # All fields zero except op_code
elif t0 in iClass1:                            # If in iClass1 it's an 0p-code plus offset (e.g., branch)
    mode = 1                                   # All class 1 instruction are mode 1 (op-code plus literal)
    binC = (mnemon[t0] << 18)+(mode << 14)+getL(t1)
                                               # Create binary code for Class1 instruction
elif t0 in iClass2:                            # If in iClass2 it's an op-code plus register number
    mode = 2                                   # All iClass2 instructions are mode 2
    binC = (mnemon[t0] << 18)+(mode << 14)+(rName[t1] << 11
                                               # Construct binary code of instruction
elif t0 in iClass3:                            # All data-processing and movement ops in iClass3
    if   (t1 in rName) and (t2[0] == '#'):  # Look for register name and literal for mode 4
        mode = 4
    elif (t1 in rName) and (t2 in rName):  # Look for register name and register name for mode 5
        mode = 5
    elif (t1 in rName) and (t2 in rNamInd):     # Look for R0,[R2]) format
        mode = 6
    elif (t1 in rNamInd) and (t2 in rName):     # Look for instruction format [R1],R2
        mode = 7
    elif (t1 in rNamInd) and (t2 in rNamInd):  # Look for two register indirect names [R1],[R2]
        mode = 8
    elif (t1[0:2] == 'M:') and (t2 in rName):
                                               # Look for memory address M: and reg name M:12,r4
        mode = 9
    elif (t1[0:2] == 'M:') and (t2 in rNamInd):  # Look for M:12,[R4] format
        mode = 10
    elif (t1 in rName) and (t2[0:2] == 'M:'):  # Look for register name and literal prefixed by M:
        mode = 11
    elif (t1 in rNamInd) and (t2[0:2] == 'M:'):
                                               # Look for register indirect name and literal prefixed by M:
        mode = 12
```

After extracting the instruction class, op-code, and mode, the final step is to get the actual register numbers and any literals. In the following fragment of code, we define the two register fields and the literal field, respectively. These are rField1, rField2, and lField and are all initialized to 0, because instructions without three fields have the corresponding bits set to 0.

Here, we use the list as a very convenient method for extracting fields rather than combined if and or operators. For example, register field 1 is used by modes 4, 5, 6, and 11. We could write the following:

```
if (mode == 4) or (mode == 5) or (mode == 6) or (mode == 11):
```

However, we can write instead, which is far easier to read:

```
if mode in [4,5,6,11]:
```

The following code shows how the three register/literal fields are evaluated:

```
binC = (mnemon[t0] << 18) + (mode << 14)    # Insert op_Code and mode fields in instruction
rField1, rField2, lField = 0, 0, 0               # Calculate register and literal fields. Initialize to zero
if mode in [4,5,6,11]: rField1 = rName[t1]  # Convert register names into register numbers
if mode in [7,8,12]:      rField1 = rNamInd[t1]
if mode in [5,7,9]:       rField2 = rName[t2]  # rField2 is second register field
if mode in [6,8,10]:      rField2 = rNamInd[t2]
if mode in [4,11,12]:     lField  = getL(t2)
                                     # if (mode==4) or (mode==11) or (mode==12): lField = getL(t2)
if mode in [9,10]:        lField  = getL(t1)
                                     # if (mode == 9) or (mode == 10): lField = getL(t1) Literal field
```

The following two lines of the code-generation logic insert the register/literal fields by shifting and executing OR on bits and append the current binary instruction, binC, to the program memory, pMem:

```
binC = binC + (rField1 << 11) + rField2 << 8) + lField
                                # Binary code with register and literal fields
pMem.append(binC)               # Append instruction to program memory
```

Features of the simulator

The simulator part of TC3 is relatively straightforward. Here, I'll simply provide a few comments on some of its features to aid in understanding the code.

1. Printing data

The number of items to be displayed increased during the simulator's development. So, we created a list of strings, one for each item to be printed, and then concatenated the items. For example, this is the print mechanism I used to display data during assembly:

```
### Display assembly details of each instruction for diagnostics
pcF  = "{0:<20}".format(" ".join(src[ic]))    # 1. instruction
icF  = 'pc = ' + "{:<3}".format(ic)          # 2. pc
binF = format(binC, "024b")                  # 3. Binary encoding
iClF = 'Class = '+ str(iClass)               # 4. instruction class
modF = 'mode = ' + str(mode)                 # 5. instruction mode. Convert mode to string
```

```
t0F  = "{:<5}".format(t0)                    # 6. token 0 (mnemonic)
t1F  = "{:<5}".format(t1)                    # 7. token 1 (register field 1)
t2F  = "{:<10}".format(t2)                   # 8. token 2 (register field 2 or literal)
print(pcF,icF,binF,iClF,modF,t0F,'t1 =',t1F,t2F)    # Print these fields
```

The `displayLevel` parameter is included to determine what information was printed during the assembly process. For example, we could write the following:

```
if displayLevel > 4: print('Binary code =', xyz)
```

This would print binary code only when debugging is required by setting the variable to 5 or greater.

2.   Implementing add with carry

When I implemented the ALU with its numbered functions, I initially forgot to include ADC, add with carry. Rather than renumbering the functions, I converted the ADD into a dual ADD/ADC operation by first performing an addition. Then, if the op-code was an ADC, add the carry bit:

```
elif fun == 1:                            # ADD:
        res = (op1 + op2)                 # Perform addition of operands
        if thisOp == 'ADC': res = res + c # If operation ADC then add carry bit
```

3.   Dealing with simple instruction classes

Here is the code used to deal with class 1 instructions. We do not have to worry about decoding the mode as there is only one mode for this class. Of course, the class could be extended (in the future) by the addition of other modes.

```
elif opClass == 1:                             # Class 1 operation instructions with literal operand
    if      thisOp == 'BRA': pc = lit          # BRA Branch unconditionally PC = L
    elif (thisOp == 'BEQ') and (z == 1): pc = lit    # BEQ Branch on zero
    elif (thisOp == 'BNE') and (z == 0): pc = lit    # BNE Branch on not zero
    elif    thisOp == 'CZN':                    # Set/clear c, z, and n flags
        c = (lit & 0b100) >> 2                  # Bit 2 of literal is c
        z = (lit & 0b010) >> 1                  # Bit 1 of literal is z
        n = (lit & 0b001)                       # Bit 0 of literal is n
```

Class 1 instructions have an op-code and literal and are generally used to implement branch operations. Notice that we compare the current instruction with a name (e.g., `'BRA'`) rather than an op-code, as we did in other simulators. The use of a table of reverse op-code-to-mnemonic translations makes life much easier.

We have added a CZN (carry zero negative) instruction, which allows us to preset condition codes; for example, CZN #%101 sets c and n to 1, and z to 0. Computers often have an operation that allows you to test condition codes, clear them, set them, and toggle (flip) them.

4. Handling literals

TC3's numeric values can be expressed in several formats, for example, binary, where we represent 8 by %1000. Literal processing in TC3 must also deal with special formats, such as M:12, which indicates a memory address. The following function performs all the literal processing and handles several formats. It can also deal with literals that are symbolic names that must be looked up in the symbol table:

```
def getL(lit8):                                    # Convert string to integer
    lit8v = 9999                                    # Dummy default
    if lit8[0:2]   == 'M:': lit8  = lit8[2:]        # Strip M: prefix from memory literal addresses
    if lit8[0:1]   == '#':  lit8  = lit8[1:]        # Strip # prefix from literal addresses
    if    type(lit8) == int: lit8v = lit8           # If integer, return it
    elif lit8.isnumeric():  lit8v = int(lit8)       # If decimal in text form convert to integer
    elif lit8 in sTab:      lit8v = sTab[lit8]      # If in symbol table, retrieve it
    elif lit8[0]   == '%':  lit8v = int(lit8[1:],2) # If binary string convert to int
    elif lit8[0:2] == '0X': lit8v = int(lit8[2:],16) # If hex string convert it to int
    elif lit8[0]   == '-':  lit8v = -int(lit8[1:]) & 0xFF
                                                    # If decimal negative convert to signed int
    return(lit8v)                                   # Return integer corresponding to text string
```

5. Result Writeback

After performing an ALU operation or a data movement, the resulting operand must be written back into the computer. However, because we have specified a two-operand CISC-style format, the result of a calculation can be written to a register (like any RISC operation), it can be written to a memory location pointed at by a register, or it can be written to a memory operation specified by its address. The following fragment of code demonstrates TC3's writeback:

```
op3 = alu(fun,op1,op2)                             # Call ALU to perform the function
if mode in [4,5,6,11]: reg[reg1] = op3             # Writeback ALU result in op3 to a register
elif mode in [7,8,12]: dMem[reg[reg1]] = op3       # Writeback result to mem pointed at by reg
elif mode in [9,10]:   dMem[lit]      = op3        # Writeback result to memory
```

Sample output

The following is a sample of the output from the simulator that demonstrates integer handling. We have written a program with six different ways of inputting a literal. In each case, we load the literal into register r0. The source program is as follows:

```
EQU www,#42
MOV r0,#12
MOV r0,#%11010
MOV r0,#0xAF
MOV r0,#-5
MOV r0,M:7
```

```
MOV r0,#www
NOP
STOP
END
```

In the following code block, we have the output of TC3. This output has been designed for the purpose of developing and testing the simulator (for example, following the assembly process):

```
Source code                          This is the tokenized source code
['MOV', 'R0', '#12']
['MOV', 'R0', '#%11010']
['MOV', 'R0', '#0XAF']
['MOV', 'R0', '#-5']
['MOV', 'R0', 'M:7']
['MOV', 'R0', '#WWW']
['NOP']
['STOP']
['END']


Equate and branch table             This is the symbol table. Only one entry
WWW        42
```

The following is the output during the assembly and analysis phase:

```
Assembly loop

MOV R0 #12       pc=0 11000001000000000001100 Class=3 mode=4  MOV   t1=R0 #12
MOV R0 #%11010   pc=1 11100000100000000011010 Class=3 mode=4  MOV   t1=R0 #%11010
MOV R0 #0XAF     pc=2 11000001000000010101111 Class=3 mode=4  MOV   t1=R0 #0XAF
MOV R0 #-5       pc=3 11000001000000011111011 Class=3 mode=4  MOV   t1=R0 #-5
MOV R0 M:7       pc=4 11000010110000000000111 Class=3 mode=11 MOV   t1=R0 M:7
MOV R0 #WWW      pc=5 11000001000000000101010 Class=3 mode=4  MOV   t1=R0 #WWW
NOP              pc=6 00000000000000000000000 Class=0 mode=0  NOP   t1 =
STOP             pc=7 00111000000000000000000 Class=0 mode=0  STOP  t1 =
END              pc=8 00111100000000000000000 Class=0 mode=0  END   t1 =


11000001000000000001100            This is the program in binary form
11000001000000000011010
11000001000000010101111
11000001000000011111011
11000010110000000000111
11000001000000000101010
00000000000000000000000
00111000000000000000000
00111100000000000000000
```

In the following code block, we have the single-step execution output. It's been edited to help fit it on the page. We printed only two memory locations for each line. The literal in the instruction and its value in r0 are printed in bold:

```
EXECUTE

MOV R0 #12     pc=0  11000001000000000001100 Class=3 mode=4
Reg=0c 00 00 00 00 00 00 00 Mem=00 C=0 Z=0 N=0


MOV R0 #%11010 pc=1  11000001000000000011010 Class=3 mode=4
Reg=1a 00 00 00 00 00 00 00 Mem=00 C=0 Z=0 N=0


MOV R0 #0XAF   pc=2  11000001000000010101111 Class=3 mode=4
Reg=af 00 00 00 00 00 00 00 Mem=00 C=0 Z=0 N=1


MOV R0 #-5     pc=3  11000001000000011111011 Class=3 mode=4
Reg=fb 00 00 00 00 00 00 00 Mem=00 C=0 Z=0 N=1


MOV R0 M:7     pc=4  11000010110000000000111 Class=3 mode=11
Reg=07 00 00 00 00 00 00 00 Mem=00 C=0 Z=0 N=0


MOV R0 #WWW    pc=5  11000001000000000101010 Class=3 mode=4
Reg=2a 00 00 00 00 00 00 00 Mem=00 C=0 Z=0 N=0


NOP            pc=6  00000000000000000000000 Class=0 mode=0
Reg=2a 00 00 00 00 00 00 00 Mem=00 C=0 Z=0 N=0


STOP           pc=7  00111000000000000000000 Class=0 mode=0
Reg=2a 00 00 00 00 00 00 00 Mem=00 C=0 Z=0 N=0
```

The complete TC3 code

We have discussed the design of TC3. Here, we present the code of a complete simulator. There are some slight differences between the descriptive fragments of code we described in the previous section and this more complete simulator. This is followed by a sample run of the simulator. The first part of the code defines the instruction modes and provides a simple source program that will be executed:

```
### TC3 CISC machine
### Demonstration register-to-memory architecture Designed 22 January 2022.
### Instruction formats and addressing modes
### Mode 0:  NOP, STOP        No operand length 1
### Mode 1:  INC R1           Single register operand
### Mode 2:  BEQ XXX          Literal operand
### Mode 3:  Reserved
```

```
### Mode 4:    MOV  r1,literal        Two-operand, register and literal
### Mode 5:    MOV  r1,r2             Two-operand, register to register
### Mode 6:    MOV  r1,[r2]           Two-operand, register indirect to register
### Mode 7:    MOV  [r1],r2           Two-operand, register to register indirect
### Mode 8:    MOV  [r1],[r2]         Two-operand, register indirect to register indirect
### Mode 9:    MOV  M,r2              Two-operand, register to memory address
### Mode 10:   MOV  M,[r2]            Two-operand, register indirect to memory address
### Mode 11:   MOV  r1,M              Two-operand, memory address to register
### Mode 12:   MOV  [r1],M            Two-operand, memory address to register indirect

### The sample test code
###          MOV   r0,#8         @ Memory locations 1 to 8 with random numbers
### Next:    RND   r5
###          MOV   [r0],r5
###          DEC   r0
###          BNE   Next
###          EQU   X,#1          @ Vector 1
###          EQU   Y,#5          @ Vector 5
###          EQU   Z,#9          @ Vector 9
###          MOV   r1,#X         @ r0 points to array X       11 0000 0100 000 000 00000001
###          MOV   r2,#Y         @ r1 points to array Y       11 0000 0100 001 000 00000101
###          MOV   r3,#Z         @ r2 points to array Z       11 0000 0100 010 000 00001001
###          MOV   r4,#6         @ r4 number of elements to add  11 0000 0100 011 000 00000100
### Loop:    MOV   r5,[r1]       @ REPEAT: Get xi             11 0000 0110 100 000 00000000
###          ADD   r5,#6         @ Add 6 to xi                11 0001 0100 100 000 00000101
###          ADD   r5,[r2]       @ Add xi + 5 to yi           11 0001 0110 100 001 00000000
###          MOV   [r3],r5       @ Store result in array Z    11 0000 0111 010 100 00000000
###          INC   r1            @ Increment pointer to array X  10 0000 0010 000 000 00000000
###          INC   r2            @ Increment pointer to array Y  10 0000 0010 001 000 00000000
###          INC   r3            @ Increment pointer to array Z  10 0000 0010 010 000 00000000
###          DEC   r4            @ Decrement loop counter     10 0001 0010 011 000 00000000
###          BNE   Loop          @ Continue until counter zero  01 0010 0001 000 000 00000100
###          STOP                                             00 1111 0000 000 000 00000000
```

The following block contains the dictionaries for instruction decoding and register lookup. We've provided reverse lookup so that you can look up a mnemonic to get its code or look up the code to get the mnemonic. Similarly, we've provided lookup for registers, such as R0 and R2, and indirect registers, such as [R0] and [R1]:

```
import random                              # Get library of random number operations
### Dictionaries and variables
mnemon = {'MOV':48,'MOVE':48,'ADD':49,'SUB':50,'CMP':51,'NOT':52,'AND':53, \
          'OR':54,'EOR':55,'ONES':56, 'MRG':57,'FFO':58,'LSL':59,'LSR':60, \
          'ADC':61,'INC':32,'DEC':33,'RND':34,'CZN':19,'TST':36,'NOP':0,   \
          'BRA':16,'BEQ':17,'BNE':18,'STOP':14,'END':15}
```

```
mnemonR = {48:'MOV',49:'ADD',50:'SUB',51:'CMP',52:'NOT',53:'AND',54:'OR',    \
           55:'EOR',56:'ONES',57:'MRG',58:'FFO',59:'LSL',60:'LSR',61:'ADC',  \
           32:'INC',33:'DEC', 34:'RND',19:'CZN',36:'TST',0:'NOP',16:'BRA',   \
           17:'BEQ',18:'BNE',14:'STOP',15:'END'}
rName   = {'R0':0,'R1':1,'R2':2,'R3':3,'R4':4,'R5':5,'R6':6,'R7':7} # Register tab
rNamInd = {'[R0]':0,'[R1]':1,'[R2]':2,'[R3]':3,'[R4]':4,' \
           '[R5]':5,'[R6]':6,'[R7]':7}                      # Indirect registers


iClass0 = ['STOP', 'NOP','END']              # class 00 mnemonic with no operands
iClass1 = ['BRA','BEQ','BNE','CZN']          # class 01 mnemonic with literal operand
iClass2 = ['INC','DEC','RND','TST']          # class 10 mnemonic with register operand
iClass3 = ['MOV','MOVE','ADD','ADC','SUB','CMP', 'NOT','AND','OR', \
           'EOR','ONES','MRG','FFO','LSL','LSR']   # class 11 mnemonic two operands


sTab = {}               # Symbol table for equates and labels name:integerValue
pMem = []               # Program memory (initially empty)
dMem = [0]*16           # Data memory
reg  = [0]*8            # Register set
z,c,n = 0,0,0           # Define and clear flags zero, carry, negative
```

The following two functions provide the ability to read integer operands in various formats, and an ALU that performs arithmetic and logic operations. Both of these functions can be expanded to provide additional capabilities:

```
def getL(lit8):                             # Convert string to integer
    lit8v = 9999                            # Dummy default
    if lit8[0:2]   == 'M:': lit8 = lit8[2:] # Strip M: prefix from memory literal addresses
    if lit8[0:1]   == '#':  lit8 = lit8[1:] # Strip # prefix from literal addresses
    if   type(lit8) == int: lit8v = lit8    # If integer, return it
    elif lit8.isnumeric():  lit8v = int(lit8)    # If decimal in text from convert to integer
    elif lit8 in sTab:      lit8v = sTab[lit8]  # If in symbol table, retrieve it
    elif lit8[0]   == '%':  lit8v = int(lit8[1:],2)   # If binary string convert to int
    elif lit8[0:2] == '0X': lit8v = int(lit8[2:],16)  # If hex string convert to int
    elif lit8[0]   == '-':  lit8v = -int(lit8[1:]) & 0xFF
                                            # If decimal negative convert to signed int
    return(lit8v)                           # Return integer corresponding to text string

def alu(fun,op1,op2):            # Perform arithmetic and logical operations on operands 1 and 2
    global z,n,c                             # Make flags global
    z,n,c = 0,0,0                            # Clear status flags initially
    if   fun == 0: res = op2                 # MOV: Perform data copy from source to destination
    elif fun == 1:                           # ADD: Perform addition - and ensure 8 bits plus carry
        res = (op1 + op2)                    #   Do addition of operands
        if thisOp == 'ADC': res = res + c    #   If operation ADC then add carry bit
    elif fun == 2: res = (op1 - op2)         # SUB: Perform subtraction
```

```
      elif fun == 3: res = op1 - op2          # CMP: Same as subtract without writeback
      elif fun == 4: res = op1 & op2          # AND: Perform bitwise AND
      elif fun == 5: res = op1 | op2          # OR: Perform bitwise OR
      elif fun == 6: res = ~op2               # NOT
      elif fun == 7: res = op1 ^ op2          # XOR
      elif fun == 8:
         res = op2 << 1                       # LSL: Perform single logical shift left
      elif fun == 9:
         res = op2 >> 1                       # LSR: Perform single logical shift right
      elif fun == 10:                         # ONES (Count number of 1s in register)
         onesCount = 0                        # Clear the 1s counter
         for i in range (0,8):                # For i = 0 to 7 (test each bit) AND with 10000000 to get msb
            if op2 & 0x80 == 0x80:            # If msb is set
               onesCount = onesCount + 1      # increment the 1s counter
            op2 = op2 << 1                     # shift the operand one place left
         res = onesCount                      # Destination operand is 1s count
      elif fun == 11:                         # MRG (merge alternate bits of two registers)
            t1 = op1 & 0b10101010             # Get even source operand bits
            t2 = op2 & 0b01010101             # Get odd destination operand bits
            res = t1 | t2                     # Merge them using an OR
      elif fun == 12:                         # FFO (Find position of leading 1)
            res = 8                           # Set default position 8 (i.e., leading 1 not found)
            for i  in range (0,8):            # Examine the bits one by one
              temp = op2 & 0x80               # AND with 10000000 to get leading bit and save
              op2 = op2 << 1                  # Shift operand left
              res = res - 1                   # Decrement place counter
              if temp == 128: break           # If the last tested bit was 1 then jump out of loop

      if res & 0xFF == 0:          z = 1      # TEST FLAGS z = 1 if bits 0 to 7 all 0
      if res & 0x80 == 0x80:       n = 1      # If bit 7 is one, set the carry bit
      if res & 0x100 == 0x100:     c = 1      # carry bit set if bit 8 set
      if (thisOp == 'LSR') and (op2 & 1 == 1): c = 1
                                              # Deal with special case of shift right (carry out is lsb)
      return(res & 0xFF)                      # Return and ensure value eight bits
```

The `trace()` function prints the state of the processor as a program is executed. This can be modified to change the amount, layout, and format of the data:

```
def trace():                                  # Function to print execution data
    cF   = "{0:<20}".format(" ".join(src[pcOld]))   # 1. instruction
    icF  = 'pc = ' + "{:<3}".format(pcOld)          # 2. pc
    binF = format(inst, "024b")                     # 3. binary code
    iClF = 'Class = '+ str(iClass)                  # 4. instruction class
    modF = 'mode = ' + str(mode)     # 5. instruction mode NOTE we have to convert mode to string
```

```
    t0F   = "{:<5}".format(t0)                          # 6. token 0 (mnemonic)
    t1F   = "{:<5}".format(t1)                          # 7. token 1 (register field 1)
    t2F   = "{:<10}".format(t2)                         # 8. token 2 (register field 2 or literal)
    rF    = 'Reg = '+ ' '.join('%02x' % b for b in reg) # 9. Registers in hex format
    m     = dMem[0:11]                                  # 10. First 10 memory locations
    mF    = 'Mem = '+ " ".join("%02x" % b for b in m)   # 11. Hex-formatted memory values
    ccrF  = 'C = '+ str(c) + ' Z = ' + str(z) +' N = ' + str(n) # 12. Condition codes
    x = input('>>> ')                                   # 13. Wait for keyboard input (return)
    print(cF,icF,binF,iClF, modF, rF, mF,ccrF)          # 14. Print the computer status data
    return()


testCode = "E:\\AwPW\\TC3_NEW_1.txt"    # Source filename on my computer
with open(testCode) as src:             # Open source file with assembly language program
    lines = src.readlines()             # Read the program into lines
src.close()                             # Close the source file
src = [i[0:-1].lstrip()  for i in lines ]
                                        # Remove the /n newline from each line of the source code
src = [i.split("@")[0] for i in src]    # Remove comments in the code
src = [i for i in src if i != '']       # Remove empty lines
for i in range(0,len(src)):             # Scan source code line by line
    src[i] = src[i].replace(',',' ')    # Replace commas by a space
    src[i] = src[i].upper()             # Convert to upper-case
    src[i] = src[i].split()             # Split into tokens (label, mnemonic, operands)

src1 = []                               # Set up dummy source file, initially empty
for i in range (0,len(src)):            # Read source and stop on first END operation
    src1.append(src[i])                 # Append line to dummy source file
    if src[i][0] == 'END': break        # Stop on 'END' token
src = src1                              # Copy dummy file to source (having stopped on 'END')

for i in range (0,len(src)):            # Deal with equates of the form EQU PQR 25
    if src[i][0] == 'EQU':              # If the line is 3 or more tokens and first token is EQU
        sTab[src[i][1]] = getL(src[i][2])
                                        # Put token in symbol table as integer
src = [i for i in src if i.count("EQU") == 0]
                                        # Remove lines with 'EQU' from source code (these are not instructions)

for i in range(0,len(src)):            # Add label addresses to symbol table
    if src[i][0][-1] == ':':           # If first token is a label with : terminator
        sTab.update({src[i][0][0:-1]:i}) # add it to the symbol table.

xLm = 0                                # Length of maximum instruction (for printing)
for i in range (0,len(src)):           # Step through source array
```

```
        xL = len(' '.join(src[i]))          # Get the length of each line after joining tokens
        if xL > xLm: xLm = xL               # If xL > xLm   NOTE: This facility is not used in this version


print('Source code')                        # Display tokenized source code
for i in range(0,len(src)): print(src[i])
print("\nEquate and branch table\n")        # Display the symbol table
for x,y in sTab.items():                    # Step through the symbol table dictionary structure
    print("{:<8}".format(x),y)              # Display each line as label and value


print('\nAssembly loop \n')


for ic in range(0,len(src)):                # ASSEMBLY LOOP (ic = instruction counter)
    t0,t1,t2 = '','',''                     # Prepare to assign tokens. Initialize to null string
    if src[ic][0][-1] != ':':               # If the first token doesn't end in colon, its an instruction
        j = 0                               # j = 0 for line starting with mnemonic
    else:                                   # If the first token ends in a colon it's a label
        j = 1                               # j = 1 if mnemonic is second token
    t0 = src[ic][j]                         # Set t0 to mnemonic
    if len(src[ic]) > 1+j: t1 = src[ic][j+1]    # Set t1 to single operand
    if len(src[ic]) > 2+j: t2 = src[ic][j+2]    # Set t2 to second operand
    tLen = len(src[ic]) - j - 1             # tLen is the number of tokens (adjusted for any label)

    binC = 0                                # Initialize binary code for this instruction to all zeros
    opCode = mnemon[t0]                     # Look up op-code in table mnemon using token t0
    iClass = opCode >> 4                    # Get two most significant bits of op-code (i.e., class)
    if   t0 in iClass0:                     # If in iClass0 it's a single instruction, no operands
        mode = 0                            # The mode is 0 for everything in this class
        binC = (mnemon[t0] << 18)           # All fields zero except op_code

    elif t0 in iClass1:                     # If in iClass1 it's an op-code plus offset (e.g., branch)
        mode = 1                            # All class 1 instruction are mode 1 (op-code plus literal)
        binC = (mnemon[t0] << 18) + (mode << 14)  + getL(t1)
                                            # Create binary code with operation plus address (literal)

    elif t0 in iClass2:                     # If in iClass2 it's an op-code plus register number
        mode = 2                            # All instruction are mode 2
        binC = (mnemon[t0] << 18) + (mode << 14)  + (rName[t1] << 11)
                                            # Create binary code

    elif t0 in iClass3:         # Two-operand inst. All data-processing and movement ops in iClass3
        if   (t1 in rName) and (t2[0] == '#'):
                                            # Look for register name and literal for mode 4
            mode = 4
```

```
    elif (t1 in rName) and (t2 in rName):
                            # Look for register name and register name for mode 5
        mode = 5
    elif (t1 in rName) and (t2 in rNamInd):
                            # Look for register name and register indirect name (r1,[r2])
        mode = 6
    elif (t1 in rNamInd) and (t2 in rName):
                            # Look for register indirect name and register ([r1],r2)
        mode = 7
    elif (t1 in rNamInd) and (t2 in rNamInd):
                            # Look for two register indirect names ([r1],[r2])
        mode = 8
    elif (t1[0:2] == 'M:') and (t2 in rName):
                            # Look for literal prefixed by M: and register name (M:12,r4)
        mode = 9
    elif (t1[0:2] == 'M:') and (t2 in rNamInd):
                            # Look for literal prefixed by M: and register indirect name  (M:12,[r4])
        mode = 10
    elif (t1 in rName) and (t2[0:2] == 'M:'):
                            # Look for register name and literal prefixed by M:
        mode = 11
    elif (t1 in rNamInd) and (t2[0:2] == 'M:'):
                            # Look for register indirect name and literal prefixed by M:
        mode = 12
    binC = (mnemon[t0] << 18) + (mode << 14)
                            # Insert op_Code and mode fields in the instruction


    rField1, rField2, lField = 0, 0, 0   # Calculate register and literal fields. Initialize to zero
    if mode in [4,5,6,11]: rField1 = rName[t1]
                            # Convert register names into register numbers rField1is first register
    if mode in [7,8,12]:    rField1 = rNamInd[t1]
    if mode in [5,7,9]:     rField2 = rName[t2]     # rField2 is second register field
    if mode in [6,8,10]:    rField2 = rNamInd[t2]


    if mode in [4,11,12]:   lField  = getL(t2)
                                # if (mode == 4) or (mode == 11) or (mode == 12): Get literal
    if mode in [9,10]:      lField  = getL(t1)
                                # if (mode == 9) or (mode == 10):    lField = getL(t1) Literal field


    binC = binC+(rField1 << 11)+(rField2 << 8)+lField
                                # Binary code with register and literal fields added
pMem.append(binC)                   # Append instruction to program memory in pMem
```

```
###   Display the assembly details of each instruction (this is for diagnostics)
      pcF   = '{0:<20}'.format(' '.join(src[ic]))  #1. instruction
      icF   = 'pc = ' + '{:<3}'.format(ic)          #2. pc
      binF  = format(binC, '024b')                  #3. binary code
      iClF  = 'Class = '+ str(iClass)               #4. instruction class
      modF  = 'mode = ' + str(mode)                 #5. instruction mode NOTE convert mode to string
      t0F   = '{:<5}'.format(t0)                     #6. token 0 (mnemonic)
      t1F   = '{:<5}'.format(t1)                     #7. token 1 (register field 1)
      t2F   = '{:<10}'.format(t2)                    #8. token 2 (register field 2 or literal)
      print(pcF,icF,binF,iClF,modF,t0F,'t1 =',t1F,t2F)  # Print these fields

print('\nEXECUTE \n')
### EXECUTE LOOP     # reverse assemble the binary instruction to recover the fields and execute the instruction
pc = 0                                    # Reset the program counter to 0
run = True                                # run flag: True to execute, False to stop (stop on END or STOP)
while run == True:                        # MAIN LOOP
    op1, op2, op3 = 0,0,0                 # Initialize data operands
    inst = pMem[pc]         # Fetch current instruction. inst is the binary op-code executed in this cycle
    pcOld = pc                            # Remember current pc for printing/display
    pc = pc + 1                           # Increment program counter for next cycle
    iClass = inst >> 22                   # Extract operation class 0 to 3 (top two bits)
    opCode = (inst >> 18)   & 0b111111    # Extract the current op-code
    mode   = (inst >> 14)   & 0b1111      # Extract the addressing mode
    reg1   = (inst >> 11)   & 0b0111      # Extract register 1 number
    reg2   = (inst >>  8)   & 0b0111      # Extract register 2 number
    lit    = inst           & 0b11111111  # Extract the 8-bit literal in the least significant bits
```

The following is the instruction execution part of the program. Note that instructions are executed in the order of their class:

```
### EXECUTE THE CODE
    thisOp = mnemonR[opCode]               # Reverse assemble. Get mnemonic from op-code
    if iClass == 0:                        # Class 0 no-operand instructions
        if thisOp == 'END' or thisOp == 'STOP': run = False
                                           # If END or STOP clear run flag to stop execution
        if opCode == 'NOP': pass           # If NOP then do nothing and "pass"
    elif iClass == 1:                      # Class 1 operation
                                           # Class 1 branch and instr with literal operands
        if    thisOp == 'BRA': pc = lit    # BRA Branch unconditionally PC = L
        elif (thisOp == 'BEQ') and (z == 1): pc = lit  # BEQ Branch on zero
        elif (thisOp == 'BNE') and (z == 0): pc = lit  # BNE Branch on not zero
        elif thisOp == 'CZN':              # Set/clear c, z, and n flags
            c = (lit & 0b100) >> 2         # Bit 2 of literal is c
            z = (lit & 0b010) >> 1         # Bit 1 of literal is z
```

```
            n = (lit & 0b001)                    # Bit 0 of literal is c

    elif iClass == 2:                            # Class 0 single-register operand
        if  thisOp == 'INC': reg[reg1] = alu(1,reg[reg1],1)
                                                 # Call ALU with second operand 1 to do increment
        elif thisOp == 'DEC': reg[reg1] = alu(2,reg[reg1],1)     # Decrement register
        elif thisOp == 'RND': reg[reg1] = random.randint(0,0xFF)
                                                 # Generate random number in range 0 to 0xFF
        elif thisOp == 'TST':                    # Test a register: return z and n flags. Set c to 0
            z, n, c = 0, 0, 0                            # Set all flags to 0
            if reg[reg1] == 0:               z = 1       # If operand 0 set z flag
            if reg[reg1] & 0x80 == 0x80: n = 1           # If operand ms bit 1 set n bit

    elif iClass == 3:                            # Class 3 operation: Two operands.
        if  mode in [4,5,6,11]: op1 = reg[reg1]
                                                 # Register, literal e.g. MOVE r1,#5 or ADD r3,#0xF2
        elif mode in [7,8,12]:      op1 = dMem[reg[reg1]]
                                                 # Register, literal e.g. MOVE r1,#5 or ADD r3,#0xF2
        elif mode in [9,10]:        op1 = lit  # MOV M:12,r3 moves register to memory
        if  mode in [4,11,12]:      op2 = lit  # Mode second operand literal
        elif mode in [5,7,9]:       op2 = reg[reg2]
                                                 # Modes with second operand contents of register
        elif mode in [6,8,10]:      op2 = dMem[reg[reg2]]
                                                 # Second operand pointed at by register

        if thisOp == 'MOV' : fun = 0             # Use mnemonic to get function required by ALU
        if thisOp == 'ADD' : fun = 1             # ADD and ADC use same function
        if thisOp == 'ADC' : fun = 1
        if thisOp == 'SUB' : fun = 2
        if thisOp == 'AND' : fun = 4
        if thisOp == 'OR'  : fun = 5
        if thisOp == 'NOT' : fun = 6
        if thisOp == 'EOR' : fun = 7
        if thisOp == 'LSL' : fun = 8
        if thisOp == 'LSR' : fun = 9
        if thisOp == 'ONES': fun = 10
        if thisOp == 'MRG' : fun = 11
        if thisOp == 'FFO' : fun = 12
        op3 = alu(fun,op1,op2)                   # Call ALU to perform the function

        if  mode in [4,5,6,11]: reg[reg1]       = op3
                                                 # Writeback ALU result in op3 result to a register
        elif mode in [7,8,12]:   dMem[reg[reg1]] = op3
```

```
                                                    # Writeback result to mem pointed at by reg
        elif mode in [9,10]:        dMem[lit]        = op3
                                                    # Writeback the result to memory

    trace()                                         # Display the results line by line
```

A sample run of TC3

Here is the output from a sample run of TC3. We have provided the source code that is executed, the equate and branch table, the assembled code, and then the output of a run:

1. Source code

```
['MOV', 'R0', '#8']
['NEXT:', 'RND', 'R5']
['MOV', '[R0]', 'R5']
['DEC', 'R0']
['BNE', 'NEXT']
['MOV', 'R1', '#X']
['MOV', 'R2', '#Y']
['MOV', 'R3', '#Z']
['MOV', 'R4', '#6']
['LOOP:', 'MOV', 'R5', '[R1]']
['ADD', 'R5', '#6']
['ADD', 'R5', '[R2]']
['MOV', '[R3]', 'R5']
['INC', 'R1']
['INC', 'R2']
['INC', 'R3']
['DEC', 'R4']
['BNE', 'LOOP']
['STOP', '00', '1111', '0']
```

2. Equate and branch table

```
X       1
Y       5
Z       9
NEXT    1
LOOP    9
```

3.   Assembly loop

```
MOV R0 #8      pc=0    11000001000000000001000 Class=3 mode=4 MOV t1=R0 #8
NEXT: RND R5 pc=1    10001000101010000000000 Class=2 mode=2 RND    t1=R5
MOV [R0] R5  pc=2    11000001110001010000000 Class=3 mode=7 MOV    t1=[R0]   R5
DEC R0         pc=3    10001001000000000000000 Class=2 mode=2 DEC    t1=R0
BNE NEXT       pc=4    01001000010000000000001 Class=1 mode=1 BNE    t1=NEXT
MOV R1 #X      pc=5    11000001000010000000001 Class=3 mode=4 MOV    t1=R1     #X
MOV R2 #Y      pc=6    11000001000100000000101 Class=3 mode=4 MOV    t1=R2     #Y
MOV R3 #Z      pc=7    11000001000110000001001 Class=3 mode=4 MOV    t1=R3     #Z
MOV R4 #6      pc=8    11000001001000000000110 Class=3 mode=4 MOV    t1=R4     #6
LOOP: MOV R5 [R1]  pc=9    11000001101010010000000 Class=3 mode=6
MOV    t1=R5       [R1]
ADD R5 #6      pc=10   11000101001010000000110 Class=3 mode=4 ADD    t1=R5     #6
ADD R5 [R2]  pc=11   11000101101010100000000 Class=3 mode=6 ADD    t1=R5     R2]
MOV [R3] R5  pc=12   11000001110111010000000 Class=3 mode=7 MOV    t1=[R3]   R5
INC R1         pc=13   10000001000100000000000 Class=2 mode=2 INC    t1=R1
INC R2         pc=14   10000001001000000000000 Class=2 mode=2 INC    t1=R2
INC R3         pc=15   10000001001100000000000 Class=2 mode=2 INC    t1=R3
DEC R4         pc=16   10001001010000000000000 Class=2 mode=2 DEC    t1=R4
BNE LOOP       pc=17   01001000010000000001001 Class=1 mode=1 BNE    t1=LOOP
STOP 00 1111 0 pc=18   00111000000000000000000 Class=0 mode=0
STOP  t1=00       1111
```

4.   EXECUTE

We have provided only a few lines of the traced output and reformatted them to fit on the page.

```
>>>
MOV R0 #8              pc = 0    11000001000000000001000
Class = 3 mode = 4
Reg = 08 00 00 00 00 00 00 00
Mem = 00 00 00 00 00 00 00 00 00 00 00
C = 0 Z = 0 N = 0

NEXT: RND R5           pc = 1    10001000101010000000000
Class = 2 mode = 2
Reg = 08 00 00 00 00 8f 00 00
Mem = 00 00 00 00 00 00 00 00 00 00 00
C = 0 Z = 0 N = 0

MOV [R0] R5            pc = 2    11000001110001010000000
Class = 3 mode = 7
Reg = 08 00 00 00 00 8f 00 00
```

```
Mem = 00 00 00 00 00 00 00 00 8f 00 00
C = 0 Z = 0 N = 1


DEC R0              pc = 3    10000100100000000000000
Class = 2 mode = 2
Reg = 07 00 00 00 00 8f 00 00
Mem = 00 00 00 00 00 00 00 00 8f 00 00
C = 0 Z = 0 N = 0


BNE NEXT            pc = 4    01001000010000000000001
Class = 1 mode = 1
Reg = 07 00 00 00 00 8f 00 00
Mem = 00 00 00 00 00 00 00 00 8f 00 00
C = 0 Z = 0 N = 0


NEXT: RND R5        pc = 1    10001000101010000000000
Class = 2 mode = 2
Reg = 07 00 00 00 00 35 00 00
Mem = 00 00 00 00 00 00 00 00 8f 00 00
C = 0 Z = 0 N = 0
```

> **Note**
> Output not displayed to save space

In the next section, we'll look at one component of simulators in greater detail, the ALU.

Arithmetic and Logic Unit (ALU)

And now for something different. We have used an ALU in all the simulators. Here, you will learn about the ALU in greater detail and about its testing.

The following Python code demonstrates the implementation of an 8-bit, 16-function ALU. We have added several *contemporary operations* that some computers provide, such as modulus, minimum, and maximum. The alu function is called with the op, a, b, cIn, and display parameters. The op parameter is in the range 0 to 15 and defines the function. The a and b parameters are two 8-bit integers in the range 0 to 255, cin is a carry in, and display is a flag. When display is 0, no data is printed. When display is 1, the inputs and results are printed by the function. This feature is for debugging.

This code demonstrates the use of Python's if...elif construct to decode the arithmetic operation. We have also included a *dictionary structure* that enables us to print out the operation code by name. In this case, the dictionary is allOps and is written as follows:

```
AllOps = {0:'clr', 1:'add',2:'sub',3:'mul'}      # just four entries to make easy reading.
```

Another feature is that we can easily print data in binary form. The `print (bin(c))` operation prints c in binary form. However, because we are using 8-bit arithmetic and wish to see leading zeros, we can force an 8-bit output by using the zfill; that is `print (bin(c).zfill(8))` method.

Alternatively, we can use `print('Result', format(c,'08b'))` to print the c variable as an 8-bit binary string.

A Python function can return multiple values as a *tuple*. A tuple is a Python list of immutable values that cannot be changed; for example, if you write return (c, z, n, v cOut), you are returning a tuple that consists of the function we calculated and the z, n, v, and cOut flags. These can't be changed, but they can be assigned to variables in the calling program; take the following example:

```
result,Zero,Neg,oVerflow,carry = alu(0,A,B,0,1)
```

Note the calculation of overflow. The v-bit is set if the sign bits of the two operands are the same and the sign bit of the result is different. Overflow is valid only for addition and subtraction. The modulus function returns a positive value if the input parameter is negative in two's complement terms. We do this by inverting the bits and adding 1.

```
# This function simulates an 8-bit ALU and provides 16 operations
# It is called by alu(op,a,b,cIn,display). Op defines the ALU function
# a,b and cIn are the two inputs and the carry in
# If display is 1, the function prints all input and output on the terminal
# Return values: q, z, n, v, cOut) q is the result
def alu(op,a,b,cIn,display):
    allOps = {0:'clr', 1:'add',2:'sub',3:'mul',4:'div',5:'and',6:'or', \
              7:'not', 8:'eor', 9:'lsl',10:'lsr', 11:'adc',12:'sbc', \
              13:'min',14:'max',15:'mod'}
    a, b = a & 0xFF, b & 0xFF              # Ensure the input is 8 bits
    cOut,z,n,v = 0,0,0,0                   # Clear all status flags
    if   op == 0:    q = 0                 # Code 0000 clear
    elif op == 1:    q = a + b             # Code 0001 add
    elif op == 2:    q = a - b             # Code 0010 subtract
    elif op == 3:    q = a * b             # Code 0011 multiply
    elif op == 4:    q = a // b            # Code 0100 divide
    elif op == 5:    q = a & b             # Code 0100 bitwise AND
    elif op == 6:    q = a | b             # Code 0100bitwise OR
    elif op == 7:    q = ~a                # Code 0111 bitwise negate (logical complement)
    elif op == 8:    q = a ^ b             # Code 0100 bitwise EOR
    elif op == 9:    q = a << b            # Code 0100 bitwise logical shift left b places
    elif op == 10:   q = a >> b            # Code 0100 bitwise logical shift right b places
    elif op == 11:   q = a + b + cIn       # Code 0100 add with carry in
    elif op == 12:   q = a - b - cIn       # Code 0100 subtract with borrow in
    elif op == 13:                         # Code 1101 q = minimum(a,b)
        if a > b: q = b
```

```
            else:       q = a
        elif op == 14:                          # Code 1110 q = maximum(a,b)
            if a > b: q = a                     # Note: in unsigned terms
            else:       q = b
        elif op == 15:                          # Code 1111 q = mod(a)
            if a > 0b01111111: q = (~a+1)&0xFF  # if a is negative q = -a (2s comp)
            else:       q = a                   # if a is positive q =    a
# Prepare to exit: Setup flags
        cOut = (q&0x100)>>8                      # Carry out is bit 8
        q    = q & 0xFF                          # Constrain result to 8 bits
        n    = (q & 0x80)>>7                     # AND q with 10000000 and shift right 7 times
        if q == 0: z = 1                         # Set z bit if result zero

        p1 = ( (a&0x80)>>7)& ((b&0x80)>>7)&~((q&0x80)>>7)
        p2 = (~(a&0x80)>>7)&~((b&0x80)>>7)& ((q&0x80)>>7)
        if p1 | p2 == True: v = 1                # Calculate v-bit (overflow)

        if display == 1:                         # Display parameters and results
            a,b = a&0xFF, b&0xFF                 # Force both inputs to 8 bits
            print('Op =',allOps[op],'Decimals: a =',a,' b =',b, \
                  'cIn =',cIn,'Result =',q)
            print('Flags: Z =',z, 'N =',n, 'V =',v, 'C =',cOut)
            print('Binaries A =',format(a,'08b'), 'B =',format(b,'08b'), \
                  'Carry in =',format(cIn,'01b'), 'Result =',format(q,'08b'))
            print ()
        return (q, z, n, v, cOut)                # Return c (result), and flags as a tuple
```

Testing the ALU

We will now demonstrate testing the ALU. A while loop is created and two integers are inputted using Python's keyboard input function and the .split() method to divide the input string into substrings. For example, you can enter add 3 5 to perform the addition of 3 and 5. A null input (i.e., a return) ends the sequence.

I have arranged the code so that you can see only the parameters entered as needed for the operation, for example, add 3,7, mod 5, or sbc 3 4 1. To make it easier to test logic functions, you can enter parameters in binary (%10110) or hexadecimal ($3B) format.

A feature of the test code is that I use a reverse dictionary. This allows you to enter a function by its name, rather than number.

The following is the code I used to test the ALU:

```
#### MAIN BODY
def literal(lit):
    if    lit.isnumeric(): lit =  int(lit)        # If decimal convert to integer
    elif lit[0] == '%': lit =  int(lit[1:],2)      # If binary string convert to int
```

```
        elif lit[0:1]== '$': lit =  int(lit[1:],16)    # If hex string convert to int
        elif lit[0]  == '-': lit = -int(lit[1:])&0xFF  # If negative convert to signed int
        return(lit)
opsRev = {'clr':0,'add':1,'sub':2,'mul':3,'div':4,'and':5,'or':6,        \
          'not':7,'eor':8,'lsl':9,'lsr':10,'adc':11,'sbc':12,            \
          'min':13,'max':14,'mod':15}
x,y,op1,op2,cIn = 0,0,0,0,0                             # Dummy value prior to test in while loop
while True:
    x = input('Enter operation and values ')
    if x == '': break                                  # Exit on return
    y = x.split()                                      # Divide into tokens
    print (y)                                          # Show the input
    fun = opsRev[y[0]]                                 # Convert function name into number
    if len(y) > 1: op1 = literal(y[1])                 # One parameter
    if len(y) > 2: op2 = literal(y[2])                 # Two parameters
    if len(y) > 3: cIn = literal(y[3])                 # Three parameters
    q, z, n, v, cOut  = alu(fun,op1,op2,cIn,1)         # Call the ALU function
                                                       # Repeat until return entered
```

Here's some sample output from a test run:

```
Enter operation and values add 25 $1F
['add', '25', '$1F']
Operation =  add Decimals: a = 25  b = 31 cIn = 0 Result = 56
Flags: Z = 0 N = 0 V = 0 C = 0
Binaries A = 00011001 B = 00011111 Carry in = 0 Result = 00111000

Enter operation and values add %11111111 1
['add', '%11111111', '1']
Operation =  add Decimals: a = 255  b = 1 cIn = 0 Result = 0
Flags: Z = 1 N = 0 V = 0 C = 1
Binaries A = 11111111 B = 00000001 Carry in = 0 Result = 00000000

Enter operation and values add 126 2
['add', '126', '2']
Operation =  add Decimals: a = 126  b = 2 cIn = 0 Result = 128
Flags: Z = 0 N = 1 V = 1 C = 0
Binaries A = 01111110 B = 00000010 Carry in = 0 Result = 10000000

Enter operation and values add 7 -2
['add', '7', '-2']
Operation =  add Decimals: a = 7  b = 254 cIn = 0 Result = 5
Flags: Z = 0 N = 0 V = 0 C = 1
Binaries A = 00000111 B = 11111110 Carry in = 0 Result = 00000101
```

```
Enter operation and values add 128 -2
['add', '128', '-2']
Operation =  add Decimals: a = 128  b = 254 cIn = 0 Result = 126
Flags: Z = 0 N = 0 V = 1 C = 1
Binaries A = 10000000 B = 11111110 Carry in = 0 Result = 01111110

Enter operation and values and $A7 %11110001
['and', '$A7', '%11110001']
Operation =  and Decimals: a = 167  b = 241 cIn = 0 Result = 161
Flags: Z = 0 N = 1 V = 0 C = 0
Binaries A = 10100111 B = 11110001 Carry in = 0 Result = 10100001

Enter operation and values lsl %11100011 2
['lsl', '%11100011', '2']
Operation =  lsl Decimals: a = 227  b = 2 cIn = 0 Result = 140
Flags: Z = 0 N = 1 V = 0 C = 1
Binaries A = 11100011 B = 00000010 Carry in = 0 Result = 10001100

Enter operation and values
```

A final example: TC4

In this example, we provide a new simulator that introduces you to some new elements of Python, such as the ability to include the date and time. This final example of a computer simulator brings some of the things we have discussed together and creates a simulator with a 32-bit instruction memory and a 16-bit data memory. Consequently, this is not a von Neumann machine because it has different program and data memories. TC4 incorporates several modifications to demonstrate both simplifications and additions.

We'll present the code first and then add some comments via the labels that indicate points of interest. Shaded parts of the code have comments following the code:

```
import re                          # Library for regular expressions for removing spaces    (See 1)

from random import   *             # Random number library
import sys                         # Operating system call library
from datetime import date          # Import date function                                   (See 2)


bPt = []                           # Breakpoint table (labels and PC values)
bActive = 0


today = date.today()               # Get today's date                                       (See 2)
print('Simulator', today, '\n')


deBug, trace, bActive  = 0, 0, 0   # Turn off debug, trace and breakpoint modes             (See 3)
```

```
x1 = input('D for debug >>> ')        # Get command input
if x1.upper() == 'D': deBug = 1        # Turn on debug mode if 'D' or 'd' entered
x2 = input('T or B')                   # Get command input
x2 = x2.upper()                        # Convert to upper-case
if x2 == 'T': trace = 1                # Turn on trace mode if 'T' or 't' entered
elif x2 == 'B':                        # If 'B' or 'b' get breakpoints until 'Q' input        (See 4)
    next = True
    bActive = 1                        # Set breakpoint active mode
    while next == True:                # Get breakpoint as either label or PC value
        y = input('Breakpoint ')
        y = y.upper()
        bPt.append(y)                  # Put breakpoint (upper-case) in table
        if y == 'Q': next = False
    if deBug == 1:                     # Display breakpoint table if in debug mode
        print ('\nBreakpoint table')
        for i in range (0,len(bPt)): print(bPt[i])
        print()
```

```
print()
```

The `memProc()` function deals with the data memory and allows you to store data in memory and even ASCII code. This function processes assembler directives:

```
def memProc(src):                                     # Memory processing
    global memPoint, memD                             # Deal with directives
    for i in range(len(src)):                         # and remove directives from source code
        if src[i][0] == '.WORD':                      # Test for .word directive
            lit = get_lit(src[i],2)                   # Get the literal value
            sTab.update({src[i][1]:memPoint})         # Bind literal name to the memory address
            memD[memPoint] = lit                      # Store the literal in memory
            memPoint = memPoint + 1                   # Move the memory pointer on one word
        if src[i][0] == '.ASCII':                     # .ASCII: test for an ASCII character
            sTab.update({src[i][1]:memPoint})         # Bind name to memory address
            character = ord(src[i][2])                # Convert character to numeric form
            memD[memPoint] = character                # Store the character in memory as ASCII code
            memPoint = memPoint + 1                   # Move the memory pointer on
        if src[i][0] == '.DSW':                       # Test for .DSW to reserve locations in memory
            sTab.update({src[i][1]:memPoint})         # Save name in table and bind to memory address
            memPoint = memPoint + int(src[i][2])      # Move memory pointer by space required
    src = [i  for i in src if i[0] != '.WORD']        # Remove .word from source
    src = [i  for i in src if i[0] != '.ASCII']       # Remove .ASCII from source
    src = [i  for i in src if i[0] != '.DSW']         # Remove .DSW from source
    memD[memPoint] = 'END'                            # Add terminator to data memory (for display)
    return(src)
```

The `get_reg()` function determines the number of a register. It first looks in the symbol table to determine whether the name is symbolic. Otherwise, it extracts the register number from the predicate:

```
def get_reg(pred,p):                    # Extract a register number from predicate
    reg = pred[p]                       # Read token p is the predicate
    if reg in sTab:                     # Check if this is a symbolic name
        reg = sTab.get(reg)             # If symbolic name read it from symbol table
        reg = int(reg[1:])              # Convert register name into number
    else: reg = int(reg[1:])            # If not symbolic name convert name into number
    return(reg)                         # Otherwise return the register number
```

The `get_lit()` function extracts a literal from the predicate. As in the case of register names, it is able to deal with symbolic values by first looking for the name in the symbol table. If there is no symbolic name, the text is converted into the appropriate integer by observing and dealing with any prefixes:

```
def get_lit(pred,p):                                         # Extract literal from place p in predicate
    global sTab                                              # We need the symbol table
    lit = pred[p]                                            # Read the literal from the predicate
    if lit in sTab:                                          # If literal is in symbol table, look it up
        lit = int(sTab.get(lit))
    else:                                                    # Convert literal format to an integer
        if   lit[0]    == "%": lit = int(pred[-1][1:],2)     # If prefix % then binary
        elif lit[0:2] == "0X": lit = int(pred[-1][2:],16)
                                                             # If prefix 0X then hexadecimal
        elif lit[0].isnumeric(): lit = int(pred[-1])         # If numeric get it
        elif lit[0].isalpha(): lit = ord(lit)                # Convert ASCII character to integer
        elif lit[0:2] == "0X": lit = int(pred[-1][2:],16)
                                                             # If prefix 0X then hexadecimal
        else:  lit = 0                                       # Default (error) value 0
    return(lit)
```

The `display()` function takes care of displaying data after each instruction has been executed. In this case, the data values are converted into hexadecimal format and turned into strings:

```
def display():                              # Print the state after each instruction
    thisOp = ' '.join(src[pcOld])           # Join this op-code's tokens into a string
    a =[format(x,'04x') for x in r]         # Format registers into hex strings
    b = (' ').join(a)                       # Join the hex strings with a space
    f1 = f'{pcOld:<4}'                      # Format the PC as a string
    f2 = f'{thisOp:<18}'                    # Format the instruction to fixed width
    print('PC =',f1,'Reg =',b,'Z =',z,'N =',n,'C =',c,f2)        # Print the data
    return()
```

The `alu()` function performs arithmetic operations. This example is very rudimentary and provides only basic operations. Since we have covered ALU elsewhere, it's not necessary to be comprehensive. You can easily add new functions yourself:

```
def alu(a,b,f):      # ALU for addition/subtraction and flag calculation          (See 6)
# a and b are the numbers to add/subtract and f the function
        global z,c,n                        # Make flags global
        z,c,n = 0,0,0                        # Clear flags initially
        if f == 1: s = a + b                 # f = 1 for add
        if f == 2: s = a - b                 # f = 2 for subtract
        s = s & 0x1FFFF                      # Constrain result to 17 bits
        if s > 0xFFFF: c = 1                 # Carry set if 17th bit 1
        if 0x8000 & s == 0x8000 : n = 1      # Bit 15 set to 1 for negative
        if s & 0xFFFF == 0: z = 1            # Zero flag set to 1 if bits 0-15 all 0
        s = 0xFFFF & s                       # Ensure 16-bit result
        return(s)

codes = {"STOP":(0,0),"NOP":(0,1),"RND":(1,4),"BRA":(2,5),"BEQ":(2,6),          \
         "BNE":(2,7),"MOV":(3,8),"LDRM":(4,9),"LDRL":(4,10),"LDRI":(7,11),       \
         "LDRI+":(7,12),"STRM":(4,13),"STRI":(7,14),"STRI+":(7,15),              \
         "ADD":(5,16),"ADDL":(6,17),"SUB":(5,18),"SUBL":(6,19),                  \
         "AND":(5,20),"ANDL":(6,21),"OR":(5,22),"ORL":(6,23), "EOR":(5,24), \
         "EORL":(6,25),"CMP":(3,26),"CMPL":(4,27),"LSL":(3,28),                  \
         "LSR":(3,29),"ROL":(3,30),"ROR": (3,31), "BSR":(2,32),                  \
         "RTS":(0,33),"PUSH":(1,34),"POP":(1,35),"BL":(2,36),"RL":(0,37),    \
         "INC":(1,48), "DEC":(1,49), "PRT":(1,3), "BHS": (2,71) }

# Style Code Format (a,b) where a is the instruction style and b is the actual op-code
# 0      Zero operand                        STOP
# 1      Destination register operand        INC   R0
# 2      Literal operand                     BEQ   5
# 3      Two registers: Rd, Rs1              MOV   R2,R4
# 4      Register and literal Rd L           LDR   R6,23
# 5      Three registers: Rd, Rs1, Rs2        ADD  R1,R2,R3
# 6      Two registers, literal Rs, Rd1, L    ADDL R1,R2,9
# 7      Indexed, Rd, Rs, L                   LDRI R4,(R6,8)
# 8      UNDEFINED


testFile = 'E:/ArchitectureWithPython/TC4_test.txt'   # Source filename on my computer
with open(testFile) as myFile:           # Open source file with assembly language program
    lines = myFile.readlines()           # Read the program into lines
myFile.close()                           # Close the source file (not actually needed)
lines = [i[0:-1]  for i in lines ]       # Remove the /n newline from each line of the source code
```

```
src = lines                          # Copy lines to variable scr (i.e., source code)

if deBug == 1:                       # If in debug mode print the source file        (See 3)
    print('Debug mode: original source file')
    for i in range(0,len(src)): print(i, src[i])      # Listing file
```

Here, we carry out the usual cleaning up of the source text in the assembly language file and prepare the text for later parsing and analysis. Note that we use a regular expression to remove multiple spaces. This is a feature we do not use in this book, but it is worthwhile investigating if you are doing extensive text processing:

```
for i in range(0,len(src)):          # Remove comments from source
    src[i] = src[i].split('@',1)[0]  # Split line on first occurrence of @ and keep first item

src = [i.strip(' ') for i in src ]       # Remove leading and trailing spaces
src = [i for i in src if i != '']        # Remove blank lines
src = [i.upper() for i in src]           # Convert lower- to upper-case
src = [re.sub('+', ' ',i) for i in src ] # Remove multiple spaces        1
src = [i.replace(', ',' ') for i in src] # Replace commas space by single space
src = [i.replace('[','') for i in src]   # Remove [ in register indirect mode
src = [i.replace(']','') for i in src]   # Remove [
src = [i.replace(',',' ') for i in src]  # Replace commas by spaces
src = [i for i in src if i[0] != '@']    # Remove lines with just a comment
src = [i.split(' ')  for i in src]       # Tokenize


if deBug == 1:                           # If in debug mode print the source file
    print('\nProcessed source file\n')
    [print(i) for i in src]
# Initialize key variables
# memP program memory, memD data memory
sTab = {}                                # Set up symbol table for labels and equates
memP = [0] * 64                          # Define program memory
memD = [0] * 64                          # Define data memory
memPoint = 0                             # memPoint points to next free    location

[sTab.update({i[1]:i[2]}) for i in src if i[0] == '.EQU']
                                         # Scan source file and deal with equates

src = [i  for i in src if i[0] != '.EQU']   # Remove equates from source
src = memProc(src)                          # Deal with memory-related directives

for i in range (0,len(src)):             # Insert labels in symbol table
    if src[i][0][-1]== ':': sTab.update({src[i][0][0:-1]:i})
                                         # Remove the colon from labels
```

```
print('\nSymbol table\n')
for x,y in sTab.items(): print("{:<8}".format(x),y)        # Display symbol table

if deBug == 1:
    print("\nListing with assembly directives removed\n")
    for i in range(0,len(src)):                    # Step through each line of code
        z = ''                                     # Create empty string for non-labels
        if src[i][0][-1] != ':': z = '        '
                                                   # Create 8-char empty first spaced
        for j in range(0,len(src[i])):             # Scan all tokens of instruction
            y = src[i][j]                          # Get a token
            y = y.ljust(8)                         # Pad it with spaces with a width of 8 characters
            z = z + y                              # Add it to the line
        print(str(i).ljust(3),z)                   # Print line number and instruction

if deBug == 1:                                     # Display data memory for debugging
    print("\nData memory")
    [print(memD[i]) for i in range(0,memPoint+1)]  # print pre-loaded data in memory
    print()


#### MAIN ASSEMBLY LOOP
if deBug == 1: print('Assembled instruction\n')    # If in debug mode print heading  4
```

Now, we execute the code. The program counter is first initialized to 0. Of course, we could have started at any arbitrary point or even provided assembly language directives to preset the pc. After setting the pc, we read an instruction and parse it.

```
pc = 0
for pc in range(0,len(src)):
    rD,rS1,rS2,lit = 0,0,0,0                        # Initialize operand fields
    if src[pc][0][-1] != ':':                       # Extract mnemonic and predicate
        mnem  = src[pc][0]
        if len(src[pc]) > 1: pred = src[pc][1:]     # Check for single mnemonic only
        else: pred = '[]'                           # If only mnemonic with no predicate
    else:
        mnem  = src[pc][1]                           # For lines with a label
        if len(src[pc]) > 2: pred = src[pc][2:]      # Get predicate if one exists
        else: pred = '[]'                            # If only mnemonic, no pred
    if mnem in codes:
        opFormat = codes.get(mnem)                   # Read of op-code format of mnemonic
    else: print('Illegal opcode ERROR, mnem')        # Display error message
```

Now, we can use `opFormat` to extract the required parameters from the predicate:

```
# OP-CODE FORMATS
    if opFormat[0] == 1:                        # Type 1 single register rD: inc r0
        rD = get_reg(pred,0)
    if opFormat[0] == 2:                        # Type 2 literal operand: BEQ 24
        lit = get_lit(pred,-1)
    if opFormat[0] == 3:                        # Type 3 two registers dD, rS1: MOV r3,R0
        rD  = get_reg(pred,0)
        rS1 = get_reg(pred,1)
    if opFormat[0] == 4:                        # Type 4 register and literal Rd, lit: LDRL R1,34
        rD  = get_reg(pred,0)
        lit = get_lit(pred,-1)
    if opFormat[0] == 5:                        # Type 5 three registers Rd, Rs1 Rs2: ADD    R1,R2,R3
        rD  = get_reg(pred,0)
        rS1 = get_reg(pred,1)
        rS2 = get_reg(pred,2)
    if opFormat[0] == 6:                        # Type 6 two registers and lit Rd, Rs1 lit: ADD    R1,R2,lit
        rD  = get_reg(pred,0)
        rS1 = get_reg(pred,1)
        lit = get_lit(pred,-1)
    if opFormat[0] == 7:                        # Type 7 two registers and lit Rd, Rs1 lit: LDR    R1,(R2,lit)
        rD  = get_reg(pred,0)
        pred[1] = pred[1].replace('(','')       # Remove brackets
        pred[2] = pred[2].replace(')','')
        rS1 = get_reg(pred,1)
        lit = get_lit(pred,-1)
    if opFormat[0] == 8:                        # Type 8 UNDEFINED
        pass
```

In this example of a simulator, we create the binary code to be executed. The various parameters extracted from the predicate have to be moved into the appropriate place to create the final binary code, `binCode`:

```
    opCd     = opFormat[1] << 25      # Move op-code to left-most 7 bits
    rDs      = rD          << 22      # Move destination reg into place
    rS1s     = rS1         << 19      # Move source reg 1 in place
    rS2s     = rS2         << 16      # Move source reg 2 in place
    binCode=opCd|rDs|rS1s|rS2s|lit    # Assemble the instruction by combining fields
    memP[pc] = binCode                # Store 32-bit binary code in program memory

    if deBug == 1:                    # If in debug mode show the binary output of the assembler
        a1 = f'{pc:<4}'               # Format for the PC (4 chars wide)
        a2 = format(binCode,'032b')   # Create 32-bit binary string for op-code
        a3 = f'{mnem:<5}'             # Format the mnemonic to 5 places
```

```
        a4 = f'{rD:<4}'                   # Format source register to 4 places
        a5 = f'{rS1:<4}'
        a6 = f'{rS2:<4}'
        a7 = f'{lit:<6}'
        print('PC =',a1,a2,a3,a4,a5,a6,a7,src[pc])  # Assemble items and print them
# CODE EXECUTE LOOP
print('\nExecute code\n')
```

This block initializes variables, registers, memory, and the stack pointer before we enter the code execution loop. Note that we create a stack with 16 entries. The stack pointer is set to 16, which is one below the bottom of the stack. When the first item is pushed, the stack pointer is pre-decremented to 15, the bottom of the available stack area:

```
r = [0] * 8                             # Register set
stack = [0] * 16                        # stack with 16 locations              See 7

sp = 16                                 # stack pointer initialize to bottom of stack + 1
lr = 0                                  # link register initialize to 0
run = 1                                 # run = 1 to execute code
pc = 0                                  # Initialize program counter
z,c,n = 0,0,0                           # Clear flag bits. Only z-bit is used

while run == 1:                         # Main loop

    instN = memP[pc]                    # Read instruction
    pcOld = pc                          # Remember the pc (for printing)
    pc = pc + 1                         # Point to the next instruction
    op   = (instN >> 25) & 0b1111111    # Extract the op-code (7 most-significant bits)
    rD   = (instN >> 22) & 0b111        # Extract the destination register
    rS1  = (instN >> 19) & 0b111        # Extract source register 1
    rS2  = (instN >> 16) & 0b111        # Extract source register 2
    lit  = (instN      ) & 0xFFFF       # Extract literal in least-significant 16 bits
    rDc  = r[rD]                        # Read destination register contents)
    rS1c = r[rS1]                       # Read source register 1 contents
    rS2c = r[rS2]                       # Read source register 2 contents
```

Here, the instructions are executed. Note we used an `if` statement for each instruction. This was used during the initial development phase. In practice, an if...elif structure would be more suitable:

```
# Instruction execution
    if op == 0b0000001:          # NOP    Nothing to see here ... it's NOP so just drop out
        pass
    if op == 0b0000100:          # RND    # RND r0 generates random number in r0
        r[rD] = randint(0,0xFFFF)
```

```
if op == 0b0000101:              # BRA      # Branch to the label or literal. Absolute address
    pc = lit
if op == 0b0000110:              # BEQ      # Branch on zero flag
    if z == 1: pc = lit
if op == 0b0000111:              # BNE      # Branch on not zero
    if z != 1: pc = lit
if op == 0b1000111:              # BHS      # Branch on unsigned higher or same      (See 8)
    if c == 0 : pc = lit
if op == 0b0001000:              # MOV      # Copy one register to another
    r[rD] = rS1c
if op == 0b0001001:              # LDRM     # Load register from address in memory
    r[rD] = memD[lit]
if op == 0b0001010:              # LDRL     # Load register with a literal
    r[rD] = lit
if op == 0b0001011:              # LDRI     # Load register indirect with offset; LDRI r1,[r2,4]
    r[rD] = memD[rS1c + lit]
if op == 0b0001100:              # LDRI+    # Auto-indexed. Increment pointer after use  (See 9)
    r[rD] = memD[rS1c + lit]
    r[rS1] = rS1c + 1
if op == 0b0001101:              # STRM     #
    memD[lit] = rDc
if op == 0b0001110:              # STRI     # Store register indexed
    memD[rS1c + lit] = rDc
if op == 0b0001111:              # STRI+    # Auto indexed
    memD[rS1c + lit] = rDc
    r[rS1] = rS1c + 1
if op == 0b0010000:              # ADD      # r1 = r2 + r3
    r[rD] = alu(rS1c,rS2c,1)
if op == 0b0010001:              # ADDL     # r1 = r2 + literal
    r[rD] = alu(rS1c,lit,1)
if op == 0b0010010:              # SUB
    r[rD] = alu(rS1c,rS2c,2)
if op == 0b0010011:              # SUBL
    r[rD] = alu(rS1c,lit,2)
if op == 0b0010100:              # AND
    r[rD] = (rS1c & rS2c) & 0xFFFF
if op == 0b0010101:              # ANDL
    r[rD] = (rS1c & lit) & 0xFFFF
if op == 0b0010110:              # OR
    r[rD] = (rS1c | rS2c) & 0xFFFF
if op == 0b0010111:              # ORL
    r[rD] = (rS1c | lit) & 0xFFFF
if op == 0b0011000:              # EOR (XOR)
```

```
            r[rD] = (rS1c ^ rS2c) & 0xFFFF
  if op == 0b0011001:                              # EORL (XORL)
            r[rD] = (rS1c ^ lit) & 0xFFFF
  if op == 0b0011010:                              # CMP
            diff = alu(rDc,rS1c,2)
  if op == 0b0011011:                              # CMPL
            diff = alu(rDc,lit,2)
  if op == 0b0011100:                              # LSL
            r[rD] = (rS1c << 1) & 0xFFFF
  if op == 0b0011101:                              # LSR
            r[rD] = (rS1c >> 1) & 0xFFFF
  if op == 0b0011110:                              # ROL
            bitLost = (rS1c & 0x8000) >> 16
            rS1c = (rS1c << 1) & 0xFFFF
            r[rD] = rS1c | bitLost
  if op == 0b0011111:                              # ROR
            bitLost = (rS1c & 0x0001)
            rS1c = (rS1c >> 1) & 0xFFFF
            r[rD] = rS1c | (bitLost << 16)
```

In the following code we've included stack-based operations for the sake of demonstrating stack usage and for versatility:

```
  if op == 0b0100000:       # BSR
      sp = sp - 1
      stack[sp] = pc
      pc = lit
  if op == 0b0100001:                              # RTS
      pc = stack[sp]
      sp = sp + 1
  if op == 0b0100010:                              # PUSH                (See 7)
      sp = sp - 1
      stack[sp] = rDc
  if op == 0b0100011:                              # POP                 (See 7)
      r[rD] = stack[sp]
      sp = sp + 1
  if op == 0b0100100:                              # BL branch with link (See 10)
      lr = pc
      pc = lit
  if op == 0b0100101:                              # RL return from link
      pc = lr
  if op == 0b0110000:                              # INC
      r[rD] = alu(rDc,1,1)
  if op == 0b0110001:                              # DEC
```

```
        r[rD] = alu(rDc,1,2)
    if op == 0b0000011:      # PRT r0 displays the ASCII character in register r0          See 11
        character = chr(r[rD])
        print(character)
    if op == 0b0000000:                        # STOP
        run = 0
# END OF CODE EXECUTION Deal with display

    if bActive ==1:                            # Are breakpoints active?
        if src[pcOld][0] in bPt:               # If the current label or mnemonic is in the table
            display()                          # display the data
        if str(pcOld) in bPt:                  # If the current PC (i.e., pcOld) is in the table display
            display()
    if trace == 1:                             # If in trace mode, display registers
        x = input('<< ')                       # Wait for keyboard entry (any key will do)
        display()                              # then display current operation
    elif bActive != 1: display()               # If not trace and not breakpoints, display registers
    if run == 0:                               # Test for end of program              See 12
        print('End of program')                # If end, say 'Goodbye'
        sys.exit()                             # and return
```

Comments on TC4

We have not provided a detailed discussion of this program because it follows the same pattern as earlier simulators. However, we have highlighted some of its principal features. The following numbers correspond to the numbers (at the end of the comment field) in the shaded lines of the code:

1. Call regular expressions library. This is a library that handles regular expressions that offer a very powerful means of processing text. In this example, we use only one simple example of regular text processing.

2. The `src = [re.sub(' +', ' ',i) for i in src ]` Python expression uses a regular expression to remove multiple spaces from a text string. We have included this to point you in the direction of regular expressions for more sophisticated text manipulation.

3. The `from datetime import date` operation imports a method date from datetime that can be used to display the date and time. This is useful for labeling your output during a run.

4. TC4 has an optional debugging facility. We can select three options. Entering 'D' provides a debugging facility by printing the source program as it is processed. We can see the original source code, the source code without comments and assembly directives, and the processed version, which includes the binary output after assembly. The 'T' option provides a line-by-line trace function that executes a line of code each time the *Enter* key is pressed. The 'B' option supports breakpoints where the output is printed only at a breakpoint. The breakpoint may be a label, a mnemonic, or the PC value. Note that in breakpoint mode, only breakpoint lines are displayed.

5. Entering T or B at the prompt can be used to set up a trace mode or enter instructions or PC values into the breakpoint table. Unusually, this is performed once at the beginning of the program and not during the execution phase.

6. The function processes the source code and deals with assembly directives related to setting up the data memory, for example, loading data values with the .WORD directive. It also supports storing an ASCII character in memory and reserving a named memory location for data.

7. The most important directive is .WORD, which stores a numeric value in memory and gives that address a symbolic value. For example, if the next free data memory location were 20, then the .WORD TIME 100 expression would store the number 100 at memory location 20 and bind the name time to 100. The .DSW (define storage word) directive simply reserves memory locations for future data access and names the address of the first location; for example, if the current memory location is 10, then .DSW XYZ 5 frees five memory locations (10, 11, 12, 13, and 14) and binds the names XYZ to 10. The memory pointer is moved to 15, the next free location. The memPoint variable is the memory pointer that keeps track of where data is to be stored in data memory during the assembly phase. The .ASCII directive is there for demonstration purposes. The .ASCII PQR directive would store the ASCII code for the character 'T' in memory.

8. These directives are removed from the source code after they have done their job.

9. We have created a very simple ALU that implements only add and subtract. This was done to keep the program small and concentrate on more interesting instructions in this final example. Simple logic operations are directly implemented in the code execution of the program, in the style

```
if thisOpcode == 'AND': result = a & b.
```

10. TC4 provides several stack operations (push and pull). We initially create a separate stack. TC4's stack does not use the data memory. This feature is for demonstration and can be expanded.

11. Real computers normally contain a far wider range of conditional branches than we have in this book. Here, we demonstrate one such branch operation, BHS, which means branch if higher or same. This operation forces a branch if two values are compared and x > y or x = y. Note that this applies to unsigned numbers (i.e., not two's complement). This condition is met if the carry bit, c, is 0 after a comparison. BHS and BCC (branch on carry 0) are synonyms. For example, if x = 1000 and y = 0100, x > y if the numbers are unsigned (4 > -8) and y > x (8 > 4) if the numbers are signed.

12. The LDRI+ operation performs a pointer-based load register operation and then increments the pointer register.

13. We have provided an interesting branch and return operation like that of the ARM's branch with link. The BL operation jumps to a target address and saves the return address in a special register called the link register, rl. At the end of the subroutine, the RL (return from link) instruction returns to the instruction after the call. This mechanism allows only one call, because a second call would overwrite the return address in the link register.

14. To demonstrate direct printing, the PRT operation displays the character corresponding to the ASCII code in the register; for example, if R1 contains 0x42, the PRT R2 operation would display B on the console.

15. When the program has been executed, the `sys.exit()` library function exits the program.

16. Here's an example of code that can be executed by TC4. It's been badly set out in order to test TC4's ability to process text:

```
@ TC4_test
@ 31 Oct 2021
        .equ abc 4
.word aaa abc
.word bbb 5
.dsw   dataA 6                 @ data area to store numbers
.word  end 0xFFFF

 ldrl  r0,0xF
 addl  r1,r7,2
 bl lk
back:  rnd r0
        ldrl  r3,dataA         @ r3 points at data area
        ldrm  r4,bbb           @ r4 contains value to store
 ldrl  r5,4                    @number of words to store
loop:  nop                     @
        bsr sub1
        dec r5
 bne loop
 stop

sub1: stri r4,[r3,0]
    inc r3
    addl  r4,r4,2
    cmpl  r4,9
    bne skip
    addl  r4,r4,6

skip:   rts

lk: ldrl  r6,%11100101
        andl  r7,r6,0xF0
    rl
```

This example ends the section of this book on designing simulators in Python. In the next part, we'll look at a real computer.

Summary

In this chapter, we have extended our overview of simulator design. We started with one of the simplest simulators of them all, the *zero-address machine*; that is, the *stack computer*, TC0. This simulator is not a true computer, because it does not include conditional and branch operations. However, it demonstrates the use of the stack as a means of performing chained calculations.

We then looked at the instruction set architecture (IAS) of a classic 8-bit computer, with its simple one-address instruction format, where all operations are applied to a single accumulator (i.e., register) and the contents of a memory location or a literal.

The one-address machine is followed by the simulation of a multi-register CISC ISA that allows operations between two registers or between a register and the contents of a memory location. The simulator we developed had a 22-bit address just to demonstrate that you can have instructions of any width.

We also looked at the simulator of an ALU to further demonstrate the way in which arithmetic operations can be simulated.

Finally, we presented a register-to-register machine with separate data and instruction memories.

In the next chapter, we'll change course and introduce the ARM-based Raspberry Pi microprocessor, which can be used to write programs in Python, and learn how to program a real 32-bit ARM microprocessor in assembly language.

Part 2:
Using Raspberry Pi to Study a Real Computer Architecture

Now we will turn our attention to a real computer – the ARM that is embedded at the heart of the Raspberry Pi single-board computer. We begin by looking at the Raspberry Pi itself and explain how you can enter an assembly program, execute it, and observe its execution by examining registers and memory during the process of executing instructions. Then, we look at the ARM computer in greater detail. First, we examine the ARM's instruction set, and then we demonstrate its addressing modes and how it accesses memory. Finally, we provide an in depth-coverage of the way in which subroutines are handled by the ARM.

This section comprises the following chapters:

Raspberry Pi: An Introduction

In previous chapters, we introduced the digital computer and explained its operation at the instruction set level. Now you will learn about a real, low-cost computer that was designed for educational purposes.

In this chapter, we introduce Raspberry Pi, which is based on the popular ARM microprocessor. We describe its instruction set architecture and demonstrate how you can use it to run assembly language programs in debugging mode. The highlights of this chapter are as follows:

- An introduction to Raspberry Pi's operating system
- Using the GCC ARM assembler and linker
- Debugging ARM assembly language programs

This is not a handbook for Raspberry Pi. We are interested only in using it to enter assembly language programs, run them, and observe their behavior. We do not cover Raspberry Pi's Windows-style GUI because it is very similar to the corresponding PC and macOS user interfaces. Moreover, the Raspberry Pi operating system includes utilities and a web browser.

Technical requirements

This chapter is based on the Raspberry Pi 4. The software we use should also be compatible with the earlier 3B model. In order to use Raspberry Pi, you will need the following:

- Raspberry Pi 4 (available with 2 GB, 4 GB, and 8 GB DRAM)
- Raspberry Pi 5V 3A power supply
- USB mouse
- USB keyboard
- Wi-Fi internet connection
- Video display with micro HDMI lead
- 32 GB Class 10 micro SD card pre-loaded with NOOBS (see the note at the end of this section)

All these items are available on Amazon or from Raspberry Pi suppliers. You can get the operating system pre-loaded onto a micro SD card, or download the operating system and preload it onto your own card using a PC or Mac. The Raspberry Pi web page at `https://www.raspberrypi.org/` provides full details about this computer including getting started, setting up, and loading the operating system on your own card.

The text was written using **NOOBS (New Out Of the Box Software)**. The Raspberry Pi Foundation no longer supports NOOBS and recommends that you download the latest version of the operating system using Raspberry Pi Imager, which runs under macOS, Windows, and Ubuntu. You can find the necessary information at `https://www.raspberrypi.org/`.

The ARM code we use in this book is designed to run on a Raspberry Pi with a 32-bit operating system.

Raspberry Pi basics

Microcomputers have been around since the 1970s. In the 1970s, several systems aimed at the enthusiast based on the Z80, 6502, and 6809 8-bit microprocessors appeared. Operating systems, apps, and the web didn't exist then.

Then, in the late 1970s, Intel introduced the 8086 and Motorola its 68000 16-bit CPU (the 68000 microprocessor actually had a 32-bit instruction set architecture, but Motorola marketed it initially as a 16-bit machine. In my view this was a catastrophic marketing mistake. 16-bit computers were a giant leap up from their 8-bit predecessors for two reasons. First, the technology had advanced, permitting designers to put far more circuitry on a chip (i.e., more registers, more powerful instruction sets, etc.), and second, processors were far faster due to the reduction in feature size (i.e., smaller transistors). Finally, the declining cost of memory meant that people could run larger and more sophisticated programs.

In the 1960s, the giant corporation IBM was famous for its large-scale data-processing machines. However, IBM wanted a change of direction and IBM's engineers decided to build a PC around Motorola's 68000 processor. Unfortunately for Motorola, a version of that chip wasn't yet in production. Intel released the 8088, an 8-bit version of its 16-bit 8086 processor with an 8-bit data bus that made it easy to create a low-cost microcomputer using 8-bit peripherals and memory components. The 8088 still had a 16-bit architecture but was able to interface to 8-bit memory and I/O devices.

IBM formed a relationship with Intel, and the IBM PC in all its beige-colored splendor arose in 1981. Unlike Apple, IBM created an open architecture that anyone could use without paying a royalty. And a million PC clones flowered. The rest is history. However, the PC and Apple's Mac left a hole in the market: an ultra-low-cost computer that the young, the student, the experimenter, and the enthusiast can play with. Raspberry Pi plugs this gap.

Low-cost computing has been around for a long time. For a few dollars, you can buy a greeting card that plays "Happy Birthday" when you open it. High-performance computing is more expensive. The cost of a computer often lies not in the processor but in the supporting cast of components and systems required to convert a microprocessor into a computer system – in particular, the graphics and display interface, the memory interface, and the communications interface (input/output). That's why the Raspberry Pi has been such an amazing success. On a tiny, low-cost board, you have all the peripherals and interfaces that you need to create a complete system comparable to a PC (although not in terms of performance).

To turn the board into a fully-fledged microcomputer, you need only a low-cost power supply and the very same mouse and keyboard you would use with a PC. Indeed, many people use peripherals left over from PCs and other computers they have lying around. I bought a 2-to-1 HDMI switch to interface my 4K monitor to both my PC and Raspberry Pi. You just press a button and the display switches from PC to Raspberry Pi. The Raspberry Pi uses an open source operating system with vast amounts of free software. No more having to take out a mortgage for Office or Photoshop.

The Raspberry Pi was an outstanding success and rapidly created a very large and enthusiastic following. It found applications at all levels of education from kindergarten to PhD. Over the years, improved versions of Raspberry Pi were introduced, as well as truly minimal versions that could be used as dedicated embedded processors for a few dollars.

Figure 9.1 illustrates the Raspberry Pi 4 that was used while writing this book. The first Raspberry Pi Model B appeared in 2012 with 256 MB of DRAM, USB ports, and Ethernet, but no wireless communications. By 2019, the Raspberry Pi 4 was available with 2 USB 2.0 and 2 USB 3.0 ports, on-board Wi-Fi 502.11ac, Bluetooth 5, and Gigabit Ethernet, plus dual-monitor support via 2 micro HDMI ports capable of supporting 4K displays. The principal features of the RPi 4 are as follows:

- The powerful ARM CPU (Quad core Cortex-A72 64-bit architecture)
- Audio (sound processing system)
- Video display and graphics logic system (you just need to plug the card into a monitor)
- DRAM main memory (2, 4, or 8 GB)
- Non-volatile flash memory with the operating system (not normally included)
- Mouse and keyboard USB ports
- Wi-Fi (both 2.4 and 5.0 GHz bands)
- Bluetooth 5.0
- Ethernet port
- A general I/O port for directly interfacing with external hardware

Figure 9.1 – The Raspberry Pi 4 (Image by Laserlicht / Wikimedia Commons / CC BY-SA 4.0)

The Raspberry Pi board is not normally sold with an operating system. It has a micro-SD port into which you have to insert a memory card containing a suitable operating system. You can buy a card with the OS already installed, or load one of the freely available variants from the web onto a card (using your PC or Mac) and plug it into the Raspberry Pi.

The classic operating system used by computer scientists in academia is Unix, which was developed at AT&T's Bell Labs in the late 1960s by a team that included Ken Thomson and Dennis Richie (two of the most significant players in computer science history). Unix was one of the first operating systems to become portable – that is, to run on different types of computers.

A strong thread in the history of computer science is open software – that is, software developed by a community of individuals that is freely available, such as the Python programming language and the LibreOffice application package, which provides much of the functionality of Microsoft's Office suite.

In the 1980s, the Free Software Foundation led by Richard Stillman led the development of the GNU operating system, which was designed to provide an open source version of Unix. In 1991, Linus Torvalds released an open source component of GNU, its kernel, called Linux.

Today, the Linux kernel plus the GNU tools and compilers have become a free, open source alternative to proprietary operating systems such as Windows. GNU/Linux is available in different flavors (distributions written by various groups with the same basic structure but different features). The original official Raspberry Pi operating system was called *Raspbian* and is based on a version of Debian Linux optimized for Raspberry Pi.

Unix and Linux operate in a *command-line mode* – that is, operating system instructions are entered in text form (just like Microsoft's DOS). Unix, Linux, and DOS all now have user-friendly graphical inputs that make use of the mouse as a key input device. The most famous of these graphical inputs is Microsoft's Windows operating system.

Raspberry Pi now includes both a Windows-based version of Linux and a text-based command-line interface that is used to invoke some of the tools required to assemble and execute ARM assembly language programs. This chapter provides a very short introduction to RPi's Linux operating system.

The Raspberry Pi operating system includes several packages that are very relevant to this book. For example, the Thonny Python IDE provides an **integrated development environment** (**IDE**) for Python and software to edit, assemble, debug, and run Python programs.

Another useful package is the Geany editor, which has built-in support for more than 50 programming languages. You can get Geany at `https://www.geany.org/`.

There is also a Terminal emulator window that lets you operate in the Linux command-line mode – a feature that is useful when working with the ARM assembly language utilities. *Figure 9.2* shows the Raspberry Pi screen on a 4K monitor with several windows open.

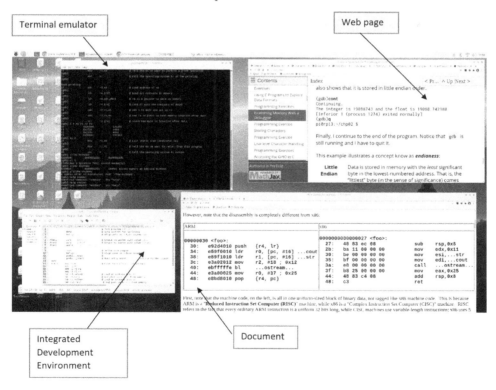

Figure 9.2 – Screenshot of Raspberry Pi's multiple windows

While writing this book, I was also introduced to Visual Studio Code, which is an editor and debugging platform. Visual Studio Code is free and available on Linux, macOS, and Windows platforms. *Figure 9.3* shows an example of a session using Visual Studio Code to write a Python program.

```python
symTab  = {}                                          # Label symbol table

prog    = []                                          # progS is the source program.

for i in range (0,len(progS)):                        # Process source code for equates

    thisLine = progS[i].split()                       # split on spaces (ok for equate and label)

    if len(thisLine) > 1 and thisLine[1] == 'equ':    # Is this an equate?

        symTab.update({thisLine[0][0:-1]:thisLine[2]}) # Store label

    else: prog.append(progS[i])                       # Append to prog unless equate


for i in range (0,len(prog)):                         # Process source code

    prog[i] = prog[i].replace(',',' ')                # Remove commas

    prog[i] = prog[i].split(' ')                      # Tokenize
```

Figure 9.3 – A VS Code session while developing a Python program

I must thank Graeme Harker for encouraging me to use VS Code. Had I discovered VS Code earlier, I would probably have stuck to that.

Now that we've introduced the ubiquitous Raspberry Pi that can form the basis of a computer system with the addition of a mouse, keyboard, and display, we are going to introduce its operating system.

However, we do not delve too deeply. In order to use the Raspberry Pi to enter, run, and debug ARM assembly language, you need to know only a few basic elements of the operating system. Moreover, even though the Raspberry Pi has a Unix-based command-line operating system, it includes a graphical interface that behaves very much like Windows or macOS.

Basics of the Raspberry Pi operating system

In this section, you will learn how to use the Raspberry Pi to create an ARM assembly language program, assemble it into code that can be executed, and then run it on the Raspberry Pi. In the next chapter, we will look at the ARM architecture in greater depth.

We do not devote much time discussing RPi's operating system because the world is full of websites devoted to Linux. We will cover the absolute minimum to help you use some of the commands that may be helpful. Most readers will use a graphical interface to perform editing, web searches, and running programs such as

Python. We will introduce the basic concepts of Linux's filing system and the command-line instruction necessary to assemble and run a source file written in the ARM assembly language. Unfortunately, the names of Unix/Linux commands are not intuitive.

Figure 9.4 illustrates the basic concepts of the Linux hierarchical operating system, with a node at each level that can support *child* nodes at a lower level; for example, `Desktop` is a child of the `pi` node.

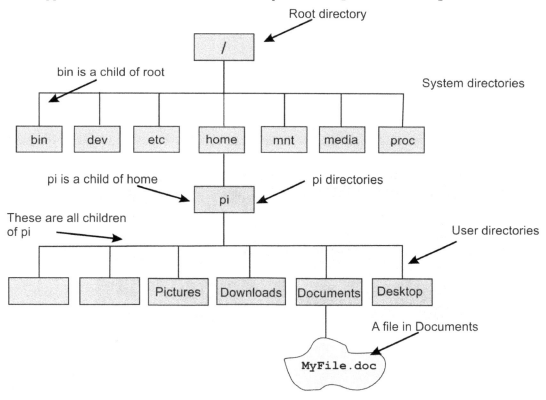

Figure 9.4 – The Raspberry Pi file structure

The top-level folder is / and is called the *root folder*. The / backslash is used to navigate the filing system very much like the Windows equivalent. A big difference between Linux and Windows is that, in Linux, you don't have to specify the disk on which the file resides (e.g., Windows invariably uses `c:/` for operating systems files). In *Figure 9.4*, the `MyFile.doc` file is a text file whose location is `/home/pi/Documents/MyFile.doc`.

Directory navigation

If you press the enter key, Raspberry Pi responds with an "*I am here*" prompt, as shown in this example:

pi@raspberrypi:**/var/log/apt $**

This prompt gives the device name and the path to the current directory (in bold font in this example). You can change the active directory with the cd (*change directory*) command, as shown in this example:

```
cd ..            # This means change directory to parent (the node above)
cd home
cd pi
cd Desktop
```

To list the files and subdirectories in the current directory, you can use the ls command (*list files*).

The ls -l /home/pi command generates the following output that gives permissions (what you can do with them), their size, and creation dates. *Figure 9.5* demonstrates this command.

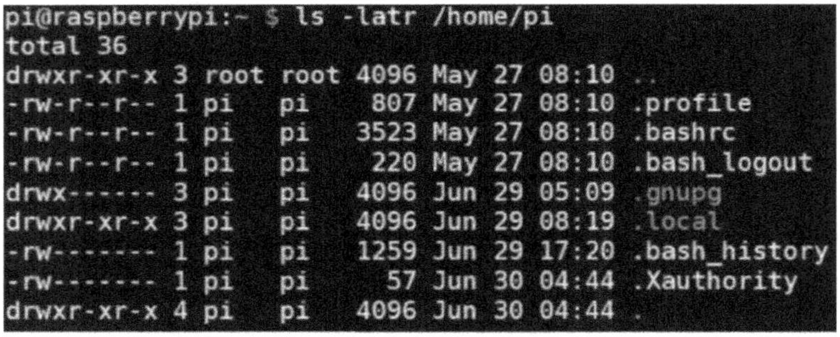

```
pi@raspberrypi:~ $ ls -latr /home/pi
total 36
drwxr-xr-x 3 root root 4096 May 27 08:10 ..
-rw-r--r-- 1 pi   pi    807 May 27 08:10 .profile
-rw-r--r-- 1 pi   pi   3523 May 27 08:10 .bashrc
-rw-r--r-- 1 pi   pi    220 May 27 08:10 .bash_logout
drwx------ 3 pi   pi   4096 Jun 29 05:09 .gnupg
drwxr-xr-x 3 pi   pi   4096 Jun 29 08:19 .local
-rw------- 1 pi   pi   1259 Jun 29 17:20 .bash_history
-rw------- 1 pi   pi     57 Jun 30 04:44 .Xauthority
drwxr-xr-x 4 pi   pi   4096 Jun 30 04:44 .
```

Figure 9.5 – The Raspberry Pi File Structure

The ls command has several options; for example, ls ~ indicates a list in the home directory. In Linux, the tilda, ~, indicates the home directory. Similarly, ls -t indicates list files by date and time created.

File operations

We now introduce some of Linux's basic file commands. The pwd command looks as if it should mean *password*. Actually, it means *print working directory* and displays the contents of the current directory. It's a "*where am I?*" command. Entering pwd will generate a response such as /home/pi.

To create a new subdirectory, you use the mkdir command. Typing mkdir newFolder creates a subdirectory called newFolder in the current directory.

If you enter mkdir /home/pi/newFolder, it will create the subdirectory in pi.

One of Linux's more confusing command names is `cat`, which lists the contents of a file. The name `cat` means `catalog`; for example, `cat /home/pi/firstExample.txt` displays the contents of the `firstExample.txt` file on the console as a text file.

To delete or *remove* a file, you use `rm`; for example, `rm tempData.py` deletes the `tempData.py` file in the current subdirectory. You can remove an entire directory with `rm -r`. This deletes the current directory and is not reversible. It is a dangerous command. The alternative is `rm -d`, which removes the current directory *only if it is empty* (i.e., you must first delete its contents).

Linux has a help command, `man` (i.e., manual) that provides details of another command; for example, `man ls` would provide details of the `ls` command.

In general, when working with Raspberry Pi, most users will be using the graphical interface. However, we will be using the command-line input to set up the Raspberry Pi and assemble, debug, and execute assembly language programs.

Installing and updating programs and packages

Having set up the RPi, you need to maintain it (i.e., install and update software). The following two commands retrieve new packages and update your software. It's a good idea to run them occasionally to get new updates. Note that `sudo` stands for *superuser do* and is required for operations that may be restricted to the administrator because they can harm the system if used inappropriately. The term `aptget` obtains and installs packages (`apt = Advanced Package Tool`):

```
sudo apt-get update       # Downloads the packages you have in your configuration source files
sudo apt-get upgrade      # Updates the packages
```

> **Note**
> sudo apt-get update updates packages but does not install them.

To install a new package on Raspberry Pi, you use the `apt-get install` command; for example,

`sudo apt-get install vim` installs the `vim` editor package.

Linux provides a shutdown command that ends a session in an orderly manner:

`sudo shutdown -h now`   Stop and enter the halt state

The -h parameter indicates *enter the halt state*, and the now parameter indicates an immediate halt. A command to shut down is `sudo shutdown -r now`. To reboot Raspberry Pi, you can enter either of the following two commands. These commands have the same effect on a single-user system. You would use `shutdown -r` on a multi-user system:

```
sudo shutdown -r now
sudo reboot
```

However, most Raspberry Pi users will shut down Raspberry Pi using a mouse from its GUI. Indeed, the only time it's necessary to use the text-based input mode is when assembling, linking, and debugging assembly language programs.

You can apply a delayed shutdown; for example, sudo shutdown -h 30 will shut down the RPi after 30 minutes. You can shut down at a specific clock time with, say, sudo shutdown -h 22:30, which shuts down at 10:30 P.M. A delayed shutdown command can be rescinded (canceled) by sudo shutdown -c.

Creating and editing an assembly language program

Let's go through the steps needed to create an ARM program on the Raspberry Pi and then execute it before we look at the ARM processor in greater detail. Although we haven't introduced the ARM assembly language yet, the actions of the instructions we use are self-evident.

First, you have to create an assembly language program in text form with a .s file type. There are many text editors and the one you choose is a personal preference. I initially used Geany, which is an IDE for languages such as C. I later used Thonny on my desktop PC. Both Geany and Thonny are excellent tools. If you create a text file on a desktop PC (or any other device), you simply change the .txt extension to .s to make it compatible with RPi's assembler.

Figure 9.6 shows the initial Geany screen:

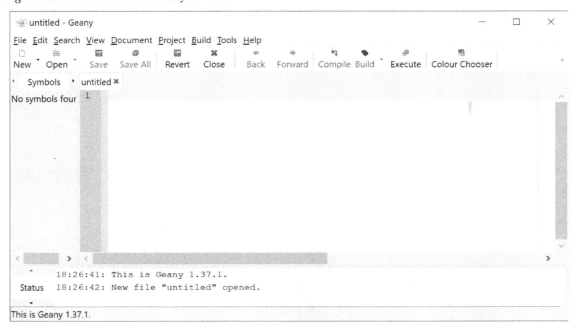

Figure 9.6 – Geany text editor window

Figure 9.7 shows a Geany window after we've created an ARM assembly language program:

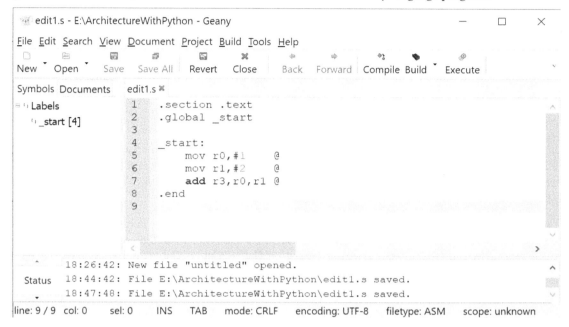

Figure 9.7 – Geany window – note that add r3,r0,r1 adds r0 to r1 and puts the sum in r0

In the following program, the text in bold font indicates an assembler directive that tells the assembler about the program's environment and how to deal with the allocation of memory space:

```
.section .text      @ .text indicates a region of code (not data)
.global _start      @ .global indicates that this label is visible to external objects
_start:             @ _start is the entry point to this program

    mov r0,#1       @ Load r0 with 1. mov copies an 8-bit value into a register
    mov r1,#2       @ Load r1 with 2
    add r3,r0,r1    @ Add r0 and r1 and put result in r3

.end                @ .end indicates the end of the program. It is optional
```

Note that ARM uses mov to load a literal and not ldr (as you might expect).

Assembling ARM code

Before we can look at the ARM architecture in depth, we will demonstrate how you write a program and run it. The Raspberry Pi's Debian-based operating system includes GCC, the *GNU Compiler Collection*, which can compile both C programs and assembly language programs. We do not deal with C here.

The two GCC commands we need to assemble the source `myProg.s` text file are as follows:

```
as -o myProg.o myProg.s
ld -o myProg myProg.o
```

The first command, `as`, takes the assembly language *source* file, `myProg.s`, and creates an *object* code file, `myProg.o`. The second command, `ld`, invokes a *linker* that uses the object file to create a binary code file, `myProg`, that can be executed. The `-o` option is necessary to build an output file. You can then run the assembled binary code program by typing `./myProg`.

Although a *single* assembly language program can be assembled to create binary code, programs are often written in modules (files) that are fitted together. These files may be written by different programmers or even library programs. They are individually assembled to create files that the linker combines to create the final binary code that can be executed. In this text, we do not make full use of the linker's facilities; all assembly language programs are single files.

Following the linking operation, an executable binary program is created. Let's now type the following:

```
./myProg ; echo $?
```

The `myProg` binary code is executed and a message is displayed. A semicolon in Linux allows two commands to be put on the same line; the two operations are *execute a program* and *display a message*.

The `echo $?` command prints a message from the executed program. The print command is `echo` and `$?` indicates the actual message to be printed. In this case, the `$?` command returns the exit status of the last command. You can print other messages; for example, `$3` prints the contents of register `r3`.

Note that if a program crashes or goes into an endless loop (non-responsive), you can enter `control-C` to escape and return to the OS level.

Debugging assembly language

We will now introduce the ARM debugger that lets you monitor the execution of a program and trace code just as we did with the simulators of *Chapter 6* and *Chapter 7*.

What we want is the ability to monitor the execution of an assembly language program, a task that we've already done when running Python computer simulators. We can do this with a *debugger*, called `gdb`, which is part of the GCC compiler suite. Consider the following example:

```
as -g -o myProg.o myProg.s      # Assemble myProg.s Note the -g parameter
ld -o myProg myProg.o           # Link myProg.o to create source code myProg
gdb myProg                      # Run the debugger
```

The -g parameter in the assembler section generates information for later use by the gdb debugger.

gdb is a very powerful tool with the facilities required to debug a program. We are going to look at only these facilities that allow us to run an ARM assembly language program and observe its execution, line by line. We begin by listing some of gdb's commands. These commands can be abbreviated; for example, the quit command can be entered as q. In *Table 9.1*, we put the required part of the command in bold, and the part of the command that can be omitted in gray, such as **q**uit. Note the difference between next and step. These are the same except when they encounter a *function*. Step traces all the operations in a function, whereas next treats the function as a single instruction and does not trace it.

When you load a program into gdb, nothing appears to happen. If you try to look at your assembly language code or the registers, you will get an error message. You must explicitly run the program first.

Command	Effect
quit	Quit: leave the gdb debugger and return to the shell. Ctrl + D also exits gdb.
list	List: list the program being debugged.
run	Run: execute the program. The program will run to completion or to a breakpoint.
break	Breakpoint: Execution runs until a breakpoint is encountered. The breakpoint can be a line number, an address, or a label.
info r	Info: show registers. This command displays register contents.
info b	Info: show breakpoints. This displays breakpoints.
continue	Continue: resume execution after a breakpoint.
delete	Delete: remove a breakpoint. Enter d <number> to remove a specific breakpoint.
next	Single step (execute one instruction). This does not trace a function.
step	Single step including all the operations in a function.
file <name>	Load a binary code file into gdb for debugging.

Table 9.1 – Basic gdb commands

Let's write and debug an ARM program on the Raspberry Pi. We haven't covered the ARM architecture yet. You don't need to know a lot about the ARM to follow the example because it's similar to the RISC architectures we simulated in *Chapter 6*. The ARM is a 32-bit computer with an RSIC architecture; that is, it is a load/store computer and the only memory accesses allowed are load and store. Operations on data are register-to-register using three operands – for example, add r1, r2, r3. The ARM has 16 registers, r0 to r15. Registers r0 to r12 can be treated as general-purpose (i.e., they all behave in the same way). Registers r13, r14, and r15 have specific functions.

Pseudo instructions – a key concept

The ARM assembler includes *pseudo-instructions* that are not part of the ARM's **instruction set** (**ISA**). A pseudo-instruction is a form of shorthand that is replaced by the assembler with actual instructions. For example, suppose a computer lacked a `clr r0` instruction that loads `r0` with 0. A pseudo-instruction, `clr r0`, could be devised and the assembler could automatically replace it with the `sub r0,r0` operation, which has the same effect.

Pseudo-instructions make the programmer's life easier; for example, the ARM's `adr r0,abc` pseudo-instruction loads a 32-bit address, ABC, into `r0`. Such an instruction does not exist; the assembler replaces adr with the appropriate ARM instructions.

An example of an ARM program

Suppose we wish to generate the sum of the cubes of numbers from 1 to 10. The following ARM code implements this algorithm. It also uses the ARM's four-operand *multiply and accumulate*, `mla`:

```
        mov   r0,#0          @ Clear the total in r0
        mov   r1,#4          @ FOR i = 1 to 4 (count down)
Next:   mul   r2,r1,r1       /* Square a number */
        mla   r0,r2,r1,r0    @ Cube the number and add to total
        subs  r1,r1,#1       @ Decrement counter (and set condition flags)
        bne   Next           @ END FOR (branch back on count not zero)
```

The label field beginning in the first column (bold in the preceding code) provides a *user-defined* tag that must be terminated by a colon. The label field is followed by the instruction consisting of an operation and any required operands. It doesn't matter if there is more than one space after commas in argument lists. The text following the @ symbol is a comment field and is ignored by the assembler. The GCC compiler also supports the C language style of comments: text delimited by /* */ characters, as this example shows.

Table 9.2 describes some of the ARM's instructions. There is only one surprise here; the `mla` *multiply and add instruction* that specifies *four* registers. It multiplies two registers together and adds a third register, and then puts the sum in a fourth register; that is, it can calculate A = B + C.D:

Instruction	ARM mnemonic	Definition
Addition	add **r0**,r1,r2	$[r0] \leftarrow [r1] + [r2]$
Subtraction	sub **r0**,r1,r2	$[r0] \leftarrow [r1] - [r2]$
AND	and **r0**,r1,r2	$[r0] \leftarrow [r1] \wedge [r2]$
OR	orr **r0**,r1,r2	$[r0] \leftarrow [r1] \vee [r2]$
Exclusive OR	eor **r0**,r1,r2	$[r0] \leftarrow [r1] \oplus [r2]$
Multiply	mul **r0**,r1,r2	$[r0] \leftarrow [r1] \times [r2]$

Instruction	ARM mnemonic	Definition
Register-to-register move	`mov r0,r1`	[r0] ← [r1]
Literal-to-register move	`mov r0,#0xAB`	[r0] ← 0xAB Move 8-bit literal
Compare	`cmp r1,r2`	[r1] − [r2]
Branch on zero to label	`beq label`	[PC] ← label (jump to label if z = 1)
Branch on not zero to label	`bne label`	[PC] ← label (jump to label if z = 0)
Multiply and add	`mla r0,r1,r2,r3`	[r0] ← [r1] x [r2] + [r3]
Load register from memory	`ldr r0,[r1]`	[r0] ← [[r1]]
Store register in memory	`str r0,[r1]`	[[r1]] ← [r0]
Call the operating system	`svc 0`	Request an operation from the OS

Table 9.2 – ARM data processing, data transfer, and compare instructions

Some computers always update condition codes after an operation. The ARM does not automatically update its status flags after an operation; you have to command a status update by appending s to the appropriate mnemonic. For example, add `r1,r2,r3` performs an addition without updating status flags, whereas adds `r1,r2,r3` updates status flags. This is not yet a program. The following provides the code and assembly language directives needed to run it on the Raspberry Pi:

```
        .global _start          @ Provide entry point
_start: mov     r0,#0           @ Clear the total in r0
        mov     r1,#10          @ FOR i = 1 to 10 (count down)
Next:   mul     r2,r1,r1        /* Square a number. Note the C style comment */
        mla     r0,r2,r1,r0     @ Cube the number and add to total
        subs    r1,r1,#1        @ Decrement counter (set condition flags)
        bne     Next            @ END FOR (branch back on count not zero)

        mov     r7,#1           @ r7 contains 1 to indicate a leave request
        svc     #0              @ Call operating system to exit this code
```

We've added an assembly language directive, .global, that declares the _start label as being *visible* outside this fragment of code. The GCC linking process links together separately assembled modules and inserts the appropriate addresses of the labels in the code.

By declaring a label as global, you are telling the linker that this label is visible to other modules and they can refer to it. Labels without a global directive are local to the current module and invisible to all other modules; that is, you could use the same label in two modules and there would not be a conflict.

The _start label indicates the point at which execution begins. The linker and operating system deal with storing the program in memory; that is, you don't have to worry about where it is going to be actually stored in the computer's physical memory.

Finally, the last two operations (shaded) provide a means of getting back to the operating system level once the code has been executed. ARM has an `svc` instruction, which stands for *service call* and is used to invoke the operating system. Most computers have an operation such as `svc` and it has many names – for example, *software interrupt*. This instruction calls the operating system and supplies one or more parameters. The parameter can be part of the instruction itself or it can be loaded into a register. When the operating system detects a service call, the parameter is read and the appropriate operation is performed. This action is entirely system dependent; that is, it is part of the operating system and not part of the computer's architecture.

In this case, the specific function required by the service call is pre-loaded into `r7`. This mechanism is part of the Raspberry Pi's operating system.

Key points to note about the assembly language program are as follows:

- Comments are preceded by an @ symbol (or the C language /*   */ book ends)
- Assembler directives are preceded by a period
- Labels begin in the first column and are terminated by a colon
- An `.end` directive can be used to terminate the assembly language (it's optional)
- The `.global` directive provides a label that indicates the entry point of the program

Using the Raspberry Pi debugger

We can now run an ARM assembly language program and observe its execution, line by line, using gdb. When you load a program into gdb, nothing appears to happen. If you try to look at your assembly language code or the registers, you will get an error message. You must explicitly run the program first.

Consider the fragment of code in *Figure 9.8*. This is a screenshot of the program after it's been loaded into the Geany editor. It's just a set of instructions and directives intended to demonstrate the steps involved in creating and testing an assembly language program. Here, we are using the Geany editor. The program demonstrates the following assembly language directives:

- `.data`   Defines a memory region where variables and constants are stored.
- `.text`   Defines a region of code (i.e., the assembly language).
- `.word`   Allows you to store a number in memory and give the location a symbolic address.
- `.balign`   Aligns code and text on a 4-byte boundary. Required because instructions are 32 bits.
- `.asciz`   Creates an ASCII text string terminated by zero in memory and gives it a name.
- `.global`   Makes a label visible to the linker. Otherwise, it is private to this module.

The `balign` operation is required because memory is byte addressed and ARM instructions are 4 bytes long. Consequently, instruction addresses must be 0, 4, 8, 12, 16, 20, and so on. If you put data elements in memory that are not multiples of 4 bytes (32 bits) between instructions, the program will crash. The `balign` instruction pads out any data you store with zeros to ensure that the next free address is on a 4-byte boundary.

Note that the code in *Figure 9.8* uses a *pseudo-instruction*. The instruction `ldr` **r4**, =Alan3 loads r4 with the 32-bit literal, `Alan3`. The assembler will automatically substitute the necessary ARM code to perform this operation.

The next step is to assemble and link the code, which we called a4.s (I got fed up with typing long names and called the source program a4.s). We can do this with the following:

```
pi@raspberrypi:~ $ cd Desktop                    # Change to Desktop directory
pi@raspberrypi:~/Desktop $ as -g -o a4.o a4.s    # Assemble the program a4.s
pi@raspberrypi:~/Desktop $ ld -o a4 a4.o         # Now link it to create executable
pi@raspberrypi:~/Desktop $ ./a4 ; echo $?        # Run the executable program a4
```

The text in bold is my input. These lines change the working directory to Desktop where my source program is, and then assemble and link the source program. The final line, `./a4 ; echo $?`, runs the program and prints its return value (showing it's been successfully executed by printing 4, the value in r0).

Figure 9.8 – The demonstration program in the Geany editor

The following four lines demonstrate how we call the gdb debugger and set a breakpoint. Text in bold font indicates lines entered from the keyboard. The other text is the debugger's output:

```
pi@raspberrypi:~/Desktop $ gdb a4
Reading symbols from a4...done.
(gdb) b _start
Breakpoint 1 at 0x10074: file a4.s, line 14.
```

Entering a breakpoint is done by b <breakpoint>, where the breakpoint is a line number or a label. Here, it's _start. If we run the code, it executes instructions up to the breakpoint. The next few lines are as follows:

```
(gdb) run
Starting program: /home/pi/Desktop/a4
Breakpoint 1, _start () at a4.s:14
14     _start: mov r0,#4           @ Enter here (first instruction)
```

Note that you can continue from a breakpoint by entering c (i.e., continue) and execution will continue to the next breakpoint.

After entering a run command, the debugger begins execution and prints the next line to be executed – that is, the line labeled by _start. The gdb instruction i r (information registers) displays the ARM's registers as follows:

```
(gdb) i r
r0          0x0          0
r1          0x0          0
r2          0x0          0
r3          0x0          0
r4          0x0          0
r5          0x0          0
r6          0x0          0
r7          0x0          0
r8          0x0          0
r9          0x0          0
r10         0x0          0
r11         0x0          0
r12         0x0          0
sp          0xbefff390   0xbefff390
lr          0x0          0
pc          0x10074      0x10074 <_start>
cpsr        0x10         16
fpscr       0x0          0
```

cpsr and fpscr are both status registers that contain information about the state of the processor.

All registers have been initialized to zero automatically by the system software, except r13, r15 (sp, pc), and the two status registers. We can now start tracing the code, executing instructions one by one with the step command, s 1. You can just hit enter to trace the next instruction, as the following output demonstrates. If you were to type si 2 (or s 2), you would step two instructions:

```
(gdb) si 1
15            mov r1,#9
(gdb)
16            add r2,r0,r1
(gdb)
17            sub r3,r2,#3
(gdb)
18            ldr r4,=Alan3          @ Load an address into r4
(gdb)
19            ldr r5,[r4]            @ And pick up a word from memory
```

Let's look at the registers using the i r command. We have removed registers from this list that haven't changed to make it easier to read. Register contents are given in hex and decimal formats:

```
(gdb) i r
r0            0x4                   4
r1            0x9                   9
r2            0xd                   13   Note: r2 is expressed in hex and decimal
r3            0xa                   10
r4            0x200a0               131232
r5            0x0                   0
pc            0x10088               0x10088 <_start+20> Note: 20 bytes from start
```

Finally, we will continue stepping until the code has been executed. You can step just by using the *enter* key after the first si 1 command:

```
(gdb) si 1
21            mov r7,#1             @ Prepare to exit
(gdb)
22            svc 0                 @ Go
(gdb)
[Inferior 1 (process 1163) exited with code 04]
```

The gdb executes the move and supervisor call instruction and exits the simulation. What have we learned? This example demonstrates the following:

- How to create an ARM assembly language program
- How to assemble and link it
- How to load it into the gdb debugger
- How to set breakpoints and run the code until a breakpoint is reached
- How to display the contents of registers at any point in a program
- How to step through the code line by line

Tracing execution and displaying memory

An important facility of a debugger is the ability to step through the code and display registers while executing a program. This allows you to follow the execution of a program and detect errors. The gdb debugger incorporates this facility via its **Text User Interface (TUI).** You don't need to explicitly invoke the TUI because you can use its facilities within gdb. The most important TUI facility is its ability to display a code window and a register window by entering `layout regs`.

Figure 9.9 provides a demonstration of the TUI with three panels. The upper window is the register window (the registers that have changed are highlighted; in this case, it's `r7`). The middle panel displays the program code, with the next instruction to be executed highlighted. Each line includes the memory address of the code in hexadecimal form and as a distance from the `start` label.

Note that the code continues after my last instruction, `svc`. This is because the disassembler reads a block of memory and displays it as code (even if it is not part of your program). In this case, the data we entered in memory with the `.word` directive is read and displayed as the corresponding ARM instruction. Remember that the debugger does not know whether a binary value in memory is an instruction or user data. If it reads a data value corresponding to an instruction op-code, it prints that op-code.

The disassembled instructions display their address in memory in hex form; for example, the first instruction is at `0x10074`. This address is determined by Raspberry Pi's operating system. As you can see, each instruction has an address 4 bytes greater than the previous one because the ARM is a 32-bit machine with 32-bit, or 4-byte, instructions; hence the need for the align directive that forces the next instruction or data onto a specific boundary.

The bottommost panel contains the commands you enter. In this case, I've used `si 1` to step through the instructions.

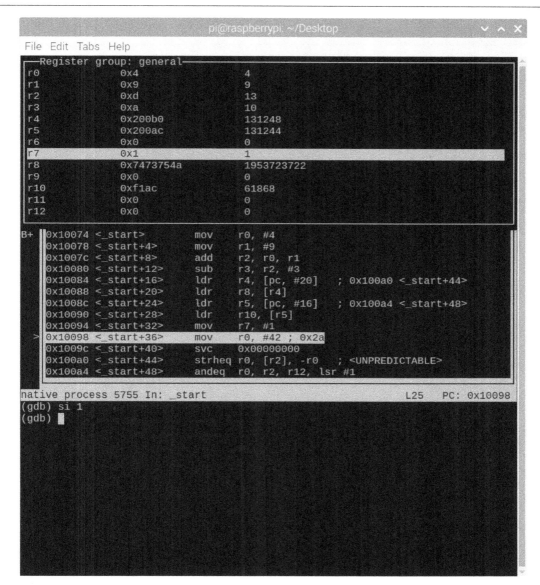

Figure 9.9 – The TUI showing registers and memory contents

Let's look at another example of an assembly language program and its debugging. This example is designed only for demonstration purposes. It doesn't do anything useful. Our intention is to demonstrate the features of an ARM assembly language program running under the GCC assembler and the gdb debugger. *Table 9.3* gives some of GCC's most common assembler directives.

GCC Assembly directive	Action
`.text`	Indicates a program segment containing code
`.data`	Indicates a program segment containing data
`.global` label	Makes the label visible to the linker
`.extern` label	Makes the label visible outside the file
`.byte` byte1,byte2, ...	Defines one or more bytes of data and stores them in memory
`.hword` hw1,hw2, ...	Defines 1 or more 16-bit halfwords and stores them in memory
`.word` w1,w2, ...	Defines 1 or more 32-bit words and stores them in memory
`.space` bytes,fill	Fills a block of memory with a given value (e.g., `.fill 64,0xFF`)
`.balign 4`	Aligns next address to a 4-byte boundary (you can also use 2, 4, 8, and 16)
`.ascii "any string"`	Stores an ASCII string in memory
`.asciz "any string"`	Stores an ASCII string in memory terminated by 0
`.equ` symbol, value	Equates the symbolic name to its value (e.g., `.equ hours 24`)
`.end`	Marks the end of a program

Table 9.3 – GCC ARM assembler directives

We have presented a more detailed explanation of some of the features of the program; these are of the form
@ PRINT STRING @:

```
                                    @ Test function calls and memory access
        .text                       @ Program (code) area
        .global  _start             @ Provide entry point and make it known to linker
        .equ     v1,0xAB            @ Test equate directive

_start:  mov     r0,#23             @ Just three dummy operations for debugging
         mov     r1,#v1             @ ARM assembler uses # to indicate a literal
         add     r2,r0,r1
```

@ PRINT STRING ON CONSOLE @

```
        ldr     r1, =banner        @ Test display function (this is a pseudo-instruction)
        mov     r2,#15             @ Number of characters to print 13 plus two newlines)
        mov     r0,#1              @ Tell the OS we want to print on console display
        mov     r7,#4              @ Tell the OS we want to perform a print operation
        svc     0                  @ Call the operating system to do the printing
```

@ USING ADR @

```
            adr     r3,v3               @ Load address of v3 into register r3 (a pseudo-instruction)
            ldr     r4,[r3]             @ Read contents of v3 in memory

                                        @ Read from memory, increment and store in next location
            ldr     r0,adr_dat1         @ r0 is a pointer to dat1 in memory
            ldr     r1,[r0]             @ Load r1 with the contents of dat1
            add     r2,r1,#1            @ Add 1 to dat1 and put in r2
            add     r3,r0,#4            @ Use r3 to point to next memory location after dat1
            str     r2,[r3]             @  Store new data in location after dat1
```

@ EXITING THE PROGRAM @

```
            mov     r0,#0               @ Exit status code (0 indicates OK)
            mov     r7,#1               @ Tell the OS we want to return from this program
            svc     0                   @ Call the operating system to return
```

@ THE ADDRESS VECTOR @

```
adr_dat1: .word     dat1                @ Generate an address for dat1 in the memory area

v2:       .word     0xFACE              @ Dummy data
banner:   .ascii    "\nTest printing\n" @ String to print. Note newlines "\n"
                                        @ This string has 15 characters (13 ASCII two newlines)
          .balign 4                     @ Align data (0 inserted because the string is 15 chars)
v3:       .word     0x1111              @ Dummy test data
          .space    4,0xAB              @ Reserve 8 bytes of storage and fill with 0xAB
          .word     0x2222
          .data                         @ Data segment
test:     .word 0xbbbb
dat1:     .word 0x1234

          .end                          @ End of this program
```

This code illustrates several points – for example, the use of assembler directives such as .equ, which binds a symbolic name to a value. I've shaded interesting blocks of code so that we can discuss them.

We have used ARM's pseudo-instructions. These are adr **r3**,v3 and ldr **r1**,=banner. These both load 32-bit addresses into a register. Such instructions don't exist. The ARM assembler chooses real instructions to perform the required actions.

@ PRINT STRING @

The first block demonstrates how we can print data from an assembly program. Well, in fact, we can't print the data but we can ask the operating system to do it for us. Most processors have an instruction called a *software interrupt* (or a system call, a trap, an exception, or an *extra code*). All these terms refer to the same thing: an instruction inserted by the programmer that invokes the operating system. In the case of ARM, it's the svc instruction (previously called swi). When used by Linux, this instruction is called with the parameter 0 – that is svc 0.

The system call is entirely operating-system-dependent and tells the operating system what it needs by passing parameters in registers. We are going to print a string of characters on the display. The Raspberry Pi OS needs the location of the string in memory to be passed in register r1, the number of characters to print in register r2, the type of the display in r0, and the operation to be performed (printing) in r7.

The address of the text to be printed, banner, is loaded into r1 by ldr **r1**, =banner. This pseudo-instruction takes an address specified by =<address>. In the program, we have used the .ascii directive to store the string to print in memory. The string is text with \n at each end, which corresponds to the newline character. Note that the newline character code is 1 byte, although it is represented in the program by \n. Unless a string or other data item stored in memory is a multiple of 4 bytes, you must follow it with a .balign 4 to ensure that the next instruction falls on a word boundary.

@ USING ADR @

The second block demonstrates the use of an adr pseudo-instruction with adr **r3**, v3. We are going to load register r3 with the address of a variable we've called v3 and loaded into memory with a .word directive. One practical consideration is that when you disassemble the code, you will not see adr; you'll see the actual code that the ARM assembler translated it into.

Putting the address of the v3 variable into a register means we can use that register as a pointer with a load instruction; for example, ldr **r4**, [r3] loads the value of the variable (i.e., 0x1111) into r4. If you wish to modify that variable, you might think that you could store it back in memory with str **r5**, **[r3]**. Sadly not! The adr instruction generates code that allows you to access only the current segment of the program. That segment is read-only because it contains the code. You cannot alter memory in that segment. If you wish to modify memory, you have to use a different technique, as we will soon see.

@ EXITING THE PROGRAM @

After an assembly language program has been executed to completion, it is necessary to return to the operating system level. Register r7 is loaded with an exit code of 1 and an svc 0 instruction executed to call the operating system. By convention, programmers load register r0 with their own exit code before exiting. An exit code of 0 is often used to indicate all went well, and an exit code of 1 indicates it didn't.

@ THE ADDRESS VECTOR @

You can't use the `adr` pseudo-instruction to write to read/write memory that is in a different segment to the code part of a program. This dilemma exists in all code development systems and is not peculiar to the ARM GCC environment. The ARM processor will allow you to read memory and write to memory anywhere within the logically addressable memory space. However, the ARM *operating system* does not let you write to regions of read-only memory or other forbidden areas. The trick is to create a pointer to the variable and store that pointer in the code segment.

Consider the following assembler directive. This stores a 32-bit `dat1` value in memory at location `adr_dat1`. By convention, some programmers indicate that an item is a pointer (i.e., address) by prefixing its name with a marker (typically `adr`). This is not a rule but a convention:

Figure 9.10 - Creating a pointer to a data value

We have created a name, `adr_dat1`, which is the *address* of the address of our target variable. The value stored is the address of the actual variable, `dat1`. So, when we write the instruction `ldr r0,adr_dat1`, the *address* of `dat1` is loaded in register `r0`. That is, register `r0` now points to `dat1`.

In the data section headed by `.data`, we have the following:

```
dat1:       .word 0x1234    @ The value 0x1234 is stored in memory at address dat1
```

This stores the `0x1234` value in memory and gives it the name `dat1`. As we have seen, that name is used to create the address of the variable in the code section by the following:

```
adr_dat1: .word    dat1
```

The next step is to run the code. We've done this and have provided an edited output from the session (removing empty prompt lines between operations and some text) in *Listing 9.1*:

```
pi@raspberrypi:~ $ cd Desktop
pi@raspberrypi:~/Desktop $ as -g -o t1a.o t1a.s
pi@raspberrypi:~/Desktop $ ld -o t1a t1a.o
pi@raspberrypi:~/Desktop $ gdb
GNU gdb (Raspbian 8.2.1-2) 8.2.1
(gdb) file t1a
Reading symbols from t1a...done.
(gdb) b _start
```

```
Breakpoint 1 at 0x10074: file t1a.s, line 7.
(gdb) r 1
Starting program: /home/pi/Desktop/t1a 1

Breakpoint 1, _start () at t1a.s:7
7     _start: mov    r0,#23          @ Just three dummy operations for debugging
(gdb) si 1
8             mov    r1,#v1
9             add    r2,r0,r1
11            ldr    r1,=banner     @ Test display function (r1 has address of a string)
12            mov    r2,#15         @ Number of characters to print 13 plus two newlines)
13            mov    r0,#1          @ Tell the OS we want to print on console display
14            mov    r7,#4          @ Tell the OS we want to perform a print operation
15            svc    0              @ Call the operating system to do the printing
Test printing
17            adr    r3,v3          @ Load address of v3
18            ldr    r4,[r3]        @ Read its contents in memory
21            ldr    r0,adr_dat1    @ r0 is a pointer to dat1 in memory
22            ldr    r1,[r0]        @ Load r1 with the contents of data1
23            add    r2,r1,#1       @ Add 1 to dat1 and put in r2
24            add    r3,r0,#4       @ Use r3 to point to next memory location after dat1
25            str    r2,[r3]        @ Store new data in location after dat1
(gdb) i r r0 r1 r2 r3
r0            0x200e8               131304
r1            0x1234                4660
r2            0x1235                4661
r3            0x200ec               131308
(gdb) si 1
28            mov    r0,#0          @ Exit status code (indicates OK)
29            mov    r7,#1          @ Tell the OS we want to return from this program
30            svc    0              @ Call the operating system to return
(gdb) x/2xw 0x200e8
0x200e8:      0x00001234    0x00001235
(gdb) si 1
[Inferior 1 (process 7601) exited normally]
```

Listing 9.1 – A debugging session

Accessing memory

We have demonstrated how you can step through a program and display registers as instructions are executed. For example, gdb lets you display the contents of registers r0 to r3 using the i r r0 r1 r2 r3 command. We will now demonstrate how the contents of memory locations can be displayed.

In *Listing 9.1*, we single-step the code through the first few instructions (memory access and store operations) and then, after line 25, we can see that the address of the dat3 variable is 0x200e8. Suppose we want to check that its value is 0x1234, and that the next word location 4 bytes on, 0x2008c, contains the 0x1235 value.

You might reasonably expect that the gdb command to read the memory location is m 0x200c. As you can see from *Listing 9.1*, the command is the rather less memorable:

`x/2xw 0x2208    Read the contents of two memory locations`

The memory access command is **x/** and the three required parameters are **2xw**. These are as follows:

- 2   The number of memory locations to be displayed.
- x   The format of the data. x indicates hexadecimal.
- w   The width of the data (number of bytes). w indicates a 4-byte 32-bit word.

The available formats are as follows:

- o   octal
- d   decimal
- x   hexadecimal
- u   unsigned integer
- s   string
- b   byte

The data display sizes are as follows:

- b   byte
- h   halfword (16 bits)
- w   word (32 bits)
- g   double word (giant word of 8 bytes or 64 bits)

Consider these examples:

- x/1xw 0x1234   Print one 4-byte word in hex form at address 0x1234
- x/6xh 0x1234   Print six 2-byte values in hex form at address 0x1234
- x/3db 0x1234   Print three one-byte values in decimal form at address 0x1234
- x/9sb 0x1234   Print nine one-byte characters in string form at address 0x1234

In the next section, we are now going to look at the ARM GCC assembler in a little more detail. For example, we will introduce the ARM's assembler directives that control the allocation of memory to a program.

Features of the GCC ARM assembler

We will begin this section by looking at how memory space can be reserved for constants and variables. We have already seen that literals in the ARM assembly language are prefixed by a # symbol. Numbers are regarded as decimal unless prefixed by 0x, which indicates hexadecimal – for example, mov r0, #0x2C. ASCII characters are indicated by using single quotes, as in this example:

```
        cmp     r0,#'A'                 @ Was it a letter 'A'?
```

Two important assembler directives are .equ, which binds a name to a value, and .word, which allows you to preload memory with data before a program runs. The .equ directive is very easy to understand; it binds a numeric value to a name. Consider the following:

```
    .equ   Tuesday, 2
```

This assembly directive binds the name Tuesday to the value 2. Whenever you write Tuesday, the assembler replaces it with 2. The GCC ARM .word assembler directive reserves memory space for constants and variables; that is, it declares a variable (or constant) and initializes it. Consider the following example:

```
    .equ    Value1,12        @ Associate name Value1 with 12
    .equ    Value2,45        @ Associate name Value2 with 45
    .word   Table,Value1     @ Store the 32-bit word 12 in memory at address Table
    .word   Value2           @ Store the word 45 in memory
    .word   Value2 + 14      @ Store 45 + 14 = 59 in memory (you can use expressions)
```

The .word directive reserves a 32-bit word (i.e., 4 bytes) of storage in memory and loads whatever value the expression to the right of .word yields into that location. In this case, we've bound Value1 to the number 12 and, therefore, the binary value 00000000000000000000000000001100 will be stored at this location. The next memory location used is the next free location (i.e., storage directives store data in memory sequentially).

The *location counter* is advanced by four bytes so that the next .word or instruction will be placed in the next word in memory. The term *location counter* refers to the pointer to the next location in memory when a program is being assembled and is similar, in concept, to the program counter.

You don't have to use 32-bit values in the ARM programs. The .byte and .hword assembler directives store a byte and a 16-bit halfword in memory, respectively, as in this example:

```
Q1:     .byte       25              @ Store the byte 25 in memory
Q2:     .byte       42              @ Store the byte 42 in memory
Tx2:    .hword      12342           @ Store the 16-bit halfword 12,342 in memory
```

Although you could use .byte to store text strings in memory, it would be very clumsy because you would have to look up the ASCII value of each character. The GCC ARM assembler provides a simpler mechanism. The .ascii directive takes a string and stores each character as an 8-bit ASCII-encoded byte in consecutive memory locations. The `.asciz` command performs the same function but inserts an 8-bit binary byte of all 0s as a terminator:

```
Mess1: .ascii    "This is message 1"    @ Store string memory
Mess2: .asciz    "This is message 2"    @ Store string followed by 0
       .balign  4                       @ Align code on word boundary
```

Because the ARM aligns all instructions on 32-bit word boundaries, the `.balign 4` directive is required to align whatever follows on the next word boundary (the 4 indicates a 4-byte boundary). In other words, if you store three 8-bit characters in memory, the `.balign 4` command skips a byte to force the next address to a 32-bit boundary. Note that `.balign 2` forces alignment on a halfword boundary (you can use `.balign 16`, or any other power of 2, to force the next memory access to be appropriately aligned).

The following ARM code demonstrates storage allocation and the use of the `.balign 4` directive:

```
        .global  _start          @ Tell the linker where we start from
        .text                    @ This is a text (code) segment
_start: mov      r0,#XX          @ Load r0 with 5 (i.e., XX)
        mov      r1,#P1          @ Load r1 with P1 which is equated to 0x12 or 18 decimal
        add      r2,r0,r1        @ Just a dummy instruction
        add      r3,r2,#YY       @ Test equate to ASCII byte (should be 0x42 for 'B')
        adr      r4,test         @ Let's load an address (i.e., location of variable test)
        ldr      r5,[r4]         @ Now, access that variable which should be 0xBB)
Again:  b        Again           @ Eternal endless loop (terminate here)

        .equ     XX,5            @ Equate XX to 5
        .equ     P1,0x12         @ Equate P1 to 0x12
        .equ     YY,'B'          @ Equate YY to the ASCII value for 'B'
        .ascii   "Hello"         @ Store the ASCII byte string "Hello"
        .balign  4               @ Ensure code is on a 32-bit word boundary
        .ascii   "Hello"         @ Store the ASCII byte string "Hello"
        .byte    0xAA            @ Store the byte 0xAA in memory
test:   .byte    0xBB            @ Store the byte 0xBB in memory
        .balign  2               @ Ensure code is on a 16-bit halfword boundary
        .hword   0xABCD          @ Store the 16-bit halfword 0xABCD in memory
last:   .word    0x12345678      @ Store a 32-bit hex value in memory
        .end
```

Let's assemble, link, and run this code on a Raspberry Pi using gdb. The first few lines from the terminal windows show the loading of the program, setting a breakpoint, and executing in a single-step mode:

```
pi@raspberrypi:~ $ cd Desktop
pi@raspberrypi:~/Desktop $ as -g -o labels.o labels.s
pi@raspberrypi:~/Desktop $ ld -o labels labels.o
pi@raspberrypi:~/Desktop $ gdb labels
```

```
GNU gdb (Raspbian 8.2.1-2) 8.2.1
Reading symbols from labels...done.
(gdb) b _start
Breakpoint 1 at 0x10054: file labels.s, line 3.
(gdb) run 1
Starting program: /home/pi/Desktop/labels 1
Breakpoint 1, _start () at labels.s:3
3    _start: mov      r0,#XX              @ Load r0 with 5 (i.e., XX)
(gdb) si 1
4            mov      r1,#P1              @ Load r1 with 0x12 (i.e., P1)
5            add      r2,r0,r1            @ Dummy instruction (r2 is 5+0x12=0x17)
6            add      r3,r2,#YY           @ Dummy instruction (r3 is 0x17+0x42=0x59)
7            adr      r4,test
8            ldr      r5,[r4]
Again () at labels.s:9
9    Again:  b        Again               @ Eternal endless loop (enter control-C to exit)
```

So far, so good. Let's see what the registers hold. We have deleted lines with registers that we're not interested in to make the output more readable:

```
(gdb) i r
r0              0x5                 5
r1              0x12                18
r2              0x17                23
r3              0x59                89  Note 0x59 = 0x17 + 0x42
r4              0x1007e             65662
r5              0xabcd00bb          2882339003
pc              0x1006c Current pc       0x1006c <Again>
```

Registers r0 to r3 contain what we would expect (r3 is 0x17 in r3 plus the 0x42 code for 'B' which is 0x59).

Register r4 contains 0x1007e, which is the address of the data called test: (i.e., 0xBB) in memory. That address is used to load the 0xBB constant into r5, which now contains 0xABCD00BB and not 0x000000BB as we expected. What went wrong?

The problem is that ldr loads a 32-bit value into a register from memory. 0xABCD00 is the word following 0xBB plus a null byte due to the .balign 2 statement. We should have used a special *"load a byte"* instruction, loaded four bytes and cleared three to zero, or aligned the byte correctly in memory. The great strength of a computer is that it does what you tell it. Alas, its great weakness is that…it does *exactly* what you tell it.

Next, we look at the data stored in memory using the x/7xw 0x1006c command, which displays 7 words of memory in hexadecimal form starting at address 0x1006c (we got that address from the pc in the register dump). Remember that it's the ARM's operating system that initially sets up the program counter:

```
(gdb) x/7xw 0x1006c
0x1006c <Again>:      0xeafffffe 0x6c6c6548 0x0000006f 0x6c6c6548
0x1007c <Again+16>: 0x00bbaa6f 0x5678abcd 0x00001234
```

We can also look at the data stored in memory in byte form using x/28xb 0x1006c, which displays 7 words (4 x 7 = 28 bytes) of memory in hexadecimal form starting at address 0x1006c:

```
(gdb) x/28xb 0x1006c
0x1006c <Again>:        0xfe    0xff    0xff    0xea    0x48    0x65    0x6c    0x6c
0x10074 <Again+8>:      0x6f    0x00    0x00    0x00    0x48    0x65    0x6c    0x6c
0x1007c <Again+16>:     0x6f    0xaa    0xbb    0x00    0xcd    0xab    0x78    0x56
0x10084 <last+2>:       0x34    0x12    0x00    0x00
```

Figure 9.10 provides a memory map demonstrating the allocation of memory. The bold hexadecimal addresses are the 4-byte word boundaries. You can see how the .balign directives insert zeros as padding in memory to form the required boundaries.

In the next section, we look at one of the key aspects of modern computer design – how a computer with a 32-bit word length can load a 32-bit value into a register:

000000010070	48	ASCII H start of the sequence Hello
000000000071	65	ASCII e
000000000072	6C	ASCII l
000000000073	6C	ASCII l
000000000074	6F	ASCII o
000000000075	00	Padded zero due to align
000000000076	00	Padded zero due to align
000000000077	0	Padded zero due to align
000000010078	48	ASCII H
000000000079	65	ASCII e
00000000007A	6C	ASCII l
00000000007B	6C	ASCII l
00000000007C	**6C**	ASCII o
00000000007D	0xAA	Byte 0xAA
00000000007E	0xBB	Byte 0xBB
00000000007F	00	Padded zero due to align
000000000080	0xAB	First byte of 0xABCD
000000000081	0xCD	Second byte of 0xABCD

Figure 9.10 – Allocating data to memory – the memory map

We next look at a dilemma that affects all computers: how do you load a constant (literal) that is the same size as the instruction word?

Dealing with 32-bit literals

Here, you will learn how the ARM uses a 32-bit instruction to load a 32-bit literal. A literal can't be combined with an op-code as we have done in the simulators. We will demonstrate how the ARM uses several techniques to use a 32-bit instruction to access a 32-bit literal.

The ARM has 32-bit data words and instructions. You can't load a 32-bit literal into an ARM register in one instruction because you can't specify both the operation and the data in one instruction. CISC processors chain two or more instructions together; for example, a 16-bit machine might take 2 instruction words to create a 32-bit instruction containing a 16-bit operation and a 16-bit literal. Some processors load a 16-bit literal (load high) with one instruction and then load a second 16-bit literal (load low) with a second instruction. The computer then concatenates the high and low halfword 16-bit values into a 32-bit literal.

The ARM has two pseudo-instructions that can load a 32-bit value into a register by letting the assembler generate the actual code needed to do this. The pseudo-instruction adr (load address) has the format adr $r_{destination}$,label, where label indicates a line (address) in the program. adr lets the assembler generate the appropriate machine code and relieves the programmer of some *housekeeping*. The adr uses the ARM's add or sub instruction together with *PC relative addressing* to generate the required address. Program counter-relative addressing specifies an address by its distance from the current instruction. The following code fragment demonstrates the use of adr:

```
        adr     r0,someData    @ Setup r1 to point to someData in memory
        ldr     r1,[r0]        @ Read someData using the pointer in r0
          .       .
someData: .word  0x12345678    @ Here's the data
```

The pseudo-instruction adr r0,someData loads register r0 with the 32-bit address of someData using the appropriate code generated by the assembler. You don't normally have to know how the assembler generates the actual code to implement the adr.

Another useful ARM pseudo-instruction is ldr r1, =value. In this case, the compiler generates the code that allows register r1 to be loaded with the stated value, as in this example:

```
    ldr r2, =0x12345678        @ Load a 32-bit literal into r2
```

This loads r2 with 12345678_{16}. The assembler employs a mov or mvn instruction if it can. The ARM's unusual *move* not instruction takes an 8-bit literal, inverts the bits, and moves it to a register. For example MVN r1,#0xF0 copies 0x0F to r1. Alternatively, the assembler uses an ldr r2,[pc,#offset] instruction to access the appropriate constant 12345678_{16} that is stored in a so-called *literal pool* or *constant pool* somewhere in memory. A literal pool is one or more data items embedded in code.

Let's look at how pseudo-instructions are treated by the GCC assembler development system. Consider the following fragment of code:

```
        .text
        .global _start
_start: ldr     r0,=0x12345678      @ Load r0 with a 32-bit constant
        adr     r1,Table1           @ Load r1 with the address of Table1
        adr     r2,Table2           @ Load r2 with the address of Table2
        ldr     r3,[r1]             @ Load r3 with data in Table1
        ldr     r4,[r2]             @ Load r4 with data in Table2
        ldr     r5, =0xAAAAAAAA     @ Load r5 with a 32-bit constant
wait:   mov     r0,#0               @ Goodbye message
        mov     r7,#1               @ Goodbye command in r7
        svc     0                   @ Call operating system to return
Table1: .word   0xABCDDCBA          @ Dummy data
Table2: .word   0xFFFFFFFF
```

The following is the edited output of a gdb debugger session. The code has been executed to completion and the register contents are as follows. The righthand column displays the data in decimal form:

r0	0x0	0
r1	0x10078	65656
r2	0x1007c	65660
r3	0xabcddcba	2882395322
r4	0xffffffff	4294967295
r5	0xaaaaaaaa	2863311530
pc	0x10074	0x10074 <wait+8>

The pointer registers, r1 and r2, have been loaded with the addresses of the two data elements in memory (i.e., Table1 and Table2). These pointers have been used to retrieve the two elements, and you can see from the debugger that the operation worked.

The following debugger output provides a disassembly of the code. This is not what was written. The assembler has converted the three pseudo-operations into actual ARM code (in bold font):

```
Dump of assembler code from 0x10054 to 0x10086:
    0x00010054 <_start+0>:    ldr    r0, [pc, #36]    ; 0x10080 <Table2+4>
    0x00010058 <_start+4>:    add    r1, pc, #24
    0x0001005c <_start+8>:    add    r2, pc, #24
    0x00010060 <_start+12>:   ldr    r3, [r1]
    0x00010064 <_start+16>:   ldr    r4, [r2]
    0x00010068 <_start+20>:   ldr    r5, [pc, #20]    ; 0x10084 <Table2+8>
```

The first load instruction loads register r0 with data from memory 36 bytes from the current program counter. At that location, the assembler has stored the 0x12345678 constant to be loaded.

The two adr operations generate an address by adding the distance between the pc and the data in memory. This is called *program counter relative addressing* and we will look at it in more detail later.

Let's look at the data in memory. We use the x/6xw 0x10080 gdb command to display six words of memory from address 0x10080:

```
(gdb) x/6xw 0x10080
0x10080 <Table2+4>:    0x12345678    0xaaaaaaaa    0x00001141    0x61656100
0x10090:               0x01006962    0x00000007
```

This shows the 0x12345678 constant that has been loaded in memory following the program, together with the other constants we loaded.

A note on endianism

We've not mentioned one topic yet - *endianism*. The term is borrowed from *Gulliver's Travels* where the world is divided into those who eat their boiled eggs from the big end and those who eat their eggs from the little end. This divides the world into mutually hostile big enders and little enders (it is, of course, satire).

Computers do something similar. Suppose you store the 32-bit hexadecimal value 0x12345678 in memory. If you stored this in word memory, where the address of each word differs by 1, life would be simple. But because computer memories are *byte-organized*, each memory location has an individual byte address, so successive byte addresses are 0,1,2,3,4,5,6... and successive word addresses are 0,4,8,12,16,20,24....

A consequence of byte addressing means that word 0 occupies byte addresses 0,1,2,3. Suppose we store 0x12345678 at address 0. Which end of the number do we put in first? Is it stored in bytes 0 to 3 as 12 34 56 78 or as 78 56 34 12?

Figure 9.4 illustrates three memory systems. In all three cases, memory is byte-addressed. In the 32-bit version, we have two 32-bit values representing 0x12345678 stored in memory at addresses c and 0x1014. Notice that the individual bytes of the stored word have different byte addresses. A little-endian number is arranged so that the most significant byte, 0x12, is stored in the lowest address of the word 0x1010. A big-endian number is stored with the most-significant byte at the lowest address, 0x1013.

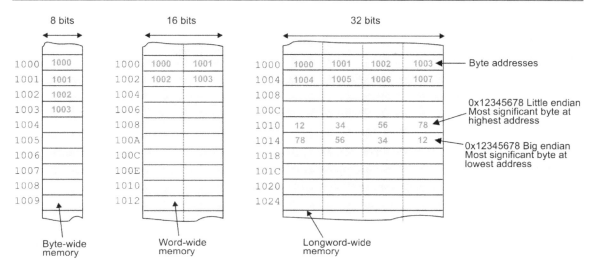

Figure 9.11 – Memory organization

Some computers are big-endian and some little-endian. Motorola microprocessors are big-endian and Intel is little-endian. ARM was originally little-endian, but it now has a bit in its CPSR status register that can be used to select the required version of endianism. By default, the ARM is little-endian.

Does the endian matter? It matters in two ways. If you are building systems or interfacing systems with mixed endianism, it matters because you must ensure that the bytes are in the correct sequence when passed from one system to another. For example, the TCP/IP protocol is big-endian. Equally, if you are performing byte and word operations on data, you have to be aware of the relationship between byte and word addresses. If you store the ASCII "Mike" at word address 0x1000 and you wanted the *"e,"* it would be at 0x1000 in a big-endian system and 0x1003 in a little-endian system.

Bringing everything together – a final example

To conclude this chapter, we provide a final example of using the Raspberry Pi to enter the ARM assembly language and run it in a debugging mode using gdb. As before, the example does not perform a useful function. Its purpose is to demonstrate addressing modes, the use of assembler directives to load data in memory, the nature of endianism, and the ability to declare variables in memory and modify them.

This example also demonstrates how memory data is displayed and how to use the memory display function to read data. We have used gdb and copied various screens during the debugging. These have been put together in what follows. We have removed some material (e.g., status registers and registers not accessed) and have slightly edited the format for readability.

The source program

The source program sets up data in memory and accesses it. We use ASCII text and numeric text as part of the demonstration. Note that an ASCII string or character using the GCC assembler requires double quotes. We also read bytes with ldrb and a halfword (16 bits) with ldrh.

The program uses `ldrb r5, [r3,#1]` to demonstrate reading bytes from a 32-bit word that is 3 bytes on from the base address of the word in r5.

The program contains dummy data stored in memory, such as 0xAAAAAAAA. We do this to demonstrate how data is stored, but mainly to help with debugging. When you display data contents in memory, these dummy values provide great markers to help you read the memory data.

Note that the word that we access in read/write memory, testRW, is in a .data section. This is initialized to 0xFFFFFFFF and is later modified:

```
        .global _start
_start: adr    r0,mike        @ r0 points to ASCII string "Mike"
        ldr    r1,[r0]        @ Read the string into r1
        ldrb   r2,[r0,#3]     @ Read byte 3 of "Mike"

        adr    r3,test        @ Point to data value 0x2468FACE in memory
        ldrb   r4,[r3]        @ Read single byte of test. Pointer in r0
        ldrb   r5,[r3,#1]     @ Read single byte 1 offset
        ldrh   r6,[r3]        @ Read halfword of test

        ldr    r7,a_adr       @ r7 points at address of testRW
        ldr    r8,=0x12345678 @ r8 loaded with 32-bit literal 0x12345678
        str    r8,[r7]        @ Store r8 in read/write memory at testRW
        ldrh   r9,[r7]        @ Read halfword of testRW
        mvn    r10,r9         @ Logically negate r9
        strh   r10,[r7,#4]    @ Store halfword in next word after testRW
        nop                   @ Just a place to stop
        mov    r0,#1          @ Raspberry Pi exit sequence
        mov    r7,#7
        svc    0

mike:   .ascii "Mike"         @ Store string as 4 ASCII characters
test:   .word  0x2468FACE     @ Save a word in memory
a_adr:  .word  testRW         @ Pointer to data in read/write memory
        .data                 @ Data section in read/write memory
nines:  .word  0x99999999     @ 0x99999999 Just dummy data
testRW: .word  0xFFFFFFFF     @
        .word  0x77777777     @ More dummy data
        .word  0xBBBBBBBB     @ More dummy data
        .end
```

The first steps are to assemble and load the program (called endian) and invoke the gdb debugger. We use bold font to indicate input from the keyboard:

```
alan@raspberrypi:~/Desktop $ as g o endian.o endian.s
alan@raspberrypi:~/Desktop $ ld o endian endian.o
alan@raspberrypi:~/Desktop $ gdb endian
GNU gdb (Raspbian 10.11.7) 10.1.90.20210103git
```

We can use gdb to set a breakpoint at _start and then run the program to that breakpoint:

```
(gdb) b _start
Breakpoint 1 at 0x10074: file endian.s, line 2.
(gdb) r
Starting program: /home/alan/Desktop/endian
Breakpoint 1, _start () at endian.s:2
2    _start: adr     r0,mike     @ r0 points to ASCII string "Mike"
```

Let's look at the program that is actually loaded into memory. This differs slightly from the one we wrote because pseudo-operations have been replaced by actual code. Note that the adr is translated into an add by taking the program counter and adding the distance of the required variable to the current pc to generate its address.

The ldr r8,=0x12345678 is translated into a load program counter relative instruction because the required constant has been loaded into memory after the end of the program:

```
(gdb) disassemble
Dump of assembler code for function _start:
=> 0x00010074 <+0>:     add    r0, pc, #60    ; 0x3c
   0x00010078 <+4>:     ldr    r1, [r0]
   0x0001007c <+8>:     ldrb   r2, [r0, #3]
   0x00010080 <+12>:    add    r3, pc, #52    ; 0x34
   0x00010084 <+16>:    ldrb   r4, [r3]
   0x00010088 <+20>:    ldrb   r5, [r3, #1]
   0x0001008c <+24>:    ldrh   r6, [r3]
   0x00010090 <+28>:    ldr    r7, [pc, #40]  ; 0x100c0 <a_adr>
   0x00010094 <+32>:    ldr    r8, [pc, #40]  ; 0x100c4 <a_adr+4>
   0x00010098 <+36>:    str    r8, [r7]
   0x0001009c <+40>:    ldrh   r9, [r7]
   0x000100a0 <+44>:    mvn    r10, r9
   0x000100a4 <+48>:    strh   r10, [r7, #4]
   0x000100a8 <+52>:    nop                   ; (mov r0, r0)
   0x000100ac <+56>:    mov    r0, #1
   0x000100b0 <+60>:    mov    r7, #7
   0x000100b4 <+64>:    svc    0x00000000
End of assembler dump.
```

This differs from the code we wrote because pseudo-operations have been replaced by actual ARM code. Note that the adr is translated into an add by taking the program counter and adding the distance of the required variable to the current pc to generate its address.

The ldr r8,=0x12345678 is translated into a load program counter relative instruction because the required constant has been loaded into memory after the end of the program.

Let's look at memory. The following shows the contents of 8 consecutive words starting with 0x100b4, which is the address of the svc 0 instruction.

Before continuing and executing the program, we will look at the contents of memory, set up by the program. Where is this data? It follows the last executable instruction, svc 0, which is at address 0x000100B4. We display the eight words from the svc in hexadecimal format:

```
(gdb) x/8wx 0x100b4
0x100b4 <_start+64>:     0xef000000    0x656b694d    0x2468face    0x000200cc
0x100c4 <a_adr+4>:       0x12345678    0x99999999    0xffffffff    0x77777777
```

You can see the 0x12345678 constant loaded by the assembler and some of the markers.

We will step through the first few instructions:

```
(gdb) si 1
3          ldr    r1,[r0]          @ Read the string into r1
4          ldrb   r2,[r0,#3]       @ Read byte 3 of "Mike"
6          adr    r3,test          @ Point to data value 0x2468FACE in memory
```

The next step is to look at the registers before the program runs to completion. We do this with gdb's i r command. There's not much to see yet (it's a partial listing), as we've executed only the first few instructions. However, r0 now contains a pointer to the ASCII text string *"Mike"* at address 0x100B8. If you look back at that address, you see that it contains 0x656b694d, which is ekiM. That's what little-endian does!

```
(gdb) i r
r0         0x100b8            65720
r1         0x656b694d         1701538125
r2         0x65               101
r3         0x0                0
r4         0x0                0
sp         0x7efff360         0x7efff360
lr         0x0                0
pc         0x10080            0x10080 <_start+12>
```

Continuing single-stepping:

```
(gdb) si 1
7          ldrb    r4,[r3]           @ Read byte of test Pointer in r0
8          ldrb    r5,[r3,#1]        @ Read single byte 1 offset
9          ldrh    r6,[r3]           @ Read halfword of test
11         ldr     r7,a_adr          @ r7 points at address of testRW
12         ldr     r8,=0x12345678    @ r8 loaded with 32-bit 0x12345678
(gdb) i r
r0              0x100b8             65720
r1              0x656b694d          1701538125
r2              0x65                101
r3              0x100bc             65724
r4              0xce                206
r5              0xfa                250
r6              0xface              64206
r7              0x200cc             131276
sp              0x7efff360          0x7efff360
lr              0x0                 0
pc              0x10094             0x10094 <_start+32>
```

Let's look at the memory in the data section. Register r7 points to the read/write data area. It starts 4 bytes before the pointer to testRW, in r7 ; that is, 0x200CC - 4 = 0x200C8. The four words beginning at that address are as follows:

```
(gdb) x/4xw 0x200c8
0x200c8:    0x99999999    0xffffffff    0x77777777    0xbbbbbbbb
```

Finally, we step through the instruction until we meet the nop at the end:

```
(gdb) si 1
13         str     r8,[r7]           @ Store r8 in read/write memory at testRW
14         ldrh    r9,[r7]           @ Read halfword of testRW
15         mvn     r10,r9            @ Logically negate r9
16         strh    r10,[r7,#4]       @ Store halfword in next word after testRW
17         nop                       @ Just a place to stop
```

```
(gdb) i r
r0              0x100b8             65720
r1              0x656b694d          1701538125
r2              0x65                101
r3              0x100bc             65724
r4              0xce                206
r5              0xfa                250
r6              0xface              64206
r7              0x200cc             131276
r8              0x12345678          305419896
r9              0x5678              22136
r10             0xffffa987          4294945159
sp              0x7efff360          0x7efff360
lr              0x0                 0
pc              0x100a8             0x100a8 <_start+52>
```

Here's our final look at the data memory. Note that 0xFFFFFFFF has been replaced with the value 0x12345678 that we wrote to memory. This demonstrates how you can access data memory using an ARM.

Note also the data value at 0x200D0 ; that is, 0x7777a987. We have changed half the word using a halfword load:

```
(gdb) x/4xw 0x200c8
0x200c8:    0x99999999    0x12345678    0x7777a987    0xbbbbbbbb
```

Summary

In this chapter, we have introduced a real computer, the Raspberry Pi. Instead of designing our own computer instruction sets, we've looked at the ARM microprocessor that is at the heart of the Raspberry Pi and most smartphones.

We introduced the basics of the Raspberry Pi and showed how to write an ARM assembly language program that can run on it. This requires an understanding of the ARM assembler and the use of the linker. We demonstrated how you can then run your ARM program instruction-by-instruction using the gdb debugger.

One important feature of Raspberry Pi's architecture we have encountered is the way in which data in memory is modified. You cannot use a str (store) instruction to modify data in memory. You must do it indirectly via a pointer to the address of the memory you wish to change. The following short program demonstrates this vital point. A data item in memory is read directly using an ldr but modified in memory using a pointer to a pointer. The key operations are in bold:

```
        .text                  @ Code section
        .global _start

_start: ldr r1,=xxx            @ Point to data xxx
        ldr r2,[r1]            @ Read the data
        adr r3,adr_xxx         @ Point to the address of the address of xxx
        ldr r4,[r3]           @ Point to the data xxx
        ldr r5,[r4]           @ Read the value of xxx
        add r5,r5,#1          @ Increment the data
        str r5,[r4]           @ Change xxx in memory

        mov r0,#0             @ Exit procedure
        mov r7,#1
        svc 0

adr_xxx: .word                @ Pointer to data xxx

        .data                 @ Data section
xxx:    .word   0xABCD        @ Initialize variable xxx

        .end
```

In order to demonstrate an ARM program, we have introduced the ARM's assembly language. Mercifully, this is not too far from the language adopted by some of the simulators. Indeed, the ARM's assembly language is not too difficult to learn, although it does incorporate some very interesting features, which we will describe in later chapters.

In the next chapter, we return to the ARM architecture and one of its most important aspects: addressing and how data is transferred to and from memory.

10
A Closer Look at the ARM

We have already introduced the ARM processor. Now, we will look at it in a little more depth. The ARM family of processors is probably the best vehicle to teach computer architecture. In particular, it is very easy to learn because of its streamlined instruction set and simple register model compared to many other microprocessors. Moreover, the ARM has some very interesting features, such as predicated execution when an instruction can either be executed or ignored, depending on the processor status. The introduction of the Raspberry Pi in computer education could not have happened at a better time because it enables students to get hands-on experience of the remarkable ARM architecture.

In this chapter, we will do the following:

- Introduce the ARM
- Describe its register set
- Examine variations in add and subtract operations
- Cover the ARM's multiplication instruction
- Introduce logical operations and shifting operations
- Explain flow control and the ARM's conditional execution

Technical requirements

Because this chapter is an extension of the previous chapter, no new hardware or software is required. All you need is Raspberry Pi, configured as a general-purpose computer. The only software needed is a text editor to create assembly language programs and the GCC assembler and loader.

Introducing the ARM

The ARM processor family has been a remarkable success story, not least because so many other microprocessors became popular for a few years and then declined into obscurity (e.g., 6502, Cyrix 486, and Itanium). At the time of its release, the Motorola 68K was widely thought of as far more elegant and powerful than Intel's 8086. Indeed, the 68K was a true 32-bit machine at a time when the 8086 was a 16-bit machine. The 68K was adopted by Apple's Mac, the Atari, and Amiga computers – all major players in the home computer market.

How could Intel's humble 8086 possibly ever have competed? Well, IBM selected the 8086 family for its new personal computer and the rest is history. Motorola later dropped out of the semiconductor business.

In the late 1980s, a new company, Advanced RISC Machines, was founded to create high-performance microprocessors. The architecture of their machines followed the register-to-register paradigm of the RISC architecture, rather than Intel and Motorola's more complicated CISC instruction sets. The ARM was born.

Not only has ARM survived when many of the earlier microprocessors failed – it has also prospered and successfully targeted the world of mobile devices, such as netbooks, tablets, and cell phones. ARM incorporates some interesting architectural features that have given it a competitive advantage over its rivals.

ARM is, in fact, a *fabless* company – that is, it develops the architecture of computers and allows other companies to manufacture those computers. The term *fabless* is derived from fab (short for fabrication).

Before we describe ARM's instructions, we will discuss its register set because all ARM data-processing instructions operate on the contents of its registers (a prime feature of the RISC computer).

Because the ARM's architecture has developed over the years, and because there are different versions of the ARM architecture in use, a teacher of it has a problem. Which version should be used to illustrate a computer architecture course? In this chapter, we will use the ARMv4 32-bit architecture, which has 32-bit instructions. Some ARM processors can switch between 32-bit and 16-bit instruction states (the 16-bit state is called the *Thumb* state). The Thumb state is intended to run very compact code in embedded control systems. We will not cover the Thumb state here.

The ARM found in Raspberry Pi 4 has a 64-bit architecture that is very different from earlier 32-bit ARMs. However, since the 32-bit ARM architecture is used in most teaching texts and Raspberry Pi 4 supports it, we will use the 32-bit architecture here. In order to be consistent with other books using the ARM to illustrate computer architecture, most of the material here is based on ARMv4T 32-bit architecture. ARM's 32-bit architectures are now referred to by the term AArch32, distinguishing them from ARM's new 64-bit architecture, AArch64.

Overview of the ARM's architecture

The ARM's architecture is interesting because it has elements of both the conventional CISC architecture such as Motorola's 68K and Intel's 32/64-bit architectures, together with the more radical streamlined RISC architecture of processors such as MIPS and RISC-V.

Here, we will examine the following:

- The ARM's register set
- Arithmetic instructions
- Special addition and subtraction instructions
- Multiplication and ARM's multiplication and addition instruction
- Bitwise instruction
- Shifting operations

We don't cover data movement operations in detail here. We have already encountered the mov operation that can be used to load a literal into a register – for example, mov r1, #12. Similarly, the str and ldr instructions load a register from memory and store a register in memory, respectively. A typical example is ldr r4, [r5] and str r0, [r9]. These two instructions use *register indirect addressing*, and we will devote the next chapter to them.

Arm register set

Unlike the popular MIPS processor with its 32 general-purpose registers, ARM has just 16 registers, r0 to r15, and a *status register*. Remarkably, the ARM's registers are not all the same – that is, some are special-purpose registers. *Figure 10.1* illustrates the ARM's register set.

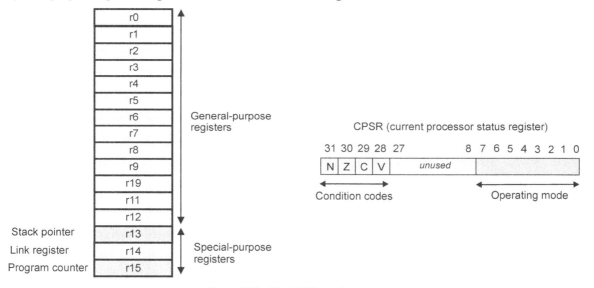

Figure 10.1 – The ARM's register set

Fourteen registers, r0 to r13, are indeed general-purpose in the sense that they all behave in the same way – for example, anything you can do with r5, you can do with r10. Registers r13, r14, and r15 are not general-purpose because they have additional functions.

Strictly speaking, r13 is a general-purpose register, but by convention, it's reserved for use as a stack pointer. If you work on a project in a team, you should respect this convention. Otherwise, you do not have to follow the convention, and you can use r13 in any way you wish.

Register r14 has an additional function imposed by the hardware. It is a *link register* and can be written lr or r14 in assembly programs. The ARM has an instruction, branch with link (bl), that lets you jump to a point in the program (i.e., a branch) and save the address of the next instruction in sequence in the link register. In other words, the instruction saves the next pc address in r14 and then jumps to the specified target. Later, you can return by copying the address in the link register to the pc with mov pc, lr or `mov 15,r14`. This is a faster subroutine call and return mechanism than the conventional `bsr` and `rts` pair of instructions that use a stack to store the return address.

Register `r15` is a truly different register from all the others and can never be used as a general-purpose register (even though you can apply some instructions to it as if it were general-purpose). Register `r15` is the *program counter* that contains the address of the next instruction to be executed and is normally written `pc` rather than `r15` in ARM code. Putting the program counter in a general register is very rare in the world of computer architecture. Note that, in practice, `pc` contains an address that is 8 bytes ahead of the current `pc` because of the way that the ARM is internally organized.

We will look at the ARM's data processing instructions first, rather than the data movement operations. We take this approach because data movement instructions are more complicated, since they involve complex addressing modes.

Arithmetic instructions

Let's begin with ARM's arithmetic instructions that perform operations on data representing *numeric quantities*:

- Addition   `add`
- Subtraction   `sub`
- Comparison   `cmp` (technically, `compare` is not a data-processing operation)
- Multiplication   `mul`
- Shifting   `lsl, lsr, asl, asr, ror, rrx`

Addition, subtraction, and comparison

Addition is a simple operation that adds two operands to generate a sum and a carryout. In decimal arithmetic, adding 4 + 5 gives 9. Adding 4 + 9 gives 13 ; that is, a result of 3 and a carry-out of 1. Computers deal with this by storing the carryout in the carry bit. ARM instructions require you to add the suffix `s` if you wish to update condition code flags after an operation – that is, you need to write `adds r1,r2,r3`.

The ARM is a 32-bit machine. How do you add 64-bit numbers? Suppose that two 64-bit numbers are A and B, where A_L is the lower-order 32 bits of A, and A_U is the upper-32 bits of A. Similarly, B_L is the lower-order 32 bits of B, and B_U is the upper-32 bits of B.

We first add A_L to B_L and record the carry. Then we add together A_U and B_U, plus any carry generated from the addition of the lower-order pair. In ARM assembler language, this is as follows:

```
adds  C_L,A_L,B_L      @ CL,AL,BL are registers, each holding the 32 lower-order bits of a word
adc   C_U,A_U,B_U      @ Add the two upper-order 32-bit registers together with the carry bit
```

The second addition, `adc`, means, *add with carry*, and adds any carry out from the previous addition. We've used C_L, A_L, B_L, and so on, rather than `r1`, `r2`, and `r3` to demonstrate that these are upper- and lower-order parts of a number distributed between two registers. We can extend this principle to perform extended-precision arithmetic with integers of any length.

The ARM also provides a simple subtract operation, sub, together with a sbc or *subtract with carry* instruction to support extended-precision subtraction, which operate like the corresponding adc.

As well as sub and sbc, the ARM has a *reverse* subtract operation, where rsc **r1**, r2, r3 perform the subtraction of r2 from r3. This instruction may seem strange and unnecessary because you can simply reverse the order of the second two registers, can't you? However, ARM lacks a *negation* instruction that subtracts a number from zero ; for example, the negative of r0 is 0 - [r0]. The reverse subtraction operation can be used to do this because rsb **r1**, r1, #0 is equivalent to neg r1.

A comparison operation compares two values by subtracting one from the other – for example, we can compare 3 with 5. Suppose the two elements being compared are A and B. If you perform A – B and the answer is zero, then A and B are equal. If the result is positive, A > B, and if it's negative, A < B. A comparison is a subtraction where you don't care about the result ; only its sign, whether it's zero, whether a carry was generated. Consider the following:

```
mov r1,#6        @ Load r1 with 6
mov r2,#8        @ Load r2 with 8
cmp r1,r2        @ Compare r1 and r2
```

The operation cmp **r1**,r2 evaluates [r1] - [r2] and updates the Z, C, N, and V bits. We can then perform operations such as beq next that branch to label next if r1 and r2 are equal. We said that you need to append s to update condition codes. Comparison operations are exceptions because setting condition codes is what they do. You can write cmps if you want, since it's the same as cmp.

There are two types of integer comparison. Consider (in 8 bits) the A = 00000001 and B = 11111111 binary values. Which is the larger? You might think that it's B, since B = 255 and A = 1. That's true. However, if these were assigned 2s complement numbers, A would be 1 and B would be -1; therefore, A is the larger. Like all processors, ARM provides two sets of branch operations, one for unsigned arithmetic and one for signed arithmetic. A programmer must select the appropriate branch depending on whether they use signed or unsigned arithmetic. The simulators we constructed earlier all provided unsigned branches only.

Multiplication

ARM's multiply instruction, mul **Rd**, Rm, Rs, generates the low-order 32 bits of the 64-bit product Rm x Rs. When using mul, you should ensure that the result does not go out of range because multiplying two m-bit numbers yields a 2m-bit product. This instruction doesn't let you multiply the contents of a register by a constant – that is, you can't perform mul **r9**, r4, #14. Moreover, you can't use the *same* register to specify both the Rd destination and the Rm operand. These restrictions are due to the implementation of this instruction in hardware. The following code demonstrates the use of ARM's multiplication to multiply 23 by 25:

```
mov     r4,#23       @ Load register r4 with 23
mov     r7,#25       @ Load register r7 with 25
mul     r9,r4,r7     @ r9 is loaded with the low-order 32-bit product of r4 and r7
```

We've already seen that ARM has a *multiply and accumulate instruction*, mla, with a *four-operand* format mla **Rd**,Rm,Rs,Rn, whose RTL definition is [Rd] ← [Rm] x [Rs] + [Rn]. The 32-bit by 32-bit multiplication is truncated to the lower-order 32 bits. Like the multiplication, Rd must not be the same as Rm (although this restriction was removed in the ARMv6 and later architectures).

ARM's *multiply and accumulate* instruction supports the calculation of an *inner-product* by performing one multiplication and addition per instruction. The inner-product is used in multimedia applications – for example, if vector **a** consists of the n components $a_1, a_2, \ldots a_n$ and vector **b** consists of the n components $b_1, b_2, \ldots, b_n$, then the *inner product* of **a** and **b** is the scalar value $s = \mathbf{a} \cdot \mathbf{b} = a_1 \cdot b_1 + a_2 \cdot b_2 + \ldots + a_n \cdot b_n$.

We will now demonstrate an application of the multiply and accumulate operations. Although we have not yet covered the ARM's addressing modes, the following example includes the instruction ldr **r0**, [r5] ,#4 that loads register r0 with an element from the array pointed at by register r5, and then it updates r5 to point at the next element (4 bytes on):

```
       mov    r4,#n        @ r4 is the counter
       mov    r3,#0        @ Clear the inner product
       adr    r5,V1        @ r5 points to v1
       adr    r6,V2        @ r6 points to v2

Loop:  ldr    r0, [r5] ,#4   @ REPEAT read a component of v1 and update the pointer
       ldr    r1, [r6] ,#4   @ Get the second element in the pair from v2
       mla    r3,r0,r1,r3    @ Add new product term to the total (r3 = r3 + r0·r1)
       subs   r4,r4,#1       @ Decrement the counter and set the (CCR)
       bne    Loop           @ UNTIL all done
```

What about division? The ARMv4 architecture lacks a division instruction as part of its basic architecture (some variants of ARM such as the ARMv7 architecture do incorporate division). If you wish to do division on the ARM, you have to write a short program that uses an iterative loop involving shifting and subtracting to perform the division (rather like pencil and paper long division).

Bitwise logical operations

The ARM provides the basic AND, OR, NOT, and EOR (exclusive or) bitwise logical operations supported by most processors. These are used to set, clear, and toggle the individual bits of a word, as we already saw when assembling instructions. There is also an unusual *bit clear* operation, bic, that ANDs its first operand with the *complement of the corresponding bits* of its second operand – that is, $c_i = a_i \wedge \overline{b_i}$.

The ARM's NOT operation is written as mvn r_d, r_s. This move instruction negates, inverts the bits of the source register and copies them to the destination register.

The following examples illustrate logical operations on r1 = 11001010_2 and r0 = 00001111_2:

Logical instruction	Operation	Final value in r2
and **r2**,r1,r0	11001010 ∧ 00001111	00001010
or **r2**,r1,r0	11001010 + 00001111	11001111
mvn **r2**,r1	$\overline{10010010}$	00110101
eor **r2**,r1,r0	11001010 ⊕ 00001111	11000101
bic **r2**,r1,r0	11001010 ∧ $\overline{00001111}$	11000000

When you design instruction sets, one of the major tasks is to construct binary codes for instructions. These operations make it easy to implement the manipulation of bits. For example, suppose variable sR1 specifies source register 1, and sR2 specifies source register 2, and we have to construct a 16-bit binary code, C, with the format xxxxx**aaa**xx**bbb**xxx. Source bits a are in sR1 and source bits b are in sR2 in the lower-order three bits.

We must insert the bits of sR1 and sR2 at the appropriate places without changing any other bits of C. In Python, we can do this with the following:

```
C = C & 0b1111100011000111    # Clear the two fields for sR1 and sR2
sR1 = sR1 << 8                # Move sR1 into position by shifting left 8 times
C = C | sR1                   # Insert sR1
sR2 = sR2 << 3                # Move sR2 into position by shifting left 3 times
C = C | sR2                   # Insert sR2
```

We can readily translate this into ARM assembly language using AND, OR, and shift operations. Assume sR1 is in r1, sR2 is in r2, and C is in register r0. Moreover, assume that the register bits are already in place in their respective registers:

```
ldr r3,=0b1111100011000111    @ Load r3 with 1111100011000111 mask
and r0,r0,r3                  @ Mask r0 to get xxxxx000xx000xxx
or  r0,r0,r1                  @ Insert r1 to get xxxxxaaaxx000xxx
or  r0,r0,r2                  @ Insert r2 to get xxxxxaaaxxbbbxxx
```

Shift operations

Python can shift bits left using the << operator, or right using the >> operator. ARM's assembly language lacks explicit instructions such as LSR or LSL that shift bits right or left. However, it does have pseudo-instructions such as lsl **r1**,r3,#4 that shift the contents of r3 four places left, transferring the result to r1. The ARM's *actual* approach to shifting is rather more unusual, complicated, and *versatile*.

The ARM includes shifting as part of conventional data operations. Consider add **r1**,r2,r3, which adds r3 to r2 and puts the result in r1. ARM allows you to shift the second operand *before* it is used in a data processing operation. You can write add r1,r2,r3, lsl r4 (see *Figure 10.2* for an explanation of the second destination field).

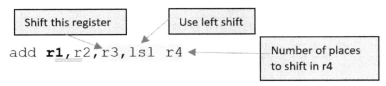

Figure 10.2 – The structure of a dynamic shift operation

This instruction takes the second source operand, r3, and performs a logical shift left. The number of left shifts is determined by the contents of r4. You can also implement a fixed shift using a constant with the following:

```
add r1,r2,r3,lsl #3
```

In this case, register r3 is shifted left by three bits before it is added to r2. A shift is called *dynamic* if the number of shifts is specified by a register, since you can change the number of shifts at runtime by changing the shift count. If the number of shifts is given by a literal (constant), it cannot be changed at runtime. This is a *static* shift.

The ARM's shift combines a data-processing operation with shifting (speeding up data processing), and it lets you specify four registers in an instruction. What do you do if you require a plain vanilla shift without including a data-processing instruction? You can use the MOV instruction, such as the following:

```
mov r1,r1,lsr #1        @ Shift contents of register r1 a single bit place right before moving
```

Today, ARM assemblers let you write the pseudo-instruction lsl **r1**,r3,#4 and automatically substitute the move instruction mov **r1**,r1,lsr #4, using a shifted second operand.

Shift types

All shifts look the same from the middle of a string of bits – that is, the bits move one (or more) places left or right. However, what happens to the bits at the end? When bits are shifted in a register, at one end, a bit will drop out. That bit can disappear into oblivion, go to the carry bit, or move around to the other end in a circular fashion. At the end where a bit is vacated, the new bit can be set to 0, 1, the same as the carry bit, or the bit that fell off the other end.

The variations in the way that the bit shifted in is treated by computers correspond to specific types of shift – *logical*, *arithmetic*, *rotate*, and *rotate through carry*. Let's look at some shift operations (*table 10.1*):

Source string	Direction	Number of shifts	Destination string
0110011111010111	Left	1	1100111110101110
0110011111010111	Left	2	1001111101011100
0110011111010111	Left	3	0011111010111000
0110011111010111	Right	1	0011001111101011
0110011111010**11**	Right	2	0001100111110101
0110011111010**111**	Right	3	0000110011111010

Table 10.1 – ARM's logical shift operations

The bits in the destination string in italic are the bits shifted in, and the bits in the source string in bold are the bits lost (dropped) after the shift. This type of shift is a *logical* shift:

- **Logical shift**: The bits shifted are moved one or more places left or right. Bits fall off at one end and zeros enter at the other end. The last bit shifted out is copied to the carry flag. *Figure 10.3* illustrates the logical shift left and the logical shift right.

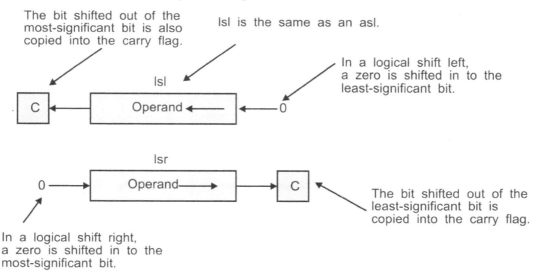

Figure 10.3 – Logical shifts

- **Arithmetic shift**: This arithmetic shift treats the number being shifted as a signed twos complement value. An arithmetic shift left is the same as a logical shift for left shifts. For right shifts, the most-significant bit is propagated right. This shift treats the operand as a signed value, which is either divided by two (shift right one bit) or multiplied by two (shift left one bit), as *Figure 10.4* demonstrates.

The purpose of an arithmetic shift is to preserve the sign of a twos complement number, when it takes part in a shifting operation that represents division by the power of 2. For example, the 8-bit value 10001111 becomes 01000111 when shifted right *logically*, but **11**000111 when shifted right *arithmetically*.

Figure 10.4 illustrates the arithmetic shift left and shift right. The ARM has an asr operation but not asl, because asl is identical to LSL – that is, you use a logical shift left because it is exactly the same as asl.

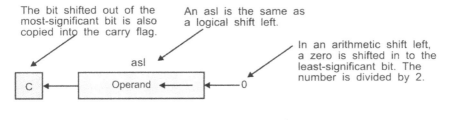

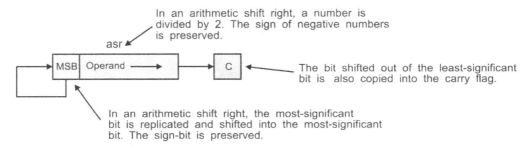

Figure 10.4 – Arithmetic shifts

- **Rotate:** A rotate treats the value to be shifted as a ring – that is, the two ends are adjacent. The bit shifted out at one end moves into the position vacated at the other end. If you apply n rotates to an n-bit value, you end up where you started. Consider the 8-bit value 01101110 being rotated left, one bit at a time:

Shift	Result	Carry out
0	01101110	0
1	11011100	1
2	10111001	1
3	01110011	0
4	11100110	1
5	11001101	1
6	10011011	1
7	00110111	0
8	01101110	0

Figure 10.5 – Example of successive rotate operations

The rotate operation is *non-destructive* – that is, no bit is lost or changed by the operation. It is very useful in operations such as counting the number of 1s in a bit string. *Figure 10.6* illustrates the *rotate* operation. Note that the ARM does *not* have a rotate right instruction – that is, there is no `ror`. Since rotate is a circular operation, shifting an *m*-bit word *p* places right is achieved by shifting 32-p places left; consequently, `ror r0,r1,#4` is achieved by `rol r0,r1,#28`.

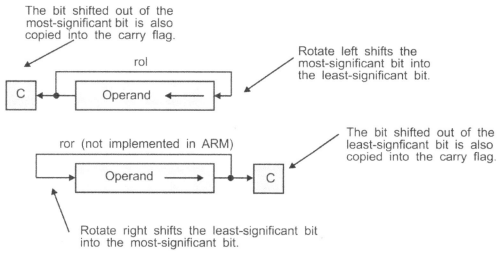

Figure 10.6 – Rotate operations (ARM does not implement ROL)

A variation of the rotate operation is the *rotate through carry*, where the carry bit is considered as part of the word being shifted – that is, an *n*-bit word becomes an *n+1* bit word. *Figure 10.7* demonstrates a rotate through carry operation, where the carry shifted out is copied into the carry bit, and the old value of the carry bit becomes the new bit shifted in. This operation is used in chained arithmetic (it's the analog of the *add with carry and subtract with borrow* operations).

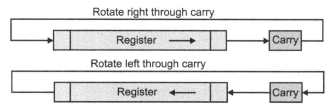

Figure 10.7 – Rotate through carry

ARM implements only the following five shifts (a programmer can synthesize the rest):

`lsl`	logical shift left
`lsr`	logical shift right
`asr`	arithmetic shift right
`ror`	rotate right
`rrx`	rotate right through carry (1-bit shift only)

rrx, which rotates bits right through carry (*Figure 10.7*), behaves differently from other shifts. First, only one direction of shift is permitted; there is no left shift through carry. Second, the ARM supports both *static* and *dynamic* shifts for all other shift operations, whereas rrx allows only one single shift.

Although there is no rotate left operation, you can readily implement it by means of a rotate right operation. The following example demonstrates the rotation, both left and right, of a 4-bit value. After four rotations, the number is unchanged. As you can see, there is symmetry between left and right rotations. For a 32-bit value, an *n*-bit shift left is identical to a 32-*n* bit shift right:

Rotate right		Rotate left	
1101	Start	1101	Start
1110	Rotate right 1	1011	Rotate left 1
0111	Rotate right 2	0111	Rotate left 2
1011	Rotate right 3	1110	Rotate left 3
1101	Rotate right 4	1101	Rotate left 4

Table 10.2 - Comparing successive left and right rotates

Consider adcs **r0**,r0,r0 (add with carry and set status flags). This adds the contents of r0 to the contents of r0, plus the carry bit, to generate 2 x [r0] + C. Shifting left is equivalent to multiplying by 2. Moving the carry bit into the least-significant position is equivalent to adding the carry bit to get 2 x [r0] + C. Appending S to the instruction forces the CCR to be updated, which ensures that any carryout is loaded into the C-bit. Consequently, adcs **r0**,r0,r0 and rlx **r0** are equivalent.

Using shift operations to merge data

In the following example, we extract the least-significant byte from each of the three registers and put them together in a new word. The literals are in a hexadecimal format. Assume that the registers are, initially, as follows:

- r1 = XXXXXX**AA**   r1 is source 1, the Xs represent don't care values
- r2 = XXXXXX**BB**   r2 is source 2
- r3 = XXXXXX**CC**   r3 is source 3
- r4 = 00**CCBBAA**   r4 is the final result

```
mov  r4,#0                    @ Clear r4
and  r1,r1,#0x000000FF        @ Clear r1 except least-significant byte
and  r2,r2,#0x0000FF00        @ Clear r2 except second byte
and  r3,r2,#0x00FF0000        @ Clear r3 except third byte
or   r4,r4,r1                 @ Copy r1 to r4. No shifting
or   r4,r4,r2 lsl #8          @ Copy r2 to r4. Shifting to second byte
or   r4,r4,r3 lsl #16         @ Copy r3 to r4. Shifting to third byte
```

The preceding code is a brute-force approach. A better alternative is as follows:

```
and  r4,r1,#0x000000FF        @ Clear r4 and insert r1 0x000000AA
or   r4,r4,r2 lsl #8          @ Insert r2, shifting left into place 0xXXXXBBAA
or   r4,r4,r3 lsl #16         @ Insert r3, shifting left into place 0xXXCCBBAA
and  r4,r4,#0x00FFFFFF        @ Insert most-significant byte 0x00CCBBAA
```

Now, consider r0 = 0x0000**AA**, r1 = 0x000000**BB**, and r2 = 0x12345678. We wish to merge the four registers to get 0x**AABB**5678. We can do this with just three instructions:

```
add  r2,r1,r2,lsl #16         @ r2 = 567800BB
add  r2,r2,r0,lsl #8          @ r2 = 5678AABB,
mov  r2,r2,ror #16            @ r2 = AABB5678
```

add r2,r1,r2,lsl #16 adds r1 to r2 after r2 has been shifted left 16 times. The 16-bit left shift moves the lower-order 16-bits of r2 into the upper-order 16-bits, and it clears the lower-order 16 bits by shifting in zeros. We've preserved the old lower-order half of r2, and we've cleared the new lower-order 16 bits ready to insert the bytes from r0 and r1. add **r2**,r2,r0,lsl #8 inserts the low-order byte of r0 into bits 8 to 15 of r2, since r0 is first shifted left by 8 bits. Since zeros are shifted into r0, this operation doesn't affect bits 0 to 7 of r2. Executing mov **r2**,r2,ror #16 performs a 16-bit rotation.

The next example of shifting demonstrates how we can implement if x < 0: x = 0. This construct sets the x variable to zero if x is negative (i.e., msb is 1); otherwise, x is unchanged. The ARM code is as follows:

```
bic r0,r0,r0,asr #31
```

The arithmetic shift right propagates the sign-bit 31 times, leaving 0x00000000 for a positive number and 0xFFFFFFFF for a negative number. The bic operation ANDs the first operand and the complement of the second. If r0 was positive, all bits are ANDed, with 1 leaving r0 unchanged. If r0 was negative, the bits are ANDed, with 0 leaving 0. Therefore, a positive x is unchanged and a negative x is set to 0.

The next section looks at a class of instruction that does not move data or process data; it determines which instruction will be executed next.

Flow control instructions

Computers execute instructions sequentially unless a branch causes a jump to an out-of-sequence instruction, or the flow of instructions is interrupted when a subroutine is called. The instruction flow is also changed when an interrupt occurs (we don't deal with interrupts here).

In this section, we will look at the following:

- Unconditional branches
- Conditional branches

Unconditional branches

ARM's unconditional branch is expressed as b target, where target denotes the *branch target address* (the address of the next instruction to be executed). The unconditional branch forces a jump (branch) from one point in a program to another. It is exactly the same as the unconditional branch we introduced earlier. The following ARM code demonstrates how the unconditional branch is used:

```
      ..   do this          @ Some code
      ..   then that        @ Some other code
    b      Next             @ Now skip past the next instructions and jump to Next:
      ..                    @ ...the code being skipped past
      ..                    @ ...the code being skipped past
Next: ..                    @ Target address for the branch, denoted by label Next
```

The ARM's branch instructions use a 24-bit literal to provide a twos complement relative offset. This is shifted left twice to create a 26-bit *byte* offset, which is added to the current program counter to obtain the 32-bit target address. The branch range is 32 MB from the current PC (in either direction). Remember that consecutive instruction addresses differ by four.

Conditional branch

ARM's conditional branches consist of a mnemonic B_{cc} and a target address. The subscript defines one of 16 conditions that must be satisfied for the branch to be taken. If the condition is true, execution continues at the branch target address. If the condition is not true, the next instruction in sequence is executed. Consider the flowing example in ARM assembly language that implements the following:

```
if x == y: y = y + 1
else:      y = y + 2


        cmp r1,r2        @ Compare x and y (r1 contains y and r2 contains x)
        bne plus2        @ If not equal, then branch to the else part
        add r1,r1,#1     @ If equal, fall through to here and add one to y
        b   leave        @ Now, skip past the else part
plus2:  add r1,r1,#2     @ ELSE add 2 to y
leave:  ...              @ Continue from here
```

The *conditional branch* instruction tests flag bits in the processor's condition code register and then takes the branch if the tested condition is true. Since the condition code register includes a zero bit (Z), negative bit (N), carry bit (C), and overflow bit (V), there are eight conditional branches based on the state of a single bit (four that branch on true and four that branch on false). *Table 10.3* defines all the ARM's conditional branches. Note that there is a branch *always* and a branch *never* instruction.

Branch instructions can be applied to *signed* or *unsigned* data. Consider the four-bit values x = 0011 and y = 1001. We want to branch if y is greater than x. Using unsigned arithmetic, x = 3 and y is 9, so y > x.

However, if we regard these as signed values, then x = 3 and y = -7, so y < x. Clearly, we have to select an unsigned comparison for unsigned arithmetic and a signed comparison for signed arithmetic.

Encoding	Mnemonic	Branch on flag status	Execute on condition
0000	EQ	Z set	Equal (i.e., zero)
0001	NE	Z clear	Not equal (i.e., not zero)
0010	CS or HS	C set	Unsigned higher or same
0011	CC or LO	C clear	Unsigned lower
0100	MI	N set	Negative
0101	PL	N clear	Positive or zero
0110	VS	V set	Overflow
0111	VC	V clear	No overflow
1000	HI	C set and Z clear	Unsigned higher
1001	LS	C clear or Z set	Unsigned lower or same
1010	GE	N set and V set, or N clear and V clear	Signed greater or equal
1011	LT	N set and V clear, or N clear and V set	Signed less than
1100	GT	Z clear, and either N set and V set, or N clear and V clear	Signed greater than
1101	LE	Z set, or N set and V clear, or N clear and V set	Signed less than or equal
1110	AL	Unconditional	Always (default)
1111	NV		Never (reserved)

Table 10.3 – ARM's conditional execution and branch control mnemonics

Some microprocessors have *synonyms* for conditional branch operations – that is, a branch condition has two mnemonics. For example, branch on carry set (bcs) can be written branch on higher or same (bhs), because C = 1 implements the (>) operation in unsigned arithmetic. Similarly, bcc can be written branch on lower (blo), because the carry clear implements an unsigned comparison that is lower.

One of the best examples of the use of conditional branching is in repetitive structures. Consider the while loop:

```
Loop:         cmp    r0,#0          @ Perform test at start of loop (exit on zero)
              beq    whileExit      @ Exit on test true
              Code   ...            @ Body of the loop
              b      Loop           @ Repeat WHILE true
whileExit:    Post-loop code...     @ Exit
```

The final section of this chapter looks at ARM's *conditional execution mechanism*, which provides a means of squashing or *annulling* instructions – that is, you can choose to run or not run an instruction at runtime. This is a feature found on very, very few processors. However, this mechanism provides the ARM with a very interesting means of speeding execution by creating compact code.

Conditional executions

Here, we will deal with just one topic, conditional executing, and we will demonstrate how you can ignore an instruction if it does not fulfill a specified criterion (related to the condition control status bits). This mechanism enables programmers to write more compact code.

Consider the `add` instruction. When the computer reads it from memory, it is executed, exactly like almost every other computer. The ARM is different; each of its instructions is *conditionally executed* – that is, an instruction is executed only if a specific condition is met; otherwise, it is bypassed (annulled or squashed). Each ARM instruction is associated with a logical condition (one of the 16 in *Table 10.3*). If the stated condition is true, the instruction is executed.

A suffix indicates conditional execution by appending `condition` – for example, `addeq r1,r2,r3` specifies that the addition is performed *only if the Z-bit in the CCR is set*. The RTL form of this operation is as follows:

```
IF Z = 1 THEN [r1] ← [r2] + [r3]
```

There is, of course, nothing to stop you from combining conditional execution and shifting, since the branch and shift fields of an instruction are independent. You can write the following:

```
addcc  r1,r2,r3, lsl r4
```

This is interpreted as follows:

```
IF C = 0 THEN [r1] ← [r2] + [r3] x 2^[r4].
```

To demonstrate the power of conditional execution, consider the following Python statement:

```
if A == B: C = D - E;
```

Translated into ARM code using conditional execution, we can write the following:

```
cmp    r1,r2      @ Compare A == B
subeq  r3,r1,r4   @ If (A== B) then C = D - E
```

After the test, the operation is either executed or not executed, depending on the result of the test. Now, consider a construct with a compound predicate:

```
if ((a == b) AND (c == d)): e = e + 1
```

```
cmp    r0,r1      @ Compare a == b
cmpeq  r2,r3      @ If a == b then test c == d
addeq  r4,r4,#1   @ If a == b AND c == d THEN increment e
```

The first line, `cmp r0,r1`, compares a and b. The next line, `cmpeq r2,r3`, executes a conditional comparison only if the result of the first line was true (i.e., a == b). The third line, `addeq r4,r4,#1`, is executed only if the previous line was true (i.e., c == d) to implement e = e + 1. Without conditional execution, we might write the following:

```
        cmp     r0,r1       @ Compare a == b
        bne     Exit        @ Exit if a =! b
        cmp     r2,r3       @ Compare c == d
        bne     Exit        @ Exit if c =! d
        add     r4,r4,#1    @ Else increment e
Exit
```

This conventional approach to compound logical conditions requires five instructions. You can also handle some testing with multiple conditions. Consider the following:

```
if (a == b)  e = e + 4;
if (a < b)   e = e + 7;
if (a > b)   e = e + 12;
```

Using the same register assignments as before, we can use conditional execution to implement this as follows:

```
        cmp     r0,r1       @ Compare a == b
        addeq   r4,r4,#4    @ If a == b then e = e + 4
        addle   r4,r4,#7    @ If a < b then e = e + 7
        addgt   r4,r4,#12   @ If a > b then e = e + 12
```

Using conventional non-conditional execution, we would have to write the following to implement this algorithm. This is rather less elegant than the previous version:

```
        cmp     r0,r1       @ Compare a == b
        bne     Test1       @ Not equal try next test
        add     r4,r4,#4    @ a == b so e = e+4
        b       ExitAll     @ Now leave
Test1:  blt     Test2       @ If a < b then
        add     r4,r4,#12   @ If we are here a > b so e = e + 12
        b       ExitAll     @ Now leave
Test2:  add     r4,r4,#7    @ If we are here a < b so e = e + 7
ExitAll:
```

In the next example, we use conditional execution to obtain the absolute value of a signed integer – that is, if the integer is negative, it is converted into the corresponding positive value. For example (in 8 bits), -2 is 11111110, which would be converted into 00000010 (i.e., +2).

We can use ARM's teq instruction **(test if equal)** that tests whether two values are equal. teq is similar to CMP, but teq does not set the V and C flags during the test. teq is useful to test for negative values *because the N-bit is set to 1 if the number tested is negative*:

```
        teq     r0,#0       @ Compare r0 with zero
        rsbmi   r0,r0,#0    @ If negative then 0 - [r0]
```

Here, the operand in r0 is tested, and the N-bit is set if it is negative and is clear if it is positive. The conditional instruction, rsbmi, is not executed if the tested operand was positive (no change is necessary). If the number was negative, the reverse substation performs 0 – r0, which reverses its sign and makes it positive.

Sequential conditional execution

Since a compare or an arithmetic operation updates the C, N, V, and Z bits, we can perform up to four conditional acts after one comparison. The following example converts uppercase ASCII-encoded characters to lowercase characters – for example, 'M' would be converted to 'm.' Bit 5 of an ASCII character is zero for uppercase letters and one for lowercase letters. Consider the code that first checks whether a character is in the range of 'A' to 'Z' and converts it to lowercase if it is:

```
cmp     r0,#'A'          @ Compare character with letter "A"
rsbges  r1,r0,#'Z'       @ Check less than Z if greater than A  Update flags
orrge   r0,r0,#0x20      @ If in "A" to "Z," then set bit 5 to force lowercase
```

The first instruction, cmp, checks whether the character is 'A' or greater by subtracting the ASCII code for 'A.' If it is, the rsbges checks that the character is less than 'Z.' This test is performed only if the character in r0 is greater or equal to 'A.' We use reverse subtraction because we want to test whether the ASCII code for Z minus the ASCII code for the character is positive. If we are in range, the conditional orr is executed, and an uppercase to lowercase conversion is performed by setting bit 5.

In the next chapter, we will look at how operands are specified – that is, we will look at addressing modes.

Summary

In this chapter, we've extended our knowledge of the ARM beyond the basic data-processing instructions we encountered in the previous chapter.

We began with the ARM's register set, which is different from almost every other processor. RISC processors generally have 32 general-purpose registers. The ARM has only 16 registers.

Two of the ARM's registers have a special purpose. Register r14 is called a *link register* and is used by the branch with link instructions to restore return addresses. Otherwise, it is a general-purpose register. Register r15 is the program counter, and that is very unusual indeed. This makes the ARM a very interesting device because you can change the program counter by operating on r15.

We also looked at shifting operations. Shifting simply involves bits moving one or more places left or right. However, as bits are in registers or memory locations, a shift involves bits moving into one and dropping out the other. The different types of shifts are determined by what happens to those bits that are shifted in or out at the ends of the number.

We discovered that the ARM has another unusual feature because it doesn't provide pure shift instructions. Instead, it can apply a shift to the second operand in a conventional data processing operation. The ARM can execute an `add r0,r1,r2, lsl r3` instruction that shifts the contents of register `r2` left by the value in `r3`. The shifted value is then added to `r1`, and the result is transferred to `r0`. This mechanism provides a *free shift* because you can do a shift and not have to pay any penalty to execute it.

Probably the most intriguing feature of the ARM is its ability to perform conditional execution – that is, before an instruction is executed, the condition code bits are checked. For example, `addeq r0,r1,r2` performs an addition only if the z-bit is set to 1. This is a very powerful operation, and you can use it to write compact code.

Sadly, it appears that conditional execution is a clever technique whose time has passed. It's not a cost-effective operation today. Conditional execution reduces the number of branches in a program and the number of clock cycles required to execute a program. Advances in computer technology have made conditional execution redundant in new CPU designs.

In the next chapter, we will look at the ARM's addressing modes – one of the highlights of this processor.

## 11

ARM Addressing Modes

Addressing modes are a fundamental part of computer architecture and are concerned with how you express the location of an operand. We introduced addressing modes in earlier chapters. Now, we will examine the ARM's rather sophisticated set of addressing modes.

The topics to be discussed are as follows:

- Literal addressing
- Scaled literals
- Register indirect addressing
- The use of two-pointer registers
- Auto-incrementing pointers

Literal addressing

The easiest addressing mode is *literal addressing*. Instead of saying where an operand is in memory, you provide the operand in an instruction (i.e., this is literally the value). Other addressing modes require you to specify where an operand is in memory. Consider the following Python expression, which has two literals, 30 and 12:

```
if A > 30: B = 12
```

We can express this fragment of Python in ARM assembly language as follows:

```
                        @ Register r0 is A and r1 is B
        cmp    r0,#30   @ Compare A with 30
        ble    Exit     @ If A ≤ 30, skip the next operation
        mov    r1,#12   @ else B = 12
Exit:
```

We can simplify this code by using conditional execution, as follows:

```
cmp    r0,#30      @ Compare A with 30
movgt  r1,#12      @ If A > 30, then B = 12
```

Scaled literals

The ARM implements 12-bit literals in an unusual way, using a technique borrowed from the world of floating-point arithmetic. Four of the 12 bits of a literal are used to scale an 8-bit constant. That is, the 8-bit constant is rotated right by twice the number in the 4-bit scaling field. The four most-significant bits of the literal field specify the literal's alignment within a 32-bit word. If the 8-bit immediate value is N and the 4-bit alignment is n, then the value of the literal is given by N rotated *right* by *2n* places. For example, if the 8-bit literal is 0xAB and n is 4, the resulting 32-bit literal is 0xAB000000 because of the eight-position right rotation (2 x 4). Remember that an eight rotate right position is equivalent to a 32 - 8 = 24 bit shift left. *Figure 11.1* demonstrates some 32-bit literals and the 12-bit literal codes that generate them.

Case	Value of 32-bit literal	Literal encoding	Rotate right	Rotate left	Code
a	00000000000000000000000 11010110	**0000** 11010110	0	0	0
b	0000000000000000000 11010110 0000	**1110** 11010110	28	4	E
c	00000000000000 11010110 0000000000	**1011** 11010110	22	10	B
d	11010110 00000000000000000000000	**0100** 11010110	8	24	4

4-bit literal alignment field determines the number of right rotations. This is doubled to give the shift value.

8-bit literal to be rotated

Figure 11.1 – ARM's literal operand encoding

You might find this rather strange. Why didn't ARM use the 12-bit literal field to provide a number in the range 0 to 4,095, rather than a number in the range 0 to 255 scaled by the power of 2? The answer is that ARM's designers determined that the scaled literals were more useful in real-world applications than unscaled numbers. For example, suppose you wanted to clear all bits of a 32-bit word, except bits 8 to 15. You would need to AND it with the literal 0b00000000000000001111111100000000 or 0x0000FF00 in hexadecimal. Using the scaling mechanism, we can take 8 bits 0x11111111 and shift them left by 8 bits (i.e., right by 24 bits) to get the required constant. However, the scaling factor n needs twice the number of rotation rights to achieve this. That is (32 − 8)/2, which is 12. Consequently, the literal stored in the 12-bit instruction field is 12,255, or CFF in hexadecimal.

Fortunately, calculating the scaling factor is something the programmer does not always have to worry about. ARM compilers take a constant and automatically generate the best instruction(s) necessary to generate it.

Register indirect addressing

We have already encountered this addressing mode where the location of an operand is held in a register. It is called register *indirect addressing* because the instruction specifies the register where a pointer to the actual operand can be found. In ARM literature, this addressing mode is called *indexed addressing*. Some people call this *base addressing*.

Register indirect addressing mode requires three read operations to access an operand:

- Read the instruction to find the pointer register
- Read the pointer register to find the operand address
- Read memory at the operand address to find the operand

Register indirect addressing is important because the contents of the register containing the pointer to the actual operand can be modified at runtime, and therefore, the address is a variable. Consequently, we can step through data structures such as tables by changing the pointer.

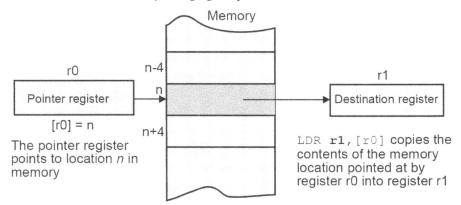

Figure 11.2 – Register indirect addressing – executing ldr r1,[r0]

Figure 11.2 illustrates the effect of ldr **r1**, [r0], where r0 is the pointer and contains the value n.

ldr **r1**, [r0] loads the contents of the memory location pointed at by register r0 into register r1.

Executing add **r0**, r0, #4 increments the contents of the pointer register r0 by 4 to point at the next word location (remember that consecutive word addresses differ by 4).

Consider the following:

```
ldr  r1, [r0]              @ Get data pointed at by r0
add  r0,r0,#4              @ Advance pointer to next word location
```

The first instruction loads r1 with the 32-bit word pointed at by r0. The second instruction increments r0 by 4 to point at the next byte in memory. Repeating this pair of instructions will allow you to step through a table of values, element by element. We will soon see that the ARM includes a mechanism to automatically increment or decrement the pointer.

The next fragment of code demonstrates how you would add together the elements of a table. Suppose that you have a table of daily expenditures you have made over four weeks. Each item is stored consecutively in a table with 4 x 7 = 28 entries:

```
         adr  r0,table         @ r0 points to the table of data (pseudo-instruction)
         add  r3,r0,#28 * 4    @ r3 points to the end of the table (28 x 4 bytes)
         mov  r1,#0            @ Clear the sum in r1
loop:    ldr  r2,[r0]          @ REPEAT: Get the next value in r2
         add  r1,r1,r2         @ Add the new value to the running total
         add  r0,r0,#4         @ Point to the next location in the table (4 bytes increment)
         cmp  r0,r3            @ Are we at the end of the table?
         bne  loop             @ UNTIL all elements added

table:   .word 123             @ Data for day 1
         .word 456             @ Data for day 2

         .word 20              @ Data for day 28
```

In this simple example, we set up a loop and step through elements from the first to the last. On each cycle, we read an element and add it to the total. The shaded lines are where the action takes place – getting an element and pointing to the next one.

The next example demonstrates both pointer-based indirect addressing and byte operations (i.e., operations on an 8-bit value rather than a full word). Suppose we want to find a given character within a string. The following code uses a *byte load instruction*, ldrb, which loads 8 bits into the destination register. We increment the pointer by 1 as we step through the string, not 4, because the values are on one-byte boundaries:

```
         ldr    r0,=String     @ r0 points at the string (using a pseudo-instruction)
loop:    ldrb   r1,[r0]        @ REPEAT Read a byte character
         add    r0,r0,#1       @ Update character pointer by 1 (not by 4)
         cmp    r1,#Term       @ UNTIL terminator found
         bne    loop
```

Pointer-based addressing with an offset

Suppose someone asks you, *"Where's the pharmacy?"* You might reply, *"It's two blocks to the left of the bank."* That's pointer-based offset addressing in everyday life. We point to the bank by giving its location in relation to something else.

The ARM allows you to specify an address using a pointer register, plus a 12-bit literal that supplies the offset. Note that this is a true 12-bit literal rather than the 8-bit scaled value used as a literal operand. The literal can be positive or negative (indicating that it's to be added to or subtracted from the base pointer). Consider `ldr r5, [r2, #160]`, where the address of the operand loaded into `r5` is the contents of `r1` plus 160.

Suppose you wanted to move a block of 24 words to a location that is 128 bytes further on in memory. Assume that the address of the block to move is at `0x400`. We can write the following:

```
        mov    r0,#0x400      @ r0 points to the block of data
        ldr    r1,#24         @ r1 contains the number of words to move
next:   ldr    r2,[r0]        @ REPEAT: Read word and put in r2
        add    r0,r0,#4       @ Point to next word
        str    r2,[r0,#128]   @ Store the word 128 bytes on
        subs   r1,#1          @ Decrement the counter and set the status bits
        bne    next           @ UNTIL all elements added
```

Unfortunately, you cannot run this directly on an ARM-based Raspberry Pi as we described because you are not allowed to modify memory in a code segment. That is an operating system limitation. To avoid this problem, you have to use pointers, as we demonstrated in *Chapter 9*. We will return to this point.

Two pointers are better than one

The register-indirect addressing mode lets you access elements in a linear data structure, such as a one-column table. Sometimes, you will have a more complex two-dimensional data structure, such as a matrix with rows and columns. In that case, two pointers can simplify programming – one pointer for the row and one for the column.

ARM provides a pointer-based addressing mode that allows you to specify an address that is the sum of two pointer registers, such as the following:

```
ldr  r7, [r0,r1]            @ Load r7 with the contents of the location pointed at by r0 plus r1
```

You can apply a shift to the second operand, such as the following:

```
ldr  r2, [r0,r1,lsl #3]     @ Load r7 with the contents of the location pointed at by r0 plus r1 x 8
```

In this case, register `r1` is scaled by 8. The scaling factor must be a power of 2 (i.e., 2, 4, 8, 16…).

Figure 11.3 illustrates pointer-based addressing with two index registers.

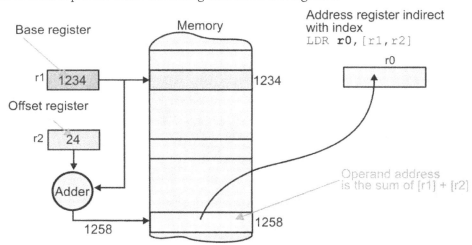

Figure 11.3 – Indexed addressing with a register offset – ldr r0,[r1,r2]

This is conceptual because we've shown one register pointing at memory (r1) and one register providing an offset from r1 (i.e., r2). However, since the final address is r1 plus r2, we could have drawn it the other way around.

Automatic indexing of pointer registers

When pointer registers are used, they are frequently used to step through data structures and are often incremented or decremented after every memory access. It would, therefore, make sense to include this action as part of the instruction.

Indeed, CISC processors invariably include automatic indexing. When RISC processors arrived with their *one instruction per clock cycle goal*, automatic indexing was dropped from the instruction set. However, this mechanism has been incorporated into ARM architecture.

ARM's automatic indexing has four variations. You can do it before using a pointer or after using a pointer. You can index up toward higher addresses or down toward lower addresses. Consider the following operations involving an index register, r0, and an increment of 4 (for one word on a byte-addressed machine). Each option is composed of a memory access and a pointer adjust action; in the first two cases, the pointer is adjusted first (pre-indexing), and in the other two cases, memory is accessed first (post-indexing). Memory accesses are given in bold:

Indexing type	First action	Second action
Pre-indexed up	[r1] ← [r1] + 4	**[r0] ← [[r1]]**
Pre-indexed down	[r1] ← [r1] - 4	**[r0] ← [[r1]]**
Post-indexed up	**[r0] ← [[r1]]**	[r1] ← [r1] + 4
Post-indexed down	**[r0] ← [[r1]]**	[r1] ← [r1] - 4

ARM indicates pre-indexing by including the offset within square brackets and appending an exclamation mark, such as the following:

```
str r4, [r0,#4]!     @ Store r4 at the address given by [r0] + 4 and then increment r0 by 4
```

The value of the pointer r0 changes *BEFORE* it is used as an offset. Let's suppose we wish to use post-indexing and increment the pointer *AFTER* it is used. In this case, the format is as follows:

```
str r4, [r0],#4     @ Store r4 at the address given by [r0] and then increment r0 by 4.
```

Here, the value of the pointer r0 changes *AFTER* it is used as an offset.

Figures 11.4 to *11.6* illustrate ARM's variations on indexed addressing. In each case, the base register is r1, the offset is 12, and the destination register is r0. These figures are summarized here:

Figure	Type	Format	Base reg before	Base reg after	Operand address
11.4	Reg indirect	ldr **r0**,[r1,#12]	[r1]	[r1]	[r1] + 12
11.5	Pre-indexed	ldr **r0**,[r1,#12]!	[r1]	[r1] + 12	[r1] + 12
11.6	Post-indexing	ldr **r0**,[r1],#12	[r1]	[r1] + 12	[r1]

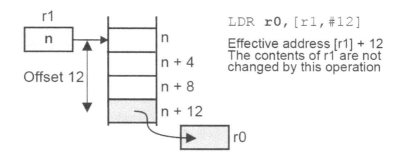

Figure 11.4 – Register indirect addressing with an offset

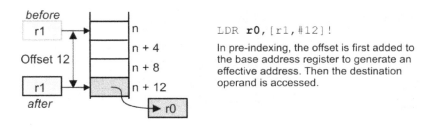

Figure 11.5 – Register indirect addressing with pre-indexing

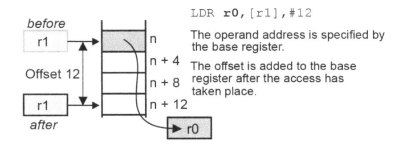

Figure 11.6 – Register indirect addressing with post-indexing

Consider the following example where we use post-indexing to move a block of data from one memory region to another. In this case, we use post-indexing by four because we move 4-byte words:

```
        adr   r0,table1      @ Source array pointer in r0. Use pseudo instruction
        adr   r1,table2      @ Destination array pointer in r1
        mov   r2,#8          @ Eight elements (words) to move
loop:   ldr   r3,[r0],#4     @ REPEAT: Get element from table 1 (post-indexing by 4)
        str   r3,[r1],#4     @ Store in table 2 (post-indexing 4)
        subs  r2,r2,#1       @ Decrement counter
        bne   loop           @ UNTIL all done
```

The two key lines of this program are the load and store instructions (shaded), where data is read from the source and copied to the destination. As we have stated, you can't run this code *directly* on Raspberry Pi without modification because of the way in which the memory space is allocated to variables. The following code demonstrates a runnable version for Raspberry Pi.

This is, essentially, the same code. As well as dealing with the memory problem, we've added assembly directives and dummy data (complete with markers that allow you to observe data in memory more easily). There's also a nop instruction. Note that some versions of ARM have a true nop and some use a pseudo-instruction. I added this as a dummy instruction to *"land on"* while testing. Remember that the address of the actual data is stored in the program area, and then a pointer is loaded with that address:

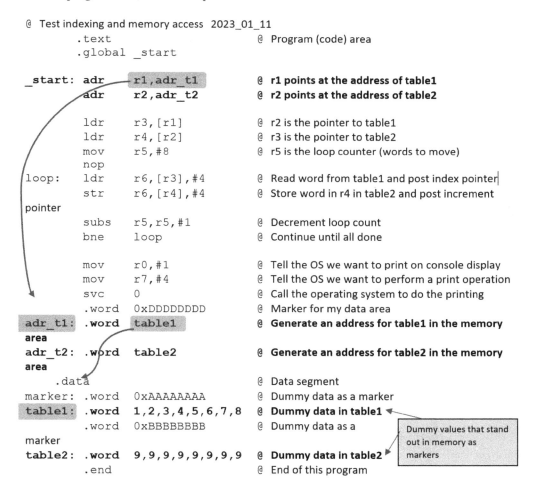

```
@  Test indexing and memory access  2023_01_11
            .text                       @  Program (code) area
            .global  _start

_start:  adr      r1,adr_t1              @  r1 points at the address of table1
         adr      r2,adr_t2              @  r2 points at the address of table2

         ldr      r3,[r1]                @  r2 is the pointer to table1
         ldr      r4,[r2]                @  r3 is the pointer to table2
         mov      r5,#8                  @  r5 is the loop counter (words to move)
         nop
loop:    ldr      r6,[r3],#4             @  Read word from table1 and post index pointer
         str      r6,[r4],#4             @  Store word in r4 in table2 and post increment
pointer
         subs     r5,r5,#1               @  Decrement loop count
         bne      loop                   @  Continue until all done

         mov      r0,#1                  @  Tell the OS we want to print on console display
         mov      r7,#4                  @  Tell the OS we want to perform a print operation
         svc      0                      @  Call the operating system to do the printing
         .word    0xDDDDDDDD             @  Marker for my data area
adr_t1:  .word    table1                 @  Generate an address for table1 in the memory
area
adr_t2:  .word    table2                 @  Generate an address for table2 in the memory
area
            .data                        @  Data segment
marker:  .word    0xAAAAAAAA             @  Dummy data as a marker
table1:  .word    1,2,3,4,5,6,7,8        @  Dummy data in table1
         .word    0xBBBBBBBB             @  Dummy data as a
marker                                                             Dummy values that stand
                                                                   out in memory as
table2:  .word    9,9,9,9,9,9,9,9        @  Dummy data in table2   markers
            .end                         @  End of this program
```

Figure 11.7 – The use of pointers when accessing read/write memory

We ran the preceding program using gbd as a debugging tool, as the following output demonstrates. In order to condense the text, we've removed unnecessary data from the display – for example, registers that are not accessed or modified.

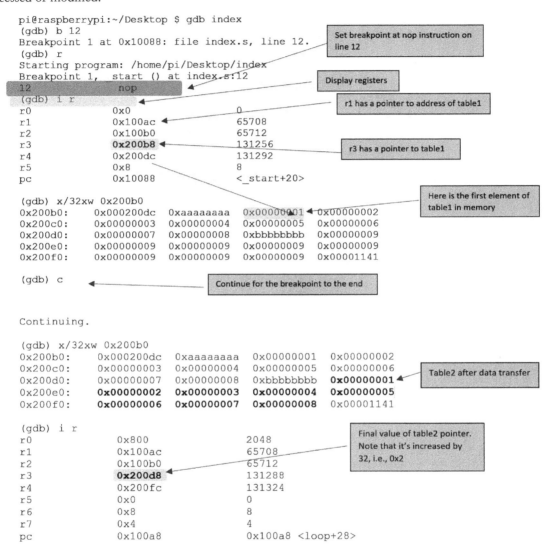

```
pi@raspberrypi:~/Desktop $ gdb index
(gdb) b 12
Breakpoint 1 at 0x10088: file index.s, line 12.          Set breakpoint at nop instruction on
(gdb) r                                                  line 12
Starting program: /home/pi/Desktop/index
Breakpoint 1,  start () at index.s:12
12              nop                                      Display registers
(gdb) i r
r0              0x0                   0                   r1 has a pointer to address of table1
r1              0x100ac               65708
r2              0x100b0               65712
r3              0x200b8               131256              r3 has a pointer to table1
r4              0x200dc               131292
r5              0x8                   8
pc              0x10088               <_start+20>

                                                         Here is the first element of
(gdb) x/32xw 0x200b0                                     table1 in memory
0x200b0:        0x000200dc  0xaaaaaaaa  0x00000001  0x00000002
0x200c0:        0x00000003  0x00000004  0x00000005  0x00000006
0x200d0:        0x00000007  0x00000008  0xbbbbbbbb  0x00000009
0x200e0:        0x00000009  0x00000009  0x00000009  0x00000009
0x200f0:        0x00000009  0x00000009  0x00000009  0x00001141

(gdb) c                                      Continue for the breakpoint to the end



Continuing.

(gdb) x/32xw 0x200b0
0x200b0:        0x000200dc  0xaaaaaaaa  0x00000001  0x00000002
0x200c0:        0x00000003  0x00000004  0x00000005  0x00000006
0x200d0:        0x00000007  0x00000008  0xbbbbbbbb  0x00000001       Table2 after data transfer
0x200e0:        0x00000002  0x00000003  0x00000004  0x00000005
0x200f0:        0x00000006  0x00000007  0x00000008  0x00001141

(gdb) i r                                            Final value of table2 pointer.
r0              0x800                 2048           Note that it's increased by
r1              0x100ac               65708          32, i.e., 0x2
r2              0x100b0               65712
r3              0x200d8               131288
r4              0x200fc               131324
r5              0x0                   0
r6              0x8                   8
r7              0x4                   4
pc              0x100a8               0x100a8 <loop+28>
```

Figure 11.8 – Using gdb to trace the program of Figure 11.7

Example of string-copying

The next example, *Figure 11.9*, uses post-indexing to copy a string from one place to another in reverse order by moving one pointer down and the other up. The destination pointer is incremented by `len-1` to point to the end of the string, initially. The following code includes assembly language directives, enabling it to run on the RPi:

```
            .equ      len,5               @ Length of string to reverse
            .text                         @ Program (code) area
            .global _start

_start:     mov       r0,#len             @ Number of characters to move
            adr       r1,adr_st1          @ r1 points at source address 1
            adr       r2,adr_st2          @ r2 points at source address 2

            ldr       r1,[r1]             @ Register r1 points to source
            ldr       r2,[r2]             @ Register r2 points to destination
            add       r2,r2,#len-1        @ r2 points to bottom of destination
Loop:       ldrb      r3,[r1],#1          @ Get char from source, increment pointer (note ldbr)
            strb      r3,[r2],#-1         @ Store char in destination, decrement pointer
            subs      r0,r0,#1            @ Decrement char count
            bne       Loop                @ REPEAT until all done

            nop                           @ Stop here
adr_st1:    .word     str1
adr_st2:    .word     str2
            .data
str1:       .ascii    "Hello"             @ Source string
str2:       .byte     0,0,0,0,0           @ Destination string
            .end
```

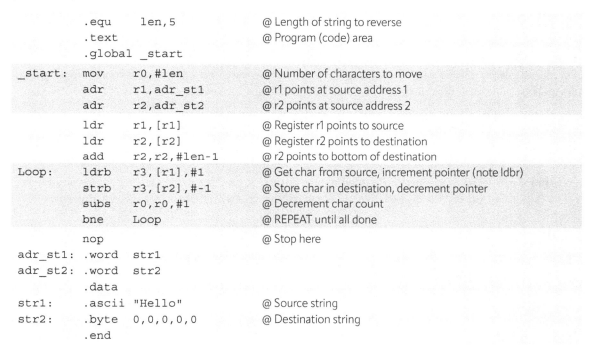
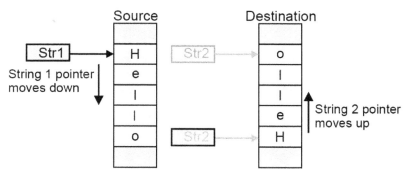

Figure 11.9 – Reversing a string

The next section looks at a variation of pointer-based addressing where the pointer is the program counter itself. Consequently, all data and programs are referenced to the location of the current program.

Program counter-relative addressing

The ARM is an unusual processor in so many ways. You can use any register (i.e., r0 to r15) as a pointer register. However, r15 is the ARM's program counter. If you use r15 as a pointer register with an index, you are saying, "*The operand is at this distance from where I am.*" Here the "*where I am*" refers to the instruction itself. *Figure 11.10* illustrates program counter-relative addressing.

Think about it. You give the address of data with respect to the program that's using it and not an absolute address in memory. If you move the program in memory, the data is still the same distance from the instructions that access it, using program counter-relative addressing. The introduction of program counter relative addressing was one of the major advances in computer architecture. By the way, most branch instructions use program counter relative addressing because the destination of a branch is specified with respect to the current instruction.

The ARM uses program counter relative addressing to load 32-bit constants. Recall that you can load only 12-bit constants with the ldr instruction. However, the assembler can pre-load a 32-bit constant in memory and then use program counter relative addressing to access it. In other words, you dump a 32-value in memory near (or within) the program and then access it using program counter relative addressing. This is the reason for pseudo-instructions. Without pseudo-instructions, you'd have to calculate the relative address between the current pc and the desired operand. Pseudo-instructions do that and make the address invisible to the programmer.

Executing ldr r0, [r15,#0x100] loads a 32-bit operand that is 0x100 bytes (0x40 or 64 words) from the contents of register r15, the program counter. The operand loaded into r0 is 0x108 bytes from the pc. Why 0x108 and not 0x100, as specified in the instruction? The additional 8 bytes are there because the program counter is incremented by 8 bytes after each instruction and, therefore, runs 8 bytes ahead of the current address.

What about program counter relative store instructions? These cannot be used. Store operations using the program counter addressing mode are not supported in the ARM. This restriction is probably because (a) a lot of code is in read-only memory and can't be changed, and (b) it would allow the modification of runtime programs.

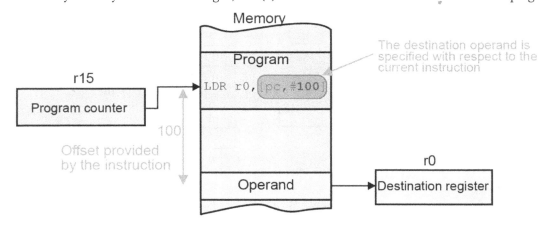

Figure 11.10 – Program counter relative addressing

Demonstration of program counter relative addressing

Consider the following text where we use two types of pseudo-instruction, both of which are designed to load a 32-bit value into a register. One is adr (load an address) and the other ldr (load a 32-bit literal):

```
        .text
        .global    _start
_start: ldr r0,=pqr
        ldr r1,=abc              @ Note the special format of the pseudo ldr
        adr r2,pqr
        ldr r3,=0x11111111

        nop
        mov r0,#0
        mov r7,#1
        svc 0
abc:    .word 0x22222222
pqr:    .word 0x33333333
        .end
```

There are three ldr instructions. Two load addresses into registers and the third, ldr, loads a 32-bit literal 0x11111111. There is an adr instruction that loads a 32-bit address into register r2. What happens when these codes are executed?

First, let's look at the source code when viewed in gdb:

```
0x10054 <_start>       ldr r0, [pc, #32]    ; 0x1007c <pqr+4>
0x10058 <_start+4>     ldr r1, [pc, #32]    ; 0x10080 <pqr+8>
0x1005c <_start+8>
0x10060 <_start+12>    ldr r3, [pc, #28]    ; 0x10084 <pqr+12>
```

Note that these differ from the source code. That's because the source code uses pseudo-instructions that are translated. For example, ldr r0,=pqr is translated into ldr r0, [pc,#32]. The source code cannot specify a 32-bit instruction. However, the translated version used a conventional load to specify the location of the actual operand 32 bits for the current value of the program counter.

add r2,pc,#20 is treated differently. Here, the 32-bit literal is generated by adding 20 to the value of the current pc, because the address to be located is 20 bytes from the current PC value.

Let's look at the registers when the code is executed up to nop using gdb. We will examine both the contents of the registers at the end of the program and then look at the memory locations. You can see the data stored in memory and the constants accessed by program counter relative addressing:

```
r0              0x00010078
r1              0x00010074
r2              0x00010078
```

```
r3                 0x11111111

(gdb)  x/8xw 0x10074
0x10074 <abc>:         0x22222222    0x33333333    0x00010078    0x00010074
0x10084 <pqr+12>:      0x11111111    0x00001141    0x61656100    0x00010069
```

In the next chapter, we will continue the theme of addressing, looking at how the ARM implements subroutines and how you can use the stack to keep track of subroutine return addresses.

Summary

Addressing modes comprise all the ways to express the location of an item in memory. Addressing modes are simultaneously the easiest and most difficult topic in assembly language programming. The concept is simple, but indirect addressing modes that use pointers may take some effort to visualize.

In this chapter, we learned about literal or immediate addressing where an operand is an actual value (it's the thing itself and not the location). Literal values are used to specify constants – for example, in x + 5, the number 5 is a literal. This is the simplest of addressing modes, and no memory location is accessed because the data is part of the instruction.

We also looked at the ARM's rather unusual way of specifying literals, by providing a value in the range of 0 to 255 and a multiplier that can multiply it by an even power of 2. You can specify 5 and store 5, 20, 80, and so on.

Much of this chapter was taken up by register indirect addressing, which has a lot of other names (indexed and pointer-based). In this case, the address is given by the contents of a register. The instruction specifies not the actual address of an operand but the register that points to it. Because you can manipulate data in a register, you can manipulate addresses and access data structures such as arrays and tables.

The ARM provides RISC-style auto-incrementing and decrementing. That means you can use a pointer and increment it or decrement it beforehand (or after it is used).

We also looked at a special form of register indirect addressing, relative addressing, where the pointer is the program counter itself – that is, the address of an operand is specified with respect to the instruction that accesses it. This means that code using program counter relative addressing can be moved around in memory without any addresses being recalculated.

In the next chapter, we will look at a topic that is fundamental to programming – the subroutine and the stack. This topic is also heavily related to addressing modes.

12

Subroutines and the Stack

A subroutine is a piece of code that is called from a point within a program and executed, and then a return is made to the instruction after the calling point. All computers use subroutines, but some computers provide a programmer with more facilities to implement subroutines than others.

In this chapter, we will look at the ARM's subroutine handling mechanisms – in particular, the following:

- The special branch and link instruction
- The stack
- A subroutine call and return
- Block move instructions

The Branch with link instruction

First, we discuss the ARM's *branch and link* instruction, `bl`, which provides a quick and easy way to call a subroutine without using a stack mechanism.

There are two basic ways of implementing subroutine calls and returns. The classic CISC approach is `BSR` (branch to subroutine) and `RTS` (return from subroutine). The typical code might be as follows:

```
        bsr abc         @ Call the subroutine on the line labeled abc
        .  .  .
        .  .  .


abc:    .  .  .         @ Subroutine abc entry point
        .  .  .
        rts             @ Subroutine abc return to calling point
```

This is simplicity in action. You call a piece of code, execute it, and return to the instruction after the calling point. Most RISC processors reject this mechanism because the subroutine call and return are complex instructions that save the return address on the stack during a call, and then pull the return address off the stack during a return. This is very convenient for a programmer but requires several CPU clock cycles to execute, and it does not fit into the one-cycle-per-instruction paradigm of the RISC processor.

The great advantage of the stack-based subroutine call/return is that you can nest subroutines and call subroutines from other subroutines, and the stack mechanism automatically deals with return addresses.

You will soon see that you can implement this mechanism yourself on an ARM, but not by using two dedicated instructions. You have to write your own code.

If you want a simple subroutine call and return (the subroutine is called a *leaf*), all you need to do is save the return address in a register (no external memory or stack is required). Then, to return, you just put the return address in the program counter – simple and fast. However, once you are in the subroutine, you can't do the same thing again and call another subroutine. Doing that would destroy your existing saved return address.

The ARM's subroutine mechanism is called *branch with link* and has the mnemonic `bl target`, where `target` is the symbolic address of the subroutine. The actual address is program counter-relative and is a 24-bit signed word that gives you a branch range of 2^{23} words from the current PC. The range is 2^{23} words in either direction from the PC (i.e., branch forward and branch back).

The branch with link instruction behaves like a branch instruction, but it also copies the return address (i.e., the address of the next instruction to be executed following a return into the link register `r14`. Let's say you execute the following:

```
bl      sub_A               @ Branch to sub_A with link and save return address in r14
```

The ARM executes a branch to the target address specified by the label `sub_A`. It also copies the program counter, held in register `r15`, into the link register `r14` to preserve the return address. At the end of the subroutine, you return by transferring the return address in `r14` to the program counter. You don't need a special return instruction; you just write the following:

```
mov     pc,lr               @ We can also write this as mov r15,r14
```

Let's look at a simple example of the use of a subroutine. Suppose that you need to evaluate the `if x > 0 then x = 16x + 1 else x = 32x` function several times in a program. Assuming that the x parameter is in register `r0`, we can write the following subroutine:

```
Func1:  cmp     r0,#0           @ Test for x > 0
        movgt   r0,r0, lsl #4   @ If x > 0 then x = 16x
        addgt   r0,r0,#1        @ If x > 0 then x = 16x + 1
        movle   r0,r0, lsl #5   @ ELSE if x < 0 THEN x = 32x
        mov     pc,lr           @ Return by restoring saved PC
```

All you need to create a subroutine is an entry point (the label `Func1`) and a return point that restores the saved address by bl in the link register.

The stack

We've already described the stack. We'll go over it again here because it's probably the single most important data structure in computing. The stack is a pile that you add things on at the top and take things off, also from the top. If you take something off the stack, it is the last thing that was added to the stack. Consequently, the stack is called a **last in first out queue** (**LIFO**), in which items enter at one end and leave in the reverse order.

Computers implement stacks by using a pointer register to point at the top of the stack. The ARM uses r13 as a stack pointer, or, to be precise, the ARM *mandates* the use of r13 as a stack pointer. You can use r0 to r13 as a stack pointer if you wish. The use of r13 is a *convention* designed to make code more readable and sharable.

There are four variations of the stack. They all do the same thing but are implemented differently. The ARM supports all four variations, but we'll use only one here for the sake of simplicity. A stack is stored in memory, which has no up or down in the normal human sense. When items are added to the stack, they can be added to the next location with a lower address or the next location with a higher address. By convention, most stacks are implemented so that the next item is stored at the *lower address*. We say that the stack grows *up* toward *lower* addresses (that's because we number lines in a book from top to bottom, with line one at the top).

The other variation in the arrangement of stacks is that the stack pointer can either point to the top item on the stack, TOS, or point to the next free item on that stack. I will cover stacks where the stack pointer points to the top item on the stack (again, this is the most common convention).

Figure 12.1 illustrates a stack used to save subroutine return addresses.

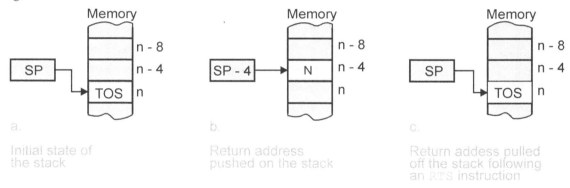

Figure 12.1 – Using the stack to save a return address, N

The stack pointer points at the top item on the stack, and when an item is added to the stack (pushed), the stack pointer is first decremented. When an item is removed from the stack, it is taken at the location indicated by the stack pointer, and the stack pointer is incremented (i.e., moved down). We can define the push and pull (pop) actions with relation to the **stack pointer** (**SP**) as follows:

```
PUSH:   [SP]    ← [SP] - 4      @ Move stack pointer up one word (up toward lower addresses)
        [[SP]]  ← data          @ Push data onto the stack. Push uses pre-decrementing.

PULL:   data    ← [[SP]]        @ Pull data off the stack by reading TOS
        [SP]    ← [SP] + 4      @ Move stack pointer down one word (pull uses post-incrementing)
```

The stack pointer is decremented and incremented by four, since we follow the ARM convention that the memory is byte-addressed and stack items are one-word long (four bytes). The next section looks in greater detail at how a subroutine is called and an orderly return is made to the calling point.

A subroutine call and return

To call a subroutine, you push the return address on the stack. CISC processors implement a subroutine call with `bsr target`. Because the ARM lacks a subroutine call instruction, you can write the following ARM code. Remember that we are dealing with 32-bit word push and pulls, and the stack must be incremented or decremented by four. Remember that r15 and SP and r13 and lr are interchangeable terms in ARM literature:

```
        sub   r13,r13,#4        @ Pre-decrement the stack pointer (r13 is used as the SP)
        str   r15,[r13]         @ Push the return address in r15 on the stack
        b     Target            @ Jump to the target address
        . . .                   @ Return here
```

There's no ARM subroutine return instruction, so you implement one with the following:

```
        ldr   r12, [r13],#+4    @ Get saved PC from stack and post-increment the stack pointer
        mov   r15,r12           @ Load PC with return address
```

The following is a simple program that sets up a call and return using this mechanism. Note that we don't set up the initial stack pointer. The ARM's operating system does that:

```
.section .text
.global _start

_start: mov   r0,#9            @ Dummy operation
        sub   sp,sp,#4         @ Decrement stack
        str   pc,[sp]          @ Save pc on stack
        b     target           @ Branch to subroutine "target"
        mov   r2,#0xFFFFFFFF   @ Return here ... this is a marker
        nop                    @ Dummy operation
        mov   r7,#1            @ Set up exit code
        svc   0               @ Leave program

target: mov   r1,#0xFF         @ Subroutine ... dummy operation
        ldr   r12,[sp],#+4    @ Pull pc off the stack
        mov   r15,r12          @ Return
        .end
```

Figure 12.2 demonstrates the output of the ARM simulator after running this code. We have included the disassembly window and the register windows. Note how the mov **r2**,#0xFFFFFFFF instruction has been transformed into the mvn **r2**,#0 operation. Recall that MVN **(move negative)** moves a literal to a register and inverts its bits. Note also how ldr r12,[sp],#+ has been renamed pop {r12}. This is equivalent to the pop stack operation (removing an item from the top of the stack).

Registers after execution of the code:

```
Register group: general
r0            0x9                    9
r1            0xff                   255
r2            0xffffffff             4294967295
r12           0x10064                65636
sp            0xbefff380             0xbefff380
lr            0x0                    0
pc            0x1006c                0x1006c <_start+24>
```

The following is an execution of the code step by step. This is an example of a subroutine call and return:

```
B+ 0x10054 <_start>        mov    r0, #9
   0x10058 <_start+4>      sub    sp, sp, #4
   0x1005c <_start+8>      str    pc, [sp]
   0x10060 <_start+12>     b      0x10074 <target>
   0x10064 <_start+16>     mvn    r2, #0
   0x10068 <_start+20>     nop                          ; (mov r0, r0)
  ^0x1006c <_start+24>     mov    r7, #1
   0x10070 <_start+28>     svc    0x00000000
   0x10074 <target>        mov    r1, #255      ; 0xff
   0x10078 <target+4>      pop    {r12}         ; (ldr r12, [sp], #4)
   0x1007c <target+8>      mov    pc, r12
```

In the next section, we will look at one of the ARM's most powerful and least RISC-like operations – the ability to move blocks of data between memory and multiple registers.

Block move instructions

In this section, we will learn how multiple registers can be moved. The fundamental concepts are as follows:

- How to specify a group of registers
- How to address memory
- How to sequence the storage of registers
- The different types of block moves

A great feature of some CISC processors was that you could push a group of registers on the stack in a single instruction. RISC processors generally don't have such an instruction because it conflicts with the one-operation-per-cycle design constraint that's at the heart of the RISC philosophy. Surprisingly, the ARM implements a block move instruction that lets you copy a group of registers to or from memory in one operation (i.e., an instruction). The following ARM code demonstrates how to load registers r1,r2,r3,r5 from memory:

```
adr   r0,DataToGo      @ Load r0 with the address of the data area
ldr   r1,[r0],#4       @ Load r1 with the word pointed at by r0 and update the pointer
ldr   r2,[r0],#4       @ Load r2 with the word pointed at by r0 and update the pointer
ldr   r3,[r0],#4       @ and so forth for the remaining registers r3 and r5...
ldr   r5,[r0],#4
```

ARM has a *block move to memory* instruction, stm, and a *block move from memory*, ldm, that copies groups of registers to and from memory. Block move instructions require a two-character suffix to describe how the data is accessed (e.g., stm**ia** or ldm**db**), as we shall see.

Conceptually, a block move is easy to understand because it is simply a *copy the contents of these registers to memory* operation, or vice versa. In practice, it is more complex. ARM provides a full set of options that determine how the move takes place – for example, whether the registers are moved from high-to-low or low-to-high memory addresses, or whether the memory pointer is updated before or after a transfer (just like a stack structure). In fact, block moves are just like the push and pull stack operations found on other computers.

Let's move the contents of registers r1, r2, r3, and r5 into sequential memory locations with stm:

```
stmia   r0!,{r1-r3,r5}    @ Note block move syntax. The register list is in braces
                          @ r0! is the destination register with auto indexing
                          @ The register list is {r1-r3,r5} r1,r2,r3,r5
```

This instruction copies registers r1 to r3, and r5 into sequential memory locations, using r0 as a pointer register with auto-indexing (indicated by the ! suffix). The **ia** suffix indicates that the index register r0 is incremented *after* each transfer, with data transfer in order of *ascending* addresses. We'll also see that this instruction can be written as stm**fd** (which is the same operation, but ARM provides two naming conventions for the same thing in their documentation).

Although ARM's block move mode instructions have several variations, the lowest numbered register is always stored at the lowest address, followed by the next lowest numbered register at the next higher address, and so on (e.g., r1, then r2, r3, and r5 in the preceding example).

Consider the following example of the block move. Because it's a little more complicated than some instructions we've encountered, we will demonstrate its execution. I've included several features that are not strictly part of the demonstration but include features I use when experimenting. In particular, I use markers in both registers and memory so that I can follow debugging more easily. For example, in the memory block, I store the data words 0xFFFFFFFF and 0xAAAAAAAA. These serve no function other than to show me, at a glance, where my data area starts and stops when I debug memory. Similarly, I use values such as `0x11111111` as words to move from registers because I can easily follow them in debugging:

```
                .text                   @ This is a code section
                .global _start          @ Define entry point for code execution
    _start:     nop                     @ nop = no operation and is a dummy instruction
                ldr     r0,=0xFFFFFFFF   @ Dummy values for testing
                ldr     r1,=0x11111111
                ldr     r2,=0x22222222
                ldr     r3,=0x33333333
                ldr     r4,=0x44444444
                ldr     r5,=0x55555555
                ldr     r0,adr_mem       @ Load pointer r0 with memory
                stmia   r0!,{r1-r3,r5}   @ Do a multiple load to memory
                mov     r10,r0           @ Save r0 in r10 (for debugging)
                ldmdb   r0!,{r6-r9}      @ Now load data from memory
                mov     r11,r0
                mov     r1,#1            @ Terminate command
                svc     0                @ Call OS to leave
                .word   0xFFFFFFFF       @ A dummy value for testing
                .word   0xAAAAAAAA       @ Another dummy value
    adr_mem:    .word   memory           @ The address of the memory for storing data
                .data                    @ Declare a memory segment for the data
    memory:     .word   0xBBBBBBBB       @ Yet another memory marker
                .space  32               @ Reserve space for storage (8 words)
                .word   0xCCCCCCCC       @ Final memory marker
                .end
```

This code sets up five registers with data that is easily visible when examining memory. Thirty-two bytes of memory are saved between two word markers at the end of the program with the `.space` directive. The start of this block is labeled `memory`, and `r0` points to it. Then the five registers are stored in memory. Instructions that carry out the block store are shaded in light gray, and the data area is shaded in dark gray.

The code we are initially interested in is for the five register loads that preset registers `r1` to `r5` with `0x11111111` to `0x55555555`, respectively. Register `r0` was set initially to `0xFFFFFFFF` just as a marker for debugging. The key instruction is **`stmia r0!,{r1-r3,r5}`**, whose purpose is to store the contents of registers `r1`, `r2`, `r3`, and `r5` in consecutive memory locations pointed at by `r0`.

The following Raspberry Pi output is from the `gdb` debugger. The source code is `blockMove1.s`. We've omitted some of the register values to make the listing more readable when registers haven't changed or haven't been used. Similarly, repetitive command lines have been omitted:

```
pi@raspberrypi:~/Desktop $ as -g -o blockMove1.o blockMove1.s
pi@raspberrypi:~/Desktop $ ld -o blockMove1 blockMove1.o
pi@raspberrypi:~/Desktop $ gdb blockMove1
```

```
(gdb) b 1
Breakpoint 1 at 0x10078: file blockMove1.s, line 6.
(gdb) r
Starting program: /home/pi/Desktop/blockMove1
Breakpoint 1, _start () at blockMove1.s:6
6              ldr    r0,=0xFFFFFFFF        @ Dummy value for testing
(gdb) i r
r0             0x0                  0          # These are the initial registers before we start
r1             0x0                  0
r2             0x0                  0
r3             0x0                  0
r4             0x0                  0
r5             0x0                  0
r6             0x0                  0
r7             0x0                  0
r8             0x0                  0
r9             0x0                  0
r10            0x0                  0
r11            0x0                  0
r12            0x0                  0
sp             0xbefff380           0xbefff380  # The OS sets up the stack pointer
lr             0x0                  0
pc             0x10078              0x10078 <_start+4>   # The OS sets up stack pointer
```

Having looked at the registers, we will now proceed to execute a series of instructions. Note that we need to enter si 1 once and then simply hit *Return* to repeat the operation:

```
(gdb) si 1
7              ldr    r1,=0x11111111       # Here we trace seven instructions
8              ldr    r2,=0x22222222
9              ldr    r3,=0x33333333
10             ldr    r4,=0x44444444
11             ldr    r5,=0x55555555
12             ldr    r0,adr_mem           @ Load pointer r0 with memory
13             stmia  r0!,{r1-r3,r5}       @ Multiple load to memory
(gdb) i r
r0             0x200cc              131276
```

Now, let's look at the registers we set up. Only registers of interest have been displayed. Note that r0 points to the data at 0x200CC. The system software is responsible for this address:

```
r1             0x11111111           286331153
r2             0x22222222           572662306
r3             0x33333333           858993459
```

```
r4              0x44444444          1145324612
r5              0x55555555          1431655765
r6              0x0                 0
```

At this point, we've set up register r0 as a pointer, and its value is 0x200cc. This value has been determined by the assembler and loader. If you refer back to the source code, we used ldr **r0**, adr_mem to load r0 via a pointer to the actual data stored in memory. This is because the software does not let us load a direct memory address.

You can see that the registers have been set up with their *easy-to-trace* values. The next step is to examine memory using the x/16xw gdb command to display 16 words of hexadecimal data:

```
pc              0x10094             0x10094 <_start+32>
(gdb) x/16xw 0x200cc
0x200cc:    0xbbbbbbbb    0x00000000    0x00000000    0x00000000
0x200dc:    0x00000000    0x00000000    0x00000000    0x00000000
0x200ec:    0x00000000    0xcccccccc    0x00001141    0x61656100
0x200fc:    0x01006962    0x00000007    0x00000108    0x0000001c
```

The two markers we've stored in memory are in bold font. Now, let's execute the stored multiple registers. Before that, we will copy the pointer to r10 (again, that is just for my own debugging purposes) so that we can see what it was before the move. After the block move instruction, we display registers of interest:

```
(gdb) si 1
14              mov     r10,r0
15              ldmdb   r0!,{r6-r9}         @ Now load data from memory
(gdb) i r
r0              0x200dc             131292
r1              0x11111111          286331153
r2              0x22222222          572662306
r3              0x33333333          858993459
r4              0x44444444          1145324612
r5              0x55555555          1431655765
r6              0x0                 0
r10             0x200dc             131292
pc              0x1009c             0x1009c <_start+40>
```

Now for the proof of the pudding. Here's the memory after the x/16xw display command. Note that the contents of the four registers have been stored in consecutive rising memory locations:

```
(gdb) x/16xw 0x200cc
0x200cc:    0x11111111    0x22222222    0x33333333    0x55555555
0x200dc:    0x00000000    0x00000000    0x00000000    0x00000000
0x200ec:    0x00000000    0xcccccccc    0x00001141    0x61656100
0x200fc:    0x01006962    0x00000007    0x00000108    0x0000001c
```

Finally, we will execute the last two commands and display the register contents:

```
(gdb) si 1
16                 mov      r11,r0
18                 mov      r1,#1        @ Terminate command
(gdb) i r
r0               0x200cc              131276
r1               0x11111111           286331153
r2               0x22222222           572662306
r3               0x33333333           858993459
r4               0x44444444           1145324612
r5               0x55555555           1431655765
r6               0x11111111           286331153        Data copied to registers
r6 - r9

r7               0x22222222           572662306
r8               0x33333333           858993459
r9               0x55555555           1431655765
r10              0x200dc              131292
```

You can see that the block move from the `ldmdb r0!,{r6-r9}` memory operation has copied the four registers from the memory and placed them in registers `r7` to `r9`.

Consider the suffix of **ldm**, which is **db**. Why `ldmdb`? When we transferred data to memory, we used the *increment after* suffix, where the pointer register is used to move the data to a memory location, and then it is incremented after the move. When we retrieve the data, we initially point at the location after the last value is moved. Consequently, to remove the items we stored in memory, we have to decrement the pointer before each move – hence the *decrement before* (db) suffix. For this reason, the instruction pair `stmia` and `ldmdb` correspond to the stack push and pull operations, respectively.

Disassembling the code

The following is a disassembly of the code for this program. It's been edited and reformatted for easier viewing. Some instructions have two lines. One line is the *original* instruction, as presented in the program. The following line is the instruction as interpreted by the assembler. This demonstrates how pseudo instructions such as `ldr r1,=0x111111` are handled.

The lines in bold require some further explanation, as shown here:

```
(gdb) disassemble /m
Dump of assembler code for function _start:
5 _start:            nop
   0x00010074 <+0>:  nop ;  (mov r0, r0)
6                    ldr    r0,=0xFFFFFFFF   @ Dummy value for testing
=> 0x00010078 <+4>:  mvn    r0, #0
```

```
7                        ldr     r1,=0x11111111
   0x0001007c <+8>:      ldr     r1, [pc, #52]    ; 0x100b8 <adr_mem+4>
8                        ldr     r2,=0x22222222
   0x00010080 <+12>:     ldr     r2, [pc, #52]    ; 0x100bc <adr_mem+8>
9                        ldr     r3,=0x33333333
   0x00010084 <+16>:     ldr     r3, [pc, #52]    ; 0x100c0 <adr_m
10                       ldr     r4,=0x44444444
   0x00010088 <+20>:     ldr     r4, [pc, #52]    ; 0x100c4 <adr_mem+16>
11                       ldr     r5,=0x55555555
   0x0001008c <+24>:     ldr     r5, [pc, #52]    ; 0x100c8 <adr_mem+20>
12                       ldr     r0,adr_mem       @ Load pointer r0 with memory
   0x00010090 <+28>:     ldr     r0, [pc, #28]    ; 0x100b4 <adr_mem>
13                       stmia   r0!,{r1-r3,r5}   @ Do a multiple load to memory
   0x00010094 <+32>:     stmia   r0!, {r1,r2,r3,r5}
14                       mov     r10,r0
   0x00010098 <+36>:     mov     r10, r0
15                       ldmdb   r0!,{r6-r9}      @ Now load data from memory
   0x0001009c <+40>:     ldmdb   r0!, {r6,r7,r8,r9}
16                       mov     r11,r0
   0x000100a0 <+44>:     mov     r11, r0
18                       mov     r1,#1            @ Terminate command
   0x000100a4 <+48>:     mov     r1, #1
19                       svc     0                @ Call OS to leave
   0x000100a8 <+52>:     svc 0x00000000
   0x000100ac <+56>:     ; <UNDEFINED> instruction: 0xffffffff
   0x000100b0 <+60>:     bge 0xfeabab60
   0x000100b4 <+0>:      andeq r0, r2, r12, asr #1
```

The following command uses x/32xw to display 32 consecutive words of memory in hexadecimal form so that we can observe what has happened in memory. Here's where our use of markers such as 0xAAAAAAAA makes it easy to recognize where we are in memory.

```
(gdb) x/32xw 0x100a8                            This displays 32 words of memory

0x100a8 <_start+52>:    0xef000000 0xffffffff 0xaaaaaaaa 0x000200cc
0x100b8 <adr_mem+4>:    0x11111111 0x22222222 0x33333333 0x44444444
0x100c8 <adr_mem+20>:   0x55555555 0xbbbbbbbb 0x00000000 0x00000000
0x100d8:                0x00000000 0x00000000 0x00000000 0x00000000
0x100e8:                0x00000000 0x00000000 0xcccccccc 0x00001141
0x100f8:                0x61656100 0x01006962 0x00000007 0x00000108
0x10108:                0x0000001c 0x00000002 0x00040000 0x00000000
0x10118:                0x00010074 0x00000058 0x00000000 0x00000000
```

Line 5 contains a `nop` instruction that does nothing (other than advance the PC to the next instruction). It can provide a placeholder for later code, or act as a debugging aid. Here, it provides a space for the first instruction to land on. The ARM lacks a `nop`, and the assembler translates `nop` to `mov r0,r0`. Like `nop`, this instruction achieves nothing!

`ldr r0,=0xFFFFFFFF` is interesting. The assembler uses ARM's `mvn` to invert the bits of the operand before moving them. If the operand is 0, the bits moved will be all 1s, which is exactly what we want.

Instruction 7 demonstrates another pseudo-operation:

```
7                          ldr       r1,=0x11111111
    0x0001007c <+8>:       ldr       r1, [pc, #52]     ; 0x100b8 <adr_mem+4>
```

The instruction requires a 32-bit literal, `0x11111111`, and that cannot be loaded as such. The compiler converts the instruction to a program counter-relative load from memory. The address is the current program counter, `0x0001007c`, plus the offset of `52` or `0x44`, plus the ARM PC's 8-byte lead. At that target address, you will find the `0x11111111` constant stored.

Instruction 12 uses a similar pseudo-instruction. In this case, it's to get the address in memory for the store multiple registers to use:

```
12                         ldr       r0,adr_mem          @ Load pointer r0 with memory
    0x00010090 <+28>: ldr        r0, [pc, #28]         @ 0x100b4 <adr_mem>
```

The code ends with `svc`, followed by the comment "*undefined*." That's because the disassembler tried to disassemble the data in memory, and it did not apply to a valid instruction.

Block moves and stack operations

Figure 12.2 to *Figure 12.5* show the four variations of block move instructions in terms of the stack type. Recall that, in this text, I use only a *full descending* full stack mode, where the stack pointer points at the top of the stack and is decremented before a new item is added. The differences between these modes are the direction in which the stack grows (up or ascending and down or descending) and depend on whether the stack pointer points at the item at the top of the stack or the next free item on it. ARM's literature uses four terms to describe stacks:

- FD   Full descending   *Figure 12.2*
- FA   Full ascending   *Figure 12.3*
- ED   Empty descending   *Figure 12.4*
- EA   Empty ascending   *Figure 12.5*

Block moves improve the performance of code by loading or storing several registers with one instruction. They are also frequently used to save registers, before calling a subroutine and then restoring them after a return from it, as the following example demonstrates. In what follows, SP is the stack pointer – that is, `r13` (you can write either `r13` or sp in the ARM assembly language).

When used by load operations, the suffix is *increment after*. When used by store operations, the suffix is *decrement before*.

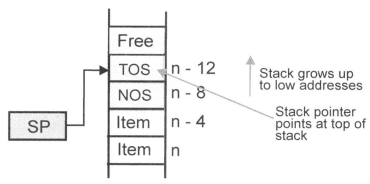

Figure 12.2 – One of ARM's four stack modes – full descending (FD, IA load, and DB store)

In a full descending stack, the stack pointer points at the item at the top of the stack (full), and when an item is added to the stack, the stack pointer is *decremented before* and when an item is removed, the stack is *incremented after*.

Consequently, we have the following:

Push r0 to r3 on the stack	`stmfd sp!,{r0-r3}`	or	`stmdb sp!,{r0-r3}`
Pull r0 to r3 off the stack	`ldmfd sp!,{r0-r3}`	or	`ldmia sp!,{r0-r3}`

As you can see, we can describe the instruction by either what it does (`db` or `ia`) or the type of stack (`fd`). It is rather unusual for assembly language designers to provide such options, and this is, initially, a little confusing.

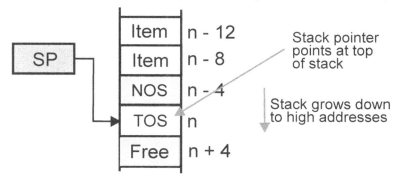

Figure 12.3 – One of ARM's four stack modes – full ascending (FA, DA load, and IB store)

In a full ascending stack, the stack pointer points at the item at the top of the stack (full), and when an item is added to the stack, the stack pointer is *incremented before*. When an item is removed, the stack is *decremented after*.

Consequently, we have the following:

Push r0 to r3 on the stack	`stmfa sp!,{r0-r3}`	or	`stmib sp!,{r0-r3}`
Pull r0 to r3 off the stack	`ldmfa sp!,{r0-r3}`	or	`ldmda sp!,{r0-r3}`

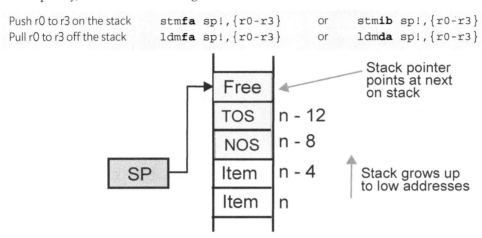

Figure 12.4 – One of ARM's four stack modes – empty descending (ED, IB load, and DA store)

In an empty descending stack, the stack pointer points at the item above the top of the stack (empty), and when an item is added to the stack, the stack pointer is incremented after. When an item is removed, the stack is decremented before. Consequently, we have the following:

Push r0 to r3 on the stack	`stmea sp!,{r0-r3}`	or	`stmia sp!,{r0-r3}`
Pull r0 to r3 off the stack	`ldmea sp!,{r0-r3}`	or	`ldmdb sp!,{r0-r3}`

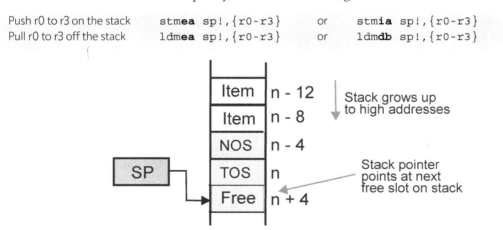

Figure 12.5 – One of ARM's four stack modes – empty ascending (EA, DB load, and IA store)

We use the `fd` block move suffix to mean *full descending*. ARM lets you use two different naming conventions for block move instructions. You can write the pair `stmia` and `ldmdb`, or the pair `stmfd` and `ldmfd`; they are the same. Yes, it is confusing:

```
                                    @ Call abc and save some registers
        bl      abc                 @ Call subroutine abc, save return address in lr (r14)
        .
abc:    stmfd   sp!,{r0-r3,r8}       @ Subroutine abc. Block move saves registers on the stack
        .
        .                           @ Body of code
        .
        ldmfd   sp!,{r0-r3,r8}       @ Subroutine complete. Now restore the registers
        mov     pc,lr               @ Copy the return address in lr to the PC
```

Since the program counter is also a user-visible register, we can simplify the code by including the PC as one of the registers we save:

```
abc:    stmfd   sp!,{r0-r3,r8,lr}   @ Save registers plus address in link register
        :
        ldmfd   sp!,{r0-r3,r8,pc}   @ Restore registers and transfer lr to PC
```

The link register with the return address is pushed onto the stack, and then at the end, we pull the saved registers, including the value of the return address that is placed in the PC, to return.

The block move provides a convenient means of copying data between memory regions. In the next example, we will copy 256 words from `pqr` to `xyz`. The block move instruction allows us to move eight registers at once, as the following code illustrates:

```
        adr     r0,pqr              @ r0 points to source (note the pseudo-op adr)
        adr     r1,xyz              @ r1 points to the destination
        mov     r2,#32              @ 32 blocks of eight words to move (256 words total)
Loop:   ldrfd   r0!,{r3-r10}        @ REPEAT Load 8 registers in r3 to r10
        strfd   r1!,{r3-r10}        @ Store the registers (moving 8 words at once)
        subs    r2,r2,#1            @ Decrement loop counter
        bne     Loop                @ Loop back until zero
```

This ends the section on Raspberry Pi and the ARM assembly language. In this book, you have learned how a computer works and what it does. We've examined instructions sets, their encoding, and their execution. In the last four chapters, we looked at high-performance architecture with an imaginative design.

Now, you should be able to write your own programs.

Summary

One of the key data structures in computing is the stack, or the LIFO queue. A stack is a queue with only one end – that is, new items enter at the same end as items leave. This single end is called the **top of stack** (**TOS**).

The stack is important because it enables the mechanization of many computing processes, ranging from dealing with arithmetic expressions to translating languages. Here, we are interested in the stack as a means of ensuring that subroutines are called and returned from in a consistent, efficient, and fool-proof manner.

A subroutine is a piece of code that can be called (invoked) from any point in a program and a return made to the calling point. This action requires the management of return addresses, and the stack is eminently suitable because the sequence of return addresses is the inverse sequence of the calling addresses – that is, the same as the order of items pushed and pulled from a stack.

We have looked at the ARM's branch and link instruction, `bl`, that can be used to call a subroutine without the overhead of the stack. However, using the branch with link a second time overwrites the return address in the link register, and you then have to use a stack to preserve previous addresses.

RISC computers, in principle, implement simple, one-cycle operations. The ARM has a very non-RISC like set of block-move instructions that allow you to move an entire group of instructions in a single operation. You can transfer up to 16 registers to or from memory in one operation. The block move lets you pass parameters to and from a subroutine via the stack.

There are four standard stack implementations. The stack pointer can point either to the item at the top of the stack, or to the free space above that item. Similarly, the stack can grow (as items are added) toward low addresses or toward high addresses. This gives four possible arrangements. However, most computers implement a stack that points to the top item on it that grows toward low addresses.

An unusual feature of the ARM's literature is that it has two naming conventions for stack organization. One convention uses the type of stack (pointing at the top or the next free item) and direction of the stack, whereas the other convention describes whether the stack is incremented/decremented before or after the operation – for example, `stmia r0!,{r2-r6}` and `stmea r0!,{r2-r6}` are identical operations.

In this book, we introduced the computer and demonstrated how it can be simulated with Python. By the end of *Chapter 8*, you should be able to design and simulate a computer instruction set, created to your own specification.

Following the design of a hypothetical teaching computer, we looked at Raspberry Pi and the ARM microprocessor at its heart. This provides an introduction to real computers. We described the ARM's instruction set architecture, explained how it operates, and explained how to write ARM assembly language programs and debug them on Raspberry Pi.

Having reached the end of this book, you might like to consider designing your own ARM simulator.

Finally, we wil provide some appendices to enable you to find some of the pieces of information you will need most frequently.

Appendices – Summary of Key Concepts

In these appendices, we will provide a brief summary of several of the aspects we introduced in this book. We will begin with an introduction to IDLE, the Python interpreter that lets you rapidly develop programs and test Python's features.

The second appendix provides a very brief summary of some of the Linux commands that you might need when developing ARM assembly language programs with Raspberry Pi.

The third appendix provides a demonstration of the running and debugging of an ARM assembly program. The purpose of this example is to bring together in one place all the steps required to debug a program.

The fourth appendix covers some concepts that can cause students confusion, such as the computer use of the terms up and down, which sometimes mean something different from the normal meaning of up and down. For example, adding something to a computer stack causes the computer stack to grow up toward lower addresses.

The final appendix defines some of the concepts that we use when discussing computer languages such as Python.

Using IDLE

The Python programs in this book have been written in Python, saved as a `.py` file, and then executed in an *integrated development environment*. However, there is another approach to executing Python that you will see mentioned in many texts. This is the Python IDLE environment (included with the Python package) that lets you execute Python code line by line.

IDLE is an interpreter that reads a line of Python as it is input and then executes it. This is very helpful if you want to test a few lines of code without going to the trouble of creating a source program.

Consider the following example, where the text in bold font is my input:

```
Python 3.9.7 (tags/v3.9.7:1016ef3, Aug 30 2021, 20:19:38) [MSC v.1929 64 bit
(AMD64)] on win32
Type "help", "copyright", "credits" or "license" for more information.
>>> x = 4
>>> y = 5
>>> print('Sum =', x+y)
Sum = 9
>>>
```

When you run a compiled Python program, the output is displayed in the run window. Here, as you can see, each input line after the >>> prompt is read and interpreted, and the result is printed.

This window is, in fact, part of the IDLE environment. This means that if your program crashes, you are able to examine variables *after* the crash. Consider the following example, where we create and run a program that contains an error:

```
# An error example
x = 5
y = input('Type a number = ')
z = x + y
print('x + y =',z)
```

If we run this program, the execution window displays the following message:

```
Type a number = 3
Traceback (most recent call last):
  File "E:/ArchitectureWithPython/IDE_Test.py", line 4, in <module>
    z = x + y
TypeError: unsupported operand type(s) for +: 'int' and 'str'
>>>
```

The Python interpreter has indicated a *type error* because we entered a string and tried to add it to an integer. We can continue in the display window and look at the x and y variables and then modify the code as follows. All keyboard input is in bold:

```
>>> x
5
>>> y
'3'
>>> y = int(y)
>>> z = x + y
>>> z
8
>>>
```

We have now located and corrected the problem. Of course, it would be necessary to edit the original Python program to correct the source code.

Because IDLE executes a statement at a time, it appears impossible to execute a loop because that requires more than one line of code. There is a way. IDLE automatically indents instructions in loops, which allows multiple statements. In order to finish (close) the loop, you must type TWO enters. Consider the following:

```
>>> i = 0
>>> for j in range(0,5):    @ Here we've started a loop
        i = i + j*j          @ Add a statement. Note the automatic indentation
```

@ Now hit the enter key twice.

```
>>> print(i)            @ We have exited the loop and added a new statement
30                      @ And here is the result
>>>
```

Instructions and commands

This appendix lists some of the popular commands you will use when running programs on Raspberry Pi:

Linux

```
cd ..                   @ Change dictionary to parent
mkdir /home/pi/testProg @ Create new file called testProg in folder pi
ls /home/pi             @ List files in folder pi
as -g -0 file.o file.s  @ Assemble source file file.s to create object file file.o
ld -0 file file.o       @ Link object file file.o
gdb file                @ Call debugger to debug file
sudo apt-get update     @ Download packages in your configuration source files
sudo apt-get upgrade    @ Updates all installed packages
```

Assembler directives

```
.text                   @ This is a code section
.global _start          @ _start is a label (first instruction)
.word                   @ Bind 32-bit value to label and store in memory
.byte                   @ Bind 8-bit value to label and store in memory
.equ                    @ .equ x,7 binds or equates 7 to the name x
.asciz                  @ Bind ASCII string to label and store (terminated by 0)
.balign                 @ .balign 4 locates instruction/data is on a word boundary
```

gdb debugger

```
file toDebug            @ Load code file toDebug for debugging
b address               @ Insert breakpoint at <address> (maybe line number or label)
x/4xw <address>         @ Display memory: four 32-bit words in hexadecimal format
x/7db <address>         @ Display memory: seven bytes in decimal format
r                       @ Run program (to a breakpoint or its termination)
s                       @ Step (execute) an instruction
n                       @ Same as step an instruction
i r                     @ Display registers
i b                     @ Display breakpoints
c                       @ Continue from breakpoint
```

Template for an ARM assembly language program

```
                    .text                @ Indicate this is code
        .global _start                   @ Provide entry point
_start: mov    r0,#0                     @ Start of the code

        mov    r0,#0                     @ Exit parameter (optional)
        mov    r7,#goHome                @ Set up leave command
        svc    #0                        @ Call operating system to exit this code

test:   .word  0xABCD1234                @ Store a word in memory with label 'test'
        .equ   goHome, 1                 @ Equate name to value
```

Running an ARM program

Here, we've put together all the information you need to run and debug a program on Raspberry Pi. We're going to take the string copying example from *Chapter 11* and go through it in more detail to provide a template for program development. This program takes an ASCII string and reverses it. In this case, the string is "Hello!!!". We have made it eight characters long so that it fits into two consecutive words (8 * 8 bits = 64 bits = 2 words).

We have located the source string, string1, in the body of the program, in the .text section, because it is only read from and never written to.

The destination, str2, that will receive the reversed string is in read/write memory in the .data section. Consequently, we have to use the technique of indirect pointers – that is, the .text portion has a pointer at adr_str2 that contains the address of the actual string, str2.

The program contains several labels that are not accessed by the code (e.g., preLoop and Wait). The purpose of these labels is to make it easy to use breakpoints when debugging by giving them names.

A final feature is the use of *markers*. We have inserted markers in memory that follow both strings – that is, 0xAAFFFFBB and 0xCCFFFFCC. These make it easier to locate data when you look at memory because they stand out.

This program tests pointer-based addressing, bytes load and store, and auto-incrementing and decrementing of pointer registers. We will step through the execution of this program using gdb's facilities:

```
        .equ   len,8                     @ Length of string to reverse (8 bytes/chars)
        .text                            @ Program (code) area
        .global _start                   @
_start: mov    r1,#len                   @ Number of characters to move in r1
        adr    r2,string1                @ r2 points at source string1 in this section
        adr    r3,adr_str2               @ r3 points at dest string str2 address in this section
        ldr    r4,[r3]                   @ r4 points to dest str2 in data section
```

```
preLoop:    add     r5,r4,#len-1        @ r5 points to bottom of dest str2
Loop:       ldrb    r6,[r2],#1          @ Get byte char from source in r6 inc pointer
            strb    r6,[r5],#-1         @ Store char in destination, decrement pointer
            subs    r1,r1,#1            @ Decrement char count
            bne     Loop                @ REPEAT until all done
Wait:       nop                         @ Stop here for testing

Exit:       mov     r0,#0               @ Stop here
            mov     r7,#1               @ Exit parameter required by svc
            svc     0                   @ Call operating system to exit program

string1:    .ascii  "Hello!!!"          @ The source string
marker:     .word   0xAAFFFFBB          @ Marker for testing

adr_str2:   .word   str2                @ POINTER to source string2 in data area

            .data                       @ The read/write data area
str2:       .byte   0,0,0,0,0,0,0,0     @ Clear destination string
            .word   0xCCFFFFCC          @ Marker and terminator
            .end
```

The program is loaded into the gdb and debugged by the following. Note that my input is in bold font:

alan@raspberrypi:~/Desktop $ **gdb pLoop**

The first step is to place three breakpoints on the labels so that we can execute code up to those points and then examine registers or memory:

```
(gdb) b _start
Breakpoint 1 at 0x10074: file pLoop.s, line 5.
(gdb) b preLoop
Breakpoint 2 at 0x10084: file pLoop.s, line 9.
(gdb) b Wait
Breakpoint 3 at 0x10098: file pLoop.s, line 14.
```

We have set three breakpoints by using b <label> three times. We can check these breakpoints by using the info b command, which displays the state of the breakpoints:

```
(gdb) info b
Num     Type           Disp Enb Address    What
1       breakpoint     keep y   0x00010074 pLoop.s:5
2       breakpoint     keep y   0x00010084 pLoop.s:9
3       breakpoint     keep y   0x00010098 pLoop.s:14
```

The next step is to run the program as far as the first instruction:

```
(gdb) r
Starting program: /home/alan/Desktop/pLoop
Breakpoint 1, _start () at pLoop.s:5
5 _start:    mov    r1,#len             @ Number of characters to move in r1
(gdb) c
Continuing.
```

There's not a lot to see here. So, we hit c to continue to the next breakpoint, and then enter i r to display the registers. Note we have not displayed registers that have not been accessed:

```
Breakpoint 2, preLoop () at pLoop.s:9
9 preLoop:   add    r5,r4,#len-1        @ r5 points to bottom of dest str2

(gdb) i r
r0        0x0             0
r1        0x8             8
r2        0x100a8         65704       Pointer to string1
r3        0x100b4         65716       Pointer to str2 address
r4        0x200b8         131256      Pointer to str2 value
sp        0x7efff360      0x7efff360
lr        0x0             0
pc        0x10084         0x10084 <preLoop>
```

Let's have a look at the data section in the code. Register r2 points at this area, and the command means four words of memory in the hexadecimal form are displayed, starting at 0x100A8:

```
(gdb) x/4wx 0x100a8
0x100a8 <string1>: 0x6c6c6548 0x2121216f 0xaaffffbb 0x000200b8
```

The three highlighted values present the string "Hello!!!" and the marker 0xCCFFFFCC. Note how these values appear *back to front*. This is a consequence of the little-endian byte ordering mode. The least-significant byte is located at the least-significant end of a word. In terms of ASCII characters, these are lleH !!!o.

We next perform a single step and display the memory in the data region. At this stage, the code had not been executed fully and this region should be as originally set up:

```
(gdb) si 1
Loop () at pLoop.s:10
10 Loop:    ldrb    r6,[r2],#1          @ Get byte char from source in r6 inc pointer

(gdb) x/4wx 0x200b8
0x200b8: 0x00000000 0x00000000 0xccffffcc 0x00001141
```

Here, you can see the zeros loaded at bytes and the marker following them. We then enter c again and continue to the Wait breakpoint when the code should have been completed. Finally, we look at the registers and then the data memory:

```
(gdb) c
Continuing.
Breakpoint 3, Wait () at pLoop.s:14
14 Wait:       nop                        @ Stop here for testing

(gdb) i r
r0              0x0                0
r1              0x0                0
r2              0x100b0            65712
r3              0x100b4            65716
r4              0x200b8            131256
r5              0x200b7            131255
r6              0x21               33
sp              0x7efff360         0x7efff360
lr              0x0                0
pc              0x10098            0x10098 <Wait>

(gdb) x/4wx 0x200b8
0x200b8:  0x6f212121 0x48656c6c 0xccffffcc 0x00001141
```

Note that the data is changed. As you can see, the order has been reversed. Again, note the effect of the little-endianism on the byte order within words. The sequence of the data is now o!!! Hell. Finally, we enter c again and the program is completed:

```
(gdb) c
Continuing.
[Inferior 1 (process 11670) exited normally]
(gdb)
```

Common confusions

The growth of computing from the 1960s to today was rapid and chaotic. The chaos arose because the technology developed so rapidly that systems became obsolete in months, and that meant much of the design was obsolete but had been incorporated in systems that were now being held back by it. Similarly, many different notations and conventions arose – for example, does MOVE A, B move A to B, or B to A? Both conventions were used at the same time by different computers. Here are a few pointers to help with the confusion.

In this book, we will largely adopt the right-to-left convention for data movement. For example, add **r1**, r2, r2 indicates the addition of r2 and r3, and the sum is put in r1. As a means of highlighting this, I often put the destination operand of an operation in bold font.

Symbols are often used with different meanings. This is particularly true of #, @, and %.

- **#**: The *hash* (or pound) sign is used in Python programs to indicate a comment field – for example, `if x > y: z = 2. # Reset z if x ever exceeds y.` The hash is used in ARM assembly language to indicate a literal value – for example, `add r0,r1,#5. @ Add the integer 5 to the contents of r1 and put in r2`.

- **@**: The *at* symbol is used to indicate a comment in the ARM assembly language.

- **%**: The *percentage sign* is used to indicate a binary value in some language – for example, `add r1,r2,#%1010` means add the literal value expressed in the binary form. Python uses the prefix `0b` to indicate binary values (e.g., 0b1010).

- **$**: In some languages, the *dollar symbol* indicates hexadecimal; for example, $A10C. Python uses the prefix `0x` to indicate hexadecimal values (e.g., 0xA10C).

- **Register indirect addressing**: A key concept in programming at the assembly language level is the pointer – that is, a variable that is the address of an element in memory. This addressing mode is called register indirect, pointer-based, or even indexed addressing.

- **Up and down**: In normal everyday use, up and down indicate the direction toward the sky (up) or toward the ground (down). In arithmetic, they indicate increasing a number (up) or decreasing it (down). In computing, when data items are added to a stack, the stack grows up. However, by convention, the address grows down as items are added. Consequently, the stack pointer is decremented when items are added to the stack and incremented when items are removed.

- **Endian**: Considerable confusion can be caused when reading a program or when interfacing one system with another because of the two standards – big endian and little endian. If you were to write `ldr r0,=0x12345678`, a big endian computer would store the bytes in byte memory at increasing addresses in the order 12,34,56,78, whereas a little endian computer would store the bytes in the order 78,56,34,12. The ARM is a little endian machine, although it can be programmed to operate in a big endian mode. In practice, this means that you must be careful when debugging programs and looking at memory dumps. Equally, you must be careful when performing byte operations on word values to ensure that you select the correct byte.

Vocabulary

All specializations have their own vocabulary, and programming is no exception. Here are a few words that you might find helpful in understanding the text and its context.

- **Compiler**: Computers execute binary programs expressed as 1s and 0s. Humans write programs in a high-level language such as Python that is close to plain English. Before a high-level language program can be executed, a piece of software called a *compiler* translates it into binary code. When you run a Python program on your computer, your source code is automatically translated into machine code by a compiler working with the operating system. Mercifully, you don't have to worry about all the actions that take place invisibly in the background during compilation.

- **Syntax error**: Like a human language, a program is made up of *sentences* that conform to a set of rules called *grammar*. If a sentence has an error, so it does not conform to the grammar, it is called a syntax error. If I said, *"I is hot"*, that would be an error of English syntax, even though the meaning (semantics) is clear. A typical syntax error in Python is $y = "4" + 1$. This is a syntax error because I'm adding two different entities that can't be added. The "4" is a character (you can print it), whereas the 1 is an integer. You can write $y = "4" + "1"$ or $z = 4 + 1$. These are both syntactically correct, and y is "41", whereas z is 5.

- **Semantic error**: Semantics is concerned with meaning. A syntax error means that the sentence is grammatically wrong even if it is syntactically correct. An example of a sentence in English with a semantic error is, *"Twas brillig, and the slithy toves did gyre and gimble in the wabe."* This is grammatically correct but does not have a meaning – that is, it's semantically incorrect. In computing, a semantic error means that your program doesn't do what you intended. A compiler can detect a syntax error but not usually a semantic error.

- **Variable**: An item of data is a variable if its value can change. If you write $age = 25$, you've created a new variable called age with the value 25. If you refer to age, the actual value will be substituted. The expression $y = age + 10$ would give y the value 35. A variable has four attributes – its name (what you call it), its address (where it's stored in the computer), its value (what it actually is), and its type (e.g., an integer, list, character, or string).

- **Constant**: A value that cannot be changed is a constant. The circumference of a circle is expressed as $c = 2\pi r$, where 2 and π are constants. Both c and r are variables.

- **Symbolic name**: We often refer to a variable or a constant by a name – for example, we call the circumference of the circle c and its radius r. We give the irrational number 3.1415926 the symbolic name π. When a program is compiled into machine code, symbolic names are replaced by actual values.

- **Address**: Information is stored in memory locations, and each location has a unique address. For example, the radius of a circle may be stored in computer memory at address 1234. A programmer normally does not have to worry about where data is actually located in memory. Translating addresses from the logical addresses used in programs to the physical addresses of memory devices is the domain of the operating system.

- **Value and location**: When we refer to the expression $c = 2\pi r$, what is r? We (humans) see r as the symbolic name for the value of the radius – say, 5. But the computer sees r as the memory address 1234, which has to be read to provide the actual value of r. If we write $r = r + 1$, do we mean $r = 5 + 1 = 6$ or do we mean $r = 1234 + 1 = 1235$? It's important to distinguish between an *address* and its *contents*. This factor becomes significant when we introduce pointers.

- **Pointer**: A pointer is a variable whose value is an address. If you modify a pointer, it points to a different location. In conventional arithmetic, we write x_i where i is really a pointer; we just call it an *index*. If we change the pointer (index) we can step through the elements of a table, array, or matrix and step through elements x_1, x_2, x_3, and x_4.

Index

U

V

Z

www.packtpub.com

Subscribe to our online digital library for full access to over 7,000 books and videos, as well as industry leading tools to help you plan your personal development and advance your career. For more information, please visit our website.

Why subscribe?

- Spend less time learning and more time coding with practical eBooks and Videos from over 4,000 industry professionals

- Improve your learning with Skill Plans built especially for you

- Get a free eBook or video every month

- Fully searchable for easy access to vital information

- Copy and paste, print, and bookmark content

Did you know that Packt offers eBook versions of every book published, with PDF and ePub files available? You can upgrade to the eBook version at packtpub.com and as a print book customer, you are entitled to a discount on the eBook copy. Get in touch with us at customercare@packtpub.com for more details.

At www.packtpub.com, you can also read a collection of free technical articles, sign up for a range of free newsletters, and receive exclusive discounts and offers on Packt books and eBooks.

Other Books You May Enjoy

If you enjoyed this book, you may be interested in these other books by Packt:

Computer Programming for Absolute Beginners

Joakim Wassberg

ISBN: 978-1-83921-686-2

- Get to grips with basic programming language concepts such as variables, loops, selection and functions
- Understand what a program is and how the computer executes it
- Explore different programming languages and learn about the relationship between source code and executable code
- Solve problems using various paradigms such as procedural programming, object oriented programming, and functional programming
- Write high-quality code using several coding conventions and best practices
- Become well-versed with how to track and fix bugs in your programs

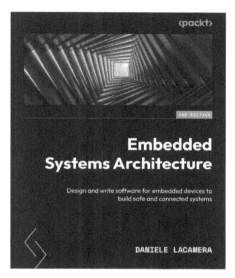

Embedded Systems Architecture - Second Edition

Daniele Lacamera

ISBN: 978-1-80323-954-5

- Participate in the design and definition phase of an embedded product
- Get to grips with writing code for ARM Cortex-M microcontrollers
- Build an embedded development lab and optimize the workflow
- Secure embedded systems with TLS
- Demystify the architecture behind the communication interfaces
- Understand the design and development patterns for connected and distributed devices in the IoT
- Master multitasking parallel execution patterns and real-time operating systems
- Become familiar with Trusted Execution Environment (TEE)

Packt is searching for authors like you

If you're interested in becoming an author for Packt, please visit `authors.packtpub.com` and apply today. We have worked with thousands of developers and tech professionals, just like you, to help them share their insight with the global tech community. You can make a general application, apply for a specific hot topic that we are recruiting an author for, or submit your own idea.

Share Your Thoughts

Now you've finished *Computer Architecture with Python and ARM*, we'd love to hear your thoughts! Scan the QR code below to go straight to the Amazon review page for this book and share your feedback or leave a review on the site that you purchased it from.

`https://packt.link/r/1-837-63667-2`

Your review is important to us and the tech community and will help us make sure we're delivering excellent quality content.

Download a free PDF copy of this book

Thanks for purchasing this book!

Do you like to read on the go but are unable to carry your print books everywhere? Is your eBook purchase not compatible with the device of your choice?

Don't worry, now with every Packt book you get a DRM-free PDF version of that book at no cost.

Read anywhere, any place, on any device. Search, copy, and paste code from your favorite technical books directly into your application.

The perks don't stop there, you can get exclusive access to discounts, newsletters, and great free content in your inbox daily

Follow these simple steps to get the benefits:

1. Scan the QR code or visit the link below

https://packt.link/free-ebook/9781837636679

2. Submit your proof of purchase
3. That's it! We'll send your free PDF and other benefits to your email directly

www.ingramcontent.com/pod-product-compliance
Lightning Source LLC
Chambersburg PA
CBHW081504050326
40690CB00015B/2920

* 9 7 8 1 8 3 7 6 3 6 6 7 9 *